'APPEASEMENT' AND THE ENGLISH SPEAKING WORLD

'APPEASEMENT'
AND THE
ENGLISH SPEAKING WORLD

BRITAIN, THE UNITED STATES, THE DOMINIONS,
AND THE POLICY OF 'APPEASEMENT',
1937–1939

by
RITCHIE OVENDALE

1975
CARDIFF
UNIVERSITY OF WALES PRESS

ISBN 0 7083 0589 X

Printed in Wales by
CSP PRINTING, ST. FAGAN'S ROAD
FAIRWATER, CARDIFF

Contents

Acknowledgements

I WOULD like to thank the following trustees for permission to use private papers in their custody: Cambridge university library and Mr. Paul Paget for the *Templewood Papers*; Mrs. Dorothy Lloyd for the extracts from the *Chamberlain Papers*; Lord Caldecote for the *Inskip Papers* in Churchill college library, Cambridge; Lady Vansittart for the *Vansittart Papers* in Churchill college library, Cambridge; Lord Zetland for the *Zetland Papers* in the India office library; the clerk of records, house of lords record office, and Viscount Samuel for the *Samuel Papers* in the house of lords record office; Major T. J. Ingram for the *Halifax Papers* in Garrowby, Yorkshire; Lord Simon for the *Simon Papers*; the trustees of the national library of Scotland for the *Elibank Papers* in the national library of Scotland, Edinburgh; the Marquess of Lothian for the *Lothian Papers* in the Scottish record office, Edinburgh. Transcripts of crown copyright records in the public record office appear by permission of the controller of H.M. stationery office.

Professor Agnes Headlam-Morley originally suggested the topic to me; her encouragement and friendship have been invaluable. I should also like to thank the following for their assistance: Professor Max Beloff, Dr. A. F. Madden, Mr. Richard Storry, Professor Jack Gallagher, Dr. Trevor Reese, Sir Keith Hancock, Mr. Rainer Tamchina, the late Professor Trefor Evans, and Professor Ieuan John and my colleagues in the department of international politics at Aberystwyth. I am grateful for the help of Michael Clarke in preparing the index. Mrs. Chris. Chadwick and the staff of Llandinam library, university college of Wales, Aberystwyth, have always been cheerful and co-operative. My research was made a good deal easier by the help of various assistants in the public record office, London, Chatham house, the Scottish record office, Rhodes house library, Oxford, and the other libraries where I have worked. I appreciate their good humour and efficiency. Desmond and Angela King have often looked after me while working on this book: I am in their debt. Above all I should like to thank my parents, Jean and Richard Ovendale, for their support over the years.

January 1975   RITCHIE OVENDALE

ABBREVIATIONS IN REFERENCES

d. – despatched, Ed. – Editorial, r. – received, r. in r. – received in registry, *Times* – *The Times*.

I

INTRODUCTION. BRITAIN, THE UNITED STATES, AND THE DOMINIONS IN 1937

Introduction. Britain, the United States, and the Dominions in 1937

IN his memoirs Lord Halifax, foreign secretary at the outbreak of the second world war, offered his considered opinion of Neville Chamberlain's achievement as prime minister:

> When war [came] . . . it found a country and Conmmowealth wholly united within itself, convinced to the foundations of soul and conscience that every conceivable effort had been made to find the way of sparing Europe the ordeal of war, and that no alternative remained. And that was the big thing that Chamberlain did.[1]

Halifax is supported in this view by Lord Templewood, a member of Chamberlain's cabinet, who wrote of the united front in the commonwealth created during Chamberlain's premiership as Britain's 'first and indispensable line of defence'.[2] Miss Hilda Chamberlain, the sister and confidant of the prime minister, touched upon another forgotten factor which influenced her brother, when she wrote that the attitude of the dominions and the United States was at that time 'all important and absolutely ignored by those who now condemn'.[3]

The authorities who have examined the decisions made in Britain on the appeasement of Europe hardly consider the influence of United States and dominion opinion.

R. W. Seton-Watson mentions only that the dominions had views on the colonial question.[4] Agnes Headlam-Morley,[5] John W. Wheeler-Bennett,[6] Lewis B. Namier,[7] Alan Bullock,[8] Hugh Trevor-Roper,[9] and A. J. P. Taylor[10] ignore the issue of commonwealth consultation. Before

---

[1] Earl of Halifax, *Fullness of Days* (London, 1957), p. 198.

[2] Lord Templewood, *Nine Troubled Years* (London, 1954), p. 389.

[3] *Templewood Papers* XIX (C) 11, Hilda Chamberlain to Templewood, 27.1.1951.

[4] R. W. Seton-Watson, *Britain and the Dictators* (Cambridge, 1938), pp. 420–4.

[5] Agnes Headlam-Morley, 'Was Neville Chamberlain's Foreign Policy Wrong?', *Listener*, XL (14.10.1948), pp. 551–3.

[6] John W. Wheeler-Bennett, *Munich: Prologue to Tragedy* (London, 1948).

[7] Lewis B. Namier, *Diplomatic Prelude, 1938–1939* (London, 1948); *Europe in Decay: A Study in Disintegration 1936–1940* (London, 1950); 'Munich Survey: A Summing up', *Listener*, XL (2.12.1948), pp. 835–6.

[8] Alan Bullock, *Hitler. A Study in Tyranny* (London, 1962).

[9] Hugh Trevor-Roper, 'Munich. Its Lessons Ten Years Later', *New York Times Magazine*, 8.8.1948. Reprinted in Francis L. Loewenheim, *Peace or Appeasement. Hitler, Chamberlain and the Munich Crisis* (Boston, 1965), pp. 158–60.

[10] A. J. P. Taylor, *The Origins of the Second World War*, Rev. Ed. (London, 1964); 'Munich Twenty Years After', *Manchester Guardian Weekly*, 30.9.1958. Reprinted in Loewenheim, pp. 158–60.

the rise of the 'revisionist school' on 'appeasement' in the 1960s it was raised in specialised works on commonwealth foreign policy by H. V. Hodson,[11] W. Y. Elliot and H. Duncan Hall, [12] Gwendolen Carter,[13] P. N. S. Mansergh,[14] and J. D. B. Miller.[15] The question went no further. Even the *Survey of International Affairs* for the years 1937–9 has only the odd reference to the commonwealth. Arnold Toynbee did contribute a separate section on the 'British Commonwealth' but he mentions only that Chamberlain, with his policy of the appeasement of Europe, represented the 'overwhelming majority of people' in the dominions.[16]

The autobiographies and biographies of the statesmen involved split into the apologists and the accusers on the issue of the influence of the dominions.

The apologists, including those who made up the so called 'inner cabinet'[17] consisting of Chamberlain,[18] Halifax,[19] Sir Samuel Hoare (Lord Templewood),[20] the home secretary, and Viscount Simon,[21] the chancellor of the exchequer, give the impression that fear of the commonwealth breaking up if there were war over certain issues was predominant in the minds of those deciding British policy.

Other members of the cabinet offer a similar explanation. Malcolm MacDonald, at different times secretary of state for the dominions and the colonies, emphasises the consideration given to the possible break up of the commonwealth.[22] Viscount Maugham, the lord chancellor, in 1944 stressed the special consideration that had had to be given to the views of

11 See D. C. Watt, 'Appeasement. The Rise of a Revisionist School?', *Political Quarterly*, XXXVI (1965), pp. 191–213; H. V. Hodson, 'British Foreign Policy and the Dominions', *Foreign Affairs* XVII (July 1939), pp. 753–63.

12 W. Y. Elliott and H. Duncan Hall, Eds., *The British Commonwealth at War* (New York, 1943).

13 Gwendolen Carter, *The British Commonwealth and World Security* (Toronto, 1947).

14 P. N. S. Mansergh, *Survey of British Commonwealth Affairs. Problems of External Policy 1913–1939* (Oxford, 1952).

15 J. D. B. Miller, *The Commonwealth and the World* (London, 1958).

16 Arnold J. Toynbee, Veronica M. Toynbee, R. G. D. Laffan, Eds., *Survey of International Affairs* 1937 2 Vols. 1938 3 Vols. 1939 Vol. 2 (Oxford, 1938–58); Arnold J. Toynbee, 'The British Commonwealth', in Arnold J. Toynbee and Frank T. Ashton-Gwatkin, Eds., *Survey of International Affairs 1939. The World in March 1939* (Oxford, 1952), pp. 21–46 at p. 37.

17 A. J. P. Taylor, 'Brummagen Statesmanship', *Observer*, 10.1.1971; Ian Colvin, *The Chamberlain Cabinet* (London, 1971), p. 146; Lord Templewood, 'The Lesson of Munich', *Listener*, XL (9.12.1948), p. 879; Colin Coote, *A Companion of Honour. The Story of Walter Elliot* (London, 1965), p. 155; R. J. Minney, Ed., *The Private Papers of Hore-Belisha* (London, 1960), p. 139.

18 Keith Feiling, *The Life of Neville Chamberlain* (London, 1946), pp. 362, 364, 379, 400; Iain Macleod *Neville Chamberlain* (London, 1961), pp. 247, 269–70; Colvin, pp. 208, 271, mentions the views of the dominions but does not evaluate their possible influence.

19 Halifax, p. 198; Earl of Birkenhead, *Halifax* (London, 1965), pp. 425–6.

20 Templewood, 'The Lesson of Munich', pp. 879–80; *Nine Troubled Years*, p. 389.

21 Viscount Simon, *Retrospect* (London, 1952), pp. 245–8, 254.

22 Malcolm MacDonald, *People and Places* (London, 1969), pp. 142–3.

the dominions.[23] Earl Winterton,[24] the chancellor of the duchy of Lancaster, and Walter Elliot,[25] the secretary of state for Scotland, quote the reluctance of the dominions to fight as an argument that no responsible minister could neglect.

Outside the cabinet, Geoffrey Dawson, the editor of *The Times*, and Lord Lothian, both of whom had been members of Lord Milner's 'kindergarten' in South Africa after the Anglo-Boer war and who moved in commonwealth circles, had misgivings that Britain would be led into a war without commonwealth support. For Dawson this was 'the vital factor'.[26] Both were members of the so called 'Cliveden set'. Michael Astor, however, in his account of the circle's activities does not mention the dominions.[27] Neither does Tom Jones, another guest at Cliveden.[28]

Viscount Samuel, although he ignores the dominions in his memoirs,[29] did consider their views important. After refusing Chamberlain's invitation to join the cabinet in October 1938, he wrote to the prime minister suggesting a committee of the privy council on national policy to include J. C. Smuts, the South African deputy prime minister, to ensure that the views of South Africa on the colonial question would be adequately made. Representatives of the dominions and India would be informed of the committee's proceedings, and might attend some meetings.[30] The Earl of Woolton, a friend of Horace Wilson, Chamberlain's adviser, did see Smuts in South Africa in 1938. Woolton told Smuts that if he made a public pronouncement that South Africa would fight, Hitler might stop.[31]

Chamberlain's principal government critics hardly mention the dominions. Winston Churchill,[32] Anthony Eden,[33] Sir Robert Vansittart,[34]

[23] Viscount Maugham, *The Truth about the Munich Crisis* (London, 1944), pp. 6, 58, 60–1; See also *At the End of the Day* (London, 1953), pp. 371, 383.

[24] Earl Winterton, *Orders of the Day* (London, 1953), pp. 240–2; Alan Houghton Brodwick, *Near to Greatness* (London, 1965), p. 232.

[25] Coote, p. 155.

[26] John Evelyn Wrench, *Geoffrey Dawson and our Times* (London, 1955), pp. 373–4; J. R. M. Butler, *Lord Lothian (Philip Kerr) 1882–1940* (London, 1960). Dawson's view was largely shared by Robin Barrington-Ward, the deputy editor of the *Times*. See Donald McLachlan, *In the Chair: Barrington-Ward of The Times* (London, 1971), pp. 102–6, and Max Beloff, 'Appeasement—For and Against', *Government and Opposition*, VII (1972), pp. 112–9 at pp. 114–5.

[27] Michael Astor, *Tribal Feeling* (London, 1963), pp. 136–47.

[28] Thomas Jones, *A Diary with Letters* (London, 1954). See also A. L. Rowse, *All Souls and Appeasement* (London, 1961); Martin Gilbert, *Plough My Own Furrow. The Story of Lord Allan of Hurtwood* (London, 1965), p. 309.

[29] Viscount Samuel, *Memoirs* (London, 1945); John Bowle, *Viscount Samuel* (London, 1957).

[30] Samuel, pp. 278–9; *Samuel Papers* A112, 1, Samuel to Chamberlain, Private and Personal 3.11.1938; 2, Confidential Memorandum by Samuel, Undated (copy); 3, Chamberlain to Samuel, 5.11.1938.

[31] Earl of Woolton, *The Memoirs of the Rt. Hon. the Earl of Woolton* (London, 1969), pp. 132–3, 140.

[32] Winston Churchill, *The Gathering Storm* (London, 1948).

[33] Anthony Eden, *Facing the Dictators* (London, 1962); *The Reckoning* (London, 1965).

[34] Lord Vansittart, 'A Morally Indefensible Agreement', *Listener*, XL (4.11.1948). pp. 675–7.

chief diplomatic adviser, Duff Cooper,[35] first lord of the admiralty until his resignation in 1938, and Harold Macmillan[36] are instances of this.

The same is true of L. S. Amery. Although a correspondent of Smuts he gives no weight to dominion influence other than to mention their views on mandates.[37] Foreign office officials and emissaries like F. T. A. Ashton-Gwatkin and Ivone Kirkpatrick ignore the dominions.[38]

The military are divided. The general officer in command of the eastern command, Edmund Ironside, reveals in his diaries: 'We could not say "If you cross the Czech frontier we will fight." It was risking the Empire and unjustifiable.'[39] Lord Ismay supports this view.[40] L. Hore-Belisha, the secretary of state for war,[41] and Basil Liddell Hart, an adviser, make no reference to the dominions.[42]

To the labour opposition, as reflected by Hugh Dalton,[43] Lord Citrine,[44] and Clement Attlee[45] the dominions did not count.

An analysis of the published memoirs and biographical material would suggest that those deciding British policy, both in the inner cabinet and the cabinet, regarded the views of the dominions as important, if not crucial. The defenders of the policy of the appeasement of Europe cite dominion opinion as a reason for its implementation, while the critics ignore the issue.

It was, however, not until the publication of articles by D. C. Watt that the question of dominion influence on British policy in the years immediately before the outbreak of war began to appear in the general works.[46] In 1961 Sir Charles Webster raised the issue but discounted the validity of the case.[47] Martin Gilbert and Richard Gott in their attack on

35 Duff Cooper 'A Cynical Act of Cold-blooded Butchery', *Listener*, XL (18.11.1948). pp, 757–8; *Old Men Forget* (London, 1953), pp. 239–40 does mention dominion views in September 1938.

36 Harold Macmillan, *Winds of Change* (London, 1966).

37 L. S. Amery, *The Unforgiving Years* (London, 1955), pp. 246–95.

38 F. T. A. Ashton-Gwatkin, 'The Personal Story of the Runciman Mission', *Listener*, XL (21.10.1948), pp. 595–7; Ivone Kirkpatrick, *The Inner Circle* (London, 1959).

39 Roderick Macleod and Dennis Kelly, Eds., *The Ironside Diaries 1937–1940* (London, 1962), p. 70, Diary, 2.11.1938.

40 Lord Ismay, *The Memoirs of General the Lord Ismay* (London, 1960), p. 92.

41 Minney, *passim*.

42 Basil Liddell Hart, *The Memoirs of Captain Liddell Hart*, 2 (London, 1965).

43 Hugh Dalton, *The Fateful Years. Memoirs 1931–45* (London, 1957).

44 Lord Citrine, *Men and Work* (London, 1964).

45 Clement Richard Attlee, *As it Happened* (London, 1964), pp. 96–104.

46 D. C. Watt, 'Der Einfluss der Dominions auf die Britische Aussenpolitik von München, 1938', *Vierteljahrshefte für Zeitgeschichte*, VIII (Jan. 1960), pp. 64–74; 'Imperial Defence Policy and Imperial Foreign Policy 1911–39: The Substance and the Shadow', 'The Influence of the Commonwealth on British Foreign Policy: the Case of the Munich Crisis', *Personalities and Policies* (London, 1965), pp. 139–74.

47 Sir Charles Webster, 'Munich Reconsidered, A Survey of British Policy', *International Affairs*, XXXVII (Apr. 1961), pp. 137–53.

'the appeasers' in 1963 do not mention the dominions.[48] The same year an American scholar, Keith Eubank, thought it worth one line.[49] His fellow countryman, William R. Rock, did not afford the dominions even that in 1966.[50] Christopher Thorne, in 1967, does mention the views expressed by the dominion high commissioners in London during the Munich crisis.[51] It was not until 1968 that Keith Robbins wrote: 'Possibly wrongly, Chamberlain still believed that Britain and the British Empire belonged together. It was taking an undue risk to make war without the certainty of dominion support.'[52] This judgment has only partially been endorsed by Esmonde M. Robertson in the survey of the historiographical debate on the origins of the second world war.[53]

Specialists on British policy writing in the 1960s, like W. N. Medlicott, do offer some analysis of dominion influence.[54] F. S. Northedge claims that 'after 1918 every major decision of British policy had to be preceded by an enquiry into the likely attitude of the British Dominions' and this was a 'major weakness in Britain's international position'. This was especially so as the vital interests of Britain and the dominions diverged.[55]

From a survey of the published literature, as Nicholas Mansergh suggests, it would seem to be an open question whether the dominions influenced or urged Britain to pursue the policy of the appeasement of Europe, or whether they were responsible for it. To show that the dominions were responsible, it would be necessary to prove that 'Chamberlain at the formative stage of a policy which he made peculiarly his own was moved to adopt it as a result of Commonwealth considerations and in response to dominion pressures'.[56] The distinction between 'responsibility' and 'influence' is important.

Consideration of the influence of United States opinion on British policy has seemingly also been stunted by the European orientation of scholars.

[48] Martin Gilbert and Richard Gott, *The Appeasers* (London, 1963).

[49] Keith Eubank, *Munich* (Oklahoma, 1963), p. 182.

[50] William R. Rock, *Appeasement on Trial. British Foreign Policy and its Critics, 1938–1939* (Hamden, Conn., 1966).

[51] Christopher Thorne, *The Approach of War 1938–9* (London, 1967), p. 74.

[52] Keith Robbins, *Munich 1938* (London, 1968), p. 329.

[53] Esmonde M. Robertson, Ed., *The Origins of the Second World War* (London, 1971), p. 22. The influence of the dominions was not considered in the general historiographical debate of the 1960s. See Robert Spencer, 'War Unpremeditated?', *The Canadian Historical Review*, XLIII (1962), pp. 136–44 for a review article of the literature. In the early 1970s, apart from a few monographs [See Rainer Tamchina, 'In Search of Common Causes: The Imperial Conference of 1937', *The Journal of Imperial and Commonwealth History*, I (Oct. 1972), pp. 79–105, and 'Commonwealth und Appeasement: Die Politik der britischen Dominions', *Neue Politische Literatur* (1972), pp. 471–89; Julian Campbell Doherty, 'Die Dominions und die Britische Aussenpolitik von München bis zum Kriegsausbruch 1939', *Vierteljahrshefte für Zeitgeschichte*, XX (1972), pp. 209–34] the dominions received only brief treatment in the general literature. [See Keith Middlemas, *Diplomacy of Illusion The British Government and Germany, 1937–39* (London, 1972), esp. p. 442; Sidney Aster, *1939 The Making of the Second World War* (London, 1973), esp. pp. 228–9].

[54] W. N. Medlicott, *Contemporary England*, (London 1967), p. 363.

[55] F. S. Northedge, *The Troubled Giant* (London, 1966), p. 627.

[56] P. N. S. Mansergh, *The Commonwealth Experience* (London, 1969), p. 282.

Several monographs do touch upon the subject.[57] The usual verdict, based on analyses of Chamberlain's attitude to Roosevelt's overture in January 1938, is that the prime minister felt that 'it is always best and safest to count on nothing from the Americans but words'.[58] A study of the foreign and cabinet office papers would suggest that the view that Chamberlain had a contempt for the United States[59] should be questioned. Perhaps the prime minister, on important issues, moulded British policy in an attempt to win over United States public opinion.

Neglect of the influence of the United States and the European orientation of scholars, has perhaps led to a distorted picture of British policy. The far east, during these years, was as much, if not more a concern, than Europe.[60] Lord Strang, at that time head of the central department of the foreign office, points to this: 'Very few seemed to be conscious of the dangerous situation in the Far East, which the government had constantly to bear in mind.'[61]

Monographs on isolationism in the United States are prolific. This study, therefore, will only attempt to analyse the phenomenon in so far as it affected British policy. Charles Tansill offers a detailed survey of United States policy in the far east and Europe in the 1930s.[62] William L. Langer and S. Everett Gleason provide an account based on the official documents[63] even though it carries the stigma of being written by one involved in the state department.[64] Selig Adler also narrates the events of the 1930s and United States reaction to them.[65] He states the administration's case.[66] A volume edited by Alexander De Conde contains essays analysing United States national interests and concepts of security during this period.[67] The contemporary influence of the literature of isolationism in the 1930s and

---

57 W. V. Wallace, 'Roosevelt and British Appeasement, 1938', *Bulletin of the British Association of American Studies*, New Series V (Dec. 1962), pp. 4–30; M. Baturin, 'The United States and Munich'. *International Affairs* Moscow, V (1959), pp. 75–81; E. L. Henson, 'Britain, America and the Month of Munich', *International Relations*, 2 No. 5 (Apr. 1962), pp. 291–301; John McVickar Haight Jnr., 'France, the United States, and the Munich Conference', *Journal of Modern History* XXXII (Dec. 1960), pp. 340–58; Roland N. Stromberg, *Collective Security and American Foreign Policy* (New York, 1963); Arnold A. Offner, *American Appeasement, United States Foreign Policy and Germany 1933–38* (Cambridge, Mass., 1969).

58 Feiling, p. 325; For a bibliography of accounts of Roosevelt's overture see Rock, pp. 23–4.

59 *Templewood Papers* XIX (C)12, Cadogan to Templewood, 26.10.1951.

60 This stricture does not apply to specialised works on the far east. See Nicholas R. Clifford, 'Britain, America and the Far East, 1937–40: a Failure in Co-operation', *Journal of British Studies*, III (1963–4), pp. 137–54; *Retreat from China* (London, 1967); Dorothy Borg, *The United States and the Far Eastern Crisis of 1933–38* (Cambridge, Mass., 1964); Bradford A. Lee, *Britain and the Sino-Japanese War, 1937–39* (London, 1973).

61 Lord Strang, *Home and Abroad* (London, 1956), p. 123. See also Birkenhead, p. 416.

62 Charles Callan Tansill, *Back Door to War. The Roosevelt Foreign Policy 1933–41* (Chicago, 1952).

63 William L. Langer and S. Everett Gleason, *The Challenge to Isolation* (London, 1952).

64 T. Desmond Williams, 'The Historiography of World War II', Robertson, pp. 53–4.

65 Selig Adler, *The Isolationist Impulse* (London, 1957), pp. 239–73.

66 Selig Adler, *The Uncertain Giant 1921–41* (New York, 1965), pp. 150–217.

67 Alexander De Conde, *Isolationism and Security* (Durham, North Carolina, 1957).

the 'fortress concept' is discussed by Robert Osgood.[68] Donald Drummond provides a narrative account of neutrality and the emergence from isolationism.[69] The neutrality legislation of the 1930s is comprehensively discussed by Robert A. Divine.[70] Manfred Jonas analyses the groups who made up and influenced the isolationist tradition, and the varieties of isolationism.[71]

There are also detailed studies of individuals involved in the neutrality debates, particularly Senators Gerald P. Nye[72] and William E. Borah.[73] Charles A. Lindbergh's journals are now published.[74] James A. Robinson has analysed the role of congress in the making of the neutrality legislation.[75]

The enigma of the role of President F. D. Roosevelt has not been resolved. Manfred Landecker argues that Roosevelt 'recognised the important role of public opinion and weighed this influence carefully in many of his political and foreign policy decision. However, he was caught in a vice between those who urged him to act more vigorously on behalf of the allies and those who insisted on the maintenance of a policy of isolation.'[76] In James MacGregor Burns's analysis Roosevelt 'tagged along with opinion'.[77] Charles A. Beard scrutinises Roosevelt's public statements and the reactions to these by congress and the press. Beard implies that Roosevelt was secretly committing his country to war.[78] Basil Rauch offers a refutation of this.[79] Robert A. Divine concludes that 'hesitancy and indecision also characterized Roosevelt's reaction to Germany's expansionist policies'. It was only by the end of 1938 that Roosevelt 'was no longer the confirmed isolationist he had been earlier in the decade'.[80]

[68] Robert Endicott Osgood, *Ideals and Self-Interest in America's Foreign Relations* (Chicago, 1953). pp. 364–80.

[69] Donald F. Drummond, *The Passing of American Neutrality 1937–41* (Ann Arbor, 1955), pp. 21–96,

[70] Robert A. Divine, *The Illusion of Neutrality* (Chicago, 1962).

[71] Manfred Jonas, *Isolationism in America 1935–41* (Ithatca, New York, 1966).

[72] Wayne S. Cole, *Senator Gerald P. Nye and American Foreign Relations* (Minneapolis, 1962).

[73] Robert James Maddox, *William E. Borah and American Foreign Policy* (Baton Rouge, 1969).

[74] Charles A. Lindbergh, *The Wartime Journals of Charles A. Lindbergh* (New York, 1970). These contain information on the so called 'Cliveden set'.

[75] James A. Robinson, *Congress and Foreign Policy-Making. A Study in Legislative Influence and Initiative* (Homewood, Illinois, 1962), pp. 24–7.

[76] Manfred Landecker, *The President and Public Opinion. Leadership in Foreign Affairs* (Washington, 1968), p. v.

[77] James MacGregor Burns, *Roosevelt: the Lion and the Fox* (London, 1956), p. 400.

[78] Charles A. Beard, *American Foreign Policy in the Making 1932–40. A Study in Responsibilities* (New Haven, 1946).

[79] Basil Rauch, *Roosevelt. From Munich to Pearl Harbor* (New York, 1950).

[80] Robert A. Divine, *Roosevelt and World War II* (Baltimore, 1969), pp. 19–20, 23.

The biographies and personal reminiscences do not illuminate.[81] Perhaps Arthur Schlesinger Jnr's. forthcoming volume will help to settle the debate.

Despite this wealth of literature little has been written on the influence of the United States on British policy. Perhaps the accepted view that Roosevelt and Chamberlain did not co-operate needs challenging.

*   *   *

Before assessing the influence of the dominions and the United States on Chamberlain's policy for the appeasement of Europe it is necessary to examine the internal situations in those countries in 1937, and the extent to which Britain calculated on their support if there were to be war.

By 1937 the international situation was unstable and war seemed likely. Hitler had occupied the Rhineland in 1936. Mussolini had moved into Abyssinia and the Spanish civil war was underway. The position of the democracies was threatened. At the beginning of the year Chamberlain piloted through parliament a renewed programme of rearmament.[82] British contingency plans were based on the assumption of dominion support.[83]

Chamberlain, soon to be prime minister, outlined his thinking to the cabinet committee on foreign policy in a memorandum dated 2 April 1937. He felt that no opportunity should be missed of reducing the international tension. Hitler had been reassuring about the peaceful intentions of Germany, and the approaches by Dr. Schacht, the German finance minister, were an invitation to general discussion.[84]

*   *   *

Before the imperial conference met in May 1937 there were several aspects of United States foreign policy of particular concern to Britain. Firstly, successive neutrality acts passed since 1935 made it unlikely that in the event of war in Europe or the far east, the United States could again be 'the arsenal of democracy'. Secondly, the United States, and particularly Cordell Hull,[85] the secretary of state, favoured the prevailing philosophy of 'economic appeasement'.[86] The essence of this idea was given by Hull

---

[81] See Samuel I Rosenman, *Working with Roosevelt* (New York, 1952), pp. 163–87; John Gunther, *Roosevelt in Retrospect* (London, 1950), pp. 325–30; Edgar Eugene Robinson, *The Roosevelt Leadership 1933–45* (New York, 1955), pp. 230–41.

[82] See Colvin, pp. 23–34.

[83] *Cab 24*, 268, C P 58 (37), Memorandum by Inskip on the Preparedness for War of Great Britain in relation to certain other Powers by May 1937, Most Secret Lock and Key, Undated; Appendix A, C O S 551, Memorandum by Chiefs of Staff Sub-Committee on Comparison of Strength of Great Britain and that of certain other Nations as at May 1937, Most Secret 9.2.1937.

[84] See Colvin, pp. 39–42.

[85] See Julius W. Pratt, *Cordell Hull 1933–44* (New York, 1964), pp. 107–38, for an Account of Hull's Trade Agreement Programme.

[86] See Allan G. B. Fisher, 'Economic Appeasement as a Means to Political Understanding and Peace', *Survey of International Affairs* 1937(1), pp. 56–109.

in a speech to the United States senate finance committee on 10 February 1937: 'In the years that lie ahead, an adequate revival of international trade will be the most powerful single force for easing political tension and averting the danger of war.'[87] This had ramifications for Britain as Hull wished to negotiate a trade treaty with that country. Any such arrangement could affect the dominions as the Ottawa agreements had established imperial preference. Britain could, however, use an Anglo-American trade treaty politically as a deterrent to the dictators. Thirdly, Britain was concerned to educate United States opinion away from isolationism. As a result consideration was given to a possible visit by Chamberlain to the United States, and the use of Malta and Gibraltar by United States vessels.

United States participation in the first world war seemed to have convinced many Americans that their boys should not again be sent to fight and die in alien countries for causes which did not concern them. The 1935 neutrality act made it mandatory for the president to proclaim the outbreak of war between foreign states and to embargo the export of arms to such states. The president had discretion in the definition of the latter, and in applying the embargo to other states as they entered the war. There were to be no private loans or credits to nations declared to be in a state of war.[88] The 1936 act allowed the president to determine when a state of war existed, but reduced executive discretion in respect of the extension of the arms embargo to belligerents entering the war subsequent to its outbreak.[89] Eden repeatedly reminded Robert W. Bingham, the United States ambassador, that this legislation favoured the aggressor as the victim, less likely to be prepared, would have its 'chief source of foreign support cut off'.[90] The 1937 legislation, as Eden pointed out to the delegates at the imperial conference, while handicapping any belligerent obtaining war material or other supplies, aided Britain as it had command of the sea and the largest purse.[91] The reason for this was the controversial 'cash and carry' clause which was introduced for a trial period of two years. This provision meant that any belligerent could purchase goods in the United States provided that it could pay for them in cash, and had the shipping

[87] Quoted by Fisher, p. 56.

[88] See Jonas, pp. 81–121, for a Discussion of this Legislation and Roosevelt's Attitude to it; Bradley Phillips, 'Current Neutrality Problems', *The American Political Science Review*, XXIX (Dec. 1935), pp. 1022–41.

[89] Whitney H. Shepardson and William O. Scroggs, *The United States in World Affairs 1936* (New York, 1937), p. 143. For a Discussion of the Shades of Opinion in the Neutrality Debate see J. W. Garner, 'Recent Neutrality Legislation of the United States', *British Yearbook of International Law*, XVII (1936), pp. 45–9. See also Jonas, pp. 122–61.

[90] *F O 371*, 20666, A448/448/45, Memorandum by Eden of a Conversation with Bingham, 18.1.1937 r. in r. 19.1.1937.

[91] Ibid., 20661, A4808/228/45, Foreign Office Minute, Extract from Eden's Address to the Imperial Conference dealing with Anglo-American Relations, Undated r. in r. 8.7.1937.

to transport them.[92] The bill had a difficult passage through congress, and the 'cash and carry' clause was probably only popular because it was a 'catchy' phrase.[93]

The importance of this move can be guaged from a draft memorandum prepared by Mr. Troutbeck in the foreign office and intended for the imperial conference. It was not circulated presumably because Vansittart complained that any leakage might harm Anglo-American relations. The memorandum suggested that policy in the United States was

> so responsive to waves of public opinion, it is perhaps not too much to hope that, provided His Majesty's Government practise a wise diplomacy, they will find United States neutrality progressively favouring themselves in any major struggle in which they may be engaged. But should this occur, it will be a direct reversal of the trend towards neutrality.[94]

A section omitted from Eden's statement to the imperial conference provides the key to British policy towards the United States. Eden was to have said that if the commonwealth and the United States drifted apart the forces for peace would have been 'incalculably weakened' both in Europe and the far east: 'If peace be the aim of our diplomacy, no greater task lies before us than to retain the goodwill of the United States.' If there were war it was impossible to exaggerate the importance of a friendly United States: the success of the British army might depend on modifications in the neutrality act. The means of improving relations with the United States were limited as the political approach was closed. Only the economic sphere remained. The 'political importance' of an Anglo-American trade treaty was immense, for, if war came, it would have 'an incalculable influence upon the final result': 'If this involves sacrifices, it is a sacrifice for peace and a sacrifice for our security.'[95]

Throughout 1936 Hull had publicly hoped for international co-operation through trade agreements. When Walter Runciman, the president of the board of trade, visited Washington in January 1937 he was told that if Britain proclaimed a programme of liberal economic relations nearly forty nations would follow and international order might be restored.[96] The state

---

[92] Anonymous, 'America: at Home and Abroad', *Round Table*, XXVII (1936–7), pp. 597–611.

[93] Cordell Hull, *The Memoirs of Cordell Hull*, 1 (London, 1948), p. 508. See *Congressional Record* 81(9), pp. 5146 ff., 29.4.1937; 81(6), pp. 2922 ff., 16.3.1937; 81(5), pp. 2248–60, 3.3.1937. For Contemporary Opinions on Neutrality Legislation see E. W. Crecraft, *Freedom of the Seas* (New York, 1935); A. W. Dulles and H. F. Armstrong, *Can We be Neutral?* (New York, 1936); P. C. Jessup, *Neutrality, Today and Tomorrow* (New York, 1936); P. Bradley, *Can We Stay out of War* (New York, 1936); Walter Lippmann, 'Rough-Hew Them how We will', *Foreign Affairs*, XV (July 1937), pp. 587–94.

[94] *F O 371*, 20666, A4581/448/45, Foreign Office Minute by Troutbeck, 10.5.1937 r. in r. 25.5.1937; Minute by Vansittart, 8.5.1937.

[95] Ibid., 20661, A4808/228/45, Foreign Office Minute, Extract from Eden's Address to the Imperial Conference dealing with Anglo-American Relations, Undated r. in r. 8.7.1937.

[96] Hull 1, pp. 520–5.

department protested to the foreign office on 17 January 1937 that the trade talks in progress between Britain and Canada impeded the programme for economic disarmament and suggested co-operation between Britain and the United States to eliminate 'these restrictions which today are stifling legitimate international trade'.[97] Runciman was told that an Anglo-American trade agreement would improve trade relations and symbolise the community of basic views and politics between the two countries. But a reduction on imperial preference rates was indispensable to successful negotiations.[98]

This suggestion was considered by the British government and taken up in informal exchanges between Chamberlain, then chancellor of the exchequer, and Henry Morgenthau, the secretary of the treasury. Although the Americans found Chamberlain official and abrupt, he was 'increasingly candid and reassuringly stiff in the face of developments on the Continent'.[99] On 6 February 1937 Chamberlain described to Morgenthau the increasing difficulties of the Blum government in France. Morgenthau, lunching with Roosevelt on 9 February raised the matter and asked whether he might approach Chamberlain for suggestions as to how to avert world financial bankruptcy as a result of the armaments race. Roosevelt agreed.[100] The British gave the message careful consideration: Chamberlain discussed the reply with Stanley Baldwin, the prime minister, and with Eden. Eden drafted the document, Chamberlain adding the insertion placing the onus for unrest on Germany.[101]

The British diplomatically insisted that it was impossible to disentangle the political and economic aspects of the problem. They offered a frank assessment of German motivations: strength so that no country could withstand German demands for European or colonial territory. The anxiety was that British rearmament would be an inadequate deterrent, and the most immediate contribution that the United States could make to world peace would be amendment of the neutrality legislation. Logistically Britain could not afford to be involved in war in Europe and the far east simultaneously. Japan, however, did not threaten Britain's very existence as did developments in Europe. Anything that the United States could do to stabilise the situation in the far east would ease Britain's position. The

[97] *Foreign Relations of the United States* (hereafter cited as '*FRUS*') 1937(2), pp. 1–2, 641.4231/47. Department of State to British Embassy, 17.1.1937; pp. 8–10, 611.4131/234½, British Embassy to Department of State, 27.1.1937.

[98] Ibid., pp. 11–3, 033.4111 Runciman Walter/12, Hull to Atherton, Telegram No. 45, 12.2.1937.

[99] John Morton Blum, *From the Morgenthau Diaries. Years of Crisis, 1928–1938* (Boston, 1959), p. 473.

[100] Blum, p. 459.

[101] Eden, *Facing the Dictators*, p. 527.

political ambitions of Germany were at the root of the economic difficulties in Europe. The proposed trade agreement between Britain and the United States might ease the situation. Mention was also made of M. van Zeeland, the Belgian prime minister's attempts to ease restrictions on international trade,[102] and of the British and French conversations on economic questions with Schacht. Formal contacts with Germany, however, had been delayed by the colonial question. The British were convinced that any common Anglo-American action would help to 'avert the menace' which threatened the world.[103]

Further informal exchanges of views took place when Norman Davis, a United States emissary, visited London. Davis was described by Sir Ronald Lindsay, the British ambassador in Washington, as being 'fundamentally friendly' to Britain, but excitable, suspicious and 'rather a bore'.[104] Eden and Davis agreed that progress towards economic and political stability would be difficult so long as Britain and the United States pursued opposing trade policies. Chamberlain also saw the need to negotiate a commercial agreement for political and economic reasons. Runciman was worried about imperial preference.[105] Eden told Bingham and Davis that Chamberlain, who was to succeed Baldwin as prime minister, ardently desired Anglo-American economic collaboration and close friendship as being vital for world peace.[106] Chamberlain, however, warned Davis that 'political appeasement' would have to come before 'economic collaboration' and disarmament. Davis saw any solution in the far east in terms of Anglo-American unity, and was told by Sir Alexander Cadogan, the deputy under secretary, of the informal conversations that the British were holding with Shigeru Yoshida, the Japanese ambassador.[107]

Eden was particularly conscious of the importance of retaining the goodwill of the United States government and public opinion in the event of a crisis. He informed Lindsay of this on 10 March. The ambassador replied that Britain should abstain from taking any initiative with the United States on a major political issue:

> America is still extraordinary youthful and sensitive. And such is the prestige today of Great Britain that co-operation with His Majesty's Government would

---

102 See *Cab 23*, 88, pp. 137–8, Cab 19 (37) 1, Secret, 28.4.1937; p. 277, Cab 24 (37) 4, Secret, 17.6.1937. For an Account of the Van Zeeland Mission see Fisher, pp. 67–78.

103 *FRUS* 1937(1), pp. 98–106, 740.00/184, Welles to Roosevelt, 27.5.1937; Enclosure 1, Memorandum from Chamberlain to Morgenthau, Undated.

104 *F O 371*, 22834, pp. 21–6, A5262/5143/45, Lindsay to Halifax, No. 857 Confidential, Transmitting Revised Record of Leading Personalities in the United States, 4.8.1939 r. in r. 16.8.1939.

105 *FRUS* 1937(1), pp. 72–4, 740.00/143, Davis to Hull, Telegram, 10.4.1937.

106 Ibid., *loc. cit.*; pp. 58–60, 740.00/125, Bingham to Hull, Telegram No. 133, 11.3.1937.

107 Borg, pp. 271, 376. Quoting from Memorandum of Conversation of Davis with Chamberlain, 26.4.1937, and Eden, 9.4.1937, *Davis Papers*.

be regarded as a compliment by the public opinion of even so powerful a state as America. But there is an even more important converse to the principle, namely, that refusal of co-operation will be regarded as a snub.[108]

Roosevelt let Eden know in March that he was thinking of an initiative to better international relations. This could only be done in close association with Britain. When Britain felt the moment was right Roosevelt hoped that he would be told.[109]

Hull wanted W. L. Mackenzie King, the prime minister of Canada, to persuade the dominions of the benefits of the United States's economic schemes, even where they cut across imperial preference. Hull spoke to Mackenzie King on 5 March 1937 but the latter did not give any opinion, or do what Hull wanted.[110]

Britain had to manoeuvre both the dominions and the United States in the discussions on the Anglo-American trade treaty.[111] In May the United States maintained that the dominions could benefit from an attitude of co-operation in this matter.[112] F. Ashton-Gwatkin felt that the arguments used to move the dominion delegates at the imperial conference should be political: 'At the price offered here it looks like the world's peace for a shilling'.[113]

Morgenthau replied to Chamberlain's memorandum of March on 1 June declaring that it was possible for Britain and the United States to direct policies 'into a channel of political and economic co-operation'. Britain could take little comfort from the political suggestions: it was the traditional policy of the United States 'not to enter into those types of agreement which constitute or which suggest alliance'; in the far east 'procedure on parallel lines and concurrently' would safeguard interests. Troutbeck of the foreign office considered the reply a 'masterpiece of negation'.[114]

Despite this damper Britain persisted in trying to convince the dominions of the benefits of the proposed trade agreement. Chamberlain, now prime minister, told Bingham that he intended to 'co-operate with the United States as far as possible'.[115] To this end Chamberlain made a moving appeal

[108] Eden, *Facing the Dictators*, p. 528.

[109] Ibid., pp. 528–9.

[110] *FRUS* 1937(1), pp. 641–8, 500.A19/61, Memorandum by Hull, 5.3.1937; *contra* Hull 1, pp. 526–8.

[111] See *D O 114*, 93, *Trade Negotiations with the United States of America. Correspondence and Papers May 1937 to May 1939*, for the details of the arrangements with the dominions of concessions on various products.

[112] *F O 371*, 20660, pp. 33–7, A3554/228/45, Lindsay to Eden, Telegram No. 133, 18.5.1937 r. in r. 19.5.1937.

[113] Ibid., p. 94, A3936/228/45, Minute by F. Ashton-Gwatkin, 24.5.1937 r. in r. 2.6.1937.

[114] Ibid., pp. 203–15, A4165/228/45, Lindsay to Halifax, Telegram No. 429 Secret, 1.6.1937 r. in r. 11.6.1937; Enclosing Memorandum by Morgenthau, Undated; Minute by Troutbeck, 17.6.1937.

[115] *FRUS* 1937(2), pp. 39–40, 611.4131/309, Bingham to Hull, Telegram No. 367, 10.6.1937 (extract).

at the imperial conference that the dominions should co-operate in the conclusion of an Anglo-American trade agreement.[116] Discussions at the imperial conference, and between dominion delegates and the officials from the board of trade, at the beginning of June revealed that Canada would consider making sacrifices in return for a *quid pro quo*. Mackenzie King said that he would handle the Canadian aspect direct with Washington. New Zealand was slightly more negative. Australia would not even go to the board of trade as nothing could be done before the Australian election in the autumn. Australia was also indulging in a tariff feud with the United States. South Africa was helpful. Mr. N. C. Havenga stated that his government attached much importance to economic appeasement. Troutbeck minuted that South Africa had never liked imperial preference, but that the price Britain would have to pay for this 'statesmanlike attitude' was unknown.[117]

After the conference Chamberlain, anxious to secure United States co-operation, worked for direct bargaining between the dominions and the United States.[118] With this in view R. G. Casey, an Australian delegate, returned via Washington and told Hull that after the election his government would do its best to facilitate any agreement.[119] But it was not until October that the British cabinet was able to offer the United States basic proposals.[120]

The difficulties experienced over the trade negotiations with the dominions and the delaying tactics of Australia in particular,[121] affected another proposal that was seen as a means of improving Anglo-American relations. Davis initiated the idea of Chamberlain or Eden visiting the United States. Bingham urged that Eden should do this as it would 'contribute greatly to the improvement of Anglo-American relations which were so vital to peace'.[122] It was intimated to Roosevelt, however,

---

[116] Ibid., pp. 40–1, 611.4131/313, Bingham to Hull, Telegram No. 384, 15.6.1937; p. 42, 611.4131/322, Memorandum by Hull, 24.6.1937.

[117] *Cab 32*, 128, p. 5, E (PD) 37 10th Mtg, Secret, 1.6.1937; *F O 371*, 20660, pp. 131–3, A4104/228/45, Foreign Office Minute by Ashton-Gwatkin on Dominions' Attitude towards Anglo-American Commercial Negotiations, 4.6.1937; pp. 144-52, A4127/228/45, Minute by Troutbeck, 11.7.1937; pp. 151–7, A4143/228/45, Minutes of a Meeting at the Board of Trade with the South African Delegates, Secret, 8.6.1937 r. in r. 11.6.1937; p. 151, Minute by Troutbeck, 12.6.1937; pp. 229–34, A4212/228/45, Record of Meeting of MacDonald, President of the Board of Trade, and Bruce, Secret, 11.6.1937 r. in r. 14.6.1937; Minute by Troutbeck, 15.6.1937; *FRUS* 1937(2), pp. 40–1, 611.4131/313, Bingham to Hull, Telegram No. 384, 15.6.1937.

[118] *FRUS* 1937(2), pp. 43–5, 611.4131/326, Bingham to Hull, Telegram No. 429, 2.7.1937.

[119] *F O 371*, 20660, pp. 160–70, A4933/228/45, Lindsay to Eden, No. 597E Confidential, 6.7.1937 r. in r. 13.7.1937; Enclosing Memorandum by Casey, 2.7.1937; Casey to Earle Page, Telegram, Unnumbered, 2.7.1937 (copy).

[120] See p. 84.

[121] *F O 371*, 20661, pp. 262–3, A4412/228/45, Minute by Troutbeck, 23.6.1937.

[122] Ibid., 20660, pp. 8–12, A3417/228/45, Memorandum by Eden of Conversation with Davis, Circulated to Baldwin, Chamberlain and Lindsay, 4.5.1937; Memorandum of Conversation with Bingham, Circulated to Baldwin, Chamberlain and Lindsay, 5.5.1937.

presumably by Davis who misunderstood a conversation with Chamberlain, that the prime minister was willing to go. Roosevelt regarded the international situation as so important that it would be of 'the greatest advantage' if Chamberlain himself went. Bingham was apprehensive as the visit of a prime minister was 'a big affair' and it would be important that something of material significance should come from it.[123] At the end of June Davis wrote to Chamberlain that an invitation would be arranged for a visit in the autumn. Foreign office officials were perturbed. A. Holman was worried that Roosevelt had a programme in mind which would include the far east, disarmament, Pacific shipping, war debts and commercial negotiations. These questions were of a delicate nature and it seemed undesirable that Chamberlain should go to the United States to discuss them unless there were a chance of further progress. Lindsay favoured a visit by Eden as the same importance might not be attached to it. It was also feared that any discussions on armaments with the United States might further limit the programme.[124] Chamberlain pointed out to Davis the difficulties of his being absent now that he was prime minister. He also thought that it might be advisable to work longer at the trade treaty and to watch developments in the European situation first.[125] Chamberlain felt that there were as good reasons for Eden not going as for himself.[126]

Sumner Welles, the under secretary of state, however, implied on 26 July that Roosevelt was interested in a visit from the prime minister and no one else.[127] On 28 July Roosevelt wrote to Chamberlain explaining that he understood that a visit in the autumn was not practicable. The president did ask whether there were any preparatory steps that might hasten the visit.[128] Eden felt a reply to this unnecessary unless Chamberlain suggested it.[129] Chamberlain did reply on 28 September pointing out that cordial relations between the democracies and the totalitarian states were not in the offing, and that there was little prospect of the situation in the far east being improved by action on the part of the western powers.

[123] Ibid., pp. 274–51, A4370/228/45, Memorandum by Eden of Conversation with Bingham, Secret, 17.6.1937; Eden to Chamberlain, Confidential, 17.6.1937.

[124] Ibid., 20661, pp. 262–70, A4412/228/45, Cleverly to Harvey, 21.6.1937; Enclosing Davis to Chamberlain, Undated (copy); Minutes by A. Holman, 23.6.1937; A. Cadogan, 23.6.1937.

[125] Ibid., A4480/228/45, Chamberlain to Davis (draft initialled by Eden); A4881/228/45, Foreign Office Minute by Harvey, Secret, 8.7.1937; Chamberlain to Davis (draft); 20662, A5473/228/45, Lindsay to Eden, Personal, 26.7.1937 (Chamberlain's Letter to Davis of 8 July posted on 22 July).

[126] Ibid., 20661, A4480/228/45, Cleverly to Harvey, Secret, 30.6.1937.

[127] Ibid., 20662, A5473/228/45, Lindsay to Eden, Personal, 26.7.1937.

[128] Ibid., A6006/228/45, Sayers to Hoyar Miller, Confidential, 18.8.1937; Minute by A. Holman, 20.8.1937; *FRUS* 1937(1), p. 113, 033.4111/338½, Roosevelt to Chamberlain, 28.7.1937, Photostatic Copy from F. D. Roosevelt Library, Hyde Park.

[129] *F O 371*, 20662, A6006/228/45, Minute by Eden, 26.8.1939.

In these circumstances I am afraid that I cannot suggest any way in which the meeting between us could be expedited, though I greatly regret this both on personal and official grounds. Perhaps the community of sentiment between our two countries as to the events in the Far East and the developments in the European situation may be doing something to create a favourable atmosphere and the conclusion of an Anglo-American commercial agreement when we have found ways of overcoming its obvious difficulties will undoubtedly be an important step in the right direction.

In my view we must wait a little longer, but I hope I need not assure you that I shall watch the course of events most carefully, as I am sure you will too, for any opportunity of furthering the purpose we both have in view.[130]

Eden agreed with Chamberlain's verdict.[131]

The British were in a difficult position over the proposal which had resulted from Davis's meddling. There was the distinct possibility that nothing concrete would follow. The effect in the United States would be disastrous and lead to a 'setback in our present cordial relations'.[132] Britain handled the issue astutely. Chamberlain carefully gave the impression that he attached considerable importance to improved Anglo-American relations. There is no evidence to suggest that Eden disagreed with Chamberlain on the advisability of the visit.

Britain, however, did not pursue proposals for improving Anglo-American relations from unofficial ambassadors like Samuel S. Levinson, a Chicago attorney who had been involved in the Kellogg pact,[133] or the financier, Barney Baruch, as they lacked official authority.[134]

As another means of furthering Anglo-American co-operation the admiralty, in July, suggested that the United States squadron in the Mediterranean be offered the use of naval and dockyard facilities in Malta and Gibralter during the prevailing situation in Europe.[135] No prior notification for such use would be necessary.[136] In September, however, the admiralty decided that the offer need not be considered for 'normal' times. The United States squadron was to be withdrawn as soon as the situation in Spain permitted.[137]

[130] Ibid., 20663, A6869/228/45, Cleverly to Hoyar Miller, Secret, 9.9.1937; *FRUS* 1937(1), pp. 131–2. 033.4111/338½, Chamberlain to Roosevelt, 28.9.1937, Photostatic Copy from F. D. Roosevelt Library, Hyde Park.

[131] Eden, *Facing the Dictators*, p. 531.

[132] *F O 371*, 20661, p. 262, A4412/228/45, Minute by A. Holman, 23.6.1937.

[133] *Lothian Papers* 338, pp. 434–6, Lothian to Halifax, 19.3.1937 (copy); p. 437, Halifax to Lothian, 23.3.1937; 341, pp. 708–11, Levinson to Lothian, Personal and Confidential, 29.4.1937; 347, p. 374, Levinson to Lothian, 23.10.1937.

[134] *F O 371*, 20663, A6550/228/45, Memorandum and Minutes on Conversation between Eden, Churchill and Baruch, Very Confidential, 31.8.1937 r. in r. 8.9.1937.

[135] Ibid., 20662, p. 250, A5298/228/45, Admiralty to Foreign Office, No. M3811/37, 26.7.1937 r. in r. 27.7.1937.

[136] Ibid., *loc. cit.*

[137] Ibid., A6519/228/45, Admiralty to Foreign Office, No. M4798/37, 8.9.1937.

Britain, in the early months of 1937 gave careful consideration to United States opinion. It was felt that the deterrent effect of Anglo-American co-operation might help to preserve peace. If there were war the importance of a friendly United States could not be exaggerated. Isolationsist sentiment in the United States made political overtures impossible and only economic moves could be pursued, in the hope that political co-operation would follow. British attitudes to the trade treaty negotiations were indicative of this policy. It is evident that Eden, Chamberlain, and the foreign office considered Anglo-American co-operation a high priority.

Relations with the United States, as the trade treaty negotiations showed, were affected by the attitude of the dominions. The position of the dominions was one which those making foreign policy could not ignore: Britain felt obliged to defend the dominions even though some members of the commonwealth did not feel that the arrangement was reciprocal.

*   *   *

By 1937 relations between Britain and the dominions were governed by different constitutional and conventional precedents to those operating in 1919. The South African parliament had given legislative enactment to the statute of Westminster, and even though Australia, New Zealand, and Canada were tardy about following this lead, their right to do so was not disputed. Ireland was a dominion 'with a difference': its government felt that it was not a dominion at all.[138] Ireland did not attend the imperial conference in 1937, and in December of that year the British cabinet considered ceasing to treat Ireland as a member of the commonwealth.[139] India had not attained the independence of dominion status and the British government had resumed control of Newfoundland.[140] In practice the dominions were not only self governing, but also fully autonomous states, equal and in no way subordinate to Britain. The British government could not, and did not, dispute the right of a dominion parliament to conduct its own external affairs, make its own defence arrangements, and to declare its right of neutrality in any future war in which Britain might be involved. It was only within the dominion parliaments that there were wrangles on these issues. The interests of the individual dominions diverged, and British statesmen had to contend with the reality that a common commonwealth policy, even in times of grave danger, could no longer be assumed, and had to be patiently sought after.[141]

[138] Mansergh, *The Commonwealth Experience*, p. 285.

[139] Colvin, p. 72.

[140] In this study I shall concentrate on the four 'major' dominions and only consider the influence of Ireland, India, and Newfoundland where it is particularly pertinent.

[141] See Mansergh, *The Commonwealth Experience*, p. 270.

This situation meant that the machinery of consultation between Britain and the dominions assumed increasing significance. By 1937 it consisted of four components.

Firstly, there were the high commissioners in London representing Canada, South Africa, Australia, New Zealand and Ireland. These high commissioners did not necessarily speak with the authority of their governments, and were mainly regarded, especially in the case of Canada, as a means through which information could be transferred. They were not members of the government, but servants. British high commissioners were reciprocally situated in Ottawa, Pretoria, Canberra and Wellington, but not in Dublin. If there were a crisis the dominion high commissioners in London were kept informed by meetings with the secretary of state for dominion affairs, and also had personal access to the prime minister and the foreign secretary. The information made available to the high commissioners was considerable, but carefully sifted, so as to present a particular picture, and occasionally contentious news was withheld. Access to information by the high commissioners became a matter of controversy between 1937 and 1939. During crises the high commissioners frequently met together as individuals and presented a united dominion front to the British government. Their influence was considerable.

The dominions office which had overall charge of the relations with the dominions was the second component. It appointed the high commissioners to the dominion capitals. These high commissioners could influence events in the individual dominions. In crises, however, it was the foreign office and the cabinet, through the secretary of state for dominion affairs, that decided British policy towards the dominions. The dominions office merely acted as a clearing agency. This, at any rate, is the situation revealed in the foreign and cabinet office papers. The role of the dominion office cannot be assessed definitely as, according to the indexes, all significant papers on foreign affairs have been destroyed under statute, presumably as there are copies in the foreign office archives.[142] Even the record of the foreign office decisions on this matter is incomplete as the dominions intelligence files for 1938 have been destroyed. The British high commissioner in the dominions relayed detailed assessments of the political situation in their various dominions, illustrated by prolific extracts from newspapers, which seemed to be taken as a gauge of opinion. These were usually passed on to the foreign office.

[142] *D O 3*, 101–4.

Thirdly, there was direct communication between prime ministers. This could take the form of telegrams relayed through the high commissioners or the dominions office. In acute crises the long distance radio telephone was used for personal conversations.

Fourthly, the imperial conference, with its secret sessions, provided an opportunity for inter commonwealth discussions on foreign affairs, defence, economic and constitutional matters. This was the best opportunity, on a level of personal contact, of achieving an agreed commonwealth policy.

On the whole the dominions, particularly Australia and New Zealand, relied for information on the international situation from the British government. The dominions did not have many legations abroad: by 1936 Canada was represented in Washington, Paris, and Tokyo; South Africa in the Hague, Brussels, Rome, Berlin, Stockholm, Paris and Lisbon; Ireland in Washington, the Vatican, Paris, Brussels, Berlin, and Madrid. New Zealand and Australia used British representatives in all parts of the world.[143] Australia did appoint a counsellor to the staff of the British embassy in Washington, but it was not until 1940 that R. G. Casey became the accredited minister in Washington.[144] Canada, South Africa, and Ireland also had departments of external affairs on a modest scale. In 1912 the Canadian department of external affairs was joined by statute to the office of prime minister,[145] but it was not until 1946 that a secretary of state for foreign affairs was appointed.[146] The South African department of external affairs was established in 1927 and the prime minister held the portfolio of minister of external affairs.[147] In Ireland there was a separate department from 1922.[148] Australia separated the department of external affairs from the prime minister's office in 1935 and took steps to build up the nucleus of a career diplomatic service this way.[149] The dominions lacked experience and expertise in the handling of their own foreign policy. Since most of the information came from the British government, the dominions without independent sources, could have their foreign policies influenced. Perhaps it is significant that the most independently minded of the dominions had the best established departments of external affairs and

[143] Mansergh, *Problems of External Policy*, p. 72.
[144] R. G. Casey, *Friends and Neighbours* (Melbourne, 1954), p. 1.
[145] Mansergh, *Problems of External Policy*, p. 71.
[146] See H. Gordon Skilling, *Canadian Representation Abroad* (Toronto, 1945,) pp. 260–7.
[147] See E. Rosenthal, *South African Diplomats Abroad* (Johannesburg, 1949).
[148] Mansergh, *Problems of External Policy*, p. 71.
[149] Casey, pp. 28–9; Earle Page, *Truant Surgeon* (Sydney, 1963), pp. 358–60; Alan Watt, *The Evolution of Australian Foreign Policy* (Cambridge, 1967), pp. 1, 21–2.

the most representatives abroad. As policy interests diverged from Britain this became more necessary.

The dominions had, however, followed the British lead in rearmament. When the decision was taken to rearm in 1934, Sir Maurice Hankey, the secretary to the cabinet and to the committee of imperial defence, had visited the various dominions. Hankey was given permission to pass on the information of the international situation which had resulted in the British programme of rearmament, and to discuss the effect on imperial defence. His mission was successful.[150]

By 1937 it was no longer possible to generalise about the commonwealth as a whole. The British government had to consider each dominion individually when it considered commonwealth support in the event of war. Mackenzie King[151] in Canada was as ardent an isolationist as some of his United States friends. In South Africa General J. B. M. Hertzog, the prime minister[152], favoured his country's neutrality, and had debated for seven years on this issue with General J. C. Smuts, the deputy prime minister.[153] J. A. Lyons, the prime minister in Australia, was faced by a vociferous and influential labour opposition pledged to fight any commitment outside Australia. Only New Zealand was happy to come to Britain's assistance in time of war but that dominion still clung to the ideal of the league of nations and openly criticised any British deviation from the covenant. For the dominions Eden's Leamington speech on 20 November 1936 was an assurance that Britain would only become entangled in Europe if it seemed that its vital interests were at stake.[154]

Internal conditions in South Africa were such that, of all the dominions, it was the one least likely to give even qualified support to British involvement in Europe. Hertzog and Smuts headed the fusion government. They

---

150 Lord Hankey, *Diplomacy by Conference* (London, 1946), pp. 131–2.

151 See J. W. Pickersgill, *The Mackenzie King Record 1939–1944* (Toronto, 1960), pp. 3–39. There is no published biography of Mackenzie King covering this period. Mansergh, *The Commonwealth Experience*, pp. 378–88, offers interesting insights into Mackenzie King's character.

152 See Oswald Pirow, *James Barry Munnik Hertzog* (Cape Town, 1958); C. M. van den Heever, *Generaal J. B. M. Hertzog* (Johannesburg, 1944]. The Abridged English Translation is not as revealing as the Afrikaans original. [C. M. van den Heever, *General J. B. M. Hertzog* (Johannesburg, 1946)]. Citations are from the Afrikaans volume. In 1967 I was refused access to the *Hertzog Papers* in the South African State Archives in Pretoria as the Custodian was away. In 1969 I was informed that the Collection had been closed. I was, however, allowed to consult the index, and am satisfied that there appears to be no material in the papers germane to this topic that is not available elsewhere.

153 W. K. Hancock, *Smuts, The Fields of Force, 1919–1950* (Cambridge, 1968), is the only biography that covers the period. See Mansergh, *The Commonwealth Experience*, pp. 370–8, for a brief essay on Smuts. In 1967 Prof. Hancock informed me that as a research student I would not be granted access to the *Smuts Papers* in the Cape Town University Library. The *Smuts Papers* in the South African State Archives in Pretoria are closed for this period. In 1967, however, I was allowed to consult the index, and am satisfied that there appears to be no material in the Pretoria collection germane to this topic. There is much valuable material in the Cape Town collection. Copies, however, of Smuts's correspondence with Lothian are to be found in the *Lothian Papers* in the Scottish Record Office, Edinburgh.

154 Anonymous, 'Power Politics and the Imperial Conference', *Round Table*, XXVII (1936–7), pp. 260–75. For Text of Speech see Anthony Eden, *Foreign Affairs* (London, 1939), pp. 163–7 esp. pp. 166–7.

had agreed to differ on the issue of the divisibility of the crown. The minority nationalist opposition party, headed by Dr. D. F. Malan, which had the avowed aim of a republic, not necessarily at once, encouraged a policy of neutrality for South Africa, and was not averse to closer relations with Germany. On these issues the nationalists did not lack sympathisers in the governing party. The small, but vociferous, dominion party, headed by Colonel C. F. Stallard, deplored any recognition of the statute of Westminster, and anxiously watched the severing of the links of empire. In the thirties racial issues in South Africa still tended to revolve around the English-Afrikaans question rather than the black-white question. The majority Afrikaner group had no link with Britain, and as early as 1914 the old Louis Botha policy of conciliation had begun to lose ground. Involvement in foreign wars was, for them, an anathema.

The South African government were prepared to co-operate with Britain on certain matters of defence. This was limited to technical assistance and the Simonstown base. A 1922 agreement recognised Simonstown as a British naval base, and the South African land and air forces were pledged to its defence for Britain in time of war.[155] In 1936 Oswald Pirow, the South African minister of defence, visited Britain and arrangements were made for an increase in South African defence equipment such as the purchase of near obsolete fighter aircraft, and for the building of a munitions factory in South Africa. After Pirow's visit the South African defence department started a survey to ascertain how industry could be mobilised for war production, and a war supplies board was established.[156] Co-operation, however, did not extend much beyond the Simonstown agreement.[157] Hertzog, in April 1937 told the house of assembly that he had never been afraid of South Africa taking part in the 'common defence of the Empire'.[158] This caused surprised comment, and the prime minister hastily claimed that he had intended to say that he was prepared to participate in discussions on empire defence.[159] Malan protested that Hertzog and Smuts had agreed to differ on the question of participation in a scheme of imperial defence.[160] Pirow, however, assured the house that South Africa was not taking part in any general scheme of empire defence. He explained

[155] Ibid., 'South Africa', Round Table, XXVII (1936–7), pp. 560–1.

[156] *Times*, 12.2.1937.

[157] *U K Parl Deb H of C* 321, col. 2915, 24.3.1937; 323, col. 1254, 6.5.1937; *Cape Times*, 3.4.1937; *Manchester Guardian*, 10.3.1937.

[158] *S A Parl Deb H of A* 1937, col. 4386, 7.4.1937.

[159] Ibid., col. 4428, 8.4.1937.

[160] Ibid., col. 4387, 7.4.1937.

that issues of defence at the imperial conference did not really affect South Africa: his visit to Britain had settled defence relations.[161]

The parliamentary debates in 1937 suggest that Hertzog's attitude to neutrality did not differ markedly from that of the republican Malan. A motion censoring a controversial article by Dr. H. J. Bodenstein, secretary to the prime minister, focussed attention on this issue. The article in the *Europäische Revue* argued that South Africa was a sovereign and independent state in the international sphere. South Africa was free to decide on its participation in any possible European war. Conveniently Bodenstein described South Africa's sphere of influence in Africa as not extending north of the equator, but including Kenya and Uganda. He probably had German colonial ambitions in mind. Hertzog considered Bodenstein's article 'excellent'.[162] In the ensuing debate Smuts shielded behind the concept of 'passive belligerency' while Hertzog seemingly took the line that South Africa, as a sovereign state, was neutral, and stood apart from any wars of the empire. On this point Hertzog and Malan were in substantial agreement. The compromise reached was that South Africa would not participate in any war except by the declaration of parliament.[163] South African attitudes tended to crystallise around the opinions attributed to Smuts and Hertzog.

Hertzog was the more consistent: a man who even before 1914 had rejected conciliation, he was in many respects the father of Afrikanerdom and had distinctly anti British traits. His attitude to Germany should be seen in the light of this. Hertzog's traditional roots were not in a liberal British democracy, but rather in the Boer republican ideal of the strong individual leader. The South African prime minister expected great things from Hitler, and hoped that the führer would stop the advance of Russia.[164]

Smuts's attitude is neither consistent nor easy to analyse. In public he stated one thing, in private he wrote another. In both cases it depended on whom he was addressing. His overriding motive seems to have been not to lose favour with anyone. Sir Keith Hancock argues that from about the middle of 1936 Smuts stopped using the word 'appeasement'. Smuts had discovered, Hancock assures us, that appeasement had come to mean a policy of propitiation pursued by the weaker party towards the stronger party. Hancock stresses that Smuts was much influenced by Churchill, but

---

[161] Ibid., cols. 4385, 4391, 7.4.1937; cols. 2501–5, 1.3.1937; *Times*, 10.5.1937.
[162] *S A Parl Deb H of A* 1937, cols. 2826, 2833–4, 2836, 5.3.1937.
[163] Ibid., cols. 2857, 2850, 5.3.1937.
[164] Pirow, p. 221.

cedes that Smuts, early in 1937, had as his guides on the European situation L. S. Amery and Lord Lothian.[165]

Lothian was a member of the Anglo-German friendship association.[166] On 16 March 1937 he wrote to Smuts anticipating the danger of a 'new phase' collective security which would involve Britain in a military alliance with France and Russia. This, Lothian thought, would 'split this country and the Empire from top to bottom'. The alternative was to find a basis of agreement with Germany, possibly allowing Germany to create 'a sort of Ottawa economic Mittel Europa'.[167]

Smuts replied that he felt it was necessary to cultivate accord between Britain and Germany: he valued the Anglo-German naval agreement; there was Hitler's goodwill and sincere desire for Anglo-German co-operation; Hitler's obsession against Russia; and the economic straits that enmeshed Germany. Smuts was an advocate of the appeasement of Europe: Hitler needed encouragement.

> He has had literally nothing from us to show to his people or to save his face as the ruler of the most powerful nation in the world.

Smuts wrote about colonial concessions to Germany, the inevitability of the *Anschluss*, of Danzig and Memel as being passing makeshifts, and of the need to make economic and financial concessions to Germany. Smuts, despite suppositions by Malan, was seemingly opposed to South Africa becoming embroiled in any European conflict. Smuts assured Lothian:

> Our South African representatives at the Imperial Conference will go all out for some way of arriving at a European settlement and will be extremely averse to South Africa or the British Commonwealth being involved in any European conflict.[168]

Publicly Smuts spoke about an 'armed Peace' which would last indefinitely.[169]

Smuts's views do seem to have influenced Lothian in some way. In May Lothian travelled to Germany to see Hitler. On his return he wrote to Eden advocating a conciliatory policy towards Germany, and a revised league system in which Britain would refuse to form part of the European regional balance, except for the defensive guarantee to France and Belgium, and

[165] Hancock, pp. 277–81.

[166] *Lothian Papers* 325, p. 28, T. P. Cornwall-Evans to Lothian enclosing List of M.P.'s who belonged to the Anglo-German Friendship, 4.2.1937.

[167] Ibid., 333, pp. 880–6, Lothian to Smuts, 16.3.1937 (copy).

[168] Ibid., 445, pp. 22–7, Smuts to Lothian, Personal and Confidential, 7.4.1937.

[169] *Cape Times*, 22.3.1937; 29.3.1937, Ed.

'return to that detachment from automatic military commitment in Europe, which has been the secret of Empire security in the past'. Lothian argued that such a form of detachment was the only basis upon which Britain would be able to find a common policy towards Europe with the dominions.[170]

Lothian, as well as circulating a memorandum of the European position as he saw it, and of the conversation that he had had in Berlin with Hitler, Goering and Schacht, to Vansittart, Inskip, Chamberlain, and Templewood, also sent copies to Mackenzie King, Casey and Hertzog for the use of these delegates to the imperial conference.[171] Significantly Lothian did not press his views on the New Zealand delegation. He also sent the memoranda to Smuts.[172]

Lothian had another ally in South Africa, the governor general, Sir Patrick Duncan who agreed with him on the European situation.[173] Before sailing for South Africa in January 1937 Duncan, a member of the Milner kindergarten, and until a shortwhile previously of the South African government, said:

> I hope you will not let these controversies in Europe pull you into commitments, even possibly with conflicts, into which it will be difficult for your Dominions to follow you. There your interests lie; there are the interests of the future.[174]

Canada did not differ markedly from South Africa on imperial defence commitments and neutrality. In March 1937 Mackenzie King visited Roosevelt and discussed a reconstituted league without sanctions which the United States might be able to join. When the Canadian prime minister saw Lindsay, Mackenzie King launched into what Lindsay described as:

> a diatribe . . . against sanctions. . . . He said that Canada was resolved to maintain neutrality in any war at any price, and that on no account would she be dragged into any hostilities. His attitude corresponded very closely to that generally adopted in America.

Vansittart minuted:

> Mackenzie King seems to lose rather than to gain in intelligence as he gets older. This is drivel, and dangerous drivel. I hope he will be sternly discouraged when he comes here from 'thinking' on these lines.[175]

---

[170] Feiling, p. 312.

[171] *Lothian Papers* 203, p. 242, Lothian to Vansittart, Confidential, 11.5.1937 (copy); p. 243, Lothian to Inskip, Confidential, 11.5.1937 (copy); p. 244, Lothian to Chamberlain, Confidential, 11.5.1937 (copy); p. 245, Lothian to Eden, Confidential, 11.5.1937 (copy); p. 246, Lothian to Templewood, Confidential, 11.5.1937 (copy); p. 247, Lothian to Mackenzie King, Confidential, 11.5.1937 (copy); p. 248, Lothian to Casey, Confidential, 11.5.1937 (copy); p. 249, Lothian to Hertzog, Confidential, 11.5.1937 (copy); pp. 252–65, Memorandum by Lothian on Visit to Berlin, 19.5.1937.

[172] Ibid., p. 250, Lothian to Smuts, 14.5.1937 (copy).

[173] Ibid., 346, pp. 246–6a, Duncan to Lothian, 19.4.1937.

[174] *Times*, 30.1.1937.

[175] *F O 371*, 20670, A2082/2082/45, Lindsay to Vansittart, 8.3.1937 r. in r. 18.3.1937 Minute by Vansittart, 31.3.1937.

As in South Africa a section of the Canadians tended to be anti British, and against any commitment by their government to foreign wars. The French Canadians had made their stand on this point clear during the 1914–8 war, and the following two decades had not mollified their rancour. A Canadian speaking to an Englishman could only play the role of a 'well-wisher'.[176] Public concern in Canada was increasing: there was a series of national radio talks and articles in *Macleans Magazine* on defence; the fourth study conference of the Canadian institute of international affairs in May 1937 took as its theme 'Canada's Defence Policy' and 'Canada and the Americans'.[177]

The parliamentary debates in 1937 revealed the Canadian government's predicament. Cabinet criticism, especially from the middle westerners concerned with social reform, was so severe that defence estimates were cut by 30 per cent. The opposition in the house was such that Mackenzie King had to hold a special caucus, at which he is said to have told his followers that they would have to vote in favour or take the consequences.[178]

Severe criticism of the government benches by the CCF, a socialist party which favoured neutrality, marked the debate. The conservatives were silent, possibly trusting that in the absence of criticism the liberal party might split on the issue of defence.[179]

At the end of January the house of commons debated a CCF motion that Canada should be neutral in the event of war regardless of who the belligerents might be. Canada should ignore any scheme for imperial defence.[180] This debate reflected the various attitudes in Canada.

The leader of the CCF, J. S. Woodsworth, gave the isolationist viewpoint. Increased defensive expenditure only foreshadows the possibility of Canada being drawn into another European war. Over 50 per cent of the people in the middle west were not of Anglo-Saxon origin. British entanglements were hardly their concern. Canada was not in immediate danger. The United States would counter any aggression towards Canada, if only for its own sake.[181]

---

[176] *Lothian Papers* 327, pp. 218–22, Loring C. Christie, Press Gallery Canadian House of Commons, to Lothian, 20.10.1936.

[177] F. H. Soward, *Canada in World Affairs, The Pre-War Years* (Oxford, 1941), p. 70.

[178] Anonymous, 'The Dominions and Imperial Defence', *Round Table*, XXVII (1936–7), p. 547.

[179] Soward, p. 41.

[180] *Can Parl Deb H of C* (1937(1)), pp. 237–41, 25.1.1937.

[181] Ibid., p. 241, 25.1.1937.

In replying Mackenzie King gave his government's stand. It would be for the Canadian parliament to say, in any situation, whether or not Canada should remain neutral. He doubted whether any Canadian government would send troops beyond the border without parliamentary sanction.[182]

Mackenzie King also offered an analysis of the divisions in Canadian public opinion. Firstly, there were those whom he labelled the imperialist school. They considered the British empire indivisible, and from this followed the need for a common defence and foreign policy. Secondly, some favoured the isolation of Canada. Mackenzie King felt that the vast majority fell into a third division between those two extremes, and favoured the policy that he supported.[183]

There was much talk of a North American 'mentality', and a feeling that Canadians should keep their own blood for their own country. Speakers from Quebec spoke of secession from the commonwealth in the event of Canadian imperial or European commitments.[184]

The defence estimates had a difficult passage: at the committee stage thirteen liberals, including twelve French Canadians, voted against them. There were murmurings in the rural constituencies, and the ticklish conscription issue was brandished in the Quebec press. In the end only 22 members out of 245 voted against the defence estimates, but this could be attributed to party discipline, and was hardly an indication of opinion in parliament or the country.[185]

Mackenzie King was the Canadian most likely to influence British policy. He was suspicious of any European or imperial entanglements. Vincent Massey, the Canadian high commissioner in London, regarded Mackenzie King as being antagonistic towards Britain.[186] In August 1936 Mackenzie King wrote to Lord Tweedsmuir, the governor general in Canada and another member of the Milner kindergarten:

> I keep wondering if some way cannot be found whereby if Europe is determined on war, she might not be left to herself, the British Empire standing outside.[187]

---

[182] Ibid., p. 250, 25.1.1937.

[183] See, for Example, Anonymous, 'The Dominions and Imperial Defence', *Round Table*, XXVII (1936–7), p. 549.

[184] *Can Parl Deb H of C* 1937(1), p. 254, 25.1.1937; pp. 551, 836, 4.2.1937; p. 937, 16.2.1937; pp. 994, 1006–7, 1023–4, 18.2.1937; p. 1055, 19.2.1937.

[185] *Times*, 17.2.1937; 24.2.1937; 26.2.1937; Anonymous, 'The Dominions and Imperial Defence', *Round Table*, XXVII (1936–7), p. 548; Soward, p. 65, See also *Can Parl Deb Sen* 1937, p. 7, 19.1.1937; p. 172, 16.3.1937.

[186] Vincent Massey, *What's Past is Prologue* (London, 1963), p. 242.

[187] *Mackenzie King Papers*, Mackenzie King to Tweedsmuir, 24.8.1936. Quoted by James Eayrs, *In Defence of Canada. Appeasement and Rearmament* (Toronto, 1965), pp. 53–4.

Mackenzie King agreed with a document drawn up by O. D. Skelton, the deputy minister of external affairs, and approved by the Canadian cabinet. The document argued that if Britain were determined on war Canada might prefer to stay out.[188]

> Is Canada to regard it as the normal thing that every generation (or less) she is to invade the Continent of Europe and join the European battle campaigns of the 20th century—so normal that she should now, in contradistinction to the 1914–18 campaign, deliberately prepare in advance? Is it to be normal that this invasion and intervention from North America should be undertaken at the outset of each European campaign, regardless of what position the United States takes? . . . Is the creation and maintenance of a Canadian nation feasible on such lines?[189]

Even if, as James Eayrs argues, Mackenzie King had overcome the 'isolationist impulse', and considering Mackenzie King's interview with Lindsay in Washington it seems unlikely that he had,[190] there is no doubt about the sentiments of other members of the Canadian delegation to the imperial conference. For example one, T. A. Crerar, a member of the cabinet, wrote in April 1937:

> Whatever we do, I feel certain that Canada will keep out of that net of a common Empire foreign policy . . . the more I see of the whole thing, the more I am certain that our destiny is on the North American continent.[191]

Canadian opinion would, in any case, inhibit Mackenzie King. The *Globe and Mail*, Toronto, justifiably argued that the defence debate had fore-stalled any commitments for imperial defence as far as Canada was concerned.[192]

The South African and Canadian delegations to the imperial conference were not likely to favour imperial co-operation on defence, and were bound to oppose any European commitments for their dominions. Both countries had embarked on limited programmes of rearmament, in many respects parallel to those initiated in Britain. But these were conceived of as necessary for their own defence. The position of Australia and New Zealand was different: both had a largely homogenous population which had its roots in Britain. Binding sentimental ties were stronger than those in South Africa and Canada. Strategically too, Australia and New Zealand

---

[188] Eayrs, p. 54.

[189] *Mackenzie King Papers*, Memorandum by Skelton for the Imperial Conference, 1937, 29.3.1937. Quoted by Eayrs, p. 54.

[190] See p. 26.

[191] *Dafoe Papers*, Crerar to Dafoe, 17.4.1937. Qoted by Eayrs, p. 55. See also *Documents on Canadian External Relations* 6, 1936–9, pp. 137–41, No. 125, Memorandum Imperial Conference 1937 Foreign Affairs and Defence, April n.d. 1937; pp. 180–8, No. 141, Memorandum Imperial Conference 1937 Defence Questions, Most Secret, 29.3.1937.

[192] *Globe and Mail*, 24.2.1937. Quoted in *Can Parl Deb Sen* 1937, p. 173, 16.3.1937.

were more vulnerable. An aggressive Japan, if unrestrained, might cause disastrous consequences for the Pacific dominions.

In Australia, however, because of the domestic situation, the government could only pursue a policy which the British considered 'weak'. The high commissioner, Sir Geoffrey Whiskard, pointed out that the coalition government had to harmonise the divergent policies of the industrial united party and the agrarian country party. It was in office only because most Australians thought that it was less undesirable than a labour combination under J. L. Lang and John Curtin. Whiskard explained that the Australian government, with a general election in the offing, was anxious to extract domestic credit from the imperial conference. The delegation would probably hope for a co-ordinated scheme of imperial defence in which 'the special problems and complete independence of Australia' would be carefully safeguarded.[193] While the government felt that Australia could not conveniently detach itself from Britain and British commitments, the opposition labour party, being socialist orientated, condemned expenditure on imperialist wars, and argued in favour of a defence policy which provided for Australian defence only. Because of the strategic vulnerability of Australia's geographical position, the labour case was more difficult to uphold than that, for instance, of the nationalist Canadians.

During the defence debate of November 1936, these opposing attitudes were obvious. One speaker blatantly stated that the first line of defence was the maintenance of a 'close relationship between the component parts of the British empire'. Mr. Archie Cameron speaking for the labour party, was alarmed by such views. He blamed it all on France, a country which had not even attempted to carry out the obligations of Versailles. He urged that the Australian delegates to the forthcoming imperial conference should impress upon Britain the need to allow France and Germany to settle their own 'eternal wrangle'.[194] Sir Archdale Parkhill, the minister of defence, described the government's policy of imperial co-operation as one of 'self-interest and self-preservation'.[195] Lyons supported, almost without qualification, the British defence white paper of February 1937. He referred to the new British defence policy as an insurance against war, and a definite contribution to the peace of the world. Although Australia's

---

[193] See Page, pp. 257–8, for an Account of the Formation of the Coalition Government. *F O 372*, T7746/104/384, Cabinet Office to Dominions Office, Political Situation in Australia, Confidential, 10.5.1937 r. in r. 19.5.1937; Minute by F. H. Cleobury, 21.5.1937; Enclosure, No. 76, Report by Whiskard, Confidential, 31.3.1937 r. 15.4.1937 (copy).

[194] *Aust Parl Deb H of R* 152, cols. 1560, 1568, 5.11.1936.

[195] Ibid., cols. 1545, 1584, 5.11.1936.

defence bill was the highest per head of the dominions, he realised that commonwealth co-operation was necessary for effective imperial defence.[196]

Australian willingness to work for imperial co-operation is discernible in Australia's preparations for the imperial conference. In November 1936, in reply to the British proposal that there should be general discussion on defence and foreign policy at the imperial conference, the Australian government suggested a review of the relations and attitudes of the dominion foreign policies to British foreign policy, and besides specifically Australian defence concerns, urged a consideration of the further development of the principle of imperial co-operation in defence.[197]

A number of significant papers were prepared by the Australian departments of defence and external affairs for the use of delegates to the conference. One on foreign policy, dated March 1937, contained ideas similar to those of Chamberlain. It stressed the need to prevent simultaneous hostile action on the part of Germany, Italy and Japan:

> Empire security demands of British foreign policy that no situation shall be allowed to arise in which Germany, in the West, Japan in the Far East, and any power, such as Italy, on the main artery between the two, are simultaneously hostile.[198]

It gave a realistic survey of the European situation, saw Germany as constituting the principal threat to world peace, and the departmental advisers considered that the maintenance of peace was dependent on wise British foreign policy backed by an increase in British military strength. In regard to the far east, however, they urged upon the British government the need, from the Australian point of view, of better relations between Britain and Japan. The possibility of assistance from the United States was not envisaged. The memoranda show that the Australian government appreciated that although close co-operation in international affairs between the commonwealth nations was a major concern of both Australia and Britain, dominions like Canada would possibly not agree. It was felt that Australia had a special role in initiating discussions on imperial defence. Parkhill, forwarding the relevant defence proposals to Casey, wrote that the British government was reluctant to originate proposals for imperial consultation, and preferred the proposals to come from the dominions. Because of their need for an impregnable Singapore imperial co-operation was particularly vital to Australia and New Zealand. The part played by Australia in commonwealth naval defence qualified it to speak 'with candour' on this.

---

[196] *Times*, 19.2.1937.
[197] Paul Hasluck, *The Government and the People 1939–1941* (Canberra, 1952), pp. 55–6.
[198] Quoted by Hasluck, p. 56.

The proposed plans also contained specific questions on British commitments. Eden's Leamington address was noted, but Australia was particularly concerned with British relations with Japan. Enquiries were to be made as to whether the prevailing accommodating policy towards Japan was temporary, pending the strengthening of British defence. Concern was shown as to whether British policy was in harmony with that of the United States in the far east.[199] These were searching enquiries on matters on which British policy was hardly formulated. On questions of principle the relevant memoranda favoured adherence to general league precepts, but realised their practical limitations in view of the recent failures of collective security.

> The future cohesion of the Empire would in a large measure depend upon the extent to which British foreign policy could command the confidence and the support of the Dominions. If that policy were based purely on European considerations, then the Dominions might well be unwilling to cooperate. Fortunately, the League of Nations and the policies enshrined in the Covenant provided a focal point for common Empire policy, and of recent years the declared policy of Great Britain and the Dominions had been based on League principles centred round the ideas of collective action, arbitration, conciliation and peace. These principles, world-wide in their scope, lessened the chance of any disruption and facilitated a consistent and unified Empire foreign policy.[200]

The Australian delegates to the imperial conference, unlike those from Canada and South Africa, went to secure imperial co-operation on defence. In the face of opposition from the other dominions Australia was willing to co-operate with Britain. After his arrival in England in May, Lyons publicly declared that Australia, following the British example, was rearming, and by this means was hoping to discharge its obligations to empire naval defence, and provide for its own local defence.[201] In Australia labour protested. The *Labor Daily*, the party's official organ, referred to a grand scheme by Whitehall to bring all the dominions to heel so that on the declaration of war, plans could be put into effect immediately. The Australian men were merely 'yes-men' to Baldwin and Eden.[202]

New Zealand, like Australia, was more inclined to support imperial co-operation than Canada or South Africa. But there were important divergences of principle in foreign policy. The official New Zealand historian, F. L. W. Wood, does his best to give the impression that the leading personalities in the dominions at that time exhibited a charming

199 Ibid., pp. 56–60.
200 Quoted by Hasluck, p. 68.
201 *Times*, 1.5.1937.
202 *Labor Daily*, 15.5.1937.

and disarming naivety.[203] Perhaps this explains the somewhat touching trust New Zealand continued to place in collective security based on the league of nations. The British government did not consider New Zealand's proposals for the reform of the league practical.[204] New Zealand, however, approved of British rearmament since it felt that Britain was determined to safeguard its position.[205]

Evidence of the close links between New Zealand and the mother country can be discerned in a controversy that raged in 1935. Speaking in parliament on external affairs the prime minister of the time, G. W. Forbes, compacently asserted that if Britain became involved in a war, New Zealand would also be involved: 'any catastrophe that affects Great Britain must inevitably affect New Zealand also, bound up as we are in the welfare of the Old Country'.[206] This statement aroused little comment, but, a few months later, Forbes, on his way to a conference in London, was reported as having told the Canadians that he saw no need for discussion on defence or foreign policy. Since New Zealanders were confident that Britain would always be on the side of peace, he felt sure that if war broke out New Zealand would act as promptly as it did in 1914. Parliamentary consultation would not be necessary.[207] Forbes was severely censored in the press for this statement, which was considered out of touch with current New Zealand thought. M. J. Savage, the leader of the labour party who, in 1937, was prime minister, made a significant statement:

> The future of the Dominions and the British Commonwealth is dependent on the will to peace. This will can be rendered wholly ineffective if unknown commitments involving the lives of our people are to be made exclusively at the will of men who may not in any way understand the objective and outlook of our people. Our youth should not be sacrificed for unknown causes and unknown policies and without reference to the representatives of the people.[208]

The leaders of New Zealand in 1937 saw their country's future linked with that of the commonwealth. Although not prepared blindly to follow Britain's lead they were less likely to place obstacles in the way of imperial defence than Canada and South Africa.

On matters of foreign policy and defence the commonwealth was divided. Colonial compensation for Germany was also a prickly subject

---

[203] See F. L. W. Wood, *The New Zealand People at War. Political and External Affairs. Official History of New Zealand in the Second World War 1939–45* (Wellington, 1958), *passim*.
[204] *U K Parl Deb H of C* 318, col. 2340, 16.12.1936.
[205] *Times*, 19.2.1937.
[206] *N Z Parl Deb* 241, p. 83.
[207] *Evening Post*, 26.4.1935. Quoted by Wood, p. 33.
[208] Ibid., 30.4.1935. Quoted by Wood, pp. 33–4.

for the dominions. From late 1936 the British cabinet had seriously considered this issue, and had noted the need to secure inter imperial agreement on the policy at the imperial conference. W. Ormsby-Gore, the secretary of state for colonies, suggested there should be no more instances of dominion statesmen irresponsibly advocating the return of other country's mandates but not of their own.[209] But at the meeting of the cabinet committee on foreign policy on 18 March 1937 MacDonald explained that the dominion position was clear. South Africa and Australia had both indicated in unmistakable language their refusal to entertain any idea of the return to Germany of former German territories of which they held the mandates. New Zealand which had the mandated territory of Samoa, had not volunteered any opinion. The South African government was opposed to any suggestion that Tanganyika should be returned to Germany. By May there was talk in the cabinet committee on foreign policy over the proposed visit of Schacht to Paris of France making the concessions, and of Gambia being ceded to France by way of compensation. Eden, however, was apprehensive of French reaction as France had pointed out that the commonwealth had received the largest share of the German colonies.[210]

At the time of the imperial conference Britain was concerned to secure the co-operation of the dominions. This was considered necessary because of the serious international situation and the likelihood of war. But the commonwealth was a diverse body, and the interests of the individual dominions did not coincide with those of the mother country. Furthermore, to improve Anglo-American relations, a primary objective of British foreign policy which could be pursued only by economic means, dominion co-operation was necessary to negotiate the proposed trade treaty. The imperial conference provided the opportunity to convince the dominions of the validity of British policy.

[209] *Cab 32*, 127, I C (36), Cabinet Committee on Imperial Conference Conclusions of 1st Meeting, Secret, 10.11.1936.
[210] *F O 371*, 20720, C2302/37/18, F P (36) 19, Memorandum by Ormsby-Gore, Lock and Key, 16.3.1937; F P (36) 7th Mtg, Minutes of 7th Meeting of Committee on Foreign Policy, Lock and Key, 18.3.1937; 20721, C3590/37/18, F P (36) 10th Mtg, Extract from Conclusions of 10th Meeting of Committee on Foreign Policy, Lock and Key, 10.5.1937; C3634/37/18, F P (36) 11th Mtg, Minutes of 11th Meeting of Committee on Foreign Policy, Lock and Key, 19.5.1937. See also John Harvey, Ed. *The Diplomatic Diaries of Oliver Harvey 1937–40* (London, 1970), p. 26, Diary, 15.3.1937; Colvin, pp. 39–42.

II

THE IMPERIAL CONFERENCE OF 1937,
AND ITS AFTERMATH

The Imperial Conference of 1937, and its Aftermath

To assess whether the dominions influenced, or were responsible for, the policy of the appeasement of Europe,[1] it is necessary to examine their stand at the imperial conference and the extent to which dominion determination to keep out of Europe was a decisive factor in encouraging or convincing Chamberlain of the need to pursue talks with Germany and Italy. Chamberlain, even before becoming prime minister, had decided that no opportunity should be missed to reduce international tension. He outlined his policy of general discussions with Germany to the cabinet committee on foreign policy on 2 April 1937.[2] There is no evidence to suggest that the attitude of the dominions caused this conclusion. Chamberlain, however, considered dominion opinion, as his chairmanship of the imperial conference shows.

In the foreign office, and in the cabinet, a psychological division persisted between those who took the dominions seriously, and others who thought in terms of the days of the British empire and assumed a certain compliance on the part of the commonwealth. Chamberlain and MacDonald were outstanding in the former category. Eden usually had a more high handed attitude.

Chamberlain showed this concern over a review by the chiefs of staff sub committee. He felt it 'undesirable to paint too black a picture for the Dominions'. Despite opposition, the report was redrafted.[3]

For Britain the imperial conference was vital for three reasons: to achieve commonwealth co-operation, and possibly even co-ordination in defence; to broach the difficult subject of colonial compensation to Germany; and to justify British foreign policy in Europe and the far east to the dominions.

The imperial conference met in London in May 1937 amidst the patriotic fervour of King George VI's coronation. Ireland was not represented. Lord Zetland, the secretary of state for India, was principal

---

[1] See the case made by D. C. Watt, *Personalities and Policies* (London, 1965), pp. 159–74. P. N. S. Mansergh, *The Commonwealth Experience* (London, 1969), p. 282, also raises the question.

[2] Ian Colvin, *The Chamberlain Cabinet* (London, 1971), pp. 39–42.

[3] *Cab 2*, 6(2), Committee of Imperial Defence Minutes of 288th Meeting, Secret, 11.2.1937(copy). No Dominion Representatives present.

spokesman for that country. Eden had summed up British policy towards Germany to the cabinet on 13 January 1937: it was one of 'being firm but always ready to talk'.[4] The cabinet hoped that the conference would achieve a common foreign policy for the commonwealth. Eden wanted dominion approval for the British policy of absolute commitments to Belgium and France, but less definite commitments in other cases.[5] When MacDonald, on 17 June, reported to the cabinet on the conference he explained that the British object had been to stress commonwealth co-operation, rather than the nationhood of the dominions as in previous conferences as that had given the impression abroad of growing disunity.[6]

The opening discussion at the conference were not propitious. Eden explained the British position to the principal delegates. From Eden's memoirs it would appear that he did not consider the attitude of the dominions important: they are hardly mentioned. It seems odd that a man occupying his position should need to be advised by Stanley Bruce, the Australian high commissioner in London, that it would be a good idea to elicit the view of the dominion statesmen.[7]

On 19 May Eden spoke in secret session to the imperial conference about the general international situation and the league of nations. He explained British undertakings to France and Belgium. It was vital to Britain that no hostile power should occupy the low countries or northern France, and there was an obvious advantage in all countries knowing this position. British commitments to the rest of Europe were limited to obligations under the league of nations. The position in central Europe was dangerous, similar to that in the Balkans before 1914. As Eden saw it, there were three alternatives for Britain in central Europe. Firstly, disinterest, but such a policy could only invite aggression. Secondly, a declaration of readiness to fight for Czechoslovakia or Austria if they became the victims of aggression, but such a policy went beyond league obligations and the limits of British public opinion. The third alternative was to make it clear that Britain was interested in events in central Europe. Eden had first discussed this stand with foreign ministers of central European countries and they had approved of it. This was British policy for central Europe. Eden spoke vaguely about reaffirmation of the principles of the covenant, and then went on to say that the commonwealth

---

4 *Cab 23*, 87, p. 2, Cab 1 (37) 2, Secret, 13.1.1937.

5 *Cab 32*, 127, I C (FP) 1st Mtg, Conclusions of the 1st Meeting of the Preparatory Committee on Foreign Policy and Defence, Secret, 19.3.1937.

6 *Cab 23*, 88, p. 278, Cab 2 (37) 5, Secret, 17.6.1937.

7 Anthony Eden, *Facing the Dictators* (London, 1962), p. 444.

had to rearm. The dominion delegates preferred to defer comment on this statement.[8]

On 21 May Eden dealt with Europe. He explained that *Mein Kampf* and the speeches and writings of the German leaders suggested that the main objective of Germany was the extension of German dominion to all territories where there were German populations or empty spaces to colonise. The Germans were anxious to reach an agreement with Britain. British neutrality and detachment from France would leave Germany free to pursue an expansionist policy. Eden felt that such a settlement would be immoral. German moves against Austria and Czechoslovakia were anticipated. But the more immediate danger of hostilities came from Italy rather than Germany.

> It was arguable that if Italy came to the conclusion that we had inspired the League of Nations to continue to refuse to recognise *de jure* her position in Abyssinia she might then be convinced that our rearmament was planned with a view to her destruction, and act accordingly.[9]

That afternoon the commonwealth leaders responded to this grim picture. Baldwin, who had been elected chairman of the conference, was not present. Chamberlain took his place.[10]

Mackenzie King expounded first. He explained that Canada's outlook was largely shaped by its geographical position and its special relationship with the United States. The United States, in its own interests, would intervene if Canada were attacked. Roosevelt had made this explicit in private discussions. After this, Mackenzie King seems to have acted as spokesman for the United States. He explained that the only safe calculation was if war broke out in Europe or Asia the United States neutrality acts would be put into effect. He mentioned possible United States membership of the league if the sanctions articles were removed. Mackenzie King drew a distinction between congress and the administration, and impressed that Roosevelt and Hull were convinced of the value of a policy of economic appeasement. After this Mackenzie King explained Canada's position in time of war:

> There are many forces which would make for Canadian participation in a conflict in which Britain's interests were seriously at stake. There would be a strong pull of kinship, the pride in common traditions, the desire to save democratic institutions, the admiration for the stability, the fairness, the independence that

---

[8] *Cab 32*, 128, pp. 7–9, E (PD) 37 1st Mtg, Eden's Speech on Foreign Affairs, Secret Lock and Key, 19.5.1937.

[9] Ibid., pp. 3–7, E (PD) 37 2nd Mtg, Eden's Speech on European Situation, Secret Lock and Key, 21.5.1937.

[10] James Eayrs, *In Defence of Canada. Appeasement and Rearmament* (Toronto, 1965), pp. 56–7.

characterise English public life, the feeling that a world in which Britain was weak would be a more chaotic and more dangerous world to live in. The influence of trade interests, the campaign by a part of the press, the legal anomalies of abstention, the appeal of war to adventurous spirits, would make in the same direction.

On the other hand opposition to participation in war, any war, is growing. It is not believed that Canada itself is in any serious danger. It is felt that the burdens left by our participation in the last war are largely responsible for the present financial difficulties. There is wide impatience, doubtless often based upon inadequate information, with the inability of Continental Europe to settle its own disputes. The isolationist swing in the United States, its renunciation of war profits and neutral rights in order to keep out of war, have made a strong impression on Canadian opinion. In some sections of the country opinion is practically unanimous against any participation in either a League or a Commonwealth war. There is outspoken rejection of the theory that whenever and wherever conflict arises in Europe, Canada can be expected to send armed forces overseas to help solve the quarrels of continental countries about which Canadians know little, and which they feel, know and care less about Canada's difficulties, and particularly so if a powerful country like the United States assumes no similar obligation. No policy in Canada is more generally accepted than that commitments of any kind, involving possible participation in war, must have prior and specific approval by parliament.

Mackenzie King explained that any attempt to reach a decision on these matters in advance would precipitate a controversy that might destroy Canadian unity. He ended:

I shall not attempt to forecast what the decision would be in the event of other parts of the Commonwealth actually being at war. Much would depend on the circumstances of the hour, both abroad and at home—upon the measure of conviction as to the unavoidability of the struggle and the seriousness of the outlook, and upon the measure of unity that had been attained in Canada. That is not the least of the reasons why we consider peace so vital, for the preservation of peace is as vital for the unity of the Commonwealth as for the unity of Canada.

Mackenzie King was followed by Casey who spoke for the Australian delegation. The Australian delegates felt that Germany should be allowed to achieve its limited objectives of incorporating German speaking people in the reich.

This involved *qua* Austria the 'Anschluss'. It concerned the 3,000,000 Germans in Czechoslovakia and the Germans in Danzig, Memel and other localities.

As regards Austria, a conservative solution might be that Great Britain should cease to offer any further opposition to the realisation of the 'Anschluss' provided always that Germany could attain this objective peaceably and without the shedding of blood.

This would split Germany and Italy. If this led to a claim for a German port on the Adriatic, the cession of Trieste would hardly create a grave danger to Britain or to the rest of the commonwealth. Casey elaborated further:

> It seemed clear that if Czechoslovakia was menaced by Germany, Great Britain would not be prepared to go to war in defence of the independence of Czecho-slovakia. If this was the true position, would it not be very much fairer to the smaller countries, and particularly to those in Central and Eastern Europe that the position should be explained to them without possibility of misunderstanding?

Savage then read to the conference what Zetland called 'a sermon on the immorality of British foreign policy'. Savage prefaced the New Zealand statement with the qualification that although what he had to say was critical of British policy this was not criticism of the objectives, but of the means. He then went on to speak of a commonwealth foreign policy, as distinct from a British foreign policy which would have to be founded on a moral basis which was universally acceptable such as the collective peace system of the league of nations. The prevailing situation where information was supplied to the dominions, was very different from actual consultation. Then followed searing criticism of the British policy in Abyssinia. British inaction at the time of the occupation of the Rhineland and the acceptance of German enfringement of treaties were also scathingly attacked. New Zealand wanted the adoption of a twofold policy:

> Firstly, that the Commonwealth (through the League of Nations) take the initiative in inviting a world-wide consideration of international affairs, both political and economic, and, secondly, that at the same time the Commonwealth take the initiative in inviting as many Powers as possible to join in realistic support of the Covenant of the League.

Zetland probably expressed the British view of Savage's statement when he wrote:

> It was only too obvious that the solution of these problems appears to be much simpler to those who live at a comfortable distance from such disturbing and dynamic personalities as Mussolini and Hitler than it does to those who, like His Majesty's Government in the United Kingdom, have to live in close contact with them.

Hertzog took a different line. He questioned why Germany and Italy should be looked upon as a menance to the peace of the world. Versailles was responsible for the dictatorial governments of these countries. He maintained that the peace of Europe could only be firmly re-established and secured if Britain were prepared to approach Germany in the same cordial and tolerant spirit as it had shown in its dealings with France. Britain should stop giving indirect support to the Franco-Soviet pact, and had no right to stop Austria from expressing its self determination and joining with Germany. There had to be partial restitution of Germany's colonies. Hertzog warned that so far as South Africa was concerned there was no need for a European war.

> If war were to arise because of England's persistence to associate herself with France in an Eastern or Central European Policy calculated to threaten Germany's existence; or because of unwillingness to redress the wrongs arising from the Treaty of Versailles, South Africa could not be expected to have any share or part in such a war.

Hertzog did say that:

> If the peace of Europe could be secured by returning to Germany some of her former Colonies, South Africa would be prepared to contribute to such a settlement.

If, however, a really friendly spirit were shown to Germany by Great Britain, and if France could be persuaded to abandon its anti German mentality, Hertzog was confident that these three great nations could fully safeguard the peace of Europe.

When reporting to the British cabinet after the conference, MacDonald said that these statements had had a 'depressing effect'. It had been hoped, however, that 'with education and patient communication of the facts' all parties would get into line. He claimed that that was what had actually happened: the attitude of the dominions had gradually swung towards that of Britain. There was not 'complete identity of views', but there was a 'spirit of co-operation'.[11]

Eden did justify British policy on 22 May to the imperial conference delegates on the grounds that it was not based entirely on expediency. Britain's policy was not founded on 'peace at any price'. Eden assured Hertzog that Britain had not entered into fresh commitments in central Europe, and had no inclination to interfere there. But the situation needed watching. Hertzog's strictures on Versailles were, perhaps, unfair. And geography prevented British relation with Germany from being as intimate as they were with France. Britain desired a *rapprochement* with Germany, and the position was hopeful in that the present French government was more disposed to be friendly to Germany than its predecessors had been. Hertzog responded cordially by saying that his observations had not been intended as a reflection on the conduct of British foreign policy. Lyons gave the assurance that Australia believed that Britain had exerted the 'maximum of restraint and good sense' in Europe. Lyons, however, did incline to Hertzog's view that there might be a lessening of the 'degree of

---

11 *Cab 32*, 128, pp. 5–21, E (PD) 37 3rd Mtg, Lock and Key, 21.5.1937; *Zetland Papers* 8, pp. 70–4, No. 14, Zetland to Linlithgow, 19.5.1937 (copy); *Cab 23*, 88, p. 279, Cab 24 (37) 5, Secret, 17.6.1937.

restraint that Britain had hitherto exercised on Germany', especially with reference to Austria. The leader of the Australian delegation then made what might have been for the British a hopeful statement:

> There could be no possible doubt that if some great disaster happened to Britain, there could be no hope or future for any of the other members of the Commonwealth and it was, therefore, in the supreme interests of everyone of them, as well as in the interests of the whole world and of Britain herself, that the component parts of the Commonwealth should stand firmly and solidly together. As he had said, Australia was in complete agreement with Britain's foreign policy and he only ventured to express the hope that it might be possible for something to be done on the lines which General Hertzog had suggested.

Mackenzie King and Hertzog were also concerned about the Franco-Soviet pact. Hertzog felt that the Germans considered that the pact meant a partial encirclement of their country with a view to war. Eden explained that it was inconceivable that the French would initiate any attack against Germany. Russia, occupied by internal problems, would not approve. Britain had tried to prevent that pact from becoming a military alliance, and Eden was able to assure Mackenzie King that Britain did not have a moral obligation towards France if France were to go to the assistance of Russia.[12]

Britain did make moves to win New Zealand around. MacDonald saw Walter Nash on 28 May and impressed on the New Zealand delegate that there had been general agreement on policy between Britain and the dominions with the exception of New Zealand. This was an optimistic interpretation by MacDonald. New Zealand's attitude seemed to be that everything should be subordinated strictly to carrying out the letter of the covenant. This observation seemed to shock Nash, and he retaliated by suggesting that, in fact, the views of New Zealand were closer to those of Britain than were the views of any other dominion. Nash explained that while the New Zealand government felt that Britain had not carried out proper league policy on some occasions, New Zealand would never make this criticism public. Nash probably gave his country's viewpoint when he said that New Zealand would be behind Britain always. If Britain were at war, New Zealand would be at war.[13] Despite this meeting MacDonald explained to the committee on foreign policy and defence on 1 June that it was hoped that the imperial conference delegates would face up to the realities of the situation, but he still anticipated difficulties with New

---

[12] *Cab 32*, 128, pp. 3–11, E (PD)37 4th Mtg, Lock and Key, 22.5.1937.

[13] Ibid., 127, E (B) (37) 22, Note by MacDonald on New Zealand Delegations Views regarding Foreign Affairs, Secret, 28.5.1937. For the use of British Representatives only. Not circulated to the Dominions.

Zealand. MacDonald did not think that Eden would be able to make much of an impression on Messrs. Savage and Nash.[14]

Eden was absent in Geneva, and the conference concerned itself with matters other than foreign affairs, until his return early in June. During this time Baldwin resigned and, as was predicted, Chamberlain assumed the responsibilities of prime minister, and also the chair at the imperial conference. Chamberlain significantly remarked to Eden that, in contrast to Baldwin, he intended to make his influence felt in foreign affairs.[15]

On 3 June Eden again addressed the conference. He described the alarming events in Spain and then concentrated on British attitudes to *Anschluss*: it would be wrong for Britain to encourage the *Anschluss* and a statement indicating British disinterest in central Europe would have this effect. If Austria did want a union with Germany Britain would not necessarily oppose it. But, Eden argued, this was no solution to central European problems: *Anschluss* would have repercussions on Poland, Czechoslovakia and Yugoslavia. British policy was to gain time in the interests of peace.

Eden did not convince the dominion leaders: Hertzog reiterated his complaint about British partiality towards France:

> This applied especially to the United Kingdom's opposition to the 'Anschluss' which was a source of very strong complaint in Germany and was held to be the negation of self-determination and the principles of the League. . . . He [Hertzog] would not of course suggest that we ought to encourage Germany to march with Austria tomorrow. He would simply say that we ought to refrain from giving Germany the impression that we were hostile to her desires.

N. C. Havenga, the South African minister of finance, harped upon the onerous provisions of Versailles. Mackenzie King hopefully observed that British policy seemed to be 'neither to encourage Germany to expand nor to encourage other countries to resist'. Eden had to add that Britain was also bound by article 80 of the treaty of Versailles. Savage spoke again of a world conference, while Chamberlain tried to mollify the argument by saying that:

> He himself to a large extent sympathised with the desire for the 'Anschluss'. Proposals of this kind, however, had to be thought of in the light of their probable reactions on the remainder of Europe.[16]

The imperial conference did issue a communique on foreign policy. When Eden described the alarming situation in Spain on 1 June it might

14 Ibid., p. 1, E (B) (37) 4th Mtg, Conclusions of 4th Meeting of British Delegates, Secret, 1.6.1937.
15 Eden, pp. 444–5.
16 *Cab 32*, 128, pp. 5–12, E (PD) 37 12th Mtg, Secret Lock and Key, 3.6.1937.

have been expected that Hertzog and Mackenzie King would have been the most agitated. But it was Lyons who pleaded that the conference should at once issue a statement of commonwealth support for the British government's efforts to 'secure world appeasement and peace'. Mackenzie King tried to dampen Lyons's fervour. The Canadian prime minister said that he attached great importance to the commonwealth presenting a united front, but that if such a resolution became the subject for debate in dominion parliaments it could only impair any united front. Chamberlain settled the dispute by undertaking, on behalf of the British delegation, to draw up a draft suitable for publication. If the conference could agree on terms for a public pronouncement, it would 'be a very impressive thing'.[17] It took three days to draw up this draft, and a further three to revise it. Altogether six editions were made.[18] Chamberlain's eventual synthesis almost met with success.

Skelton, however, minuted his disapproval to Mackenzie King:

Don't like this—it covers all foreign policy really.[19]

Indeed Zetland wrote:

Most of the meetings are now taken up with reservations by Mr. Mackenzie King in connection with any statement by the Conference which can possibly suggest that the members of the Commonwealth have undertaken to co-operate in any matter whatsoever! You will have yourselves observed indications . . . of fissiparous tendencies on the part of liberal party in Canada, and the Canadian prime minister is suffering from a bad attack of cold feet in consequence.[20]

Mackenzie King, however, perhaps impressed by Chamberlain, or by the urgency of the situation, no longer seems to have been so resolutely opposed to a common front. It was Savage who objected: he was proud to be numbered amongst those who were prepared to use force on behalf of peace and of the league. In reply to an accusation by Savage that the Canadian delegation came close to wanting to weaken the power of the league Mackenzie King said that he could not agree to any declaration which stated that the dominions based their policy upon 'principles laid down by the League of Nations', as this covered collective security in which the Canadian government no longer believed. This was an open breach

[17] Ibid., pp. 5–8, E (PD) 37 10th Mtg, Secret Lock and Key, 1.6.1937.

[18] Ibid., 130, E (FP) 37 1st Mtg, Secret Lock and Key, 8.6.1937; E (FP) 37 2nd Mtg, Secret Lock and Key, 8.6.1937; E (FP) 37 3rd Mtg, Secret Lock and Key, 8.6.1937; E (FP) 37 4th Mtg, Secret Lock and Key, 9.7.1937.

[19] Quoted by Eayrs, p. 58.

[20] *Zetland Papers* 8, p. 105, No. 24, Zetland to Linlithgow, Private, 13.6.1937. See also Kenneth McNaught, 'Canadian Foreign Policy and the Whig Interpretation: 1936–1939', *Report of the Canadian Historical Association* (1957), pp. 43–54, for a discussion of the significance of 'unity' in Canada and Mackenzie King's philosophy on this.

between two members of the commonwealth on a fundamental issue. A way out was provided by the use of a footnote recognising the right of each member state to support its statement of policy as submitted to the league assembly in September 1936. This covered Savage's misgivings. The British delegation, however, unhappily pointed out that any practised reader of the communique would realise that there was a fundamental disagreement amongst the members of the commonwealth.[21]

The communique issued by the conference on foreign affairs was so full of reservations that it could hardly be said to represent a common front. The commonwealth had the preservation of peace as its first objective. Settlements of differences among nations and the adjustment of national needs were to be sought by 'methods of co-operation, joint inquiry and conciliation'. The commonwealth unanimously declared that their armaments would not be used for purposes of aggression. Each of the commonwealth governments would have to take such measures of defence as they considered necessary, for their security. This was clearly not a co-operative venture. Mention was made of the need to increase the stability of economic and financial conditions in the world. This could be taken as a statement in favour of economic appeasement. Lastly there came what might be considered as a pledge of appeasement by members of the commonwealth:

> Finally the Members of the Conference, while themselves firmly attached to the principles of democracy and to parliamentary forms of government, decided to register their view that differences of political creed should be no obstacle to friendly relations between Governments and countries, and that nothing would be more damaging to the hopes of international appeasement than the division, real or apparent, of the world into opposing groups.[22]

Colonial compensation for Germany was another concern of the conference and when, at a most secret meeting of the leading delegates on 2 June, the question was broached, dominion response was not encouraging. Admittedly the presentation of the British case was odd. The dominion prime ministers were not told initially about the British and French attitude about the possibility of meeting German colonial claims by surrendering mandates over Togoland and the Cameroons.[23] This was probably because of the fear of leakage. Ormsby-Gore spoke about the British public being united in opposition to any restoration of

---

[21] *Cab 32*, 130, E (FP) 37 2nd Mtg, Secret Lock and Key, 8.6.1937; E (FP) 37 3rd Mtg, Secret Lock and Key, 8.6.1937; E (FP) 37 4th Mtg, Secret Lock and Key, 9.7.1937.

[22] *Cmd 5482, Imperial Conference. 1937. Summary of Proceedings* (June 1937), pp. 14–6.

[23] *F O 371*, 20721, C4135/37/18, Imperial Conference E (GC) 37, Observations on Minutes of Imperial Conference Meeting of 4 June 1937, 8–9.6.1937.

the German colonies. He felt that to transfer any of the five and a half million people in mandated territories to any other power against their will would be to do a great moral wrong and, in his opinion, any government in Britain which attempted to do so would be split internally and could not survive.

Mackenzie King made no observations. Casey opposed giving up New Guinea and Nauru. Savage said something about colonial compensation being suitable if it were part of a general settlement.[24] Earlier Hertzog had made ambiguous statements about a South African contribution, but when pressed by Eden on the matter he had been evasive.[25] At this meeting Hertzog suggested that Germany had a right to a voice in the mandates question and although South Africa would oppose any transfer of South West Africa, if the restitution of Tanganyika could bring peace to Europe, South Africa would not stand in the way. Hertzog felt that if only Togoland and the Cameroons were restored, Germany would not be satisfied. If nothing were done in the near future South Africa would approach Germany directly as it was felt essential to develop South West Africa and to settle its future.

Chamberlain tried to settle doubts by explaining that the British government had not decided on a policy of colonial compensation. The British prime minister suggested, however, that the dominions should not 'close their minds to the possibility of a general settlement which might include the return to Germany of territories'.[26]

Foreign office officials were concerned that the dominions, and Hertzog in particular, had been left under the misapprehension that approaches had been made to Germany about colonial compensation. They considered it wrong to leave the dominions with the impression that Germany had little interest in colonial compensation. Chamberlain apparently settled these doubts at a dinner with dominion representatives, on 15 June. No minutes were made of this occasion.[27]

Efforts to secure a joint defence scheme for the commonwealth were not successful. At the end of February 1937 the British chiefs of staff had drawn up a review of imperial defence, in preparation for the conference, outlining schemes to facilitate co-operation amongst the members of the

---

24 *Cab 32*, 128, pp. 9–10, E (PD) 37 11 Mtg, Most Secret Lock and Key, 2.6.1937.

25 *F O 371*, 20721, C3989/37/18, Foreign Office Minute on German Colonial Situation, 26.5.1937.

26 *Cab 32*, 128, pp. 10–12, E (PD) 37 11th Mtg, Most Secret Lock and Key, 2.6.1937.

27 *F O 371*, 20721, pp. 237–40, 34135/37/18, Harvey to Hoyer Millar, 20.9.1937; Minutes by O. E. Sargent, 8.6.1937; Cadogan, 9.6.1937; Eden, 9.6.1937.

commonwealth. A basic premise of this report was that the commonwealth could not survive a British defeat. Dominion assistance, at least in the form of munitions, was anticipated in the event of a war against Germany. Dominion preparedness was to be encouraged, as immediate reinforcements would be more welcome than those received six months after the outbreak of hostilities. There were also more specific schemes for dominion assistance in the far east and the Mediterranean. Significantly it was stressed that the ability of any dominion to help did not constitute any commitment for that dominion. Rearmament was vital, as the danger of war was seen as being in inverse proportion to the strength which the commonwealth was believed to represent. This report was circulated to the dominions.[28]

Inskip, on 24 May, pointed out to the delegates that the British rearmament programme was defensive, and intended for the defence of the commonwealth and trade routes: Britain could not act as the guardian of universal security. He did suggest that the dominions should consider developing their internal capacity for the production of munitions and war materials. Mackenzie King even objected to a possible scheme of defence centralisation. His policy was to keep Canada united. Canadian public opinion would not support larger defence appropriations and was opposed to extraneous commitments. In contrast to this Australia proposed extended defence efforts.[29] Savage said that New Zealand 'would welcome and indeed asked for a co-ordinated system of defence for the Commonwealth'. Havenga refused to get involved: South Africa's defence matters had been settled by Pirow's visit to London the previous year.[30] The British delegation on 9 June submitted a draft document on imperial defence. The final communique hardly resembled the original. Significantly the Australian delegation, which had come to the conference with such detailed proposals on defence, thought that the memorandum would serve. Mackenzie King, however, cited numerous objections. One paragraph gave the impression that 'the United Kingdom were undertaking a supervision over the training and equipment of the whole Empire'. The Australians preferred the original to Mackenzie King's proposed amendment, as did Chamberlain. It was, however, Mackenzie King's stand that prevailed. The Canadian prime minister similarly objected to a paragraph

28 *Cab 24*, 268, C P 73 (37), Memorandum by Inskip, Secret, 26.2.1937; 1305–B, Review of Imperial Defence by the Chiefs of Staff Sub Committee as amended by the Committee of Imperial Defence at their 289th Meeting on 25.2.1937, Secret, 22.2.1937; *Cab 23*, 87, p. 25, Cab 10 (37) 11, 3.2.1937; *Cab 2*, 6(2), Committee of Imperial Defence Minutes of 288th Mtg, Secret, 11.2.1937 (copy), No Dominion Representatives present.
29 *Cab 32*, 128, pp. 4–17, E (PD) 37 5th Mtg, Secret Lock and Key, 24.5.1937.
30 Ibid., pp. 3–4, E (PD) 37 6th Mtg, Secret Lock and Key, 25.5.1937.

about the importance of safeguarding 'the maritime communications of the Empire'. This gave an impression of empire forces, and any such implication would make it impossible for the Canadian government to obtain defence appropriations. The Australians demurred, unsuccessfully, preferring the original draft. One paragraph of the report had been included almost as a sop to the Australian point of view. But even this did not escape modification by Mackenzie King. Any impression of unified or co-operative action by the commonwealth in defence matters was weakened.

The draft read:

> In the course of the discussions, the Conference found general agreement among their members that while it is the sole responsibility of the several Parliaments of the British Commonwealth to decide the nature and scope of their own defence policy, the security of each member of the Commonwealth can be increased by co-operation so far as each Government and Parliament may be prepared to go on such matters on the free interchange on information concerning the state of their naval, military and air forces, the continuance of arrangements already initiated for concerting the defences of ports, and measures for co-operation if and when the Governments of the British Commonwealth may so decide, between the forces of the several members of the Commonwealth in defence of communications and other common interests.

Mackenzie King stated flatly that the wording 'the continuance of arrangements already initiated' was unacceptable: it would arouse suspicions in Canada of agreements on commitments. Both Australia and New Zealand supported the retention of the original draft, unsuccessfully. The impression of unity was marred by following 'arrangements already initiated' with 'by certain members of the Commonwealth' in the final draft.

Mackenzie King was equally resolute over the last paragraph of the British draft. He could not face a Canadian parliament with a report which said that representatives of the dominions frequently attended meetings of the committee of imperial defence. Canada, emphatically, was not represented on the committee of imperial defence. Mackenzie King was keen to see defence strengthened and co-operation improved, but the idea of a committee in London would not meet with Canadian support. Savage tried to argue that the delegates were discussing imperial defence, and he could therefore not see any objection to a committee of imperial defence. Hertzog sided with Mackenzie King against the Australians and New Zealanders: the South African prime minister pointed out that words like 'Empire' and 'Defence Committee' had always created difficulties at imperial conferences. Perhaps it would be better to avoid them. Once again Mackenzie King prevailed.[31]

The British delegation had been hoping for a more definite commitment by the commonwealth to co-operate in imperial defence. The final communique did not imply such a commitment. Mention was made of the British rearmament programme and it was noted that commonwealth parliaments had made provision for similar measures. Attention was drawn to the facilities offered by the committee of imperial defence for those countries that wished to make use of them. There was co-operation on a more technical level with regard to standardisation of training and equipment, and uniformity of administrative practice in such matters. Reference was also made to the advantages of co-operation in the production and supply of munitions, raw materials and food. But the co-operation seemed to end there. Britain could rely on Australia and New Zealand for support in matters of commonwealth defence, but Canada and South Africa were determined to remain aloof from any commitments. Although the dominions were willing to increase their defence expenditure in their own interests, there were obstacles in the way of any imperial defence scheme.[32]

In November 1937, with the reorganisation of the committee of imperial defence, it was arranged that there would be more meetings to which the dominion high commissioners or their deputies, were not invited. Only the high commissioners from Australia, South Africa and New Zealand attended these meetings in any case. The position was understood by the dominion high commissioners and prime ministers.[33] British contingency planning in November 1937 still envisaged support from Australia, New Zealand and Canada.[34] Perhaps, in the eyes of the British military, the imperial conference had not changed the situation materially.

MacDonald was rather optimistic when he reported to the cabinet on 17 June that the policies of the members of the commonwealth were closer than they had been before the conference. He explained that:

> The Australian Prime Minister, of course, had never expressed any doubts. Mr. Savage, the Leader of a Labour Government in New Zealand, which was rather inclined to criticise our foreign policy, had said roundly one day that if the

[31] Ibid., 130, E (D) 37 1st Mtg, Secret Lock and Key, 10.6.1937; E (D) 37 2nd Mtg, Secret Lock and Key, 11.6.1937.
[32] *Cmd 5482*, pp. 16–20.
[33] *Cab 24*, 273, C P 284 (37), No. 1376–B, Note by Inskip on a proposed Reorganisation of the Committee of Imperial Defence, Signed M. P. A. Hankey, Secret, 3.11.1937.
[34] Ibid., C P 296(37), No. 1366–B, Report by Chiefs of Staff Sub Committee on Comparison of Strength of Britain with certain other Powers at January 1938, Most Secret Lock and Key, 12.11.1937.

United Kingdom was at war New Zealand would be at war whether the issue was right or wrong. General Hertzog on the previous evening had said that after taking part in four Imperial Conferences he had on the present occasion felt for the first time a feeling of kinship with ourselves. Mr. Mackenzie King was about to visit Germany where he would see Herr Hitler. After expressing sympathy with Hitler's constructive work and telling him of the sympathy which was felt with Germany in England, he intended to add that if Germany should ever turn her mind from constructive to destructive efforts against the United Kingdom all the Dominions would come to her Britain's aid and that there would be great numbers of Canadians anxious to swim the Atlantic! No doubt we should have our difficulties with the Dominions in the future, but the Conference had been a great stride forward in the direction of unity. He thought much of the success was due to the skilful and attractive Chairmanship of the Prime Minister.

Chamberlain confirmed MacDonald's general impressions, and added that he felt that the personal relations established would prove of incalculable value in the future.[35]

When the prime ministers returned to their various dominions, however, it seemed that little had changed. In South Africa Hertzog and his governing clique favoured a *rapprochement* with Germany. Questioned on his arrival Hertzog argued that there was no 'warmindedness' among the European nations. Their rearmament was for defence and should be regarded as a guarantee of world peace.[36] In his next public speech on 28 September Hertzog championed isolation. His premise was that the tension in Europe was caused by Versailles.

> In these circumstances, can America or any other state outside Europe be blamed if it conscientiously refrains from taking part in any European affair which may be calculated in any way to affect European international problems?

It was not for South Africa to become involved in righteous crusades, or to go to the assistance of any part of the empire, unless its own vital interests were at stake.

> Let South Africa continue her membership of the League but let her never forget that she is not a part of Europe, and that she should never identify herself with the spirit and aspirations of Europe to the detriment of her own interests or against her own free judgment, or in a manner which adversely affects her independence of action.
>
> South Africa's co-operation with Europe, where and how she shall co-operate, either in peace or in war, are at present questions which South Africa and South Africa alone must decide. The test according to which these decisions must be made may never be other than the interests of South Africa itself.[37]

---

35 *Cab 23*, 88, pp. 278–80, Cab 24 (37) 5, Secret, 17.6.1937.
36 *Cape Times*, 6.7.1937.
37 Ibid., 29.9.1937; 30.9.1937, Ed.

More open sentiments were expressed by Charles te Water, the South African high commissioner in London, on a visit to Canada in September. Te Water said that South Africa would be prepared to discuss the colonial question with Germany and the other powers concerned. Hertzog stated that te Water was not speaking for the South African government, but that South Africa was not opposed to friendly discussions of German colonial desires.[38] A month later, Pirow spoke on the colonial issue. A request was made in the British house of commons that the British government make it clear that it would not support Pirow's alleged advocacy of the surrender of African colonies to Germany. The Marquess of Harington, parliamentary under secretary for the dominions, pointed out that Pirow's comments had to be seen in the context of his whole speech. Pirow had advocated the promotion of a closer relationship between Germany and South Africa, and Germany and the British empire on the basis of equality and a fair settlement of the colonial question.[39] Pirow hinted his sympathies when he spoke to the Afrikaner national student organisations. He referred to democracy as setting a premium on selfishness and exploitation, and as being inductive to sterility and waste of time. The idealistic alternatives to democracy were fascism or communism. Pirow had no time for communism. The implication, as Stallard pointed out, was that Pirow preferred fascism.[40] A significant clique of the South African leaders not only favoured the appeasement of Europe, but were more than sympathetically inclined towards Germany. Indeed F. H. Cleobury in the foreign office noted:

> Col. Stallard and his party always strike us as rather wrong-headed, but they are a useful counter-balance to the Malanites, and they probably act as a check on any desire General Hertzog may have to beat the Malanites by stealing the Malanite programme.[41]

In Canada a slight drift away from isolationism was discernible after the imperial conference. Canadian press reaction tended to be relief that no definite action had been taken by the imperial conference.[42] The change in Mackenzie King's attitude was the important result. He was more sympathetically inclined to the possibility of Canada going to Britain's aid if Britain were the victim of aggression. His favourable impression of

38 Ibid., 16.9.1937, Ed.

39 Ibid., 4.11.1937.

40 Ibid., 1.10.1937; 16.10.1937.

41 *F O 372*, 3203, T15785/344/385, No. G91/52, Price to Dunbar, 16.11.1937 r. in r. 17.11.1937; Minute by F. H. Cleobury, 18.11.1937.

42 Toronto *Globe and Mail* (Independent Liberal), Montreal *Gazette* (Conservative), Ottawa *Journal* (Conservative), and Ottawa *Citizen* (Liberal). Quoted by *Times*, 18.6.1937.

Chamberlain seems to have been responsible for this. After his return to Canada Mackenzie King wrote to a mutual friend in England:

> I marvel at the splendid manner in which he [Chamberlain] measures up to the exceptional obligations of his high office. He had my best of wishes and most sympathetic understanding in all that he undertakes. When you are again talking with him, tell him, at all costs, to keep the Empire out of war.[43]

One should not lose sight of the significance of the last sentence. In the same letter he wrote:

> If the British Empire can be kept out of war, it will be able to take care of itself. . . . If drawn into war, I firmly believe disruptive forces will begin to operate which will be beyond the control of all concerned.[44]

After the imperial conference Mackenzie King paid brief visits to France, Belgium, and Germany. Speaking at the Paris exhibition he seems to have made certain claims for Canada, which, in view of his statement to the commonwealth prime ministers during the foreign affairs discussion, were surprising. There was some dispute as to what Mackenzie King actually said. The Reuter account was later questioned. It read:

> We like to manage our own affairs but any threat to England would immediately bring Canada to her side.[45]

The Canadian press account was more general:

> We like to manage our own affairs, we co-operate with other parts of the British Empire in discussing questions of British interests. The fact that we have our own representatives in other countries is evidence of that liberty and freedom which above all we prize and were it imperilled from any source whatever, would bring us together again in preservation of it.[46]

Perhaps, for reasons of internal politics, Mackenzie King was reluctant that the impression given by the Reuter account should stand. On the other hand it might have been intended as a warning to the dictators. Chamberlain used the Reuter interpretation in one of his political speeches.[47] Mackenzie King, however, assured the Canadian house of commons the following year that the Canadian press report had given the correct interpretation.[48]

After Paris Mackenzie King went to Germany. He told the Canadian house of commons in 1944 that the object of his visit was to tell Hitler

---

[43] *Mackenzie King Papers*, Mackenzie King to Greenwood, 6.10.1937. Quoted by Eayrs, p. 60.
[44] Ibid., p. 54.
[45] *Times*, 3.7.1937.
[46] Gwendolen Carter, *The British Commonwealth and International Security* (Toronto, 1947), p. 278.
[47] Speech to the National Government Demonstration, Albert Hall. *Times*, 9.7.1937.
[48] F O 371, 21630, C2807/317/62, No. f705/24, Dominions Office to Foreign Office, 6.4.1938 r. in r. 9.4.1938; Enclosing copy of Telegram from High Commissioner in Canada No. 62 of 2.4.1938.

that if there were a war of aggression Canada would be at Britain's side.[49]
Mackenzie King had spoken to MacDonald about his European trip on
21 June 1937: he had stressed how strong the isolationist movement was
in Canada and that he was going to Germany as he was anxious to allay
the suspicion that the British were always anxious to meet the French and
avoided meeting the Germans.[50] Hitler saw Mackenzie King on 29 June
and seemingly mesmerised the Canadian visitor. After reading Mackenzie
King's report, O. E. Sargent of the foreign office minuted with Vansittart's
concurrence:

> It is curious how easily impressed and reassured Hitler's visitors are when Hitler
> tells them that Germany needs to expand at somebody else's expense but of course
> does not want war![51]

According to Mackenzie King's account Hitler was told:

> If the time ever came where any part of the Empire felt that the freedom which
> we all enjoyed was being impaired through any act of aggression on the part of
> a foreign country it would soon be seen that all would join together to protect
> the freedom which we were determined should not be imperilled.[52]

He also let Hitler know how impressed the dominion prime ministers had
been with Chamberlain: they had expected to find a man with rigid views
but had been delighted to discover his liberal and broadminded outlook.
When Mackenzie King saw Goering he apparently went further in indicating the unity of the commonwealth in the event of German aggression.
Goering enquired whether Canada would aid Britain if that country tried
to prevent a union of Austria and Germany. The general was told that
Canadian action would be determined by 'fair play and justice'.[53]

Mackenzie King also saw von Neurath and wrote to Eden how
impressed he had been with both Goering and von Neurath. They were
men 'with whom it should be possible to work with a good deal of trust
and confidence'. Sir Nevile Henderson, the British ambassador, was a
'first rate person for Berlin and had the confidence of the German
administration'.[54] At W. Strang's suggestion it was explained to Mackenzie
King that the British government did not feel the time was appropriate to
renew their invitation to von Neurath, and because of the state of public

[49] *Can Parl Deb H of C* 1944(6), p. 6275, 11.8.1944.

[50] *F O 371*, 20750, C6349/5187/18, Pitblado to Caccia, Secret, 2.9.1937 r. in r. 9.9.1937; Enclosing copy
of Note by MacDonald of Interview with Mackenzie King, 21.6.1937.

[51] Ibid., C5187/5187/18, Mackenzie King to Eden, Personal and Confidential, 6.7.1937 (copy); Minute
by O. E. Sargent, 25. 7.1937; Minute by Vansittart, 26.7.1937.

[52] Ibid., p. 4, Memorandum by Mackenzie King of Interview with Hitler, 29.6.1937.

[53] Ibid., pp. 13–4.

[54] Ibid., Mackenzie King to Eden, Personal and Confidential, 6.7.1937 (copy).

opinion it would be impossible for Goering to visit Britain, but Henderson had managed to establish contact with the general.[55]

When the Canadian prime minister finally sailed for home he carried with him a lasting impression of two men whom he thought could preserve the peace of Europe: Chamberlain and Hitler. Writing to Chamberlain on 6 July Mackenzie King expressed his confidence:

> I continue to have you and your great problems much in my thoughts. It will require immense patience and forebearance to save some appalling situations but I am returning to Canada with the feeling that you and your colleagues are whooly aware of that fact, and will be equal to the situation.[56]

Chamberlain replied reassuringly:

> You may in any event be assured that we shall continue with patience and persistence, our present endeavour to bring peace and order into a disturbed Europe.[57]

After Mackenzie King landed in Canada he saw the British high commissioner, Sir Francis Floud. Floud reported that Mackenzie King had been 'completely hypnotised' by his reception in Germany and he doubted even whether Hitler had been warned along the lines suggested by the Canadian prime minister.[58]

Back in Canada Mackenzie King was careful to stress that the purpose of the imperial conference had been discussions and review, not decision and action. In a broadcast to the nation he stated that the delegations at the conference were unanimous in declaring the complete freedom of action of each government in foreign affairs and defence.[59] All these assertions suited the isolationist demands of the Canadian parliament. Mackenzie King was convinced that Canadian opinion would not stand any mention of involvement in Europe. Whether he felt very differently is open to question. He did urge Chamberlain to keep the commonwealth out of war 'at all costs', and probably his confidence in the British prime minister stemmed from the impression that Chamberlain was the man most able to achieve this. Mackenzie King was influential in Canada, and Chamberlain had acquired a significant convert.

55 Ibid., Minute by W. Strang, 21.7.1937; Chamberlain to Mackenzie King, Personal and Confidential, 29.7.1937 (copy).

56 Ibid., Mackenzie King to Chamberlain, Personal and Confidential, 6.7.1937 (copy).

57 Ibid., Chamberlain to Mackenzie King, Personal and Confidential, 29.7.1937 (copy).

58 Ibid., C6349/5187/18, Pitblado to Caccia, Secret, 2.9.1937 r. in r. 9.9.1937; Enclosing Sir Francis Floud to Sir Henry Batterbee, 9.8.1937 (copy).

59 *Times*, 10.7.1937; 21.7.1937.

Before returning to Australia Lyons saw Mussolini and urged upon Chamberlain the need to meet the duce.[60] Lyons faced a barrage of criticism from his opposition labour party. Even during the imperial conference the marked division in Australian opinion could be noted in the press. The official organ of the labour party, the *Labor Daily*, impolitely referred to Lyons being 'ready to promise the world', especially if it committed Australia in advance to 'any ill-considered world adventure in war'.[61] The Australian defence proposals were referred to as Parkhill's 'Plan for War',[62] and the *Labor Daily* urged the declaration of Australia's neutrality. Such ideas, however, were regarded by newspapers like the *Sydney Morning Herald* and the *Advertiser* (Adelaide) as an illusion.[63]

At the end of July, Curtin, the labour leader, let it be known, unequivocally, that his party's policy was 'against participation in foreign wars and for the reservation of all Australia's strength for defence of the land in which we live'.[64] The congress of the Australasian council of trade unions held in Melbourne in July went further. It resolved: to organise the masses against war; to oppose the rearmament policies of the British and Australian governments; to support a policy of collective security through the league of nations; and to 'secure democratic control of the army inside Australia' in which was implicit labour's opposition to conscription and labour camps.[65] Curtin repudiated these decisions: the parliamentary labour party was not prepared to go so far. The parliamentary debates during August reflected the division of opinion. Curtin and his labour supporters maintained that there should be no defence commitments outside Australia,[66] while Lyons defended Australia's defence policy on the grounds that the commonwealth stood for peace, and the 'maintenance of friendship with all the nations of the world, to the exclusion of none'. In assessing this 'patriotic' stand by the governing party, it should be remembered that they were conscious of Australia's vulnerable strategic position. Lyons had been one of the most forceful proponents of the appeasement of Europe at the imperial conference.

Foreign policy and defence issues predominated in the election campaign which Lyons fought on his return. Curtin based his labour attack on the

[60] Enid Lyons, *So We take Comfort* (London, 1965), pp. 259–62.

[61] *Labor Daily*, 17.5.1937.

[62] Ibid., 27.8.1937.

[63] Ibid., 24.5.1937; 25.5.1937; *Sydney Morning Herald*, 21.5.1937, Ed; *Advertiser*, 16.6.1937.

[64] *Melbourne Herald*, 30.7.1937. Quoted by Anonymous, 'The Defence of Australia', *Round Table*, XXVIII (1937–8), p. 129.

[65] Ibid., 23.7.1937. Quoted in *Aust Parl Deb* 1937, p. 166, 16.8.1937.

[66] *Aust Parl Deb* 1937, pp. 102–9, 117.

platform that Australia could not influence European affairs, and that his country's best contribution to the commonwealth would be self reliance in its own defence. Robert Menzies, the attorney general, campaigning for the government, challenged labour on the ground that they were isolationist, and not prepared to co-operate with Britain. Lyons was prepared to risk the election on this issue, and on 28 September, pronounced that a policy of isolation from Britain would be suicidal.[67] At the end of October Lyons's government was returned for a third term of office, a precedent in Australian history.[68] Hasluck points to the complexities of this election and to the internal difficulties of the labour party which could be used, and were used by labour, to account for their defeat.[69] Despite this qualification the election seems to have been fought mainly on commonwealth co-operation and defence. This issue preoccupied the party leaders in their final campaign speeches.[70] Lyons stated that he took the favourable vote as an endorsement of his government's policy of co-operation with Britain. Curtin saw the election as a victory for labour's opposition to foreign entanglements since the new government was pledged to oppose conscription.[71] *The Times* considered the election results a victory for continuity in defence policy, and for commonwealth co-operation.[72]

On the whole the New Zealand press expressed disappointment in the smallness of the tangible results of the conference.[73] In his report to parliament Savage did little to dispel this.[74] Significantly, in the speech from the throne in September it was stressed that the New Zealand government reaffirmed its attachment to the principles of the covenant, and of collective security.[75] The opposition supported this.[76]

The imperial conference had done little to change the attitude of the dominion statesmen on the issues of invilvement in Europe, and imperial defence commitments. Their response to Eden's survey of international affairs was not a resolution to take a definite stand against possible aggression, but rather an appeal for the appeasement of Europe. New Zealand was an awkward exception.

---

67 Paul Hasluck, *The Government and the People 1939–1941* (Canberra, 1952), pp. 84–5.
68 *Times*, 25.10.1937.
69 Hasluck, pp. 85–6.
70 *Times*, 23.10.1937.
71 Ibid., 25.10.1937.
72 Ibid., 26.10.1937.
73 *Wellington Post, Dominion*. Quoted in *Times*, 18.6.1937.
74 *N Z Parl Deb* 248, pp. 473–6, 29.9.1937.
75 Ibid., p. 2, 9.9.1937.
76 Ibid., pp. 477, 483.

D. C. Watt argues that dominion determination to keep out of Europe was a decisive factor in encouraging Chamberlain to pursue his policy of the appeasement of Europe. The evidence cited for this is that two moves in that direction, namely the invitation to Baron von Neurath, the German foreign minister, to visit London, and Chamberlain's first private letter to Mussolini followed immediately on the close of the conference.[77] In Watt's view this is a discernible change in the attitude of a man who had initially urged rearmament.

An examination of Chamberlain's speeches, however, suggests that he had consistently favoured the appeasement of Europe, and had urged rearmament as a means of achieving this. In January 1937 Chamberlain stressed:

> We have our own ideas as to the best way our country can be governed. We have no desire or intention to try to force those ideas on the people of other countries. . . . We most earnestly desire political appeasement. We shall do everything that lies in our power to assure it.[78]

Chamberlain left an explanation of his policy in his diary. Writing on 19 February 1938 he explained what he had hoped to achieve:

> From the first I have been trying to improve relations with the 2 storm centres, Berlin and Rome. It seemed to me that we were drifting into worse and worse positions with both, with the prospect of having ultimately to face 2 enemies at once.

The factors that convinced him of the need for this policy, at least in retrospect, were the weakness of France, the unreliability of the United States, and the cost of rearmament. The stand of the dominion prime ministers at the imperial conference is not mentioned.[79] Chamberlain noted that because of these factors he made friendly references to Germany in two speeches but though this seemed to be appreciated it elicited no response.[80] Baron von Neurath was invited to visit Britain and, at first, the invitation was accepted. Eden wrote to Lothian on 1 June that he hoped that this visit would 'accomplish much good work in clearing each other's minds of any misconceptions which may exist as to our policies'.[81] There was, however, no question of negotiations but only of conversations.[82] The plan was cancelled by Hitler. Chamberlain noted in his diary: 'For the time the way to Berlin was blocked'.[83]

---

[77] Watt, pp. 156, 165.
[78] *Times*, 30.1.1937.
[79] Quoted by Keith Feiling, *The Life of Neville Chamberlain* (London, 1946), p. 322.
[80] Ibid., p. 329.
[81] *Lothian Papers* 337, pp. 352–4, Eden to Lothian, 18.6.1937.
[82] Ibid., *loc. cit.*
[83] *Chamberlain Papers*, Diary, 19.2.1938.

Italy still remained, but then Italy was not Chamberlain's first preoccupation. Feiling quotes the prime minister's first thought as being: 'If only we could get on terms with the Germans, I would not care a rap for Musso [*sic*]'.[84]

The chance to disengage Italy from the axis came in July. Until June British defence preparations had been based on the assumption that Italy 'could not be counted on as a reliable friend but in present circumstances need not be regarded as a probable enemy'. On 15 June 1937 Eden circulated to the committee of imperial defence a memorandum suggesting that Italy should be considered as a 'possible enemy'. The committee considered this on 5 July and recommended to the cabinet that Italy should be omitted from the cabinet decision of 15 November 1933 which stated that there should be no defence expenditure to meet attacks from Italy, France or the United States. Chamberlain recalled when the cabinet discussed this issue on 14 July that the cabinet had agreed on 8 July that the best way of countering the 'disquieting attitude' of the Italian governmen was to cultivate better relations with Germany.[85] Then on 2 July Sir Eric Drummond, the ambassador in Rome, wrote to Vansittart that Mussolini, despairing of Britain's friendship, might decide on war with Britain in the immediate future. Drummond did not think that Mussolini would do this but suggested precautions. Eden, on 14 July, recommended to the cabinet the need to show signs of rearmament in the Mediterranean. Halifax also suggested that Eden should send a personal letter to Mussolini.[86]

On 21 July there seemed to be a sudden reversal of Italian policy. Count Grandi, the Italian ambassador in London, saw Eden and mentioned what an excellent press the foreign secretary's speech of 19 July in the house of commons had had in Italy. He gauged the time right to pass on a message from Mussolini to the prime minister. Mussolini, Grandi said, had emphasised his desire for a permanent friendship with Britain.[87]

Chamberlain was sceptical of this advance.[88] He had, however, been prepared by reports from British representatives in Italy that

84 Quoted by Feiling, p. 329.

85 *F O 371*, 21160, R5186/1/22, Foreign Office Minute by Mr. Nichols on some recent Developments in Anglo-Italian Relations, including certain Conclusions reached by the Cabinet and the Committee of Imperial Defence, Secret and Confidential, 29.7.1937; *Cab 23*, 89, pp. 10–2, 30 (37), Lock and Key, 14.7.1937.

86 *F O 371*, 21160, R5186/1/22, Foreign Office Minute by Mr. Nichols on some recent Developments in Anglo-Italian Relations, including certain Conclusions reached by the Cabinet and the Committee of Imperial Defence, Secret and Confidential, 29.7.1937.

87 Eden, pp. 448–50.

88 Quoted by Feiling, p. 330.

Mussolini's German connection was not his first choice. The Czechs had also passed on similar information.[89]

At the meeting between Chamberlain and Grandi on 27 July it emerged that Mussolini wanted *de jure* recognition of the Italian conquest of Abyssinia. Chamberlain would only justify this as part of a general scheme of reconciliation. He wrote a letter to Mussolini: the British government was ready to start conversations.[90] Chamberlain did not show the letter to Eden as he had the 'feeling that he [Eden] would object to it'. The duce welcomed the proposed conversations. It was the British hope that they would start in September. Chamberlain recalled, retrospectively:

> At that time Eden and I both recognised (and the Italians apparently agreed) that the formal recognition of their Abyssinian conquest, to which they attached great importance, must follow on some declaration by the League that Abyssinia was no longer an independent State . . . we thought that the League might, if conversations went well, be willing to make such a declaration at their next meeting.[91]

From the Eden memoirs it would seem that Eden had reservations. Eden saw in Mussolini the tactics of a Machiavelli. In September Chamberlain complained that the foreign office persisted in seeing a Machiavelli in the duce.[92]

Chamberlain, however, maintained his policy. On 8 September, when arguing for *de jure* recognition of Abyssinia, the prime minister told the cabinet:

> He [Chamberlain] had regarded the lessening of the tension between this country and Italy as a very valuable contribution towards the pacification and appeasement of Europe. A return to normal friendly relations between ourselves and Italy would undoubtedly weaken the Rome-Berlin axis and it might be anticipated that in the event of a dispute between ourselves and Germany the attitude of Italy would be very different from what it is at present.[93]

There were serious obstacles. Italian submarine activities in the Mediterranean, and Mussolini's boasts of Franco's capture of Santander had meant difficulties in the league. Franco would not co-operate, and Britain could not pursue the matter on its own.

[89] Ibid., *loc. cit.*

[90] *F O 371*, 21160, R5186/1/22, Foreign Office Minute by Mr. Nichols on some recent Developments in Anglo-Italian Relations, including certain Conclusions reached by the Cabinet and the Committee of Imperial Defence, Secret and Confidential, 29.7.1937.

[91] Quoted by Feiling, pp. 330–1.

[92] Eden, pp. 456–7; Feiling, p. 331.

[93] *Cab 23*, 89, p. 32, Cab 34 (37) 8, Secret, 8.9.1937.

Chamberlain was anxious that Mussolini should not think the Anglo-Italian conversations dead. There was a possibility that Italy might be amenable at the Nyon conference, which was meeting to discuss shipping in the Mediterranean, on the understanding that its wants would be satisfied by the league. The prime minister admitted that Eden had difficulty in going as far as he, himself, would like to go on this matter. MacDonald pointed out that it would be difficult to guarantee Geneva's action. There was likely to be opposition from one or two dominion delegates who were devotees of the league. But he did concede that it might be possible to persuade even New Zealand if the conference were successful. Convincing support for Chamberlain in the cabinet, however, came from the first lord of the admiralty, Duff Cooper, who pointed out that British foreign policy had to be based on the state of armaments. Britain could not fight Italy, Germany and Japan at the same time, and, for this reason, Mussolini's friendship was important.[94] It was always stressed that any settlement with Italy had to be seen as part of the general appeasement of Europe.[95]

Italy's attitude prevented further developments. Italy refused to attend the Nyon conference. Agreement on the patrolling of the Mediterranean was reached, and this was welcomed in the dominions and the United States, but, predictably, Italy was resentful.[96] On 22 September Mussolini gave the assurance that no more volunteers would be sent to Spain, and against mounting anti British Italian propaganda, complained of the delay in the Anglo-Italian negotiations. Chamberlain, however, was consistent in his foreign policy aims. He wrote:

> Mussolini had been more than usually insolent with his offensive remarks about bleating democracies, and his outrageous allusions to the Colonies. But Anthony should never have been provoked in to a retreat which throws Germany and Italy together in self defence, when our policy is so obviously to try to divide them.[97]

During October moves in the direction of Anglo-Italian conversations were made. There was the possibility that Ciano might attend the Brussels conference, and exchange opinions with Eden there. They came to nothing.[98] As Eden explained to the cabinet on 13 October both Italy and Britain recognised that Spain stood in the way of any conversations,

94 Ibid., pp. 32–40.
95 *Cab 24*, 271, C P (210) 37, Memorandum by Eden on the present phase in Anglo-Italian Relations, and the Question of the final Recognition of Italian Sovereignty in Abyssinia, September 1937.
96 Eden, pp. 459–70.
97 Quoted by Feiling, p. 332.
98 Eden, p. 474.

and *de jure* recognition of Abyssinia was linked to the Spanish question in the league.[99]

An examination of Chamberlain's European policy during the first few months of his office suggest that he was not greatly influenced by the dominions in his decision to approach Germany and Italy. Probably the statements of several of the delegates to the imperial conference did help to confirm Chamberlain in a course of action that he had already decided upon. But there is no record in the foreign office papers of any of these moves being taken because of dominion pressure. The imperial conference convinced Chamberlain that his policy of preserving peace in Europe was was the right one, but to say that it caused him to embark upon it is probably an exaggeration.

[99] *Cab 23*, 89, p. 13, Cab 37 (37) 3, Secret, 13.10.1937.

III

EDEN AND THE FAR EAST, 1937

Eden and the Far East, 1937

WHILE Chamberlain was preoccupied with furthering the appeasement of Europe, Eden, until his resignation in February 1938, concentrated on the explosive situation in the far east. The foreign secretary, however, did not see the far east as an end in itself: he records in his memoirs:

> I did not regard Europe and the Far East as separate problems; but if, as I had to accept, there was to be no effective American participation in Europe for the present, it seemed reasonable to hope that we could mount and prosecute a joint policy in the Far East.[1]

Anglo-American co-operation and United States involvement in Europe were Eden's first priorities, and it was here that he and Chamberlain diverged.[2] Chamberlain believed that some settlement with the dictators was feasible, and a vague chance of the United States moving out of isolation should not be allowed to jeopardise this end.

Both Britain and the United States had traditional interests in the far east, but there had been friction between the two powers during the Manchurian crisis of 1931, and co-operation after that had not been significant.[3] Before July 1937 it appeared that United States interest was lagging behind that of Britain.[4] Britain made separate advances to the Japanese, and in 1936 talks were opened between Yoshida Shigeru, the Japanese ambassador in London, and the foreign office.[5] They were closely watched by the United States: it was concerned about the recognition of any 'special interest' or 'special position' of any power in the far east.[6] By July 1937, however, Cadogan was able to assure Bingham that he was not hopeful of the outcome of these talks.[7]

There was also the proposal made at the imperial conference by the Australian prime minister, for a regional understanding and pact of non aggression by the countries of the Pacific, based on league principles. This would commit Japan to respect the territory of British colonial possessions

---

[1] Anthony Eden, *Facing the Dictators* (London, 1962), p. 523.

[2] See John Harvey, Ed., *The Diplomatic Diaries of Oliver Harvey 1937–1940* (London, 1970), p. 49, Diary, 2.10.1937.

[3] See Nicholas R. Clifford, *Retreat from China* (London, 1967), pp. 1–17.

[4] *Foreign Relations of the United States* (hereafter cited as '*FRUS*') 1937(3), pp. 36–7, 711.93/350, Johnson to Hull, Telegram No. 108, 9.3.1937.

[5] *U K Parl Deb H of C* 323, col. 1253, 6.5.1937.

[6] *FRUS* 1937(3) pp. 103–4, 741.94/101a, No. 1757, Hull to Bingham, 24.5.1937

[7] Ibid., pp. 115–6, 741.94/111, Grew to Hull, Telegram No. 165, 23.6.1937.

and of Australia and New Zealand.[8] At the time this proposal received much publicity. The outbreak of hostilities between China and Japan, however, ended the Yoshida conversations, and forestalled any Pacific pact. In any case, for the latter, the co-operation of the United States was necessary, and it was not forthcoming.[9]

On 7 July Japanese infantry clashed with troops of the Chinese 29th army. Negotiations resulted in an agreement on 11 July, but fighting flared up again. A confrontation between Japan and China was imminent.[10] The United States suggested that Britain restrain the Japanese by threatening to discontinue their conversations with Yoshida.[11] Both Britain and the United States made independent but simultaneous protests and the United States asked the British for a frank exchange of information and views.[12] The British complied: Eden warned Yoshida of the serious effects which events in north China might have on Anglo-Japanese discussions,[13] and on 21 July he told the house of commons that he had let the Japanese know that the moment was not opportune for conversations.[14]

For Eden the Marco Polo bridge incident was an opportunity. On 12 July he saw Bingham, and enquired whether the United States would like to suggest any joint *démarche*.[15] The next day the foreign secretary went further and asked Hull whether he would be prepared to instruct the United States ambassadors in Nanking and Tokyo to co-operate with their British counterparts in urging restraint in those capitals.[16] The state department's response set the tone that the United States was to maintain throughout the crisis. The United States memorandum merely stressed the importance of close co-operation in exchanging information and views, and of working on parallel lines.[17] Stanley Hornbeck, the far eastern adviser in the state department, told Lindsay that it was his government's desire to co-operate with the British. Co-operation on parallel but independent lines, however, would be more effective than would joint or

[8] Ibid., p. 126, 741.94/111, Hull to Grew, Telegram No. 102, 1.7.1937.

[9] Cordell Hull, *The Memoirs of Cordell Hull*, 1 (London, 1948), pp. 531–2.

[10] See James B. Crowley, 'A Reconsideration of the Marco Polo Bridge Incident', *Journal of Asian Studies*, XXII (May 1963), pp. 277–91; Dorothy Borg, *The United States and the Far Eastern Crisis of 1933–1938* (Cambridge, Mass., 1964), pp. 276–81. For an account of British strategy during the far eastern crisis of 1937 see W. R. Louis, *British Strategy in the Far East 1919–39* (Oxford, 1971), pp. 238–50.

[11] *FRUS* 1937(3), p. 144, 793.94/8738, Memorandum by Hornbeck, 12.7.1937.

[12] Ibid., pp. 147–8, 793.94/8749, Hull to Bingham, Telegram No. 291, 12.7.1937.

[13] Ibid., pp. 154–5, 793.94/8750, Bingham to Hull, Telegram No. 465, 13.7.1937; *F O 371*, 20950, F4084/9/10, Eden to Lindsay, Telegram, 12.7.1937 r. in r. 14.7.1937 (draft).

[14] *FRUS* 1937(3), pp. 240–1, 793.94/8908, Bingham to Hull, Telegram No. 497, 21.7.1937.

[15] *F O 371*, 20950, F4084/9/10, Eden to Lindsay, Telegram, 12.7.1937 r. in r. 14.7.1937 (draft).

[16] *FRUS* 1937(3), pp. 158–9, 793.94/8777, British Embassy to Department of State, 13.7.1937.

[17] Ibid., pp. 159–60, 793.94/8785, Department of State to British Embassy, 13.7.1937.

identical representations.[18] Norman Davis was probably closer to the truth when he explained to the British ambassador that his government was reluctant to 'get mixed up with all Europe in the Far East'.[19]

Eden was not restrained by this polite rebuff. On 20 July he saw Bingham and explained the need for joint action to obviate the impression that the British were more interested than the United States. Bingham encouragingly told him that he thought it would be easier to collaborate with the United States in the far east than in Europe.[20]

Bingham, however, was a friend of Eden and believed in Anglo-American co-operation. On 21 July he made a suggestion on his own responsibility, to the foreign secretary, that the British government approach the United States with a proposal of a joint Anglo-American embargo on Japanese trade.[21] Eden was keen, but felt that any such suggestion needed to be preceded by a favourable United States response to a British request for a joint approach to China and Japan to suspend troop movements.[22] Chamberlain did not like Bingham's proposal.[23] Lindsay, too, referred to it as 'nonsense': congressional approval would be necessary for any embargo, and was unlikely.[24] In any event the United States politely rebuffed the British request for joint action.[25]

Both the British and the United States men on the spot doubted whether the Japanese government would welcome an offer of foreign mediation.[26] Some foreign office officials also doubted the wisdom of pointed representations.[27] But Eden felt that there was something more at stake than merely peace in the far east, and pressed for 'joint' rather than 'parallel' action. Chamberlain also told the cabinet that 'joint' action was likely to produce more results than simultaneous and parallel representations.[28] Discussions

---

[18] Ibid., pp. 160–1, 793.94/8786, Memorandum by Hornbeck, 14.7.1937.

[19] *F O 371*, 20950, F4160/9/10, Lindsay to Foreign Office. Telegram No. 184, 15.7.1937 r. 16.7.1937 (decypher).

[20] Ibid., F4301/9/10, Eden to Lindsay, Telegram No. 684, 20.7.1937 r. in r. 21.7.1937. *Contra FRUS* 1937(3), pp. 224–5, 793.94/8875, Bingham to Hull, Telegram No. 489, 20.7.1937; pp. 227–8 793.94/9068, Memorandum by Hornbeck, 21.7.1937.

[21] *F O 371*, 20950, F4301/9/10, Unnumbered, Eden to Lindsay, Telegram, Most Secret and Personal, 21.7.1937, Copy to Prime Minister only.

[22] Ibid., F4301/9/10, Unnumbered, Eden to Lindsay, Telegram, Most Secret and Personal Copy to Prime Minister only, 21.7.1937 (following above in file); F4302/9/10, Eden to Lindsay, Telegram, Most Immediate, 20.7.1937 r. in r. 21.7.1937 (draft).

[23] Eden, pp. 532–3.

[24] *F O 371*, 20951 F4463/9/10, Unnumbered, Lindsay to Eden, Telegram, Immediate Secret, 23.7.1937 (decypher)

[25] Ibid., F4463/9/10, Unnumbered, Eden to Lindsay, Telegram, Most Secret and Personal, 28.7.1937; *FRUS* 1937(3), pp. 226–7, 793.94/8920, British Embassy to Department of State, 20.7.1937.

[26] *FRUS* 1937(3), pp. 231–2, 793.94/8888, Grew to Hull, Telegram No. 216, 21.7.1937.

[27] *F O 371*, 20950, F4317/9/10, Lindsay to Foreign Office, Telegram No. 194, 20.7.1937 r. in r. 21.7.1937; Foreign Office Minutes attached.

[28] *Cab 23*, 89, p. 8, Cab 32 (37) 5, Secret, 28.7.1937.

on far eastern policy, however, were between Eden and the foreign office, and bypassed the cabinet.[29]

The United States took the view that the impression that there had been a failure of Anglo-American co-operation was a 'misconception'.[30] Chamberlain told the cabinet that the United States did not object 'in principle to joint representations'.[31]

Eden was undeterred by persistent United States rebuffs, and as the situation in the far east deteriorated, he again, on 28 July, asked whether there should not be 'joint' Anglo-American representations to China and Japan.[32] But, from the British point of view the record of Anglo-American co-operation in this sphere over the next month was, as minuted by Vansittart, 'melancholy'.[33] On 3 August Vansittart suggested there might be a joint Anglo-American offer of 'good Offices' to the antagonists, but the United States felt that such an offer had been made already.[34] There were separate confidential approaches, but these served as an example of established Anglo-American 'parallel' action in the far east.

When fighting broke out in Shanghai[35] in the middle of August the United States again stepped back. Asked by the British whether they would accept joint responsibility for protection of foreigners at Shanghai, if the Chinese and Japanese agreed to withdraw their armed forces to positions occupied before the outbreak of hostilities,[36] the United States replied that the Japanese response to the proposal had already disposed of any 'possible assumption of a joint responsibility'. In any case, to avoid misunderstanding 'it should not be expected that this government [United States] would be favourably inclined toward any project envisaging military or policy responsibility over and above those which relate to the

---

[29] Ibid., p. 23, Cab 30 (37) 13, Secret, 14.7.1937; p. 4, Cab 31 (37), Secret, 28.7.1937.

[30] *U K Parl Deb H of C* 326, cols. 1811–4, 19.7.1937, Hugh Dalton's Speech; *F O 371*, 20951, F4620/9/10, Eden to Lindsay, Telegram No. 717, 28.9.1937 r. in r. 29.7.1937; *FRUS* 1937(3), pp. 286–8, 793.94/9043, Bingham to Hull, Telegram No. 509, 28.7.1937; pp. 289–90, 793.94/9043, Hull to Bingham Telegram No. 322, 29.7.1937.

[31] *Cab 23*, 89, Cab 32 (37) 5, Secret, 28.7.1937.

[32] *F O 371*, 20951, F4620/9/10, Eden to Lindsay, Telegram No. 717, 28.9.1937 r. in r. 29.7.1937; *FRUS* 1937(3), pp. 286–8, 793.94/9043, Bingham to Hull, Telegram No. 509, 28.7.1937; pp. 289–90, 793.94/9043, Hull to Bingham Telegram No. 322, 29.7.1937.

[33] *F O 371*, 20954, F5868/9/10, Foreign Office Memorandum by Mr. Ronald on Sino-Japanese Dispute and Anglo-American Co-operation, 27.8.1937; Minute by Vansittart, Undated.

[34] Ibid., *loc. cit.*; *FRUS* 1937(3), pp. 319–20, 793.94/9151, Bingham to Hull, Telegram No. 521, 3.8.1937; pp. 327–8, 793.94/9151, Hull to Bingham, Telegram No. 334, 5.8.1937; pp. 339–40, 793.94/9217, Bingham to Hull, Telegram No. 531, 6.8.1937.

[35] Clifford, pp. 22–3.

[36] *F O 371*, 20954, F5868/9/10, Foreign Office Memorandum by Mr. Ronald on Sino-Japanese Dispute and Anglo-American Co-operation, 27.8.1937; *FRUS* 1937(3), pp. 444–5, 793.94/9756, British Embassy to Department of State, 18.8.37.

already existing missions of its armed forces now present in China'.[37] On 21 August Hull even complained of embarrassing British pressure for United States co-operation.[38] Hornbeck's advice was such that Mr. Ronald of the foreign office minuted on 27 August:

> Mr. Hornbeck is no doubt right when he says that, if we want U.S. co-operation, we must consult the State Depart. [*sic*] before taking action: I would go further and say that we must always frame our approach to the State Depart. [*sic*] in such a way that any action which may ultimately be taken may be represented as an American idea acted on through American initiative. And we must never complain if the State Depart. [*sic*] act without consulting us, as over Tsingtao.[39] In other words we must be prepared to take all the knocks and get none of the credit. But Anglo-American co-operation being so important, I venture to think that we should be wise to submit to this, humiliating though it may be.[40]

This succinctly summed up the British position.

United States reticence, however, did not discourage British efforts to achieve joint action. Chamberlain, according to a minute of 12 August, felt that 'if the U.S. had been willing to come in with us, a joint move earlier might have had some success'.[41] He, Eden and Halifax issued a communique late in August on the far east observing 'with satisfaction the close collaboration that has been maintained with other governments, especially the American and the French'. The United States *chargé* in London, Herschel Johnson, took objection to remarks in *The Times* on this.[42] But Halifax, Eden and Chamberlain decided to renew efforts to get the United States to participate in a 'joint declaration'.[43]

At the end of August when Eden saw Johnson to discuss means of meeting the proposed Japanese blockade of the China coast, the foreign secretary stressed the need for Anglo-American co-operation.[44] The United States, however, found the British proposals embarrassing: there was the neutrality legislation to consider.[45] In September the usual line of action was

[37] *FRUS* 1937(3), pp. 449–50, 793.94/9756, Department of State to British Embassy, 19.8.1937; p. 455, 793.94/9643, British Embassy to Department of State, 20.8.1937; p. 456, 793.94/9643, Department of State to British Embassy, 21.8.1937.

[38] *F O 371*, 20954, F5868/9/10, Foreign Office Memorandum by Mr. Ronald on Sino-Japanese Dispute and Anglo-American Co-operation, 27.8.1937; *FRUS* 1937(3), pp. 464–7, 793.94/9980, Memorandum by Hornbeck, 24.8.1937.

[39] The United States made independent representations through their ambassador at Nanking about the deteriorating situation in Tsingtao without consulting the British. See *F O 371*, 20954, F5868/9/10, Foreign Office Memorandum by Mr. Ronald on Sino-Japanese Dispute and Anglo-American Co-operation, 27.8.1937.

[40] *F O 371*, 20954, F5683/9/10, Lindsay to Foreign Office, Telegram, 24.8.1937 d.25.8.1937 (decypher); Foreign Office Minute by Mr. Ronald, 25.8.1937.

[41] Ibid., F5868/9/10, Foreign Office Memorandum by Mr. Ronald on Sino-Japanese Dispute and Anglo-American Co-operation, 27.8.1937.

[42] *FRUS* 1937(3), pp. 480–1, 793.94/9711, Johnson to Hull, Telegram No. 558, 26.8.1937.

[43] Ibid., pp. 485–8, 793.94/9732, Grew to Hull, Telegram No. 321, 27.8.1937.

[44] *FRUS* 1937(4), pp. 439–40, 793.941112/9, Johnson to Hull, Telegram No. 569, 31.8.1937.

[45] Ibid., pp. 441–3, 793.94112/9, Hull to Johnson, Telegram No. 374, 1.9.1937.

taken over the Japanese seizure of Pratas reef,[46] and there was consultation about possible Japanese bombing of Nanking.[47] Parallel representations were made over the continued use of sections of the international settlement at Shanghai as a base for Japanese military operations.[48]

The attitudes of the British and United States representatives in Japan are important in the light of the stands taken by their respective governments. Sir Robert Craigie, the newly appointed British ambassador to Tokyo, while travelling to Japan had an informal talk on the general situation with Mr. Key, the second secretary to the United States legation in Ottawa. Craigie explained that he had not gone to Washington in case the Japanese considered that his presence was indicative of a scheme for concerted Anglo-American action against them. Indeed, Craigie tended to look at the matter from the internal situation in Japan, rather than from that of leading the United States away from its isolationist tendencies. His views were more in line with the state department than with the foreign office. Craigie felt that the way to strengthen the hands of the civilian and moderate groups in Japan was for Britain and the United States to refrain from exerting any joint or concerted action against the Japanese government. Britain and the United States should inform each other, but act independently. The action taken would probably be identical. The Japanese should know that Britain and the United States held common views on the far east. Craigie did mention that an 'important and influential' group in the foreign office saw the chief hope of curbing the Japanese in joint Anglo-American action. Craigie disagreed with this section and felt that the United States government had been wise to discourage joint action.[49]

Craigie's views coincided with those of Joseph Grew, his United States counterpart. Grew felt that strict neutrality, and staying out of the far eastern mess, should be the objects of United States policy.[50] On 22 September it seems that Craigie and Grew agreed that parallel action by the

[46] *FRUS* 1937(3), p. 523, 793.94/10043, Johnson to Hull, Telegram No. 593, 13.9.1937; pp. 523–4, 793.94/10043, Hull to Johnson, Telegram No. 392, 14.9.1937.

[47] Ibid., p. 533, 793.94/10146a, Acting Secretary of State to Johnson, Telegram No. 394, 20.9.1937; p. 535, 793.94/10152, Johnson to Hull, Telegram No. 601, 20.9.1937; p. 549, 793.94/10231, Johnson to Hull, Telegram No. 606, 24.9.1937.

[48] Ibid., pp. 555–6, 793.94/10260, Hull to Gauss, Telegram No. 427, 28.9.1937; pp. 560–1, 793.94/10419, British Embassy to Department of State, 1.10.1937; pp. 568–9, 793.94/10419, Department of State to British Embassy, 2.10.1937.

[49] Ibid., pp. 401–4, 793.94/9509, Memorandum by Key, 13.8.1937; Copy transmitted by the Minister in Canada to the Department of State in Despatch No. 1553, 17.8.1937 r. 19.8.1937. I have been unable to find any record of this in the British documents.

[50] Waldo H. Heinrichs, *American Ambassador* (Boston, 1966), pp. 241–2.

United States and Britain was more likely to be effective than identical action would be.[51]

Inspired by a suggestion from the economist, J. M. Keynes, the British tried to press the United States into a boycott of Japanese goods. Cadogan had told Johnson earlier in September that the British could not send forces to the far east 'in sufficient strength to command the situation'. For this reason, as the cabinet was aware, United States co-operation was vital. The state department, however, made it clear on 5 October that the United States would not get involved in any armed conflict: it had to be guided by the neutrality legislation.[52]

Any hope of closer Anglo-American co-operation in the far east was nearly dashed by the response of isolationist sentiment in the United States to Roosevelt's 'quarantine speech' at Chicago on 5 October. Roosevelt himself inserted the controversial 'quarantine' reference. He said:

> It seems to be unfortunately true that the epidemic of world lawlessness is spreading. When an epidemic of physical disease starts to spread, the community approves and joins in a quarantine of the patients in order to protect the health of the community against the spread of the disease.[53]

Reaction in the United States was immediate and vociferous: a telegraphic poll of congress revealed a majority of two to one against common action in the far east.[54]

Certain newspapers and officials, however, approved Roosevelt's moral. Henry Stimson, a former secretary of state, wrote to the *New York Times* urging that the United States and Britain should stop helping Japanese aggression by providing that country with materials. He also called the neutrality legislation a policy of 'amoral drift.'[55] The *New York Times* wrote of a realisation that the United States would not 'either with honor or with safety, play the role of the hermit in the modern world'.[56] Dorothy Borg claims that 'any dispassionate estimate of the evidence at the administration's command did not justify the assumption that . . . there was "hardly a voice raised to express agreement with the President's views" '.[57] Certainly V. A. L. Mallet, the counsellor at Washington, gave some foreign

---

[51] *FRUS* 1937(3), pp. 591–3, Enclosure in 793.94/11020, Grew to Hull, Draft Telegram, 6.10.1937; Telegram sent for Record Purposes.
[52] *F O 371*, 21015, F7822/6799/10, Keynes to Jebb, 29.9.1937; F8142/6799/10, Foreign Office Memorandum by J. W. Nicholls, r. in r. 20.10.1937.
[53] Hull 1, p. 545.
[54] Ibid., *loc. cit.*
[55] *Times*, 8.10.1937.
[56] *New York Times*, 7.10.1937, Ed.
[57] Borg, pp. 387–98.

office officials the impression that press reaction to the Chicago speech was 'surprisingly favourable'.[58] A. Holman of the foreign office, however, analysed the press comment as being 'cautious rather than favourable'.[59] The state department considered that reaction was hostile and determined United States foreign policy accordingly.

Britain was cautious. Chamberlain told the cabinet on 6 October that the government should not allow itself 'to be manoeuvred into a position in which it could be said that the United States had offered to co-operate in economic sanctions if the United Kingdom would join them and that we were standing in the way of such action'. The cabinet also discussed the risk of war that sanctions posed, and the prime minister pointed out that the United States might have to be asked whether it would co-operate in defending British possessions in the far east. Chamberlain felt that, for the moment, 'President Roosevelt had rather embarrassed the situation, but he did not underrate the importance of this statement, especially as a warning to the Dictator Powers that there was a point beyond which the United States would not permit them to go. Consequently, if embarrassing to-day, the speech might prove useful later on.'[60]

Chamberlain saw the need for some public response. On 8 October he spoke of the British government being whole heartedly with Roosevelt's call for a concerted effort for peace.[61] Privately the prime minister wrote: 'Seeing that patients suffering from epidemic diseases do not usually go about fully armed . . . something lacking in his analogy . . . when I asked U.S.A. to make a joint *démarche* at the very beginning, they refused.'[62]

At the cabinet meeting on 6 October Eden suggested that it would be necessary to take diplomatic action.[63] Eden, consistently determined to enmesh the United States in the far east, and, if possible, Europe, was seemingly anxious to seize this opportunity. But Sumner Welles told Mallet on 12 October that he interpreted quarantine 'as a remote and vague objective'. Emphasis should be placed on the last sentence: 'America hates war. America hopes for peace.'[64] On the same day Wickham Steed saw Hull and Roosevelt, and had a conversation which Vansittart minuted

[58] *F O 371*, 20667, A7544/448/45, No. 928, Mallet to Foreign Office, 12.10.1937 r. in r. 20.10.1937; Minutes, 21.10.1937.

[59] Ibid., Minute by A. Holman, 21.10.1937.

[60] *Cab 23*, 89, pp. 6–9, Cab 36 (37) 5, Secret, 6.10.1937.

[61] *Times*, 9.10.1937.

[62] Keith Feiling, *The Life of Neville Chamberlain* (London, 1946), p. 325.

[63] *Cab 23*, 89, p. 7, Cab 36 (37) 5, Secret, 6.10.1937.

[64] *F O 371*, 21019, F7792/7240/10, Mallet to Foreign Office, Telegram No. 340, Immediate, 12.10.1937 r. in r. 13.10.1937 (decypher).

that Eden should find 'enlightening'. Roosevelt explained that his words had been meant to educate United States public opinion and 'to show the world in which direction that opinion is running'. But the president stressed that there were three things which he wanted the British government not to do:

(1) It should not speak or think or act as though it were possible for me to be in any way an exponent of British Foreign Office policy.

(2) It should never forget I cannot march ahead of our very difficult and restive American public opinion; and

(3) It must not try to push me in any way to the front or to thrust leadership upon me. . . . I cannot and shall not try to impose anything upon our people or the world. I will seek most earnestly to co-operate with all nations that are working for freedom and for peace.

Holman minuted on 18 October:

This shows very clearly that nothing concrete can be expected at present from the U.S.A. and that much harm may be done by the Press and public bodies trying to force the pace.[65]

Chamberlain carefully supervised the British enquiries that went to Washington, and saw Eden on the morning of 12 October so that no telegram was despatched which Eden 'had not seen and approved'.[66] The telegram eventually sent instructed Mallet to express British concern that public opinion in Britain and in the United States 'should too hastily and too easily assume that quarantine means economic sanctions without the risk of war'.[67] The United States was asked whether, in the event of its considering a joint imposition of a boycott against Japan, it had taken into account the possibility that Japan would take retaliatory action, possibly aggressive action, against the United States and those taking part in the boycott. Welles also assured Mallet that Roosevelt was not considering immediate application of quarantine measures: the intention of the president was that the United States should undertake to co-operate with the other signatories of the nine power treaty to find a solution of the Chinese situation, through an agreement satisfactory to all the signatories of the treaty.[68] After this, Eden, in a telephone conversation with Welles, offered Britain's whole hearted co-operation. Of course, there was no longer any misconception on the part of the British about the meaning of the Chicago speech.[69]

65 Ibid., 20663, A7441/228/45, Mallet to Foreign Office, Telegram No.344, 13.10.1937 r. in r. 15.10.1937 (decypher); Foreign Office Minutes, 15.10.1937; Minute by Holman, 18.10.1937; Minute by Vansittart, 14.10.1937.

66 Ibid., 21019, F7477/7240/10, Vansittart to Eden, 11.10.1937.

67 Ibid., Eden to Mallet, Telegram, Most Immediate, 12.10.1937 (cypher, draft).

68 *FRUS* 1937(3), pp. 600–2, 711.00 Pres. Speech, Oct. 5 1937/100, Memorandum by Welles, 12.10.1937.

69 Ibid., pp. 608–9, 793.94 Conf./51, Memorandum by Welles, 14.10.1937.

During October the United States co-operated with the league. At the end of August China had decided to lay its case before the league: China wished to invoke article XVII of the covenant, which could lead to sanctions against Japan. Under British and French pressure the Chinese modified their stand and referred the matter to the far east advisory committee, a body formed during the Manchurian crisis and which could include a United States representative. But on 27 September this committee passed a resolution condemning Japanese bombing and ended any possibility of Japanese co-operation with the league.[70]

Eden explained British impotence to the cabinet on 29 September: the state department was not anxious for joint Anglo-American action; any approach on Britain's part would embarrass the United States government, and perhaps interfere with the prevailing good relations; consequently he thought that British policy should be 'to take no step without the support of the United States of America'. There was also the difficulty of the attitude adopted by the New Zealand delegation at Geneva, one which coincided with that of the labour opposition in Britain. MacDonald had had to exercise a restraining influence on the New Zealand representatives and had impressed on them that if the British government were to adopt the policy they proposed, they would soon have to extricate both New Zealand and themselves from a dangerous situation.[71]

On 21 September Bruce resurrected his imperial conference plan of a conference of powers with interests in the Pacific, to allow the league 'to transcend the limitations of its present membership'.[72] Britain feared that this might embarrass the United States. To forestall Chinese impatience, on 4 October Lord Cranborne, modified Bruce's plan proposed a conference of the signatories of the nine power treaty of which the United States was one. He later explained to Leland Harrison that there had been no time to consult Washington on this.[73] Eden told the cabinet on 6 October that this move would give 'the fullest scope to the United States of America to give any co-operation they could'. Chamberlain was anxious: if Britain were involved in the far east, the dictators might move in Europe.[74]

Reviving the nine power treaty involved the United States.[75] British attempts, however, to force any initiative on the United States were

---

[70] See Clifford, pp. 36–7.
[71] *Cab 23*, 89, pp. 14–5, Cab 35 (37) 4, Secret, 29.9.1937.
[72] *League of Nations Official Journal*, Aug.–Sept. 1937, pp. 653–5.
[73] Clifford, p. 37.
[74] *Cab 23*, 89, pp. 5–12, Cab 36 (37) 5, Secret, 6.10.1937.
[75] Eden, p. 608.

thwarted. Brussels was settled on as the venue, but the state department objected to invitations issued 'at the request of the American and British Governments'.[76]

The foreign office was confronted with what sanctions against Japan might mean. The official's attitude is summed up in a minute by Gladwyn Jebb of 8 October:

> I think that the principle to be applied to the whole problem is essentially simple: *half-measures are far worse than useless and full measures mean war.*[77]

The cabinet discussed the matter on 13 October. Chamberlain emphasised the need to reach agreement with the United States representatives to the conference. Roosevelt had used 'quarantine' in such a way that he could escape any interpretation of boycott. But the British opposition might interpret the phrase as an offer to impose economic sanctions, and might suggest that the British government were standing in the way of an effective restraint on Japan. Chamberlain had discussed the matter with Eden, and he thought that they had agreed on certain conclusions: effective sanctions were impossible without a risk of war; ineffective sanctions would result in 'prolonged bitterness and ill-will'; even if sufficient countries imposed economic sanctions against Japan, Chamberlain doubted whether they would operate in time to serve China; there was also the danger that Japan, encouraged by Italy and Germany, might make a retaliatory attack. With the situation in Europe Britain could not send a fleet to the far east. Sanctions were only possible if the United States would guarantee that it would 'face up to all the consequences which might fall on nations with large interests in the Far East.' Even then it was impossible to foresee how long public opinion in the United States would maintain that position.

Eden had a different emphasis. The foreign secretary felt that Anglo-American co-operation was vital, and, in the unlikely event of the United States being prepared to impose sanctions, he felt that Britain should take the risk and do likewise.

MacDonald was more cautious. Some of the dominions were signatories of the nine power treaty, and he felt that it was necessary to get into line with them even before approaching the United States.[78]

The foreign office was divided on how to approach the United States. There was departmental criticism of one draft on the grounds that it gave

[76] Hull 1, pp. 550–1; Clifford, p. 38.

[77] *F O 371*, 21015, F8142/6799/10, Foreign Office Memorandum by J. W. Nichols, r. in r. 20.10.1937; Minute by Jebb, 8.10.1937.

[78] *Cab 23*, 89, pp. 13–21, Cab 37 (37) 3, Secret, 10.10.1937.

too optimistic an impression as to the possible efficiency of sanctions. The United States section felt that it was too pessimistic, and would provide an excessive 'cold douche' to United States ardour.

The British dilemma is cogently expressed in a minute by Jebb of 15 October:

> In my view sanctions would almost certainly mean war and the U.S.A. is not now prepared to fight, even with the British Empire as an ally. Therefore there will in fact be no sanctions. But the extent to which the U.S. are 'coming out of their shell' is really remarkable, and we must do everything to see that they do not—as in 1932 and 1935—retire into it again, perhaps for good and all, on the grounds, however unjustified, that 'England has let us down'. It is vital therefore for us to take the risk of saying that we are prepared to go to any length if they will stand by us; and it is highly desirable to suggest that we would be prepared to do something more than they are prepared to do: in fact to set them an example. Nor is the risk involved by such a policy so very great, for if *per impossibile* the U.S. found themselves involved in a war between us and Japan they would automatically become our ally in the event of trouble in Europe.
>
> At the same time it is equally desirable not to queer the pitch of President Roosevelt by giving the impression that we are anxious to apply sanctions and thereby to jockey him into a military alliance. Any such suggestion would no doubt play into the hands of our enemies in America and ruin our relations with Japan.[79]

In the end a vague memorandum was sent to the state department, laying stress on sanctions, and showing more optimism as to their outcome. Mallet was told of the British government's real intention but the dominions were only sent a summary of what went to the state department. As R. A. Wiseman of the dominions office pointed out, there was the danger of adverse dominion reaction, if, because of a leakage, it had became known that Britain was discussing the possibility of sanctions with the United States without first consulting the dominions.[80]

The method of informing the dominions was, as foreign office officials observed, unfortunate: the dominions were left with the impression that the telegram sent to them was a reasoned statement of the British government's views, whereas, in actuality, it was drafted 'solely for consumption in the United States'.[81]

---

[79] *F O 371*, 21015, F8143/6799/10, Foreign Office Minute on Economic Pressure against Japan, 13.10.1937 r. in r. 20.10.1937; Minutes by Jebb, 15.10.1937; Holman, 15.10.1937; X. R. Ronald, 19.10.1937.

[80] Ibid., *loc. cit.*; Minutes of Inter Departmental Meeting held at the Foreign Office, 13.10.1937.

[81] Ibid., F8615/6799/10, Minutes on Telegraphic Correspondence between the Dominions Office and the Dominions, 28.10.1937 r. in r. 28.10.1937.

New Zealand 'got hold of the wrong end of the stick' and had to be dealt with by the dominions office, but otherwise the only serious misunderstanding came from South Africa.[82]

South Africa insisted that the Brussels conference was not competent to discuss either assistance to China, or pressure on Japan. Foreign office officials were concerned that if Britain let South Africa know its true motives, South Africa might pass the information on to the United States. But in the end it was decided that the high commissioner in South Africa should explain confidentially to Hertzog the reason for the controversial telegram was that Britain did not want to discourage the tendency in the United States to emerge from isolation, and also to guard against a repetition on 1932, when the United States maintained, without justification, that British reluctance to take effective action prevented the United States from giving full support to the league.[83]

Canada felt that sanctions were outside the scope of the conference, but understood that there was no prospect of overwhelming support for them. The Canadian government also warned that overt assistance to China would give rise to the same situation as sanctions.[84] Jebb of the foreign office considered this reply 'extremely satisfactory'.[85]

The Australian view was that the Brussels conference could only consider 'mediation'. Any 'other measures' should first be submitted to the league.[86] Jebb thought this 'on the whole quite sensible' and Australia was assured that it was not intended that the Brussels conference should take matters out of the hands of the league.[87]

In this instance the dominions were able to influence British policy in the direction that Britain wanted. Jebb minuted, tongue in cheek, on 28 October:

[82] Ibid., Minute by Jebb, 28.10.1937. I could not trace copies of the correspondence with New Zealand, No. F 8236 and F8363.

[83] Ibid., F8614/6799/10, Dominions Office to Foreign Office, No. F 10/3, 28.10.1937 r. in r. 28.10.1937; Enclosing South African Government to Dominions Office, Telegram No. 25, Confidential, 26.10.1937 (copy); Minute by R. P. Heppel, 28.10.1937; F8615/6799/10. Minutes on Telegraphic Correspondence between the Dominion Office and the Dominions, 28.10.1937 r. in r. 28.10.1937; Minutes by Jebb, 28.10.1937; A. Cadogan, 28.10.1937; Vansittart, 29.10.1937; Foreign Office to High Commisioner in South Africa, Telegram, Undated (draft).

[84] Ibid., F8614/6799/10, Dominions Office to Foreign Office, No. F10/3, 28.10.1937 r. in r. 28.10.1937; Enclosing Canadian Government to MacDonald, Telegram No. 61, Confidential, 27.10.1937 (copy); Minute by R. P. Heppel, 28.10.1937.

[85] Ibid., F8615/6799/10, Minutes on Telegraphic Correspondence between the Dominions Office and the Dominions, 28.10.1937 r. in r. 28.10.1937; Minute by Jebb, 28.10.1937.

[86] Ibid., Minute by R. E. Heppel, 28.10.1937; Enclosing Australian Government to Dominions Office, Telegram No. 85, 28.10.1937 (copy).

[87] Ibid., Minute by Jebb, 28.10.1937; Telegram to Australian Government, Undated (draft).

Generally speaking, we seem to have put ourselves in the excellent tactical position of allowing the Dominions to torpedo a 'sanctions' policy in advance before definitely committing ourselves one way or the other.[88]

United States reaction to the mention of sanctions was also considered by the foreign office as satisfactory.[89] Washington felt that the question of sanctions' did not arise in a conference which had for its objective the finding of a solution of the conflict in the Far East by agreement'.[90] Chamberlain was able to tell the cabinet on 20 October that it was clear that the United States 'had no intention of taking any decisive action in the Far East'.[91]

Eden hoped that Hull would lead the United States delegation to the Brussels conference, but, it was felt that the secretary of state could not be away for such a time, and the task fell to Norman Davis, an adviser in whom Roosevelt was supposed to have confidence.[92] Foreign office officials thought that Davis was 'unreliable' and seemingly even stupid.[93] Davis was sole delegate, but Hornbeck and Pierrepont Moffat accompanied him as advisers.[94] Some foreign office officials felt that Hornbeck could not be placed in the same category as Davis, but Sir J. Pratt had a poor opinion of Hornbeck's intelligence.[95] Moffat distrusted British manoeuvres.[96]

This did not augur well for Eden's hopes. Even Roosevelt seems to have been annoyed with Britain. Davis received his instructions from the president. Roosevelt said that the British cabinet should recognise that there was such a thing as public opinion in the United States. Davis was to emphasise that the United States was not prepared to take joint action with the league, or to take the lead in any future moves. Because of public opinion the United States could not afford to be made a 'tail to the British kite'.[97]

This stand was made clear to Britain before the conference. On 28 October Bingham saw Eden and gave him a message from Roosevelt. The

[88] Ibid., F8615/6799/10, Minutes on Telegraphic Correspondence between the Dominions Office and the Dominions, 28.10.1937 r. in r. 28.10.1937; Minute by Jebb, 28.10.1937.

[89] Ibid., *loc. cit.*

[90] *FRUS* 1937(4), pp. 97–8, 632.6231/261, Memorandum by Welles, 21.10.1937; pp. 114–6, 793.94 Conference/128, Bingham to Hull, Telegram No. 674, 28.10.1937.

[91] *Cab 23*, 89, p. 10, Cab 38 (37) 4, Secret, 20.10.1937.

[92] Hull 1, pp. 551–2.

[93] *F O 371*, 21017, F9293/6799/10, No. 14, British Delegation Brussels to Foreign Office, 8.11.1937 r. in r. 10.11.1937; Minutes by Foreign Office Officials, 16.11.1937.

[94] Nancy Harrison Hooker, Ed., *The Moffat Papers* (Cambridge Mass., 1956), p. 156.

[95] *F O 371*, 21017, F9293/6799/10, No. 14, British Delegation Brussels to Foreign Office, 8.11.1937 r. in r. 10.11.1937; Minutes by Foreign Office Officials, 16.11.1937; Hooker, p. 159.

[96] Clifford, pp. 176–7.

[97] Hull 1, pp. 551–2; *FRUS* 1937(4), pp. 85–6, 793.94 Conference/73d, Memorandum from the File of President Roosevelt's Secretary, apparently of Views for Norman H. Davis, who visited the President who visited the President at Hyde Park before attending the Brussels Conference, Photostatic Copy from the F. D. Roosevelt Library, Hyde Park.

president felt that the British should not take the lead at the conference, and should not make any effort to push the United States into the lead. British attempts to pin down the United States to a precise interpretation of the Chicago speech had been 'objectionable and damaging'.[98]

Then Eden made a statement in the house of commons on 31 October, probably in line with Chamberlain's instructions to present the object of the Brussels conference as 'appeasement',[99] which caused trouble. Eden said: 'to get the full co-operation on an equal basis of the United States Government in an international conference, I would travel, not only from Geneva to Brussels, but from Melbourne to Alaska'.

Eden also mentioned that the initiative for holding the conference had come from the United States. This was seen as a further British attempt to push the United States out in front.[100]

On 2 November, before the conference started, Eden, MacDonald and Cadogan met Davis and his advisers. The accounts of what transpired are confused, but it seems that Eden stressed that Britain was ready for fullest co-operation with the United States. Davis supposed that there had been enough talk of sanctions. He could not agree to joint action. Public opinion in the United States felt that Britain had larger interests in the far east than the United States, could not protect them, and was trying to manoeuvre the United States into doing so. The United States would have to 'bear the brunt'. Eden denied this. Britain could send a few ships to the far east.[101] Davis did tell Eden on 4 November that public opinion in the United States would develop, and seemed to hint that if Japan continued to be recalcitrant 'it might be prepared to consider the possibility of action'.[102] On 6 November Davis suggested a form of sanctions against Japan similar to those which had been implemented against Italy: 'we will just refuse to buy Japanese goods'. Eden explained the risks involved.[103] Hornbeck made a similar suggestion to MacDonald on 8 November.[104] Foreign office officials like H. W. Thomas considered these half measures no good at all, whereas Jebb took the line that Britain should be willing to

[98] *FRUS* 1937(4), pp. 114–6, 793.94 Conference/128, Bingham to Hull, Telegram No. 674, 28.10.1937.

[99] *Cab 23*, 89, p. 10, Cab 38 (37) 4, Secret, 20.10.1937.

[100] Eden, p. 536; Hooker, pp. 161–2.

[101] *F O 371*, 21016, F9046/6799/10, Clive to Foreign Office, Telegram No. 76, 2.11.1937 d. 3.11.1937 r. in r. 4.11.1937 (decypher); *FRUS* 1937(4), pp. 145–7, 793.94 Conference/776, Davis to Hull, Telegram No. 10, 2.11.1937 r. 3.11.1937.

[102] *F O 371*, 21016, F9072/6799/10, Clive to Foreign Office, Telegram No. 78, 3.11.1937 d. 4.11.1937 r. in r. 5.11.1937 (decypher).

[103] Ibid., 21019, F9293/7240/10, Eden to Lindsay, Telegram, 6.11.1937. r. in r. 9.11.1937 (draft).

[104] Ibid., 21017, F9293/6799/10, British Delegation Brussels to Foreign Office, Telegram No. 14, Memorandum by MacDonald, 8.11.1937 r. in r. 10.11.1937.

co-operate with the United States 'in this, as in any other initiative, provided only that we both exchanged assurances of mutual support'.[105]

On 9 November Davis made proposals to Eden as to what could be done if the Japanese refused to co-operate. Eden pointed out that if Britain and the United States supplied arms in large quantities to China, Japan would be likely to react. Davis then thought that Anglo-American solidarity could be shown by a refusal to recognise Japanese aggression in China or Manchuria. Eden lauded the significance of any common Anglo-American decision at Brussels. Davis's third suggestion was that Britain and the United States should refuse to take Japanese products. Davis hoped that Roosevelt would be prepared to ask congress to suspend the neutrality act.[106] Foreign office officials were not impressed: some thought Davis's suggestions were 'impracticable'. Jebb, however argued again that if co-operation were achieved on the third suggestion, and should any action lead to war, the United States would be Britain's ally in the far east, and if there were trouble in Europe, Britain would then have the United States at its side. Knowledge of this, he felt, would be an effective deterrent to precipate action by the European dictators. Vansittart agreed, but officials like A. Holman and A. W. Orde were more hesitant.[107]

Eden, however, saw his chance. He wired Lindsay asking for his view of Davis's third suggestion. Significantly this was a restricted document and was not circulated to the cabinet, or even to Chamberlain. Vansittart, however, was allowed to see it. The foreign secretary made a strong case, similar to that advanced by Jebb:

> Having in mind the vital importance for the future of maintaining and developing the present trend of Anglo-American relations, I naturally wish to take all possible steps which may lead to close Anglo-American co-operation, whether in Europe or in the Far East.

Eden felt that joint Anglo-American action along the lines suggested by Davis might be the foundation for later co-operation in Europe. Because of the situation in Europe Britain would be unable to deploy a vast naval force in the far east, and would have to insist on a guarantee being forthcoming for the possessions of those applying sanctions. The United States would be implicated neatly. If the United States were prepared to give such a guarantee, the French and the Russians had agreed to join in the international action. Eden also felt sure of dominion compliance. The foreign

---

105 Ibid., Minute by H. W. Thomas, 11.11.1937; Minute by Jebb, 16.11.1937.
106 Ibid., F9385/6799/10, Clive to Foreign Office, Telegram No. 64, 9.11.1937 r. 11.11.1937 (*en claire*).
107 Ibid., Minutes by Jebb, 12.11.1937; A. Holman, 12.11.1937; A. W. Orde, 13.11.1937; Vansittart, 13.11.1937.

secretary, however, did have doubts as to whether Davis had put the matter clearly to Roosevelt.[108]

Lindsay had been so surprised, already, by the cabled reports of Eden's interviews at Brussels, that he had called on Wilson, the assistant secretary of state, to check the accounts confidentially.[109] The ambassador was quick to point out that sanctions were 'hardly in the atmosphere at all' in the United States.[110] On 13 November Lindsay called on Welles to clarify the position. Any hopes that Eden might have had were dampened. Welles said that the president was unlikely to request the repeal of the neutrality act as it affected the far east, and there was no need even to consider possibilities like economic sanctions against Japan, or fleet movements by the United States, Britain and France in the Pacific.[111] Davis was discouraged by Washington from making further suggestions along these lines.[112]

Japan refused the second invitation to go to Brussels, the conference recessed for a week, and the problem arose of how to bring it to a close.[113] On 15 November Davis made further suggestions to the British to which foreign office officials minuted objections.[114] As Lindsay pointed out the United States could do nothing without congressional legislation.[115] The British cabinet was worried that the Chinese would ask for German and Italian mediation. Eden warned of the effect on India and Burma of Japanese predominance in China.[116]

In the end, on 21 November, the British and United States delegations drafted a report consisting of platitudes. The conference was suspended: the powers would not take risks to stop Japan.[117]

Co-operation between the United States and British delegations at Brussels had been excellent, but it could not lead to much. The British

[108] Ibid., F9736/6799/10, Harvey to Hoyer Millar, 10.11.1937; Enclosing Eden to Lindsay, Telegram No. 2, Immediate Very Confidential Lock and Key, 10.11.1937 (cypher); Minutes by Foreign Office Officials, 11.11.1937.

[109] *FRUS* 1937(4), pp. 160–2, 793.94 Conference/234, Memorandum by Wilson, 6.11.1937; See also Eden, pp. 537–8.

[110] *F O 371*, 21017, F9682/6799/10, Lindsay to Eden, Telegram No. 1, Very Confidential, 11.11.1937 r. in r. 18.11.1937 (decypher).

[111] Ibid., F9683/6799/10, Lindsay to Eden, Telegram N. 2, Very Confidential, 13.11.1937 r. 14.11.1937 r. in r. 18.11.1937 (decypher); Lindsay to Eden. Telegram No. 3, Very Confidential, 13.11.1937 r. 14.11.1937 r. in r. 18.11.1937; *FRUS* 1937(4), pp. 152–5, 793.94 Conference/251, Memorandum by Welles, 13.11.1937.

[112] Ibid., F9548/6799/10, Eden to Lindsay, Telegram No. 510, 14.11.1937 (draft).

[113] Clifford, p. 42.

[114] *F O 371*, 21017, F9629/6799/10, No. 29, British Delegation Brussels to Foreign Office, 15.11.1937 r. in r. 16.11.1937; Minute by O. W. Orde, 19.11.1937.

[115] Ibid., F9665/6799/10, Lindsay to Foreign Office, Telegram No. 398, Immediate No Distribution, 16.11.1937 r. 17.11.1937 r. in r. 17.11.1937 (decypher).

[116] *Cab 23*, 90, pp. 7–10, Cab 42 (37) 4, Secret, 17.11.1937.

[117] Clifford, p. 43.

were prepared to take action in the far east provided the United States would co-operate and defend British possessions there. Indeed Eden saw this as his chance: if there were war in the far east under these circumstances, and the European dictators seized the opportunity to make trouble in Europe, the United States would inevitably be involved alongside Britain in Europe as well as in the far east. Eden would have achieved his principal foreign policy aim. Seemingly, however, Eden did not have the prime minister's or the cabinet's support for such a scheme, as the telegram in which it was outlined to Lindsay was not circulated to them. In any case it was thwarted immediately by state department reaction to any suggestion of sanctions. Indeed the attitude of the state department was such that Davis was advised by Hull not to go to London on the way back.[118]

Perhaps a more satisfactory aspect of the conference was the agreement achieved amongst the dominions. MacDonald saw Jordan on 29 October in London before they both left for Brussels and impressed on the New Zealand delegate that the conference was not meeting to consider whether sanctions should be imposed against Japan. Jordan, after much argument, agreed that sanctions would be out of place.[119] At Brussels there were frequent meetings between the dominion and British delegates at which policies were thrashed out. These were so successful that Eden was able to report on 13 November that 'co-operation between all Commonwealth delegations could scarcely have been more complete and Dominion delegations have kept in step with us from the beginning'. Jordan continually urged strong action against Japan, and said that New Zealand was prepared to play its part. But even he was eventually made to understand that British policy was dependent on that of the United States. Both Bruce, the Australian delegate, and Dr. Gie, the South African delegate, had instructions from their governments to oppose anything in the nature of sanctions. If, however, the United States and Britain agreed jointly to do something along such lines, they felt sure that their governments would support it. Senator Dandurand of Canada would not commit himself on this aspect, but it seemed that Canada would join in any action which both the United States and Britain agreed upon.[120] If Eden's scheme for the far east had been put into effect, the dominions would have supported it.

[118] *FRUS* 1937(4), p. 230, 793.94 Conference 296, Hull to Bullitt, Telegram No. 50, 26.11.1937.

[119] *F O 371*, 21017, F9478/6799/10, Cabinet Office No. F P (36) 38, 4.11.1937, Cabinet Committee on Foreign Policy New Zealand and the Brussels Conference, Memorandum by MacDonald, 29.10.1937.

[120] Ibid., 21016, F9085/6799/10, No. 5, British Delegation Brussels to Foreign Office, 4.11.1937 r. in r. 5.11.1937, Record of Meeting of Dominion Representatives, 2.11.1937; 21017, F9509/6799/10, No. 19, British Delegation Brussels to Foreign Office, 12.11.1937 r. in r. 13.11.1937, Record of Meeting of Dominion Representatives, 10.11.1937; F9510/6799/10, No. 20, British Delegation Brussels to Foreign Office, 12.11.1937 r. in r. 13.11.1937, Meeting of Dominion Representatives, 11.11.1937; F9519/6799/10, Clive to Foreign Office, Telegram No. 90, 13.11.1937 r. in r. 15.11.1937 (decypher).

In the broader field of Anglo-American co-operation Hull and Roosevelt were growing increasingly anxious about the proposed trade treaty. Little had been achieved in the previous few months and the state department was virtually employing this as a threat. Bingham, on 28 October, let Eden know that time was short. If there were no agreement, United States public opinion would react, and further Anglo-American co-operation would be difficult.[121] On 27 October the cabinet considered a report by the committee on trade and agriculture on this matter. Some of the dominions were being obstreperous. The report recommended that a more specific and substantive offer should be made to the United States. If the United States agreed that such an offer formed the basis for negotiation the dominions could then be told if they withheld their consent they would be responsible for blocking further progress. MacDonald warned the cabinet that the dominions might be awkward, but if given reasonable warning, this could be avoided. Intricate financial manoeuvring and negotiation with the dominions on such matters as fixed prices for apples meant that by the middle of November Hull was able to announce that the United States and Britain had agreed to begin negotiations for a reciprocal tariff treaty.[122]

Anglo-American action in the far east was still envisaged after Brussels.[123] By the end of November the situation in the far east had deteriorated. Trouble arose in the Chinese maritime customs, first at Tientsin, and then at Shanghai where the Japanese authorities had seized the customs vessels. Eden told the cabinet on 24 November that the Japanese were taking British property, and Britain did not have the force to resist. Chamberlain pointed out that Britain could not exert forceful pressure on the Japanese without the co-operation of the United States. The prime minister had no objection to Eden approaching the United States government as to whether they would be prepared to send ships to the far east if Britain did likewise, but he felt sure that the reply would be that United States interests did not justify the despatch of ships.[124] Eden made an approach, and Welles noted this as a reversal of earlier British policy. Only ten days previously Lindsay had explained that because of the European situation Britain was not in a position to deploy its forces to far

---

[121] *F O 371*, 20663, A7765/228/45, Memorandum by Eden of Conversation with Davis, 28.10.1937 r. in r. 29.10.1937; *FRUS* 1937(4), pp. 114–6, 793.94 Conference/128, Bingham to Hull, Telegram No. 674, 28.10.1937.

[122] *Cab. 23*, 90, pp. 10–8, Cab 39 (37) 7, Secret, 27.10.1937; Appendices to Cab 39(37), Mallet to Foreign Office, Telegrams No. 371, No Distribution, 26.10.1937 r. 27.10.1937 r. in r. 28.10.1937 (decypher). See also *D O 114*, 93, *passim.; New York Times*, 19.11.1937, Ed.

[123] See Nicholas, pp. 44–6.

[124] *Cab 23*, 90, p. 8, Cab 43 (37) 5, Secret, 24. 11.1937.

eastern waters. Welles observed that consequently any forceful measure would mean an overwhelming display of United States naval force.[125] The state department was also kept informed by Grew of 'British ineptitudes, both of action and of statement' in the far east.[126] United States public opinion, as Lindsay warned on 30 November, was still strongly isolationist: the situation in Shanghai had merely caused pronouncements in congress in favour of non intervention, and statements by people like Senator Pittman that United States interests were comparatively unaffected.[127]

This was the situation when the Panay incident occurred, and months of careful preparation by Eden were put to the test. On 12 December a Japanese fieldgun battery attacked HMS *Ladybird* at Wuhu. At the same time Japanese aircraft bombed and sank the United States gunboat, *Panay* in the Yangtse.[128]

Eden immediately saw Johnson, and lamented that this was the sort of incident he had feared might happen if there were no restraint on the Japanese government provided by evidence of joint Anglo-American determination. Eden understood the difficulties that the state department faced in taking any move which could be interpreted as 'joint action' with the British, but stressed that such action was most likely to produce results. He requested that Lindsay be consulted before the United States took any final decision.[129] Johnson felt that the British hoped for some positive United States action, such as the moving of the fleet.[130] Eden seems to have anticipated that the United States would mobilise its fleet, and was anxious that the British should know in advance so that they could take similar action.[131] Lindsay does not appear to have mentioned this when he saw Welles.[132]

Eden was disappointed. The state department protested independently to Japan on the evening of 13 December. The reason for this step, offered to the British, that this was done to forestall a Japanese apology and thus there was no time for consultation, was hardly convincing. Foreign office

[125] *FRUS* 1937(3), pp. 724–5, 693.002/4112/3, Memorandum by Welles, 27.11.1937.

[126] Ibid., pp. 792–4, 793.94/11841, No. 2696, Grew to Hull, 11.12.1937 r. 27.12.1937.

[127] *F O 371*, 20667, A8790/448/45, No.1053, Lindsay to Foreign Office, 30.11.1937 r. in r. 7.12.1937.

[128] Eden, pp. 541–2; See Manny T. Koginos, *The Panay Incident: Prelude to War* (Purdue, 1967), *passim*.

[129] *F O 371*, 21021, F11086/10816/10, No. 1159, Memorandum by Eden of Conversation with Johnson, 13.12.1937 r. in r. 16.12.1937; *FRUS* 1937(4), pp. 490–1, 394.115 Panay/28, Johnson to Hull, Telegram No. 1767, 13.12.1937.

[130] *FRUS* 1937(4), pp. 494–5, 394.114 Panay/43, Johnson to Hull, Telegram No. 772, 13.12.1937; *F O 371*, 21021, F10961/10816/10, Minute by Cadogan, 13.12.1937 r. in r. 14.12.1937.

[131] *F O 371*, 21021, F10961/10816/10, Eden to Lindsay, Telegram No. 591, Most Immediate, 13.12.1937 (draft).

[132] Ibid., F10976/10816/10, Lindsay to Foreign Office, Telegram No. 464, Most Immediate, 13.12.1937.

officials minuted: 'The American administration are *afraid* of co-operation with us, and will always try to avoid it.'[133]

Lindsay called on Hull on 14 December to say that Eden was 'disappointed'. The ambassador reiterated a request for joint action. Hull spoke of the slow process of educating United States public opinion.[134]

On 14 December Eden had consultations with Chamberlain and Duff Cooper. They decided to mention to Washington the possibility of the despatch of a battle fleet to far eastern waters. It was hoped that the United States government would do the same, and in that event, naval staff conversations would be desirable. Britain could only act with United States support.

Cabinet discussion on 15 December watered down this proposed telegram. Chamberlain suggested something short of sending the fleet, possibly mobilisation. The thorny question of Italy and the Mediterranean was also raised. Duff Cooper pointed out that if the British fleet went to the far east the French would have to look after the Mediterranean, and the French were then likely to have apprehensions about the safety of the Atlantic. But at this point in the discussion a telegram from Lindsay was read. Lindsay warned that Roosevelt and Hull had been doing their best to bring public opinion around to realising the dangers of the situation, but certainly were not in a position to adopt measures like those which the cabinet were discussing. Despite this Chamberlain took a surprisingly firm line. The prime minister pointed to the loss of prestige for the democracies in the far east. He felt that some action should be taken to restore the situation, and though realising the difficulties that the United States government had with public opinion, he wondered whether they would not consider mobilisation as a first step. Eden warned that 'mobilisation' was a formidable word, and suggested that a phrase like 'an improved state of readiness of the fleet' might seem less shocking to United States ears. MacDonald also mentioned that it might be wise to inform the dominions, and to approach Australia and New Zealand to see if they would co-operate in any such venture. The cabinet even discussed whether Britain could act on its own, but Chamberlain pointed out that the forces were not adequate, and any such move might make it more difficult for the United States to co-operate afterwards.

---

[133] Ibid., F10984/10816/10, Lindsay to Foreign Office, Telegram No. 468, Immediate, 14.12.1937 decypher); Minutes by J. Thyne Henderson, 14.12.1937; Minutes by C. W. Orde, 15.12.1937.

[134] Ibid., F10976/10816/10, Eden to Lindsay, Telegram No. 594, Most Immediate No Distribution, 14.12.1937 (cypher); F11048/10876/10, Lindsay to Eden, Telegram No. 470, Important Very Confidential No Distribution, 14.12.1937 r. 15.12.1937 r. in r. 15.12.1937.

Accordingly a telegram was sent to Lindsay on 15 December asking him to approach the state department on the lines of the cabinet discussion.[135] But Hull and his advisers did not think that the United States was in a position to send forces to the far east. Isolationist sentiment was too strong.[136]

At this stage a new factor was introduced by the United States: the possibility of sanctions. This alarmed Chamberlain. Morgenthau telephoned Sir John Simon, the chancellor of the exchequer, with the knowledge and approval of Roosevelt. Morgenthau said that his message was for Chamberlain and Simon alone, and that he was operating through the treasury rather than through diplomatic channels. A probable reason for this was the attitude of state department officials, and the prevailing isolationist sentiment in the United States. Simon was not only cautious, but suspicious, irritable and aloof.

Morgenthau outlined the proposition: the trading with the enemy act gave the president the authority to declare a national emergency, with the idea of keeping the United States quarantined against war. This would mean exchange control involving bank credits and gold movements. The United States needed co-operation for such a policy against Japan.

Simon hedged.[137] This subject later became a corollary to the naval discussions between Britain and the United States.

Chamberlain was not impressed by Morgenthau's proposal. The prime minister told the cabinet on 22 December that the British difficulty lay not in 'Roosevelt's goodwill, but in his failure to appreciate the needs of the situation'. A blockade was impossible if not supported by force.[138] By 21 December Chamberlain and Eden had made their attitude to the Japanese situation clear to the United States. The British could not co-operate in monetary action against the Japanese without special parliamentary legislation, and without first consulting the dominions. This was a polite, but firm, refusal of the Morgenthau overture.[139]

The opportunity for a firm United States stand passed on 23 December when the state department officially accepted the full apology tended by

---

[135] *Cab 23*, 90, pp. 5–12, Cab 47 (37) 3, 4, Secret, 15.12.1937; *F O 371*, 21021, F10976/10816/10, Eden to Lindsay, Telegram No. 607, Very Confidential No Distribution, 15.12.1937 (cypher); F11056/10816/10, Lindsay to Eden, Telegram No. 469, 14.12.1937 r. in r. 15.12.1937.

[136] *F O 371*, 21021, F11215/10816/10, Lindsay to Eden, Telegram No 485, 17.12.1937 r. 18.12.1937 r. in r. 20.12.1937.

[137] John Morton Blum, *From the Morgenthau Diaries Years of Crisis 1928–1938* (Boston, 1959), pp. 485–92.

[138] *Cab 23*, 90, Annex to Cab 48 (37) 5, Most Secret, 22.12.1937.

[139] Blum, p. 492.

the Japanese for the *Panay* incident.[140] The pressure of public opinion in the United States partially explains the attitude of the state department over the *Panay* incident. Observers noted American opinion as being strongly isolationist: the *Panay* incident inflamed emotions, but showed that the public would resist any strong preventive policy.[141] An effort was made to force the Ludlow war referendum resolution through congress. This would have meant shackling the executive since it made a referendum majority assent necessary for a declaration of war, except when the territory of the United States was invaded and its citizens were attacked.[142] In the foreign office J. G. S. Beith minuted: 'The fact that a crank like Mr. Ludlow got 218 signatures is significant of isolationism in the U.S.'[143] Roosevelt, his foreign policy advisers and many newspapers possibly favoured a stronger, more positive United States policy. But their views merely contrasted with the mass opinion.

Against this background it is possible to understand United States reaction to statements about Anglo-American co-operation in the British house of commons. On 21 December, the foreign policy debate was marked, as Johnson observed, by 'the almost unanimous awareness of the key position occupied by the United States and the equally unanimous desire to obtain American co-operation which means American support'.[144] Eden played up the extent of Anglo-American co-operation. He did, however, say that there was no question of treaty entanglements between Britain and the United States.[145] In February 1938, speaking in the senate, William E. Borah made oblique references to Eden's statement in an attempt to suggest that there was a possible alliance between the United States and Britain. Eden assured Hull that he had made no statement that could lead to this kind of accusation.[146]

The gain from the *Panay* crisis was the Anglo-American naval staff conversations. A week before the *Panay* incident Eden had telegraphed Lindsay that the cabinet was considering how to make Britain's power felt in the far east. It was arranged that Lindsay should have a secret interview with Roosevelt on the night of 16 December, and for the meeting Lindsay

[140] Joseph C. Grew, *Turbulent Era. A Diplomatic Record of Fifty Years 1904–1945* 2 (Boston, 1952), p. 1294.

[141] Anonymous, 'Warp and Woof of American Policy', *Round Table*, XXVIII (1937–8), pp. 297–310 at p. 299; *New York Times*, 15.12.1937.

[142] *New York Times*, 17.12.1937.

[143] *F O 371*, 20667, A9406/448/45, No. 1107, Lindsay to Foreign Office, 12.12.1937 r. in r. 30.12.1937; Minute by J. G. S. Beith, 4.1.1938.

[144] *FRUS* 1937(3), pp. 830–2, 793.94/11767, Johnson to Hull, Telegram No. 800, 22.12.1937.

[145] *New York Times*, 3.2.1938, Ed.

[146] *FRUS* 1938(3), p. 63, 711.41/377a, Hull to Johnson, Telegram No. 50, 2.2.1938; pp.69–70, 711.41/378, Johnson to Hull, Telegram, 5.2.1938.

was authorised to mention British readiness to make a substantial contribution to any naval display, up to eight or nine capital ships, provided that the United States would do likewise, or the less drastic step of getting the fleet into a greater state of readiness, and staff conversations. At the secret meeting Roosevelt took up the matter of staff conversations. The president favoured an arrangement like that in 1916–7 when an exchange of secret information had been established between the admiralty and the navy department. He hoped to send a suitable person to London to further the matter. Roosevelt had in mind a blockade of Japan which might take eighteen months to become effective, if there were further Japanese outrages, presumably on United States property. But he was against an Anglo-American naval demonstration as it would have no effect on the military authorities on Japan. Mention was made of advancing the date of naval maneouvres due to begin at Hawaii in three months time, and of a visit of United States cruisers to Singapore. Lindsay did his best to encourage the latter proposal. Roosevelt was not prepared to take up the British offer for a naval demonstration in the far east, and suggested that it was more important to keep its ships to look after Europe. When Eden disclosed what had transpired to the cabinet on 22 December, he referred to the president's attitude as being 'an encouraging feature in the situation'.[147]

Roosevelt accordingly carried out his suggestions: he arranged for Captain Ingersoll of the United States navy to go to London for conversations. Eden met Ingersoll on 1 January. Ingersoll did not respond enthusiastically to Eden's mention of joint action, and suggested that they should proceed with a technical examination, after which it should be easier to consider any political decisions which might have to be taken. Eden, however, did pass on information about the opening of the new dock at Singapore, and said how much Britain would welcome the visit of United States ships there.[148]

On 3 January Ingersoll and Admiral Jones of the royal navy discussed matters. It soon transpired that Ingersoll had no definite instructions, and was in Britain more 'as a liaison officer than as a consultant.'[149] The

[147] *Cab 23*, 90, Annex to Cab 48 (37) 5, Most Secret, 22.12.1937; Eden, pp. 543–4. See also Lawrence Pratt, 'The Anglo-American Naval Conversations on the Far East of January 1938', *International Affairs*, XLVII (1971), pp. 745–63.

[148] *F O 371*, 22106, pp. 259–61, F95/84/10, No. 23, Foreign Office Minute of Conversation between Eden, Cadogan, Johnson and Ingersoll, 1.1.1938.

[149] Ibid., pp. 415–7, F95/84/10, Memorandum by Chatfield of Conversation between Jones, Wilson and Ingersoll, 3.1.1938.

foreign office, however, despite Lindsay's warnings that it would be 'undesirable to press the United States Government unduly', was anxious to find out how far any United States action would be dependent on British co-operation. There were reports in the press on 7 January of a Japanese assault on two British police officers in Shanghai. In the light of this the foreign office asked Lindsay whether, if Britain were to state that it was completing certain naval preparations short of mobilisation, the United States would proceed on parallel lines, and possibly send an advance force of cruisers, destroyers and submarines to Hawaii and the rest of the fleet to Pacific ports. Ingersoll had said that, from a technical point of view this was possible.[150]

The president agreed on 10 January that if the British government decided to issue a statement that they were completing certain naval preparations, an announcement would be made that the vessels of the United States Pacific fleet were being sent to dry dock. Soon after that the date of the Pacific manoeuvres would be advanced by two or three weeks. Significantly Chamberlain's observations on this were cautious:

> It is evident that the Americans feel themselves obliged to act with the greatest caution and to take only one step at a time. I am therefore against asking them to commit themselves to any specific action in hypothetical circs. [*sic*] and I am sure this would lead to nothing helpful. On our side I feel that this would be a most unfortunate moment to send the fleet away and I would therefore take no immediate action which would involve us in having to do so if the Japanese returned an unsatisfactory reply.[151]

Chamberlain's judgment on this issue was perceptive: the United States, partly because of public opinion, and, partly because of the effect on Japan, was anxious not to take action in the far east simultaneously with that of Britain.[152]

A positive result of the Ingersoll mission, however, was the visit of three United States cruisers to Singapore, and the informal understanding that if British and United States fleets were 'required to work together in a war against Japan', the British fleet could use United States waters, while the United States could use the waters of the British commonwealth. The British, however, were careful to explain the limitation on the latter:

> It is understood that the Government of the United Kingdom cannot definitely commit the Governments of the Dominions of the British Commonwealth to any

150 Ibid., pp. 422–3, F96/84/10, Foreign Office to Lindsay, Telegram No. 19, Immediate Very Secret No Distribution, 7.1.1938 (cypher).

151 Ibid., pp. 505–16, F407/84/10, Lindsay to Foreign Office, Telegram No. 35, 10.1.1938; Minute by Chamberlain, 11.1.1938; Eden to Cadogan, 9.1.1938; Minute by Cadogan, 11.1.1938.

152 Ibid., pp. 523–4, F531/84/10, Lindsay to Foreign Office, Telegram No. 46, 13.1.1938.

action in concert with the United Kingdom. The Admiralty feels sure, however, that Canada, Australia and New Zealand would co-operate with the United Kingdom against Japan in the circumstances under consideration.

No mention was made of South Africa, possibly because that dominion did not have significant interests in the far east, or else because the British felt that South Africa co-operation was doubtful, especially with Hertzog's declared views on neutrality. It was also agreed that, in the event of a general European war British strength in the far east would have to be reduced and 'the possible necessity of direct tactical co-operation between the United States and British Fleets would require further consideration'.[153]

The crisis that erupted in the far east in 1937 provided British statesmen and especially Eden with the opportunity of securing United States co-operation. A limiting factor on British policy, however, was the attitude of the dominions who had to be carefully consulted and educated. To achieve Anglo-American co-operation Eden was prepared to go to considerable lengths, even to concealing telegrams from his colleagues. Eden's scheme was for United States involvement alongside Britain in the far east, so that if there were war in Europe, the United States would automatically be committed alongside Britain there. Chamberlain, however, having had his original proposal for a joint Anglo-American *demarchè* in the far east refused, was trying to steer British policy more in the direction of the appeasement of Europe. He was still conscious of the possibility of Anglo-American collaboration, but did not set as much store by it as did Eden. Eden seems to have been convinced that almost everything should be sacrificed for the chance of bringing about Anglo-American co-operation. Chamberlain had different priorities, and it was this division between the two statesmen which was to result in the British cabinet crisis over Roosevelt's peace proposal in January 1938.

[153] Ibid., pp. 1–5, F716/84/10, Markham (Admiralty) to Harvey, 17.1.1938; Transmitting Copy of Staff Conversations between United States and Britain, 13.1.1938.

IV

ROOSEVELT'S OVERTURE AND
EDEN'S RESIGNATION

Roosevelt's Overture and Eden's Resignation

WHILE Eden was attempting to achieve Anglo-American co-operation in the far east Chamberlain concentrated on the appeasement of Europe. This difference of emphasis was to lead to Eden's resignation. Eden felt it futile to try to reach agreement with the dictators. The best was of averting war, or possibly even preparing for it, was to involve the United States alongside Britain in the far east, in the hope that if there were a European conflagration, the United States would automatically be committed as Britain's ally. The foreign secretary did not enlighten Chamberlain fully as to his aims.[1]

Perhaps a reason for Eden's action can be found in an observation made by Cadogan that Chamberlain 'had an almost instinctive contempt for the Americans'.[2] Cadogan's strictures are too severe: throughout his premiership Chamberlain showed concern for United States opinion, but, unlike Eden, felt that it should not be allowed to be an obstacle to a settlement with the dictators.

The partnership between Eden and Chamberlain was not happy: there was duplicity on both sides. Chamberlain, as Halifax observed, 'rather carelessly gave the appearance of side-tracking the F.O.' Chamberlain once complained to Halifax that after thinking he had reached agreement with Eden he was always seeing telegrams issued from the foreign office with a slightly different twist.[3] Horace Wilson said much the same:

> Neville had a marked affection for Anthony—always listened carefully to what he had to say: they usually ended by agreeing what to do next, but Anthony seemed to change his mind when he got back to the F.O. He was entitled to do this, no doubt, but it was not Neville's way of doing business.[4]

Cadogan felt that 'both men at the beginning were resolved to work loyally together, but differences of temperament soon began to accumulate and became intensified'. This 'tended to create in Chamberlain a certain feeling of isolation' and led to the prime minister's reliance on Horace

---

[1] See p. 81.
[2] *Templewood Papers* XIX (C) 12, Cadogan to Templewood, 26.10.1951.
[3] Ibid., Halifax to Templewood, 28.11.1951.
[4] Ibid., Wilson to Templewood, 10.7.1952.

Wilson, an industrial adviser. Chamberlain, moreover, was 'in a sense, a man of a one-track mind'.[5]

Much the same can be said of Eden. He also pursued his aims with single minded determination. It seems, too, that Eden felt insecure, and was worried about supposed intrigues in the cabinet against him.[6]

By October 1937 Chamberlain's schemes for Italy had not advanced.[7] An opportunity, however, came to improve relations with Germany, always Chamberlain's first objective. Halifax was invited to an international sporting exhibition in Berlin. Chamberlain hoped that this would be an opportunity to sound out German demands: the prime minister believed in personal contacts. There is no evidence of any attempt on Chamberlain's part to side step his foreign secretary.[8] Eden disapproved of the final arrangements which gave the impression of the British government running after the dictator. He argued with Chamberlain.[9] According to Halifax Eden was the first who wished to use the visit.[10] There were disturbing factors. Information was leaked to the press the source of which was not discovered.[11] A divergence of views was discernible: Chamberlain thought that the policy of 'getting together with the dictators was the right one'. For Eden the proposed discussions were 'rather aimless and therefore hazardous'.[12]

Halifax saw Hitler on 19 November. Halifax lacked the depth of understanding necessary to penetrate the nazi leaders.[13] The lord president on 24 November gave the cabinet an account of his visit. The Germans had no policy of immediate adventure. They were too preoccupied with building up their country. The Germans would press their aims in central Europe with 'a beaver-like persistence', but not in a form to give others cause—or probably occasion—to interfere'. Halifax thought that a basis of understanding on central and eastern Europe would not be too difficult. Hitler had raised the sensitive question of colonies, but the cabinet decided that it would be premature to initiate an examination of the question. The first step would be a discussion with the French. Halifax stressed that the

5 Ibid., Cadogan to Templewood, 26.10.1952.
6 John Harvey, Ed., *The Diplomatic Diaries of Oliver Harvey 1937–1940* (London, 1970), pp. 62–3, Diary, 5.12.1937.
7 See pp. 62–3.
8 Earl of Birkenhead, *Halifax* (London, 1965), p. 365; Earl of Halifax, *Fullness of Days* (London, 1957), p. 184; Anthony Eden, *Facing the Dictators* (London, 1962), pp. 508–9.
9 Eden, p. 512; Harvey, pp. 60–1, Diary, 16.11.1937.
10 *Templewood Papers* XIX (C) 12, Halifax to Templewood, 28.11.1951.
11 *Zetland Papers* 8, pp. 197–202, No. 48, Zetland to Linlithgow, 15.11.1937.
12 Eden, pp. 513–5; Harvey, p. 61, Diary, 17.11.1937.
13 Birkenhead, p. 372; See Birkenhead, pp. 365–74, for an Account of the German Visit.

impression should not be given of a bargain being struck as Hitler based his colonial claims on grounds of equity.[14]

From what Chamberlain wrote on 26 November, it seems that he was convinced that it would be possible to come to terms with the dictators.

> But I don't see why we shouldn't say to Germany, "give us satisfactory assurances that you won't use force to deal with the Austrians and Czechoslovakians, and we will give give you similar assurances that we won't use force to prevent the changes you want, if you can get them by peaceful means".[15]

At the end of November the British had conversations with the French. While the French would have preferred to approach Berlin first, the British favoured Mediterranean conversations as these might induce Italy to take a more stalwart line in central Europe. Chamberlain refused to believe that the Italians were naturally sympathetic to Germany. The French agreed to British negotiations with Rome.[16] Chamberlain also raised the question of the British contribution to a colonial settlement with Germany. The prime minister asked what the French government would think about a British approach to Belgium and Portugal to meet Germany's suggestion for a mandate in west Africa over Belgian and Portuguese territory in compensation for Tanganyika. Léon Delbos, the French foreign minister, considered the question as delicate, even premature: the basis of any approach should be a general consideration of the colonial question.[17]

Chamberlain stated in the house of commons that the British government had no immediate intention of extending the Anglo-French conversations to include other countries. Sir Orme Sargent minuted on 2 December that as far as colonies were concerned, that let out Belgium and Portugal. Sargent wondered, however, whether the colonial issue should not be raised with the dominion governments.[18] Eden did see Dr. Gie, the South African minister in Berlin, on 6 December. The colonial issue apparently was not discussed. Gie warned that the British government should not allow its course to be influenced by sentiment: stiff bargaining would be necessary with Germany.[19]

In December Italy resigned from the league. Eden's conversations with Grandi did not come to much.[20] The British had agreed with the French

---

[14] *Cab 23*, 90, p. 4, Cab 43 (37) 3, Secret, 24.11.1937; Addendum, pp. 1-7, Summary of the Discussions referred to in Cab 43 (37) 3, Most Secret Lock and Key, 24.11.1937.

[15] Quoted by Keith Feiling, *The Life of Neville Chamberlain* (London, 1946), pp. 332–3.

[16] Eden, pp. 516–8; Feiling, p. 334.

[17] *F O 371*, 20736, C8234/270/18, Foreign Office Memorandum of Anglo-French Conversations, 30.11.1937.

[18] Ibid., 20737, C8411/270/18, Foreign Office Minute by Sargent, 2.12.1937 r. in r. 8.12.1937.

[19] Ibid., C8407/270/18, Foreign Office Memorandum of Conversation between Eden and Gie, 6.12.1937.

[20] Eden, pp. 334–5.

that *de jure* recognition of the conquest of Abyssinia could only be given after a decision by the league. Eden told Grandi this on 2 December. Grandi spoke of *de jure* recognition as the one result his government hoped for from the proposed conversations with Britain. The import of the official Italian reply was that *de jure* recognition was fundamental for Italian opinion. At the interview with Crolla, the Italian *chargé d'affairs*, Eden took a firm line: the Italian government had shown little desire to meet the British; Italian activities in Spain, Libya and the Mediterranean were cited as examples of this.[21]

Chamberlain drew different conclusions, and was left with a freer hand to implement them when Eden went to the French Riviera at the beginning of the new year. In his diary Chamberlain recalled:

> The Berlin-Rome Axis had been greatly strengthened, Germany had signed an Anti-Comintern pact with Japan, and Italy had joined it. I told A. [Eden] that I feared we were getting ourselves into a deadlock, if we stuck to it that we could not open conversations till the League had given us permission.[22]

Halifax and Chamberlain agreed that Abyssinia should be handled through the league, but that some *de facto* recognition should be given. Chamberlain felt that such recognition should not be given unconditionally but as part of a general appeasement of Europe.[23]

While Eden was away Chamberlain took charge of the foreign office. Eden had instructed the foreign office to study the Abyssinian question. Officials produced a memorandum A, according to which Britain should trade off *de jure* recognition of the conquest of Abyssinia against concessions by Italy in Spain, Libya, Pantelleria, and Arabia. Eden wrote to Chamberlain that he did not like 'setting high moral principles against material advantages', and consequently had instructed the foreign office to produce alternative B, which he preferred. This alternative meant that Eden would go to Geneva to win Delbos's support for a joint Anglo-French declaration that the time had come for *de jure* recognition. Conversations with the Italians could then be entered with a clear conscience. Chamberlain rejected the B memorandum because 'we should be giving away our best card for nothing and we should draw down on ourselves a condemnation more scathing than that aroused by the Hoare-Laval proposals'. Memorandum A did not meet with Chamberlain's approval either:

---

21 Ibid., pp. 475–6.
22 Quoted by Feiling, p. 335.
23 Ibid., *loc. cit.*

We should approach the matter from the angle of obtaining general appeasement to which each must make its contribution and justify *de jure* on that ground which was of interest to all the Mediterranean nations and, since that sea was a danger spot, to the whole world.[24]

It was against this background that Chamberlain received a proposal from Roosevelt on 12 January which, according to Cadogan, cut across the prime minister's 'pet plan of an agreement with Italy'.[25] Chamberlain, in pursuit of the appeasement of Europe, saw the opportunity of separating Rome from Berlin, and possibly of coming to terms with both on a general European settlement. Although Chamberlain was sensitive to the need for co-operation with the United States, in January 1938, after the isolationist outburst over the *Panay* incident, it seemed improbable that the United States would involve itself in world affairs.

On 11 January Welles called on Lindsay to convey a secret message from Roosevelt for the British prime minister. Chamberlain, in a letter, referred to this message as 'a bombshell which after a 3,000 mile journey suddenly landed in my lap'.[26] Roosevelt 'proposed to issue a sort of world appeal to end international tension by a general agreement to abide by international law and order'. Certain minor powers would draw up an agenda for a conference to which all would be invited. The president intended to take the only initiative left open to him by United States public opinion. This initiative was designed to work parallel with British negotiations with the central powers. Only the British government was being informed of the scheme and Roosevelt was anxious that no other government should learn of it. The scheme would be initiated only if Roosevelt received an assurance from Chamberlain by 17 January that it had 'the cordial approval and whole-hearted support' of the British government. If the British approved, the French, the Germans and the Italians would be informed of the general outline of the scheme on 20 January, and on 22 January the plan would be announced to the diplomatic corps at Washington.

This was the plan. Roosevelt suggested that all governments should try to reach unanimous agreement on four issues: essential principles to be observed in international relations; methods for limiting armaments; the establishing of the right of all peoples to have access upon equal terms to raw materials; the establishing of rights and obligations of governments

---

[24] *Chamberlain Papers*, Diary, 19.–27.2.1938. Quoted by Iain Macleod, *Neville Chamberlain* (London, 1961), pp. 211–2; Harvey, pp. 66–8, Diary, 1.–13.1.1938.

[25] *Templewood Papers* XIX (C) 12, Cadogan to Templewood, 26.10.1951.

[26] Ibid., XIX (C) 11, Chamberlain to Hilda Chamberlain, 27.1.1938 (copy, extract).

in time of war. Roosevelt also touched upon two other ticklish questions: the inequities of the Versailles treaty; and the United States attitude to world affairs. The president spoke of:

> The traditional policy of freedom from political involvement which the United States Government has maintained and will maintain is well-known.[27]

This so called peace plan, both in its origin and in the form in which it was finally presented, seems to have been more the brain child of Sumner Welles than that of the president. For sometime, however, the president had been considering the feasibility of a dramatic meeting of the world's statesmen at sea.[28] Langer and Gleason suggest that it was Halifax's interview with Hitler which roused Roosevelt into taking up a plan for world peace.[29] The United States government, however, had been informed of the contents of the interview a month before Roosevelt made his sudden move.[30] It was Welles who drew up the detailed memorandum and submitted it to Roosevelt on 10 January 1938.[31]

Lindsay's telegram informing Chamberlain of Roosevelt's offer arrived on the morning of 12 January, and reached Cadogan in the afternoon. Cadogan immediately sent Chamberlain at Chequers the relevant documents and a minute pointing out the pitfalls in Roosevelt's plan. The under secretary did recommend that the peace plan should be welcomed.[32] Chamberlain did not agree. He recorded in his diary:

> I was in a dilemma. The plan appeared to me fantastic and likely to excite the derision of Germany and Italy. They might even use it to postpone conversations with us, and if we were associated with it they would see in it another attempt on the part of the democratic bloc to put the dictators in the wrong. There was no time to consult Anthony, for in view of the secrecy on which Roosevelt insisted in emphatic terms I did not dare to telephone.[33]

Early on 13 January two further telegrams arrived from Lindsay giving the ambassador's personal opinion. Lindsay was a former under secretary at the foreign office and ambassador to Berlin and had been in the United States for some time. He urged acceptance of the president's proposal. The ambassador considered it a 'genuine effort' and argued that American

[27] *Cab 23*, 92, pp. 1–4, Secret Addendum to Cab 1 (3), Eden's Summary of Events following Roosevelt's Message, Lock and Key, 24.1.1938; Eden, pp. 548–9.

[28] Sumner Welles, *The Time for Decision* (London, 1944), pp. 51–6.

[29] William L. Langer and S. Everett Gleason, *The Challenge to Isolation* (London, 1952), p. 24.

[30] *Foreign Relations of the United States* (hereafter cited as *'FRUS'*) 1937(1), pp. 183–5, 741.62/208, Johnson to Hull, Telegram No. 751, 3.12.1937.

[31] *FRUS* 1938(1), pp. 115–7, 740.00/276½, Memorandum by Welles, 10.1.1937 (8); Photostatic Copy from F. D. Roosevelt Library, Hyde Park, New York.

[32] *F O 371*, 21526, pp. 178–80, A2127/64/45, Cadogan to Eden, Most Secret, 13.1.1938 (draft).

[33] *Chamberlain Papers*, Diary, 19.–27.2.1938. Quoted by Macleod, p. 212.

opinion might be won round to the scheme since it combined disarmament and the relaxation of economic pressure. Like Eden, Lindsay saw the best hope of combating the dictators in winning United States support for the democracies. If Britain blocked the plan at its inception all progress made in the previous two years in the direction of Anglo-American co-operation would be lost.

> Destructive criticisms, reservations of attempts to define the issues more clearly can only accomplish very little in favour of anything you may wish to push forward while they will create a disproportionate bad impression in the thought of the Administration.[34]

Eden comments: 'The advice was authoritative and should have been compelling'.[35] It was, however, advice from a man bound up with the United States point of view. The comment is by one who had attempted in the face of continual rebuffs to gear British policy to Anglo-American co-operation.

Lindsay's message was passed on to Chamberlain. The prime minister told Cadogan to discuss the situation with Wilson. Wilson was not pleased with Roosevelt. In the draft reply that Cadogan made after this conversation it was mentioned that Roosevelt's plan might cut across British discussions that were to be started with Italy and Germany, and it was suggested that the president might consider deferring his initiative until the results of these talks were known. British support would be whole hearted, however, if the president pressed the scheme immediately. Cadogan wanted his draft to be sent to Eden in France.

Chamberlain returned to London on the evening of 13 January, and, on his own initiative, without consulting any member of the cabinet, changed this.[36] The message had been sent to Chamberlain personally, but Roosevelt had not asked for Chamberlain's support, but for the 'cordial approval and whole-hearted support of His Majesty's Government'. It could be argued that Chamberlain was not his majesty's government. Chamberlain, on this occasion, seemingly acted against the advice of the officials concerned with foreign affairs who were present at the time, and of the British government's man on the spot. Apparently, too, Chamberlain did not take the proposal light heartedly: Cadogan recorded that the prime minister viewed it with the 'gravest concern'.[37]

[34] *Cab 23*, 92, p. 3. Secret Addendum to Cab 1 (38), Eden's Summary of Events following Roosevelt's Message, Lock and Key, 24.1.1938; Eden, p. 550.

[35] Eden, p. 550.

[36] *F O 371*, 21526, pp. 178–80, A2127/64/45, Cadogan to Eden, Most Secret, 13.1.1938 (draft).

[37] Ibid., *loc. cit.*

That evening a reply was sent to Roosevelt. Chamberlain had until 17 January to do so. A possible reason for this can be found in the message that Cadogan gave to Eden:

> He [Chamberlain] asked me to explain to you [Eden] that it was impossible to consult you as to the reply to Washington, as that had to be sent off at once—in order to give time for the President to give us his reply before Monday. You will though, as I have pointed out, probably be able to give us your ideas as to what the decision should be in the event of the President's reply being unfavourable.[38]

Chamberlain's reply was considered and polite. The prime minister started by expressing the highest appreciation of the mark of confidence that Roosevelt had shown in consulting him about the plan and noted that the initiative was to run parallel to British efforts with the central powers. Chamberlain hoped for 'some improvement in the immediate future', and explained British efforts to reach a general appeasement by improving relations with the Italian and German governments. The basis in each case was that all parties should make their contribution. In the case of Italy the British government would be prepared, if possible with the authority of the league of nations, to recognise *de jure* the Italian conquest of Abyssinia, a step by which Mussolini set great store, if the Italian government were ready 'to give evidence of their desire to contribute to the restoration of confidence and friendly relations'. Following on Halifax's visit to Berlin, the British were about to see 'in what measure German aspirations might be satisfied so that they could make their contribution to a general appeasement'. Chamberlain trusted that before long conservations would be started with Germany. The prime minister said that he mentioned these facts so that the president might consider whether there were not a risk of his proposal cutting across British efforts. Chamberlain asked whether it would not be wiser to hold his hand for a short time to see what progress the British could make in beginning to tackle some of the problems piecemeal. These were only Chamberlain's reflections and he was ready to consider immediately any observations that Roosevelt might wish to make.[39]

At the same time Chamberlain pointed out to Lindsay that there were certain phrases in Roosevelt's draft plan which caused grave misgivings, especially those about traditional United States policy of 'freedom from political involvements', and the hints at a readjustment of Versailles.[40]

---

[38] Ibid., *loc. cit.*

[39] Ibid., pp. 196–8, Chamberlain to Lindsay, Telegram No. 35, Immediate Most Secret, 13.1.1938 (cypher).

[40] Ibid., p. 200, Chamberlain to Lindsay, Telegram No. 36, Immediate Most Secret, 13.1.1938 (cypher).

Lindsay saw Welles on 14 January and passed on Chamberlain's message to Roosevelt. Welles said that Roosevelt was a little disappointed, but would in a written reply to be sent on 17 January, indicate his willingness to postpone the scheme.[41] Welles afterwards described this reply as being 'in the nature of a douché of cold water'.[42] It probably was for Welles as he had thought up the plan. On 16 January Lindsay asked Hull about Roosevelt's reactions: Hull said that the president was less disappointed than he had been, and implied that he had not been particularly disappointed'.[43] Hull had never liked these sort of schemes.[44] The same impression was formed by Halifax who, when British ambassador in Washington from January 1941, had consulted the relevant files and formed the view that Roosevelt had not been as upset by Chamberlain's reply as had been made out by some.[45]

Eden returned to London on the evening of 15 January, and, after seeing the correspondence, sent a telegram to Lindsay saying that if Roosevelt was disappointed over a negative attitude Eden was convinced that that was not the impression which Chamberlain wished to convey. There were difficulties such as the short time allowed for considering so far reaching a proposal, and also that Eden and Chamberlain had not been able to consult.[46]

The next day Eden travelled to Chequers, and the subsequent interview indicated the widening gulf between the prime minister and his foreign secretary. Chamberlain recorded in his diary that Eden proposed 'that we should at once call off the idea of Italian conversations lest we should offend the U.S.A.'[47] The prime minister objected. According to Eden Chamberlain 'apparently believed with increasing conviction that our approaches to the dictators were likely to lead very soon to genuine settlements'. Eden recorded his response to Chamberlain:

My view was that we should work on parallel lines, doing our best to improve Anglo-American relations while preparing for discussions with Germany and Italy. All my instincts were against according *de jure* recognition of Mussolini's conquest of Abyssinia at the present time.[48]

[41] *Cab 23*, 92, p. 4, Secret Addendum to Cab 1 (38), Eden's Summary of Events following Roosevelt's Message, Lock and Key, 24.1.1938.
[42] Welles, p. 56.
[43] *F O 371*, 21526, p. 172, A2127/64/45, Lindsay to Foreign Office, Telegram Immediate Very Secret, 15.1.1938 d. 16.1.1938 (decypher).
[44] See, for example, Cordell Hull, *The Memoirs of Cordell Hull* 1 (London, 1948), p. 546.
[45] *Halifax Papers* A4 410 17i, Halifax to Mrs. Chamberlain, 13.5.1948 (copy).
[46] *F O 371*, 21526, p. 171, A2127/64/45, Eden to Lindsay, Telegram No. 41, Immediate Very Secret, 16.1.1938 (decypher).
[47] *Chamberlain Papers*, Diary, 19.–27.2.1938. Quoted by Macleod, p. 213.
[48] Eden, pp. 553–5.

On the day of his interview with Eden Chamberlain wrote to a correspondent in the United States. The letter suggests Chamberlain's thoughts at the time. He wrote of his attempts and disappointments trying to bring Britain and the United States together. The good will of the United States government was hampered by public opinion. 'In spite of my disappointment, I intend to keep on doing everything I can to promote Anglo-American understanding and co-operation.' He did not expect the United States to pull British chestnuts out of the fire, but both countries wanted the same fundamental objects. Co-operation between Britain and the United States was the greatest instrument in the world for the preservation of peace. Chamberlain explained that being a realist, Britain, in the absence of a powerful ally, and until its armaments were completed, had to adjust its foreign policy to circumstances. He felt that a friendly president, at a later stage, might be able to give a 'fresh stimulus' to enable the successful completion of talks with Germany and Italy.[49]

Eden, apparently, did not think that there was any future in pursuing the appeasement of Europe. He hoped that the United States might be persuaded to play a more active role. To Chamberlain Roosevelt's initiative seemed naive and woolly. Eden felt that it might well have both these qualities, 'but this did not weigh a feather in the scale beside the significance of an American intervention in Europe at this moment'.[50] Eden again explained this to Chamberlain in a letter on 17 January, though the foreign secretary expressed himself in more diplomatic terms.[51]

On 18 January Roosevelt's reply of the previous day to Chamberlain's message was received in London. In his diary Chamberlain referred to this as a 'somewhat sulky acquiescence in postponement'. It produced 'some strongly worded warnings against shocking public opinion by giving *de jure* to Italy'.[52] The president's reply does not suggest that Roosevelt was a disappointed man. He 'readily' agreed to defer his peace plan for a short while. He warned that a British surrender to the principle of non-recognition would seriously affront United States public opinion. Roosevelt's government could have no connection with the political features of the negotiations with the dictators, but he did ask to be appraised of these features which would have

a material effect upon the maintenance of those international principles and upon the policies of world appeasement which this Government endeavours to

[49] *Chamberlain Papers*, Chamberlain to Mrs. Morton Prince, 16.1.1938. Quoted by Feiling, pp. 323–4.
[50] Eden, p. 557.
[51] *F O 371*, 21526, pp. 167–70, A2127/64/45, Eden to Chamberlain, Personal and Secret, 17.1.1938 (copy).
[52] *Chamberlain Papers*, Diary, 19.–27.2.1938. Quoted by Macleod, p. 212.

support, and in particular, of those questions which have to do with treaty rights and economic and financial questions.[53]

This letter could be taken as the 'go ahead' for Chamberlain: there was direct approval of the appeasement of Europe.

But Lindsay warned that Welles had said that Roosevelt's instructions on *de jure* recognition were even more emphatic than the actual message. Roosevelt was worried that 'it would rouse a feeling of disgust; would revive and multiply all our fear of pulling the chestnuts out of the fire'.[54]

On the afternoon of 18 January Chamberlain and Eden discussed Roosevelt's message. That day Eden drafted a memorandum for Chamberlain which, in the end, was not sent, but communicated orally to the prime minister. The most significant aspects of the memorandum, however, are those which were deleted, and presumably not conveyed to Chamberlain. Eden's scheming had not changed from the time of the Brussels conference:

> The decision we have to take seems to me to depend upon the significance which we attach to Anglo-American co-operation. [What we have to choose between is Anglo-American co-operation in an attempt to insure world peace and a piecemeal settlement approached by way of problematical agreement with Mussolini.] If as is clear to me we must choose the former alternative, then it seems that we should reconsider our attitude and strongly support President Roosevelt's initiative. As you know, I do not take the view that this initiative need injure the prospects of our negotiations with Germany, which I regard as the most important of the two sets of negotiations [we were considering. In fact the closer the sympathy and co-operation between the United States and ourselves, the stronger will be our position in dealing with Germany.][55]

Chamberlain, presumably, was not convinced by Eden's arguments: Chamberlain put Europe before the United States. The two could not agree, and Chambrelain summoned the foreign affairs committee of the cabinet to lay the position before them.[56] That evening Eden told Oliver Harvey, his private secretary, that 'everything must give way to primary importance of good relations with Roosevelt and America'.[57]

The Italians timed their next move well. On 19 January Grandi made approaches about informal talks with the British which would have to

[53] *F O 371*, 21526, pp. 163–5, A2127/64/45, Roosevelt to Chamberlain, Telegram, Immediate Most Secret Special Distribution, 17.1.1938 d. 18.1.1938 (decypher); *FRUS* 1938(1), pp. 120–2, 740.00/264b, Welles to Roosevelt, 17.1.1938; 740.00/264½, Enclosure, Roosevelt to Chamberlain, Undated.

[54] *Cab 23*, 92, pp. 5–6, Secret Addendum to Cab 1 (38), Eden's Summary of Events following Roosevelt's Message, Lock and Key, 24.1.1938.

[55] *F O 371*, 21526, pp. 153–5, A2127/64/45, Eden to Chamberlain, 18.1.1938 (draft, revise); pp. 156–9, Eden to Chamberlain, 18.1.1938 (not sent, for oral communication to Chamberlain).

[56] *Chamberlain Papers*, Diary, 19.–27.2.1938. Quoted by Macleod, p. 213.

[57] Harvey, p. 73, Diary, 18.1.1937.

include *de jure* recognition of Abyssinia. That evening there was a meeting of the foreign affairs committee. Eden noticed that Inskip had noted: 'Eden's policy to line up the U.S.A., Great Britain and France, result war.' Eden argued against this claiming that such a policy would make the dictators behave themselves. Chamberlain, Halifax, Simon and Inskip felt that there was a real chance to reach agreement with the dictators, and felt that Roosevelt's plan did not amount to much since the United States would do nothing practical.

At the foreign affairs committee on 19 January Chamberlain produced a draft telegram re-explaining to Roosevelt the need for *de jure* recognition of the conquest of Abyssinia, and asking the president to use his influence with Italy to help Britain to reach agreement. Eden argued against this on the ground that the recognition of Abyssinia was not solely a British affair. Eden, overlooking the *Panay* incident, spoke of British relations with the United States from the time of the Brussels conference as having been excellent. Eden felt that talks with Italy should have to wait for Roosevelt's proposal. Chamberlain did not. Chamberlain criticised Roosevelt's plan: it would be received with shouts of laughter in nazi Germany; the four points on which the governments of the world were to agree were unrealistic. Chamberlain, in this assessment was probably influenced by Horace Wilson.

By 20 January Chamberlain had come around to agreeing to parallel action: the British negotiations with Mussolini could go on at the same time as Roosevelt's plan. Eden saw a contradiction in this in view of Roosevelt's stand on Abyssinia. The foreign affairs committee approved three draft telegrams: one asking Roosevelt to defer his initiative no longer; the second explaining to the president the British attitude on *de jure* recognition of Abyssinia, and the third asking Lindsay to see if he would obtain modifications in Roosevelt's appeal. On 21 January when Eden put these draft telegrams before the foreign affairs committee there was opposition. Chamberlain had thought that the dictators would regard the Roosevelt plan as being directed at themselves. He saw Eden's draft telegram as putting the Italian negotiations 'out of court'. A compromise was achieved: the committee agreed that there should be no commitment to Italian conversations until the reception given to Roosevelt's plan could be assessed.[58]

---

[58] *Cab 27*, 622 (1), F P (36) 17, 19.1.1938, Lock and Key; F P (36) 18, Lock and Key, 20.1.1938; F P (36) 19, Lock and Key, 21.1.1938; F P (36) 19, Lock and Key, 21.1.1938. These are references: the summaries of the discussions were placed in the cabinet secretary's standard file of committee's proceedings and have presumably been destroyed. See Ian Colvin, *The Chamberlain Cabinet* (London, 1971), pp. 85–6. For an account of what happened see Eden, pp. 565–7; Harvey, pp. 74–8, Diary, 19.–23.1.1938.

Following these discussions messages from Chamberlain were sent to Washington on the evening of 21 January. The first explained the delay on the grounds that it had been used for further consideration of the president's proposals, and that the prime minister did not feel 'justified in asking the President to delay the announcement of his scheme any longer'. Chamberlain added that he welcomed the president's initiative warmly, and would do his best to contribute to the success of his scheme, whenever Roosevelt decided to launch it.[59] It was explained to Lindsay, however, that the British did not want to share responsibility for the scheme, and the president should be conscious of the points of which they did not approve: 'the procedure to be adopted, the irritation it might cause to the dictators and Japan, and the great difficulties that may arise about the two main points of his scheme, limitation or armaments and equal access to raw materials'.[60] There was a further message explaining the British position on *de jure* recognition of Abyssinia. Chamberlain pointed out that Britain did not intend granting recognition except as part of a scheme of Mediterranean appeasement and that, therefore, Britain would not contemplate doing it until the substance of an agreement had been worked out which both sides were willing to conclude. That would take time.[61]

When Lindsay delivered this message to Welles on 22 January, it transpired that Roosevelt might modify the phrase about 'the inequities of the post-war settlement'. The traditional United States policy of freedom from political involvement would have to stay. According to Lindsay Welles said that he thought that the president would be relieved to find that Britain only contemplated the grant of *de jure* recognition as part of a general settlement with Italy, and, therefore, not in the immediate future. The ambassador reported Welles as saying: 'The President regarded recognition as an unpleasant pill which we should both have to swallow and he wished that we should both swallow it together'. The British wished to swallow it in a general settlement with Italy and the president wished to in a general settlement involving world appeasement.[62] It seems unlikely that these were Roosevelt's sentiments both in view of his previous and later stand over *de jure* recognition. Langer and Gleason claim that slanted reporting by Lindsay could account for this impression.[63] The ambassador

[59] *F O 371*, 21526, p. 152, A2127/64/45, Chamberlain to Lindsay, Telegram No. 58, Immediate Most Secret Special Distribution, 21.1.1938 (cypher).
[60] Ibid., pp. 150-1, Chamberlain to Lindsay, Telegram No. 59, Immediate Most Secret Special Distribution, 21.1.1938 (cypher).
[61] Ibid., pp. 146-9, Chamberlain to Roosevelt, Telegram No. 60, Immediate Most Secret Special Distribution, 21.1.1938 (cypher).
[62] Ibid., pp. 138-9, Lindsay to Foreign Office, Telegram, Immediate Very Secret Special Distribution, 22.1.1938 r. 23.1.1938.
[63] Langer and Gleason, p. 28.

was certainly guilty of this on one occasion.[64] Lindsay, too, does not seem to have been over concerned about United States opposition to *de jure* recognition. On 8 January he had written that it was 'hardly necessary to worry much about effect in America' of this. Lindsay felt that despite criticism in congress, the press, and disappointment among some high minded people, such action 'would be regarded as an effort to pay the necessary price of peace'.[65]

The position was finally put to the cabinet on 24 January. Eden outlined what had happened and then Chamberlain supplemented it with his own comments:

> The Cabinet would see that the Foreign Policy Committee had been placed in a dilemma. On the one hand, they very much wanted to secure American co-operation and to draw into closer relations with the United States. On the other hand, they had received these rather preposterous proposals to which the Government were asked to give whole-hearted co-operation. . . .
>
> Up to now the President's view [of the British reaction] had not been received but only the reaction of the Under-Secretary of State in Washington, whose opinion did not always reflect that of the President.

The cabinet agreed that Eden should sound out Delbos at Geneva about the French reaction to *de jure* recognition. Eden should also try to discourage any discussion of this matter by the league. The dominions were to be informed in a telegram which had to be approved by Chamberlain. To mollify certain of the dominions the term *de jure* should be avoided and one like 'recognition of the Italian position in Ethiopia' substituted.[66]

Chamberlain without waiting for Roosevelt's reaction pressed on with his plans for the appeasement of Europe. On 24 January, the same afternoon as the cabinet meeting, the committee on foreign policy discussed the proposed conversations with the German government. The main concentration was on the colonial question Chamberlain explained that examination of the colonial question could only be undertaken 'as a part and parcel of a general settlement'. The colonial question was, in German eyes, the only outstanding problem remaining between Britain and Germany. Chamberlain divulged to the committee a notion which he had been developing of 'an entirely new method of presenting the problem'. The matter should not be treated as colonial restitution but as a new experiment in colonial development. Interested powers, including Germany,

---

[64] Ibid., pp. 28–9.

[65] *F O 371*, 21526, p. 125, A2127/64/45, Lindsay to Foreign Office, Telegram No. 31, No Distribution, 8.1.1938 (attached).

[66] *Cab 23*, 92, pp. 1–2, Cab 1 (38) 1, Secret, 24.1.1938; pp. 8–9, Secret Addendum to Cab 1 (38), Chamberlain's Supplementation of Eden's Outline, Lock and Key, 24.1.1938.

would administer certain central African territories. Each power would administer its own territory subject to overriding rules to be laid down by general agreement. The discussion revealed how little the British were prepared to cede.

Eden felt it improbable that a settlement with Germany could be effected by handing over to it Togoland and the Cameroons. There was talk of a possible Belgian contribution, or British compensation to France for territory it might cede. Ormsby-Gore insisted that Sierra Leone and the Gambia could not be transferred to Germany because of the opposition of the inhabitants. He further pointed out that if Germany wanted space in which to settle surplus German population, the only suitable African territory would be South West Africa. MacDonald said that South Africa would never agree to give up that territory. South African opinion was also sensitive about Tanganyika: a threat to its communications would be posed if that country were in hostile hands. Chamberlain explained that his plan would exclude South West Africa. MacDonald then favoured Chamberlain's plan provided the southern line were drawn north of South West Africa. He did not think, however, that the Germans would look at it. In private discussions at the imperial conference with Ormsby-Gore Hertzog had explained that he was mainly opposed to the transfer of those parts of Tanganyika bordering on Portuguese territory.[67]

On 3 February the cabinet committee on foreign policy conferred with Nevile Henderson on Germany's colonial claims,[68] and subsequently the foreign office drew up a memorandum incorporating Chamberlain's suggestions for a solution of the colonial problem in Africa.[69] South Africa applied pressure. The cabinet was told on 9 February by Mac-Donald that while he was in Berlin Gie had expressed the hope that before Hitler spoke on 20 February Britain would let Germany know that it was prepared to make some suggestions to follow up Halifax's visit.[70]

Simultaneous with these advances towards Germany, feelers were put out towards Italy. While Eden was away at the league, Chamberlain, on 28 January, asked Lindsay to ascertain what United States action was proposed as it was difficult to further British policy towards Italy, Germany, and Japan, with no knowledge of Roosevelt's intentions. Lindsay's reply implied that the United States did not object to British negotiations in

[67] *Cab 27*, 623(2), pp. 1–26, F P (36) 21, Lock and Key, 24.1.1938.
[68] Ibid., pp. 1–22, F P (36) 22, Lock and Key, 3.2.1938.
[69] *F O 371*, 21679, pp. 147–54, C1305/184/18, Memorandum prepared by Foreign and Colonial Offices on Colonial Problem in Tropical Africa, 16.2.1938.
[70] *Cab 23*, 92, pp. 2–3, Cab 4 (38) 2, Secret, 9.2.1938.

Europe, provided that *de jure* recognition would only be granted as part of a general settlement.[71] Roosevelt later warned that any immediate *de jure* recognition would have 'an ill effect on Anglo-American' relations.[72] On 6 February Lindsay wired that he had been taken aback by the strong reaction on this subject from Welles, Hull and Roosevelt. He continued:

> Of course I dislike differing on such a matter from such high authorities but I did sometimes think they were laying it on rather thick. I feel sure that you will have the influence of the administration in support of your efforts if you can adhere to line of P.M.'s message, viz. that recognition can only be given in consideration of a general settlement with Italy and add perhaps that such a settlement cannot fail to bring closer an even wider appeasement. In such conditions I feel sure that administration would do all it could to influence opinion favourably .... But sentiment for isolation in general is still very strong everywhere.[73]

Early in February Eden enquired whether Roosevelt had reached any decision about when to launch his peace plan.[74] The president took a week to answer. He had decided to delay because of the acute situation in Germany where there had been changes in the hierarchy. In conveying this message Welles wondered whether there was not apathy on the part of the British government towards the peace plan. Lindsay explained that the British government was now committed to support it fully.[75] On 16 February the British were told by Lindsay that Roosevelt intended to launch his plan soon after 23 February, irrespective of what Hitler might say on 20 February.[76] Cadogan minuted that if the British were to suggest any modifications they would have to do so immediately.[77]

While Roosevelt was deliberating Grandi asked to see Chamberlain and Eden. It took some time for Eden to tell Chamberlain of the request. Eden saw Grandi and discussed *de jure* recognition. Eden did not fix any date for the opening of conversations with Italy, and suggested to Chamberlain that progress should first be made with the Spanish situation.

An unpleasant surprise from Germany intervened. Kurt von Schuschnigg, the Austrian chancellor, was summoned to Berchtesgaden, bullied,

---

71 Eden, p. 567.

72 *F O 371*, 21526, p. 126, A2127/64/45, Foreign Office to Lindsay, Telegram No. 93, Important Very Secret, 4.2.1938 (cypher).

73 Ibid., pp. 123–4, Lindsay to Foreign Office, Telegram No. 113, Important Very Secret Special Distribution, 6.2.1938 (decypher).

74 *FRUS* 1938(1), pp. 122–4, 865D.01/385, Memorandum by Welles, 2.2.1938.

75 Ibid., pp. 124–5, 740.00/290½, Memorandum by Welles, 9.2.1938 (extract).

76 *F O 371*, 21526, p. 102, A2127/64/45, Lindsay to Foreign Office, Telegram No. 121, Immediate Very Secret Special Distribution, 16.2.1938 (decypher).

77 Ibid., pp. 99–100, Foreign Office to Lindsay, Telegram No. 126, Important Very Secret Special Distribution, 18.2.1938 (decypher); Minute by Cadogan, 17.2.1938.

and forced to yield to Hitler's demands.[78] France approached Britain about a guarantee of integrity of Austria,[79] but Chamberlain was moving in another direction. He explained his motives to the cabinet on 19 February:

> It was difficult to believe that . . . the eventual result would not be the absorption of Austria and probably some action in Czecho-Slovakia. . . . He did not know what would be the reaction in the Balkans. It might lead those states to give up all hope of resistance to the hegemony of Germany. It would seem that this must be unpalatable to Signor Mussolini and that an opportunity offered to encourage him to make a more determined stand.[80]

On 16 February Perth reported that Ciano had hinted that 'something was stirring' in the way of conversations between Italy and Britain. Chamberlain decided that the time had come for him and the foreign secretary to interview Grandi. On 17 February Eden said that Cadogan had suggested that it might be better if Eden saw Grandi alone. Chamberlain recorded in his diary:

> I resisted this as I was convinced it was intended to prevent my seeing Grandi lest that should bring the conversations nearer. . . . Anthony . . . sent me a note begging me very earnestly not to commit us to any talks when I met Grandi.
>
> This note convinced me that the issue between us must be faced and faced at once.

Chamberlain anticipated a series of catastrophes if agreement were not reached with Italy which would culminate in France having to fight or submit to German domination, and in Britain almost certainly being drawn in.

On 18 February Eden and Chamberlain met Grandi. Eden was unimpressed by Grandi's assurances. Chamberlain felt that 'one opportunity after another of advancing towards peace' had been lost, and this chance should not be thrown away. He called a cabinet meeting for the following day. The prime minister was determined to stand firm even if it meant losing his foreign secretary.[81]

At the cabinet meeting Chamberlain explained the disagreement with Eden:

> He thought that there was no difference of opinion between the Foreign Secretary and himself on the desirability in principle of conversations with a view to an agreement with Italy. The issue was as to the method.

[78] *Chamberlain Papers*, Diary, 19.2.1938. Quoted by Macleod, pp. 213–4.
[79] *Templewood Papers* XIX (C) 12, Cabinet Paper R1657 (137), 3, 18.2.1938.
[80] *Cab 23*, 92, p. 5, Cab 6 (38), Secret, 19.2.1938.
[81] *Chamberlain Papers*, Diary, 19.–27.2.1938. Quoted by Macleod, pp. 214–5.

Chamberlain argued that this was the last chance. There would be repercussions on the conversations with Germany as the Italians would impress upon them that the British were unreliable. Eden questioned Mussolini's motives and opposed *de jure* recognition as it would cause 'an impression of scuttle in England and alienation of public opinion in the United States'. The foreign secretary told the cabinet that he could not recommend Italian conversations to the house and that if that were the cabinet's decision, they would have to find someone else to put it to the house.[82]

On 20 February Eden resigned. The apparent reason was disagreement over the timing of the Italian conversations. The cause was more fundamental. By February 1938 it was clear that Chamberlain and Eden wished to pursue two divergent foreign policies. Eden saw the only hope for the future in Anglo-American co-operation and felt that all should be sacrificed to this end. Hence his attitude to Roosevelt's peace plan. Chamberlain expected little from the United States, and was determined that a settlement could only be reached by the appeasement of Europe. He was becoming concerned about Austria, and the consequent need for Italian support.

This emerged at the cabinet meeting on 20 February. Eden insisted that the difficulties did not refer only to Italy and mentioned Roosevelt's peace plan.

> He had not thought that the original answer was correct, and his view was that a mistake had been made. He himself would have recommended a different course.

He feared that difference in outlook between himself and the prime minister made it impossible for him to continue as foreign secretary.[83]

At Halifax's suggestion an attempt was made to work out a compromise, but Eden insisted on standing by his decision to resign. Halifax saw behind this decision a number of factors:

> I cannot help thinking that the difference of the actual time-table of conversations was not, and never has been, the principal difference. I suspect it having been the cumulative result of a good many different things.[84]

There was, however, a veiled hint in Eden's statement to the house of commons that the real division between the prime minister and the foreign secretary was a fundamental one, one bearing on Anglo-American relations:

[82] *Cab 23*, 92, pp. 1–35, Cab 6 (38), Secret, 19.2.1938.
[83] Ibid., pp. 1–23, Cab 7 (38), Secret, 20.2.1938.
[84] *Halifax Papers* A 4 410 11i, A Record of Events connected with Anthony Eden's Resignation, 19.–20.2.1938; *Cab 23*, 92, pp. 247–9, Meeting of Ministers, Most Secret Lock and Key, 20.2.1938.

I have spoken to the House of the immediate difference that had divided me from my colleagues, but I should not be frank with the House if I were to pretend that is an isolated issue as between my right hon. friend the Prime Minister and myself. It is not. Within the last few weeks upon one most important decision of foreign policy which did not concern Italy at all, the difference was fundamental.[85]

For Eden, Roosevelt's overture was so important that in the end he staked his reputation on it.

In January, after one of his disagreements with Chamberlain on the matter, he had threatened to resign, but Chamberlain had pointed out that owing to the secrecy insisted on by Roosevelt, there could not be a pretext that could be made public.[86] The timing of the Italian conversations provided this pretext. Austria, as Cadogan suggests might have been a subconscious factor in motivating Eden,[87] but in the end it was the choice 'either Europe or the United States'.

Churchill wrote of Roosevelt's overture: 'We must regard its rejection as the loss of the last frail chance to save the world from tyranny otherwise than by war.'[88] Eden and Welles agree.[89] Most historians have endorsed their verdict.[90]

The prime minister had good reason for assuming that little of immediate practical importance could have resulted from Roosevelt's initiative. Langer and Gleason, the official United States historians conclude:

Conceivably, a really strong stand by the United States Government might have changed the course of events, but . . . nothing of that kind was ever remotely envisaged in Washington.[91]

Chamberlain believed that agreement with the dictators was possible, and fearing that if it were not achieved in the near future, Britain would be drawn into a war, he pursued this object with single minded determination. Under pressure from Eden Chamberlain did give Roosevelt the assurance of British support for his plan. Perhaps Roosevelt was deterred by Chamberlain's initial response, but it still seemed as if the plan would be launched during February. It was not until 12 March that Welles told

[85] Quoted by Eden, p. 600.

[86] *Chamberlain Papers*, Diary, 19.–27.2.1938. Quoted by Macleod, p. 213.

[87] *Templewood Papers* XIX (C) 12, Cadogan to Templewood, 18.1.1952.

[88] Winston Churchill, *The Gathering Storm* (London, 1948), p. 199.

[89] Eden, p. 568.

[90] See William R. Rock, *Appeasement on Trial. British Foreign Policy and its Critics, 1938–1939* (New York, 1966), pp. 23–4 for a bibliography of accounts of Roosevelt's overture, and historians' verdicts on it.

[91] Langer and Gleason, p. 32.

Lindsay that the thought the 'opportunity for presenting President's plan was unlikely to recur'.[92]

Although it seems that, conscious of United States isolationist opinion, Chamberlain was doubtful about any United States support over Europe and the far east he cannot be accused of not cultivating Anglo-American co-operation. The prime minister's treatment of the Irish question shows this. He hoped to activate a more friendly atmosphere in the United States by quietening a hostile and dangerous Irish opinion there.[93]

In October 1937 de Valera had suggested to MacDonald that a favourable Irish settlement would do much to win over United States opinion.[94] Lindsay saw Halifax about this matter on 6 April 1938 and stressed that the Irish element in the United States had a considerable effect on relations between Britain and the United States. Chamberlain reported to the cabinet on 13 April that Lindsay had spoken strongly to him about the valuable effect on opinion in the United States of an agreement with Ireland.[95] The United States press did greet the Irish settlement as a constructive settlement.[96]

In pursuing the appeasement of Europe in these months Chamberlain was thwarted in his moves towards Germany. Henderson saw Hitler on 3 March. On 9 March Halifax, who had succeeded as foreign secretary, explained what had transpired to the cabinet. Henderson had started by opening up the colonial question, even though in doing so he had gone beyond his instructions. But Hitler's response had been disappointing: the führer had spoken of the unconditional return of all the ex-German colonies. Chamberlain explained when further approaches were mooted that:

> It was not proposed to say that this was the last opportunity, but that it was a more favourable opportunity than might occur again.[97]

Italy was more promising. The Anglo-Italian agreement was signed in Rome by Perth and Ciano on 16 April.[98] But both New Zealand and the United States created difficulties over *de jure* recognition.

[92] *F O 371*, 21526, p. 84, A2127/64/45, Lindsay to Foreign Office, Telegram No. 153, Most Secret, 12.3.1938.
[93] Lord Templewood, *Nine Troubled Years* (London, 1954), p. 284.
[94] *Cab 24*, 271, C P 228(37), Memorandum by MacDonald of Relations with Ireland, Secret, Oct. 1937.
[95] *F O 414*, 275 XLIX, p. 135, No. 28, A2707/1/45, Halifax to Lindsay, No. 297, 6.4.1938; *Cab 23*, 93, p. 20, Cab 19 (38) 6, Secret, 13.4.1938.
[96] *F O 414*, 275 XLIX, pp. 149–50, No. 36, A3834/1/45, Lindsay to Halifax, No. 412, 9.5.1938 r. 17.5.1938.
[97] *Cab 23*, 92, pp. 1–2, Cab 10 (38) 1, Secret, 2.3.1938; pp. 4–8, Cab 11 (38), Secret, 9.3.1938.
[98] Macleod, p. 221.

Canada, Australia and South Africa did not raise objections. On 9 February the high commissioner in South Africa reported that Hertzog had told him that he felt 'no good purpose could be served by keeping pending' this matter.[99] As early as 2 February the New Zealand government let the dominions office know that they would oppose this move, and would not mollify the stand that they had taken the previous August over *de jure* recognition.[100] MacDonald on 15 March warned the cabinet committee on foreign policy that New Zealand could be expected to raise difficulties.[101] On 29 March he explained the situation to the committee. New Zealand was the only dominion likely to react violently, and unfortunately New Zealand was a member of the council of the league. But even if New Zealand or any other dominion raised difficulties MacDonald did not advise any alteration in the proposed time table. New Zealand would attach more importance to the views of Britain than of the dominions.[102] New Zealand remained adamant: on 7 April MacDonald reported that the New Zealand government had agreed not to vote against the resolution in the league council but would abstain, and press for a reference of the matter to the assembly.[103] There was more trouble with New Zealand when Chamberlain stated in the house of commons that the dominions were in agreement with Britain's general policy in foreign affairs'. The New Zealand government, though reluctant to embarrass Britain, threatened to make a public statement on the matter, which doubtless would have included their views on *de jure* recognition.[104] It took a diplomatic note from Chamberlain on 13 April to quieten them.[105] In the end the New Zealand delegate to the league abstained from voting, but had sharp words to say about British policy.[106]

Chamberlain was also anxious that the United States should be given special treatment over *de* jure recognition.[107] There is a disparity in the records over United States support for Chamberlain's Italian policy. Langer and Gleason attribute this to Lindsay's reporting.[108] As a result of

[99] *D O 114*, 87, No. 109, F43/47, High Commissioner in South Africa to Dominions Office, Secret, 9.2.1938.
[100] Ibid., No. 108, F43/42, New Zealand Government to Dominions Office, Telegram, Secret, 3.2.1938 (cypher).
[101] *Cab 27*, 623(2), p. 19, F P (36) 25, Lock and Key, 15.3.1938.
[102] Ibid., pp. 5–6, F P (36) 28, Lock and Key, 29.3.1938.
[103] Ibid., pp. 10–11, F P (36) 29, Lock and Key, 7.4.1938.
[104] *F O 371*, 21630, p. 113, C3063/317/62, F48/94, New Zealand Government to Dominions Office Telegram No . 34, Secret, 13.4.1938 d. 14.4.1938 r. in r. 19.4.1938.
[105] Ibid., p. 116, F84/94, Chamberlain to New Zealand Government, Paraphrase Telegram No, 51, Immediate Secret, 13.4.1938.
[106] *Cab 23*, 93, p. 14, Cab 22 (38) 6, Secret, 4.5.1938.
[107] *Cab 27*, 623(2), p. 5, F P (36) 28, Lock and Key, 29.3.1938.
[108] Langer and Gleason, p. 28.

a report by Lindsay of a conversation with Welles[109] Halifax wired early in March:

> I am very much gratified to learn that the President and Administration consider the procedure of His Majesty's Government to be right and I trust they may be justified in thinking that prospects are favourable. I am confident of their desire to help and we shall be sustained in our efforts by the knowledge that we have the sympathy of the United States.[110]

Welles pointed out Lindsay's misapprehension: no responsible United States official had said that they considered the stand of the British government 'to be right'. Lindsay admitted that he had probably over emphasised certain of Welles's remarks and that Halifax had probably done the same.

Chamberlain was still conscious of a possible role for the United States in his schemes. In March Halifax asked if the United States would not be prepared to assist or encourage a scheme of co-operation in Europe, political and economic. Welles said that the president had made it clear that the United States did not intend to participate in European appeasement.[111]

The British hoped for public United States approval of the Anglo-Italian agreement. Roosevelt was not enthusiastic. The subsequent United States press statement was diplomatic, but restrained: 'This Government has seen the conclusion of an agreement with sympathetic interest because it is proof of the value of peaceful negotiations.'[112]

Concern for United States opinion was shown in the final agreement in that Chamberlain made clear that the only circumstances in which British recognition of the Italian conquest of Abyssinia could be morally justified would be 'if it was shown to be an essential feature of a general appeasement'. The agreement was made contingent on a settlement in Spain, and consequently did not come into effect until November.[113]

By April 1938 Anglo-American relations were on much the same basis as they had been during 1937. The Chamberlain government was anxious to obtain Anglo-American co-operation, but this was not to be at the expense of the appeasement of Europe. Eden confronted Chamberlain with a choice: either the prime minister was to work for the appeasement of

109 Memorandum by Welles, 25.2.1938. Quoted by Langer and Gleason, pp. 28–9.
110 Quoted by Langer and Gleason, p. 29. Not printed in *FRUS*.
111 *FRUS*, 1938(1), pp. 126–30, 760F62/1312, Welles to Roosevelt, 8.3.1938; Enclosure, Memorandum by Welles, 8.3.1938.
112 Langer and Gleason pp. 30–1.
113 Macleod, p. 21.

Europe or was to strive for an Anglo-American alliance with which to confront the dictators. Chamberlain chose the former, and, perhaps, he was right. Eden's policy might have worked if the United States could be tricked into some commitment alongside Britain in the far east. But isolationist opinion was strong, and United States politicians were cautious.

V

CRISIS OVER CZECHOSLOVAKIA

Crisis over Czechoslovakia

AFTER Eden's resignation as foreign secretary Chamberlain was left to pursue the appeasement of Europe. The prime minister found Halifax, Eden's successor, a man to whom a suggestion only had to be made for it to be carried out 'with sympathy and understanding'.[1] Halifax thought himself 'very lazy and disliked work'.[2] From March to September 1938 Britain debated what it could do if Germany invaded Czechoslovakia. In these deliberations, and the revised armaments programme that followed from them, the attitude of the dominions had to be weighed against other considerations. It was important to assess the reaction of opinion in the dominions to developments in Europe. Care also had to be taken not to offend the United States. As MacDonald told his colleagues on 30 August: 'The British Commonwealth of Nations and the United States of America together were the only force which could eventually check the progress of dictatorship; one day this combination might have to fight to defeat the growing evil'.[3]

On 12 March nazi troops marched into Austria. That day Chamberlain told the cabinet that he felt that the *Anschluss* 'had to come'. The question then to be considered was how to prevent 'an occurrence of similar events in Czecho-Slovakia'.[4] Delbos had said that France would honour its engagements to Czechoslovakia, and that this would mean war.[5] The foreign office had proposed that Roosevelt be told that 'if the forces of order could not be mobilised' Czechoslovakia would suffer the same fate as Austria. Halifax stopped this as the subject 'required further exploration'.[6]

The cabinet committee on foreign policy on 18 March discussed Czechoslovakia. Halifax presented three alternatives: firstly, a 'grand alliance'; secondly, a new commitment to Europe in effect guaranteeing Czechoslovakia; or, thirdly, a negative policy of restraint on France and

---

[1] *Templewood Papers* XIX (C) 11, Chamberlain to Hilda Chamberlain, 9.7.1938 (copy).

[2] John Harvey, Ed., *The Diplomatic Diaries of Oliver Harvey 1937–1940* (London, 1970), p. 100, Diary, 23.2.1938.

[3] *Cab 23*, 94, pp. 16–7, Notes of a Meeting of Ministers, Secret, 30.8.1938.

[4] Ibid., 92, pp. 5–6, Cab 12 (38) 1, Secret, 12.3.1938.

[5] *Zetland Papers* 9, p. 52, Zetland to Linlithgow, Private, 8.3.1938.

[6] *Cab 23*, 92, pp. 5–11, Cab 12 (38) 1, Secret, 12.3.1938.

Czechoslovakia. Two principal obstacles emerged: a guarantee to Czechoslovakia might mean the end of the commonwealth; and, in any case, it would be logistically impossible to save Czechoslovakia.

MacDonald warned that the dominions office would object to Halifax's second alternative:

> He had never favoured our adopting a particular foreign policy merely in order to please the Dominions. In view of our geographical position and our many connections and interests with the Continent of Europe, he had always thought that if we came to the conclusion that a particular policy in regard to foreign affairs was a right and proper one for us to follow we ought to adopt it irrespective of the views of the Dominions. In the present case, however, we might, if we accepted the [second] alternative . . . find ourselves engaged in a European war to prevent Germans living in the Sudetan districts of Czechoslovakia from being united with Germany. On this issue the British Commonwealth might well break in pieces. Australia and New Zealand would almost certainly follow our lead. Eire would no doubt take the same line partly because she would feel that on an issue of this kind she could not take a line different from our own, but South Africa and Canada would see no reason whatever why they should join in a war to prevent certain Germans from rejoining their fatherland.

MacDonald said that he realised that this factor would have to be considered alongside other considerations, and might in the end be outweighed.

Chamberlain also opposed sending troops to Czechoslovakia: no effective troops could be sent to that country, and all Britain would achieve would be a war with Germany.

The lord president of the council, Viscount Hailsham, wondered whether it would be possible to enlist the support of the United States against policies of violence. Chamberlain 'saw no reason to suppose that the United States were prepared to intervene in Europe'.[7]

On 22 March the cabinet considered the report by the chiefs of staff sub committee on the military implications of German aggression against Czechoslovakia, the dominant conclusion of which was that no pressure which Britain and its possible allies could exercise would prevent the defeat of Czechoslovakia. The cabinet was also warned that while there was no suggestion that the foreign policy of Britain could be subordinated to the views of the dominions, a policy of further commitment would be unpopular in all the dominions except possibly New Zealand, and might lead to a crisis in commonwealth relations. France and Russia could not

---

[7] *Cab 27*, 623 pt 2, pp. 1–27, F P (36) 26th Mtg, 18.3.1938, Lock and Key; Appendix 1, Memorandum by Halifax, 18.3.1938.

help Czechoslovakia effectively either. The cabinet decided that a policy of bluff would be dangerous.[8]

Both the cabinet and the cabinet committee on foreign policy were influenced in deciding British policy towards Czechoslovakia by the attitude of the dominions. Although it was felt that it would be wrong for the dominions to dictate British foreign policy, their attitude was given consideration, and was one of the factors militating against any guarantee to Czechoslovakia.

Consequently the statement which Halifax drew up for Chamberlain to give in the house of commons mentioned that Britain could not extend its obligations and risk a grave divergence of opinion in Britain and the commonwealth.[9] The dominions were informed a day in advance of the outline of the statement.[10] R. A. Butler also met the dominion high commissioners in London on 23 March and explained the situation to them.[11] The French were warned that because of the dominions Britain could not surrender its 'liberty of decisions in advance'.[12]

On 24 March in the house of commons Chamberlain outlined the circumstances in which Britain would fight other than in its own defence or that of the commonwealth. These were: firstly, in accordance with Locarno and British traditional foreign policy, the defence of France and Belgium against unprovoked aggression; secondly, the fulfilment of specific treaty obligations to Portugal, Iraq, and Egypt; and thirdly, the assisting of a victim of aggression where the British felt that it was warranted under the covenant. This last case might cover Czechoslovakia, but there could be no automatic promise to assist France if it were called upon to help Czechoslovakia under the terms of the Franco-Czech treaty of 1925, as Britain had no vital interests in that area.[13]

The dominion governments generally approved of Chamberlain's statement. Halifax gave an assurance to this effect in the house of lords on 29 March.[14] The dominions did express opinions. On 16 March Halifax had explained to the dominion high commissioners that although Britain

---

[8] *Cab 23*, 93, pp. 1–10, Cab 15 (38), Secret, 22.3.1938.

[9] *Cab 24*, 276, p. 12, C P 75 (38), Draft by Halifax of Statement to Parliament on Situation in Central Europe, Secret.

[10] *Cab 27*, 623 Pt 2, p. 16, F P (36) 27th Mtg, Lock and Key, 22.3.1938.

[11] *F O 371*, 21630, pp. 178–89, C5055/317/62, Pitblado to Loxley, 20.5.1938 r. in r. 28.5.1938: Transmitting Corrected Copy of Note of Meeting with Dominion High Commissioners, attended by Mr. Butler on 23.3.1938.

[12] *Cab 27*, 623 Pt 2, p. 4, F P (36) 27th Mtg, Appendix, Draft Memorandum for French Government, Lock and Key.

[13] Iain Macleod, *Neville Chamberlain* (London, 1961), pp. 224–5.

[14] *U K Parl Deb H of L* 108, col. 477, 29.3.1938.

was determined not to slam the door on discussions with Germany, it might, if these failed, be found to have to take its stand 'by those peoples representing the rule of law'.[15] It transpired that Australia and South Africa opposed European commitments, Canada approved of the appeasement of Europe, and New Zealand did not feel able to comment.

Australia reacted: Lyons wired that his government felt that 'no definite commitment should be undertaken with regard to Czechoslovakia'.[16]

In contrast, Savage felt generally that 'we were so far away out here that you on the spot were far better able to judge the best course to pursue'.[17]

Hertzog, whom W. H. Clark, the high commissioner in South Africa, reported had a 'special sympathy' with Germany,[18] responded immediately.

> On behalf of South Africa I must once more insist, that the Union has no interest whatever in political questions affecting Czechoslovakia or any other Eastern European Power, and that it cannot be expected that the Union would deem herself in any way concerned in any form of warlike hostilities which may arise from such political questions. Nor can I see any reason why Great Britain should jeopardize the peace and interests of the Commonwealth by interesting herself in any of these questions to the extent of becoming a participant in a war arising out of them.[19]

Te Water conveyed this message to MacDonald on 23 March. MacDonald explained to Halifax that he had told the cabinet on 22 March that this was likely to be South Africa's attitude, and that although note should be taken of Hertzog's emphatic language, there was no need to place 'too literal an interpretation upon it'. MacDonald felt that South Africa would not come in at the beginning of any war fought to rescue Czechoslovakia or any other eastern or central European country from German clutches, 'but I am almost equally certain that South Africa would quickly come into a war in which we were involved because of an actual attack on French security'.[20]

Hertzog initially supported the German case over Czechoslovakia. On 25 March he relayed to Britain a message from Gie that so much

---

[15] *D O 114*, 94, pp. 13–4, Appendix 1, Enclosure in No. 1 Aide Memoire of a Message from Hertzog to be delivered to Halifax by te Water, 23.3.1938.

[16] *F O 800*, 310, pp. 8–9, H/IX/106, Pittblado to Caccia, 23.3.1938; Enclosing Lyons to Chamberlain, Telegram, Personal, Undated (paraphrase, copy).

[17] Ibid., pp. 1–2, H/IX/103, Galway to Halifax, 14.3.1938 (extract, copy).

[18] *F O 371*, 21679, p. 43, C2601/184/18, Batterbee to Sir O. Sargent, 4.4.1938 r. in r. 6.4.1938; Transmitting Clark to Batterbee, Confidential, 25.3.1938.

[19] *D O 114*, 94, pp. 13–4, Appendix 1, Enclosure in No. 1, Aide Memoire of a Message from Hertzog to be delivered to Halifax by te Water, 23.3.1938.

[20] Ibid., p. 13, Appendix 1, No. 1, F82/11, Memorandum by MacDonald, 23.3.1938.

importance was attached in Germany to France's ceasing to insist on coming to the aid of Czechoslovakia that 'such cessation might be regarded as a decisive factor in the search for a solution of the problems involved'. Czechoslovakia should abandon reliance on French and Russian support.[21]

On 29 March Hertzog sent a message to Chamberlain urging a revision of Versailles. Hertzog argued that France had no greater claim to security than any other European state, and had no right to stand in the way of the necessary revision of the peace treaty. If France persisted Britain should withhold support from it.[22] MacDonald saw te Water, and, in Chamberlain's words, dealt 'very sensibly with the high commissioner'.[23] MacDonald argued:

> But he [te Water] must realize that in the last resort our security was to a considerable extent bound up with that of France. If there were a war in Central Europe, which was confined to Central Europe, I could see no reason why we should intervene. But if that war spread to Western Europe, and there were a German invasion of France which threatened to overwhelm France, then, at once the security of this island was in jeopardy. That meant that the security of the whole British Commonwealth of Nations was threatened. It was quite impossible for us to take the line that the time might come when we should tell France that in no circumstances would we support her, and I did not think that Dominion statesmen ought to delude themselves into thinking that was possible even from their own point of view.

Te Water agreed that if Britain and France made a sincere attempt to settle central European problems and failed, they would have to stand together. But he did not speculate on South Africa's position in such circumstances.[24]

---

[21] Ibid., p. 14, Appendix 1, No. 2, F82/24, Aide Memoire of a Message from Hertzog to be delivered to MacDonald by te Water, 25.3.1938.

[22] Ibid., p. 16, Appendix 1, Enclosure in No. 3, Aide Memoire of a Message from Hertzog to be communicated to Chamberlain, 29.3.1938.

It is interesting to note that the office of the high commissioner in South Africa did not receive a copy of this memorandum until much later, as there was a delay which happened when the South African government replied through te Water to communications from the dominions office, and not through the high commission. M. E. Antrobus of the office of the high commission commented on 5 May:

> At the same time Ministers, though they would not dare to say so openly, do realise that a European war would almost certainly involve the Union in active participation in support of Great Britain and, therefore, as honest men they are genuinely anxious not to see Great Britain involved in any policy on which they could not wholeheartedly support her.

> What of course is interesting in the episode is that it shows that the P.M. at any rate studies the telegrams closely. One still does not know how far other ministers, with the possible exception of General Smuts, are given any opportunity of doing so. There is no system, so far as we are aware, of circulating telegrams or papers to the Cabinet.

In turn the dominions office did not inform the foreign office of Antrobus's analysis, until 29 June, when, by chance, it came out in conversation that the foreign office did not know of this despatch. [*F O 371*, 21657, C6757/42/18, Dixon to Mallet, 29.6.1938; Enclosing M.E. Antrobus to Dixon, Secret, 5.5.1938 (extract, copy).]

[23] *Premier 1*, 262, Minute by Chamberlain, 3.4.1938

[24] *D O 114*, 94, p. 15, Appendix 1, No. 3, F82/25, Note by MacDonald of a Conversation with te Water on the International Situation, 1.4.1938.

Mackenzie King wrote to MacDonald on 2 April of his admiration for the way in which Chamberlain had performed his task: 'I approve whole-heartedly of the course he had adopted, particularly his determination to get in touch with Italy and Germany. . . . I am more convinced than ever that to keep the British Empire out of a European war, is the one means of saving the Empire.'[25]

At the end of April Daladier, the new French prime minister, came to London to obtain a commitment in advance of British co-operation with France against Germany should France decide upon war. France was ready for war.[26] Foreign office officials doubted French support for this stand of Daladier.[27]

Details of these conversations were relayed to the dominions on 30 April. An outburst from South Africa followed. On 5 May the South African government warned that unless France could 'come to support some policy of European peace which will safely leave European hegemony to mature under the aegis of whichever nation of Europe may be most deserving of it', France should be warned that it did not have the support of the commonwealth. South Africa would not participate in a war over European hegemony.[28]

MacDonald discussed this message with te Water on 9 May. The high commissioner said that South African fears concerned the French: Britain's wise diplomacy commanded 'the complete support of General Hertzog and the South African Government'. MacDonald reassured te Water that Britain had refused any commitments beyond those outlined in Chamberlain's speech on 24 March. The French had agreed to make representations to Prague, similar to those of Britain, that Beneš should go as far as possible towards meeting the representations of the Sudeten Germans.[29]

The cabinet discussed the South African telegram on 11 May. Mac-Donald reminded the cabinet of Hertzog's tendency to jump to hasty conclusions.[30] Chamberlain sent the full record of the discussions with the French, together with a further reassuring telegram to Hertzog, explaining

---

[25] *F O 800*, 310, pp. 10–1, H/IX/107, Mackenzie King to MacDonald, 2.4.1938 (extract, copy).

[26] *Documents on British Foreign Policy* 3rd Series (hereafter cited as *'DBFP'*) 1, pp. 198–234 at p. 207, No. 164, C3687/13/17, Record of Anglo-French Conversations on 28 and 29 April 1938.

[27] Lord Strang, *Home and Abroad* (London, 1956), pp. 134–5.

[28] *D O 114*, 92, p. 42, Appendix 2, No. 2 F82/31A, South African Government to British Government, Telegram No. 8, Most Secret, 5.5.1938 (cypher).

[29] Ibid., pp. 16–7, Appendix 1, No. 4, F82/31A, Note by MacDonald of a Conversation with te Water on the International Situation, 9.5.1938.

[30] *Cab 23*, 93, p. 3, Cab 23 (38) 3, Secret, 11.5.1938.

that French policy was not actuated by a desire for preventive war. The French ministers had been told that the British government had to take into consideration the attitude of the dominions. It was not the British that had accepted the French view, but the French that had accepted the British.[31]

Te Water asked Lord Stanley, the newly appointed secretary of state for the dominions, for a meeting of the dominion high commissioners and the foreign secretary to discuss Czechoslovakia.[32] Menzies and Sir Earle Page also attended.[33] This meeting was occasioned by the weekend crisis of 19–22 May when there were reports of troop movements in Czechoslovakia and Germany.[34] Chamberlain felt that the Germans had made all preparations for a coup and had only been deterred by British warnings. He wrote to his sister that 'the incident shows how utterly untrustworthy and dishonest the German Government is'.[35] Britain warned Czechoslovakia that if war broke out, even if France and Britain were to come in, Czechoslovakia would be overrun by German forces. When Halifax explained British policy to the high commissioners it was obvious that every effort had been made to avoid any British entanglement. Halifax had left it to the French to tell the Czechs to withdraw their mobilisation order so that it could not be argued that Britain had a moral obligation to go to that country's support if it were attacked. Henderson had reminded the Germans of Chamberlain's statements in the house of commons on Czechoslovakia, but it had been carefully pointed out to the French that this did not mean any new obligation on Britain's part. The British solution to the Czech problem met in essence the suggestions made by Gie. Halifax hoped to get the Czechoslovakian government and the Sudeten Germans to agree to a cantonal system on Swiss lines, but he was anxious that Britain should not be involved in discussions on this as it might mean that Britain would be dragged into underwriting the settlement. Czechoslovakia would be a neutral state, and have no alliance with Russia and France.

The Australian delegates did not show sympathy for the Czechs. Bruce spoke of Benes preferring defeat to the end of the Czech domination of

---

31 *D O 114*, 92, pp. 42–4, Appendix 2, No. 3, F82/31A, British Government to South African Government, Telegram No. 13, Most Secret, 11.5.1938 (cypher).

32 *F O 800*, 310, pp. 15–7, H/IX/110, Stanley to Halifax, Personal, May 1938.

33 See Earle Page, *Truant Surgeon* (Sydney, 1963), pp. 258–9, for an account of the visit of the Australian trade mission.

34 *D O 114*, 92, pp. 17–8, Appendix 1, No. 5, F82/69, Note of a Meeting with the Dominion Representatives on 25.5.1938.

35 *Chamberlain Papers*, Chamberlain to Hilda Chamberlain, 28.5.1938. Quoted by Macleod, p. 232.

Czechoslovakia. He felt, however, that it would be necessary to tell the Czechs that the cantonal settlement was an historical development, fulfilling the intention of Versailles. Page explained that Australia wanted a politically satisfied Germany. If the Sudentenland would satisfy Germany it might be wise to give it to them.

Te Water was worried that the French were 'hanging behind'. He suggested that the problem should be looked at from the German point of view, and rather than delay the issue, it might be wise to allow the Sudeten Germans to be absorbed into the reich. Germany would not stop until this had happened. It emerged that the South African government felt that if war broke out, and first France and then Britain were involved over Czechoslovakia, it was doubtful that South Africa would come in.[36]

South Africa and Australia favoured the cession of the Sudetenland to Germany: both countries were ardent supporters of the appeasement of Europe. Canada, as was usual, was not represented at this meeting. The New Zealand delegate presumably sat in shocked silence. New Zealand, it can be assumed, disliked these proposals. The Irish delegate did not speak.[37]

Britain was limited by the attitude of the dominions. There was no question of British policy being dictated by the dominions: their opinion was rather one factor that had to be considered. In this instance it was, perhaps, a major factor, as it was feared that a British guarantee to Czechoslovakia might lead to a disintegration of the commonwealth. The only dominion governments that attempted to argue their case with any force, however, were South Africa and Australia. Nonetheless consideration was given to the attitude of the commonwealth as a whole.

During these months Chamberlain embarked upon a programme of rearmament: in this both the dominions and the United States had some role to play.

The question of accelerated rearmament came before the cabinet on 16 February. The only dominion which had indicated its willingness to co-operate with Britain to 'the maximum extent' was Australia, and in March that country became concerned about delays in delivery from Britain of armaments, aircraft and munitions.[38] The paper from the

---

[36] *D O 114*, 92, pp. 17–21, Appendix 1, No. 5, F82/69, Note of a Meeting with the Dominion Representatives on 25.5.1938.

[37] Ibid., *loc. cit.*

[38] *Cab 23*, 92, p. 1, Cab 5 (38) 1, Secret, 16.2.1938; *Premier 1*, 310, Lyons to Chamberlain, Telegram, Secret and Personal, 17.3.1938 (paraphrase); D300/69, Chamberlain to Lyons, Telegram, Secret and Personal, 28.3.1938 (paraphrase).

committee of imperial defence showed that despite increased rearmament, in 1939, with regard to aircraft, Britain would still be a good deal below the German standard.[39] MacDonald raised the question of consultation with the dominions. In supplying information to the dominions it was vital to ensure that secrets would not leak out, and also that some of the dominions would not be unduly alarmed. Hore-Belisha, the secretary of state for war, suggested that the dominions might help to defend imperial communications in peace time. But when the matter of further approaches to the dominions was discussed MacDonald pointed out that it would not be of much use to approach Canada; there were political objections to an approach to South Africa as the only points where they could help Britain garrison in time of peace were in the colonies and mandated territories in central and east Africa. It would be possible, however, to approach the Australian and New Zealand governments about the garrison of Singapore.[40] MacDonald did propose that with the new naval construction programme Australia might be asked to build a third capital ship.[41]

With the *Anschluss* the cabinet reconsidered defence matters. On 12 March Chamberlain mentioned the possibility of increasing the defence programme, but he felt that there should be concentration on the air force rather than the navy, and on an acceleration of anti aircraft defences.[42] The cabinet on 30 March discussed the suggestion of the committee of imperial defence for the purchase of militarised Douglas aircraft from the United States. The question of supplies from Canada was also raised.[43] The committee of imperial defence considered these issues the following day. Inskip pointed out that arrangements had been concluded for the establishment of a Bren gun factory in Canada in which British and Canadian requirements would be combined. He felt, however, that results could be had more quickly by expanding in Britain. The United States, as Lord Weir pointed out, was a different case: the question was rather the possibility of obtaining delivery of certain types of aircraft. The committee authorised a mission to the United States.[44]

The need for aircraft became more pressing in April when scheme 'L' for an enlarged air force was discussed by the cabinet. In two years time

[39] *Cab 24*, 274, C P (24) 38, Defence Expenditure in Future Years, Lock and Key, 8.2.1938.

[40] *Cab 23*, 92, pp. 15–48, Cab 5 (38) 9, Secret, 16.2.1938.

[41] Ibid., p. 15, Cab 9 (38) 8, Secret, 23.2.1938; *Cab 24*, 274, C P (29) 38, Memorandum by Cooper on New Naval Construction Programme, Secret, 11.2.1938.

[42] *Cab 23*, 92, pp. 6–11, Cab 12 (38) 3, Secret, 12.3.1938; pp. 8–9, Cab 13 (38) 3, Secret, 14.3.1938.

[43] Ibid., 93, pp. 8–9, Cab 17 (38) 6, Secret, 30.3.1938.

[44] *Cab 2*, 7, C I D Minutes of 317th Meeting, Secret, 31.3.1938.

although Britain would have fewer machines than Germany it should be relatively stronger. The real danger was the present.[45]

A mission went to both the United States and Canada to investigate war potential in those countries.[46] On 18 May a report was presented to the cabinet suggesting the purchase of four hundred United States aircraft costing £4,200,000. The difficulties of the neutrality act were raised,[47] but on 25 May Halifax pointed out to the cabinet that the idea of purchasing United States machines, with the implication that the United States was behind Britain had had a useful effect in Germany. Oliver Stanley, the president of the board of trade, also urged a hasty purchase of the aircraft as that might help the trade negotiations.[48]

In June the cabinet also considered the creation of a war potential for aircraft production in Canada. Lord Stanley stressed the real political value of these proposals, but warned that the mission should be technical in character and avoid politics, otherwise Mackenzie King, who was already antagonistic towards training establishments in Canada, might turn against the proposal.

Chamberlain pointed out that it would take some time for the scheme to operate, and the cost would be heavy. But the conference of ministers had taken a wider view.[49] Lord Stanley had welcomed these proposals as 'the first real indication of Canada's intention to change her policy of isolation in matters of imperial defence'. Kingsley Wood, the secretary of state for air, had also mentioned that Massey had said that this scheme would get the Canadian government to take a more active interest in other proposals for co-operation in imperial defence such as the arrangements for the recruiting and training of pilots and other Canadian air personnel.[50]

When Chamberlain presented the case to the cabinet he argued that the insurance value of the scheme in the event of prospective damage to British factories in time of war, was considerable. Another factor was that:

> If Canada could become interested in the provision of aircraft to this country the aloofness of that Dominion from Imperial defence and its disassociation from

---

[45] *Cab 23*, 93, p. 22, Cab 18 (38) 8, Secret, 6.4.1938; See *Premier 1*, 238, for Documents on the Royal Air Force Heavy Bomber Policy and the Purchase of Aircraft from the United States.

[46] Ibid., p. 26, Cab 19 (38) 8, Secret, 13.4.1938.

[47] Ibid., p. 27, Cab 24 (38) 15, Secret, 18.5.1938.

[48] Ibid., pp. 16–7, Cab 26 (38) 6, Secret, 25.5.1938.

[49] Ibid., 94, pp. 5–8, Cab 30 (38) 5, Secret, 30.6.1938; *Cab 24*, 277, C P 143 (38), Memorandum by Wood on Creation of a War Potential for Aircraft Production in Canada, Secret, 16.6.1938; See *Premier 1*, 239, for Mackenzie King's Protests about the Publicity over the Air School in Canada.

[50] *Cab 24*, 277, pp. 1–16, C P 148 (38), Conference of Ministers on Air Mission to United States and Canada, Secret, 24.6.1938. See *Documents on Canadian External Relations* 6, 1936–9, pp. 204–36 for an account of the training of pilots in Canada.

the problems of the United Kingdom might be reduced. It was not inconceivable that the whole attitude of Canada towards the defence of the Empire might be changed.

The cabinet agreed to examine what sort of aircraft should be manufactured in Canada.[51]

The cabinet agreed in principle, however, on 11 May that war material should be supplied to Portugal. MacDonald pointed out that this would mean giving Portugal priority over the dominions, and that certain arrangements to supply Canada in 1940 and 1941 would not then be carried out. Chamberlain did not think that Canada would be prejudiced, as, of all parts of the empire, it was the one most immune from risk.[52]

There was a further consideration of defence expenditure at the end of July. Increased aircraft production meant a possible cut in the navy. Duff Cooper argued against this: for the first time Britain was relying on a possible ally, France, to maintain its maritime supremacy. The position of the dominions had to be borne in mind: at the imperial conference they had been told that Britain could send a fleet to the far east. Templewood pointed out that even the new standard fleet would only just be strong enough to hold the situation on the far east and British waters at the same time. If this could not be achieved it would be a terrible shock for the dominions. He therefore deprecated the proposal to drop the new standard. Templewood suggested that pressure could be put on the dominions to contribute. He instanced Australia's friendliness towards the building of a capital ship: Australia was unlikely to do so, however, if it felt that Britain could not hold the position in the far east. Earl Stanhope, the president of the board of education, suggested that the new standard fleet should not be abandoned, but the dominions should be told that it was being slowed down for financial reasons, and it was to be hoped that they would assist.[53] It came out at the cabinet meeting on 27 July, however, that Parkhill, the Australian minister for defence, had never informed his colleagues about British representations on the capital ship issue. MacDonald, then secretary of state for colonies, said that he had the impression from talking to Menzies that Australia might build a battle cruiser. In the end the cabinet agreed not to say that the new standard programme had been discarded, although it was not to be adopted by any particular date. Even so, Duff Cooper foresaw difficulties with New Zealand and Australia, especially as

51 *Cab 23*, 94, pp. 8–11, Cab 30 (38) 5, Secret, 30.6.1938.
52 Ibid., 93, pp. 14–6, Cab 23 (38) 5, Secret, 11.5.1938.
53 Ibid., 94, pp. 16–26, Cab 33 (38) 8, Secret, 20.7.1938; *Cab 24*, 278, C P 170 (38), Memorandum by Inskip dealing with Naval Expenditure, Most Secret.

New Zealand had been under the impression that Britain had adopted the new standard.[54]

The committee of imperial defence and the cabinet in considering the defence preparations which followed on Hitler's move against Austria were careful to take the position of the dominions into account. The debate on building aircraft in Canada suggested that this should be done largely in an attempt to involve an isolationist dominion in imperial defence. It also emerged that it was imperative to avoid war at this time as British defences compared unfavourably with those of the axis powers.

No help was expected from the United States. By May 1938 the British government had instructed all its departments to proceed independently on their war plans, without looking for any help or support from the United States.[55]

British policy towards Czechoslovakia, and the programme of re-armament, was followed closely and debated both in the dominions and the United States.

In South Africa the issue of neutrality was prominent. In May a general election was fought, and although it would be wrong to say that the campaign was conducted solely on the issue of participation in a British war, this was a platform on which opponents hurled abuse, and the political press focused attention. There was no agreement among the leading parties as to what South Africa's position should be in such a contingency. The nationalists declared themselves unequivocally for isolation and non participation. The ruling united party was in a more ambiguous position. With fusion as its declared aim, it had to offer a convincing alternative for patriotic English speaking South Africa, whose sensibilities were being ruffled by the controversial national anthem issue, to the declared dominion party policy which was to stand by the mother country's side in any eventuality. Hertzog had strong sympathies for the German predicament, and these had not been shaken by the squabble over South West Africa. Smuts and Hertzog seemed to agree to differ on this issue, and, in a way, it suited the united party's purposes that they should do so. In the English speaking constituencies Smuts spoke of the likelihood of South Africa standing by Britain if called upon to do so. In the predominantly Afrikaner areas, and in the nationalist strongholds, Hertzog stressed his consistent view that it would be for parliament to decide, the

---

[54] *Cab 23*, 94, pp. 19–21, Cab 35 (38) 7, Secret, 27.7.1938.

[55] *Foreign Relations of the United States* (hereafter cited as '*FRUS*') 1938(1), p. 55, 741.62/270, Kennedy to Hull, Telegram No. 412, 16.5.1938.

implication being that a South African parliament dominated by the united party would decide against participation in a British war.[56] In the general election the united party won a resounding victory, gaining ground from both the dominion and the nationalist parties.[57]

Debate on the question was protracted into a parliamentary wrangle in August. Malan pointing to statements made by Smuts that if Britain were in danger the dominions would 'do their duty' as in 1914, and that if Britain went to war South Africa would 'not remain behind', asked if the other members of the cabinet also subscribed to that policy. A week later Smuts replied with the usual government formula that the decision to go to war rested with parliament. The references he had made had been to the situation where either Britain or part of the commonwealth was in danger or attacked. It was Smuts's personal opinion, and not the government's policy, that if

> Great Britain is attacked and comes into actual danger—not merely that she goes to war in Central Europe as an ally of France, but where England herself is attacked and is in danger—that South Africa will help her.

Smuts explained that Hertzog probably had a different personal view.[58] Hertzog in the house of assembly and at the united party congress refused to be drawn on this point, and would only indicate that he might differ from Smuts as a matter of personal opinion.[59]

During the defence debate in early September Pirow stated that it was the policy of the South African government to take part in a war whenever it was in the interests of South Africa to do so. Dominion and nationalist party representatives remarked on the conflicting statements of the minister of defence which 'differed according to the circumstances of the audience which he had to address'.[60] Pirow gave the assurance that the committee of imperial defence were 'carrying on in their own course' without consulting South Africa.[61]

Informed public comment on the Czechoslovakian question ranged from the editorial in the *Burger* headed *Will you fight for Czechoslovakia?* to severe criticisms of Chamberlain's so called appeasement policy in the *Natal Witness*.[62]

[56] *Burger*, 14.4.1938; 2.5.1938, Ed.; 5.5.1938, Ed.; 11.5.1938, Ed.; *Suiderstem*, 2.5.1938, Ed.; 12.4.1938, Ed.
[57] *Times*, 20.5.1938.
[58] *S A Parl Deb H of A* 1938, 32, cols. 1094–5, 17.8.1938; cols. 1676–80, 25.8.1938.
[59] Ibid., col. 1682, 25.8.1938; col. 1808, 29.8.1938.
[60] Ibid., cols. 2324–5, 2335–6, 7.9.1938; cols. 2412–4, 8.9.1938.
[61] Ibid., col. 2411, 8.9.1938.
[62] *Burger*, 24.5.1938, Ed.; *Natal Witness*, 15.6.1938, Ed.; 17.6.1938, Ed.

In South Africa it was Smuts rather than Hertzog who was the key figure. It was he who could be relied upon to mollify English speaking imperial sentiment. Smuts was adept at changing his façades. From his personal correspondence it would seem that he favoured Chamberlain's policy of the appeasement of Europe, and the British refusal to guarantee Czechoslovakia. Smuts wrote to Lothian on 20 May that Hitler, with Austria in his possession, had 'unlocked the door to South Eastern Europe'. There was nothing to stop Hitler's domination from eventually extending to the Bosphorus. Smuts expanded on what he thought British policy should be:

> On Great Britain is imposed the duty of a very cautious policy. She is not directly interested, and she knows all the Dominions are averse to European complications.[63]

On the point of dominion participation Smuts had written categorically to L. S. Amery two months previously:

> As regards the Dominions they will fight for Great Britain if attacked, they will not fight in the battles of Central or South Eastern Europe. I even have my doubts whether they will fight again for France and Belgium.[64]

At the end of May Smuts wrote of Germany's march to the south east being inevitable, and that Britain could only be 'an interested spectator'.[65] Lothian confirmed Smuts in this view.

> The only practical policy of the moment . . . is to do everything we can to ensure that Germany's growing influence Eastwards respects the political independence of the small nations of Eastern Europe and is extended without actual resort to violence.[66]

Smuts felt that the dominions would only go to Britain's aid if it were attacked. The dominions were not prepared to become embroiled in European squabbles. This was hardly the image of Smuts put over in the South African English speaking press, or the one given by Smuts at political meetings in English speaking centres.

Duncan also thought like Smuts. The governor general wrote to Lothian at the end of August:

> I am very concerned about it because it seems almost inevitable that if France intervenes forcibly in Central Europe we shall be pulled in too. When I say 'we' I mean 'You'. What will happen here the Lord only knows.

---

[63] *Lothian Papers* 367, pp. 872–6, Smuts to Lothian, 20.5.1938.
[64] *Smuts Papers*, Smuts to L. S. Amery, 28.3.1938. Quoted by W. K. Hancock, *Smuts. The Fields of Force, 1919–1950* (Cambridge, 1968), p. 284.
[65] *Lothian Papers* 367, pp. 872–6, Smuts to Lothian, 20.5.1938.
[66] Ibid., pp. 877–81, Lothian to Smuts, 2.6.1938 (copy).

Duncan felt that there should be no commitment by Britain to interfere in Europe. France should be told that Britain would not support it over Czechoslovakia.[67]

South Africa was not prepared to fight over Czechoslovakia, and disapproved of any British support for France on this issue.

The lord privy seal visited Australia during January and February 1938 and reported that interest in foreign affairs seemed to be increasing. Australian newspapers published full reports of foreign affairs. These were based on British sources. He reported that Australians feared Japan, but were in sympathy with British efforts to meet Germany's legitimate claims.[68]

The Australian government officially approved British policy.[69] At the end of April it revealed its acceptance of the British refusal to guarantee Czechoslovakia.[70]

The isolationist labour opposition was divided. Collings, the labour leader in the senate, said that Australia should be free of European entanglements.[71] Trade unionists urged that the dictators should be met by more active opposition, but were not prepared to fight for European causes.[72] Individual state trade unions refused to co-operate in Lyons's defence preparations.[73] When in July 1938 a 'representative' conference of the New South Wales trade unions demanded a break with the pro fascist policy of Chamberlain, and sanctions against aggressors, the bulk of the trade union movement objected.[74] Labour was not in a position to oppose Lyons effectively.

Reaction to the Czech crisis in May would suggest that Australian opinion was not wholly isolationist. While the *Age* spoke of there being no need for the commonwealth to be embroiled in war,[75] newspapers like the Melbourne *Argus* warned that war in Europe would involve Australia.[76]

[67] Ibid., 346, pp. 251–2, Duncan to Lothian, 30.8.1938.

[68] *Cab 24*, 276, pp. 185–7, C P 96 (38), Visit to Australia of Lord Privy Seal, Secret, 11.1.1938–21.2.1938.

[69] *F O 371*, 21630, pp. 83–5, C2247/317/62, No. D O 2, Dominions Office to Dunbar, 28.3.1938 r. in r. 30.3.1938; Transmitting High Commissioner in Australia to Dominions Office, Telegram No. 67, Secret, 23.3.1938 (copy).

[70] *Aust Parl Deb* 1937–8, 157, Sen, cols. 572–6, 28.4.1938; H of R, cols. 535–9, 27.4.1938.

[71] Ibid., Sen, col. 582, 28.4.1938.

[72] Anonymous, 'The Commonwealth and the Dictatorships', *Round Table*, XXVIII (1937–8), pp. 435–52; Paul Hasluck, *The Government and the People 1939–1941* (Canberra, 1952), pp. 87–9.

[73] *Times*, 4.7.1938.

[74] Hasluck, p. 89.

[75] *Age*, 24.5.1938, Ed.

[76] *Argus*, 24.5.1938; *Sydney Morning Herald*, 14.6.1938, Ed. See E. M. Andrews, *Isolationism and Appeasement in Australia, Reactions to the European Crisis, 1935–9* (Canberra, 1970), pp. 117–89 for an account of Australian press coverage during the period.

On 25 May W. M. Hughes assured the house of representatives that there were no new British commitments to Czechoslovakia, and that a peaceful solution might be possible.[77]

The issue of dominion consultation, however, was debated in Australia. In June, in London, Menzies spoke of the need to accelerate the process of consolidation and consultation between the British and dominion governments: the British people should have one and not six voices. The Australian press used this opportunity to criticise the government for failing to give a lead in international issues.[78] At the end of May, speaking in the senate, Duncan-Hughes had insisted that Australia should keep 'as closely as we conscientiously can to the foreign policy of the Old Country'.[79]

Menzies's remarks caused questions in the British house of commons about provisions for adequate consultation with the dominions, and, whether the dominions should not be given the opportunity to shape British foreign policy. Chamberlain, in reply, pointed to Menzies's own confession that international events did not always allow time for fireside chats.[80]

In August W. M. Hughes condemned the dominions office as an obstruction to effective consultation and suggested that the procedure, often followed, of messages being communicated direct by the foreign office, or circulated between prime ministers, should be adopted as the rule.[81] In July Menzies visited Germany as head of an Australian trade mission, and as Australia had no diplomatic representation in Europe, the visit probably was important for informing Australian official opinion on the German question. Before sailing for Australia on 8 August, however, Menzies harped back to the question of dominion consultation. Menzies saw two elements on which a commonwealth policy would have to depend: a British government which recognised that in matters of international policy, it was speaking for British people all over the world, and must therefore attach proper weight to dominion views; and, secondly, dominion governments which recognised responsibility for an effective contribution to commonwealth policy and security.[82] As *The Times* pointed out on 9 August giving advice meant a sharing of responsibility, and some dominions found it more convenient to allow the British government to

[77] *Aust Parl Deb* 1937–8, 157, H of R, cols. 1375–6, 25.5.1938.
[78] *Times*, 27.6.1938.
[79] *Aust Parl Deb* 1937–8, 158, Sen, cols. 1538–40, 31.5.1938.
[80] *U K Parl Deb H of C* 337, cols. 1898–9, 29.6.1938.
[81] *Times*, 9.8.1938.
[82] Ibid., *loc. cit.*

reach its decisions, and then they would decide whether to adhere to that decision or not.[83]

Australian politics were marked by a reluctance on the part of the government to allow protracted discussions of foreign policy. It would seem a fair assumption that the Australian government would not be willing to support any British entanglement over Czechoslovakia, and would favour the appeasement of Europe.

New Zealand with its belief in collective security, morality, and the league of nations, was the only dominion likely to criticise Chamberlain's Czechoslovakian policy. At Geneva British policy generally was criticised by New Zealand delegates. In May 1938 New Zealand opposed the British proposal that independent nations be authorised to decide whether to recognise the Italian conquest of Abyssinia. The same month New Zealand supported the Spanish representative's demand that his government should be allowed to purchase war materials wherever it could. New Zealand also regarded the Sino-Japanese dispute as a breach of the covenant which demanded positive action.[84]

New Zealand though the dominion most critical of British foreign policy was also the one which was unequivocally prepared to stand by the mother country. The speech from the throne in June delivered by the governor general, Viscount Galway, reaffirmed this attitude.

> My Ministers believe that if disputes between nations are to be settled by force and not by reason there is little hope of attaining international justice, and they remain convinced that the Covenant of the League of Nations offers the best, if not the only, means of establishing an ordered international life. At the same time my Ministers have continued to affirm their belief that the people of this Dominion regard themselves as one with the people of the United Kingdom, with whom, in the future as in the past, they will always stand.[85]

The opposition did not dissent from this. Indeed, if there were to have been any disagreement, it would have been expected from the labour government, who, while in opposition in 1935, had had strongly isolationist tendencies. There was opposition criticism of New Zealand's independent stand at Geneva on the ground that New Zealand, with its inadequate defence force, had no right to dictate to the 'Old Country as to what action it should take'.[86]

---

[83] Ibid., 9.8.1938, Ed.
[84] H. V. Hodson, Ed., *The British Commonwealth and the Future* (London, 1939), p. 92.
[85] *N Z Parl Deb* 1938, 251, Leg Co, p. 1, 28.6.1938.
[86] Ibid., H of R, p. 137, 1.7.1938; Leg Co, p. 6, 29.6.1938; p. 109, 1.7.1938.

The British policy of no commitment on Czechoslovakia, however, did not arouse active criticism in New Zealand: parliament did not discuss the matter specifically; and although the press reported developments it usually did not comment. Perhaps the impending general election accounted partially for the silence.[87] The general assumption was that if Britain went to war over Czechoslovakia, New Zealand would be at its side, and on this opinion was practically unanimous. Although it would be in line with the New Zealand's general attitude to approve of British support for the Czechs, there is no evidence that New Zealand pressured Chamberlain to take a firm stand on Czechoslovakia.

In Canada Mackenzie King was careful to make it clear that his government had been informed of, but not consulted on, Chamberlain's statement of 24 March.[88] The conservatives demanded a definite statement on Canadian foreign policy,[89] while a CCF member clamoured for the assurance that Canada would never participate in a foreign war without the consent of the people and not just the consent of parliament.[90] But Canadian opinion was such that Lord Tweedsmuir, the governor general of Canada, wrote to Chamberlain:

> I am delighted to see that you have British opinion solidly behind you. You certainly have Canada's. At first the Press and people were inclined to be critical, but now the feeling on your side is unanimous + cordial. You have no warmer admirer than my Prime Minister.[91]

When on 24 May Mackenzie King gave a carefully reasoned, but cautious, statement on foreign policy, there was nothing that could be detected as a significant departure from the Canadian policy pursued over the previous few years. Canada was bound by no commitments, either to remain neutral, or to engage in war. It would be for the Canadian parliament to decide on the merits of the situation:

> So far as the Canadian government is concerned, it does not consider that it is in the interest either of Canada or of the Commonwealth to tender advice as to what policy the United Kingdom should adopt week by week, or become involved in British political disputes. We have expressed no opinion on that policy, and no one in London is authorised or warranted in interpreting us as doing so.[92]

The conservative leader, Bennett, spoke for himself only, but not for his party, as the conservative foreign policy was to be finalised at a forthcoming convention. In any case Bennett's attitude had much in common

---

87 Anonymous, 'Overseas Reactions to the Crisis', *Round Table*, XXIX (1938–9), pp. 53–6.
88 *Can Parl Deb H of C* 1938(2), pp. 1935–6, 1.4.1938.
89 Ibid., p. 1935.
90 Ibid., 1938(3), p. 2878, 13.5.1938.
91 *Templewood Papers* XIX (C) 11, Chamberlain to Hilda Chamberlain, 6.4.1938 (copy).
92 *Can Parl Deb H of C* 1938(3), pp. 3177–89, 24.5.1938.

with that of Mackenzie King.[93] And the compromise resolution on foreign policy adopted by the conservative convention in July, as a result of suspicions of European entanglements expressed by French Canadian conservatives, could equally well have been drawn up by the liberals.[94]

The CCF resolutions of July 1938 were consistent with those passed by that party in previous years: the party would insist on non participation in any war 'whose purpose is really in defence of imperialist interests'.[95]

From March to September 1938 all major Canadian political groups were opposed to any Canadian commitment to Europe. Canadian orientation was more towards the geographical situation of the country as part of the north American continent than as a member of the commonwealth. The need to placate the French element was a significant factor. It does not follow that Canada was pledged to a policy of neutrality: it was rather one of no commitment.

Public opinion in the dominions had not changed from the time of the imperial conference. With the exception of New Zealand the dominions were not opposed to the *Anschluss*, felt that Germany had legitimate grievances, and were determined not to become involved in any central European conflict which was designed to prevent the Sudeten Germans from being absorbed into the reich. The British cabinet's assessment of dominion opinion was accurate. Dominion statesmen, possibly because of internal conditions, did not appear to be attempting to lead their countries toward a more committed European policy. Ironically New Zealand, committed to fight for Britain, was the one dominion which was an embarrassment to Chamberlain in his schemes to achieve European appeasement. The most loyal of the dominions was the one which could have broken a united commonwealth front on this matter. And it obediently refrained from criticism.

The fear of a dissolution of the commonwealth was still a factor in British policy in July. On 20 July Halifax in a conversation with Bonnet and Daladier outlined a possible scheme for a British mediator to be sent to Czechoslovakia to speak to Benes and the Sudeten leaders. The British, however, could not undertake any commitment beyond that stated by Chamberlain on 24 March. The reason that Halifax gave for this reluctance was the attitude of the dominions. He cited pressure from the Aga Khan

93 Ibid., pp. 3190–5, 3206–23, 24.5.1938.
94 F. H. Soward, *Canada in World Affairs. The Pre-War Years* (Oxford, 1941), pp. 103–4.
95 Ibid., pp. 105–6.

to accept no commitment that would involve the empire in war, and said that South Africa had the same attitude.[96]

Lord Runciman was appointed the mediator in question. Templewood recalls that Chamberlain felt that this attempt was worth the effort 'if only to explode the charge of obstruction that Hitler was making against the Czech government, and to prove to the British Commonwealth that every impediment to a reasonable compromise had been removed'.[97] Mackenzie King even committed himself to cabling Runciman his best wishes.[98] This action by Mackenzie King suggests foundation for Chamberlain's supposition. Mackenzie King, however, would not consent to the publication of his message.[99]

The evidence would suggest that Chamberlain's policy of refusing to commit Britain to a guarantee of Czechoslovakia, was in part due to concern that Canada, Australia and South Africa would disapprove, and that there might be a crisis in dominion relations. Dominion opinion cannot be said to have determined British policy on this issue, but it was a considerable factor. Hertzog, Mackenzie King and Lyons were among Chamberlain's most ardent supporters in his efforts to reach agreement with the dictators, and dominion opinion together with the military situation, had decided the cabinet on its policy towards Czechoslovakia.

In contrast to the dominions, the United States generally disapproved of the 'cowardly' British stand on Czechoslovakia. Kept informed of developments in British policy, United States statesmen, however, were more concerned with internal politics and the economic situation.[100]

The mobilisation crisis of May did arouse sharp comment in the United States press. The columnist, Dorothy Thompson, described the paradox: 'Now the very public who have supported our own isolation are highly indignant when Great Britain adopts something of the attitude'. Miss Thompson warned that Chamberlain's policy had 'brought British stock to an all time low' in the United States.[101]

United States opinion appeared not to be neutral. But it is questionable whether Americans were prepared to commit themselves, and how many

[96] *DBFP* 1, pp. 601–3, No. 523, C7320/1941/18, Phipps to Foreign Office, Telegram No. 480, 20.7.1938 r. 21.7.1938.
[97] Lord Templewood, *Nine Troubled Years* (London, 1954), p. 298.
[98] *Mackenzie King Papers*, King to Runcimann, Telegram, 29.7.1938. Quoted by James Eayrs, *In Defence of Canada. Appeasement and Rearmament* (Toronto, 1965), p. 63.
[99] Ibid., p. 64.
[100] Anonymous, 'America in the Balance', *Round Table*, XXVIII (1937–8), pp. 470–85; 'Wall Street and Washington', *Round Table*, XXVIII (1937–8), pp. 664–77.
[101] *New York Herald Tribune*, 20.5.1938.

even were informed of developments overseas. The British observer in the United States would tend to have a distorted view of this. New York, Boston, Washington and Chicago were the centres most seen by British visitors, and most press reports on feeling in the United States were based on reaction in those centres. Interest in foreign affairs was confined mainly to the east coast and Washington. The great middle west was stubbornly isolationist: the only memory it retained of the 1914–8 war was that its sons were conscripted and that some of them never came back from Europe.[102]

British statesmen were conscious of the effect of United States isolationism: in the Anglo-French conversations at the end of April, Chamberlain told Daladier that Britain could not count on being able to purchase ammunition from the United States to the same extent as it had during the 1914–8 war.[103]

Chamberlain remained anxious to cultivate good relations with the United States and certainly the prime minister had an excellent personal relationship with the new United States ambassador, Joseph P. Kennedy: Kennedy was one of the few foreigners with whom Chamberlain was on first name terms. The two men had almost identical views on the need to maintain peace. Chamberlain took care to keep the new ambassador informed of British policy, and Kennedy kept the state department barraged with reports of the alarming situation in Europe.[104]

The issue of Anglo-American co-operation in the far east came up again in July. The cabinet was considering the possibility of granting a loan to China, and what the effect on Japan was likely to be. Chamberlain told the cabinet on 6 July that the situation would be much improved if the United States would join Britain on this matter. There was the danger, however, that the United States would announce that it had refused a British suggestion of this kind. Chamberlain had seen Kennedy, just back from Washington, and the ambassador had given a favourable account of Roosevelt's desire to co-operate with the British government, and had also been reassuring as to Roosevelt's intentions over the application of the neutrality act, if Britain became involved in war. The prime minister suggested that Kennedy should be approached for his views on United States reaction to the loan proposed. It was decided not to approach the

---

102 *New York Times*, 15.6.1938; *Times*, 29.6.1938.

103 *DBFP* 1, pp. 198–235 at p. 203, No. 164, C3687/13/17, Record of Anglo-French Conversations on 28 and 29 April 1938.

104 Richard J. Whalen, *The Founding Father: the Story of Joseph P. Kennedy* (London, 1965), pp. 232–4.

dominions at that stage.[105] Halifax saw Kennedy but the ambassador doubted whether the United States would collaborate with Britain in giving a loan to China. Halifax and Stanley also saw Bruce, the Australian high commissioner, about this matter. Bruce felt that Australian public opinion would only favour a loan to China if it did not involve the risk of trouble with Japan. Halifax put the matter to the cabinet again on 13 July: he pointed out that if Japan reacted unfavourably, and perhaps made a move against Hong Kong, Britain would not be able to reply. The European situation was serious, and Halifax had been impressed by Kennedy's comment 'that the British Empire had enough trouble on its hands at the moment without gratuitously taking on more'. Consequently because of the lack of United States and dominion support, and the possible attitude of Japan, the cabinet decided to abandon the proposed financial support for China.[106]

Britain was still anxious to cultivate Anglo-American co-operation. This can be guaged from a comment by Mr. F. Ashton-Gwatkin, head of the economic relations of the foreign office, on his return from a six weeks visit to the United States:

> In a play which I saw in London some years ago, a young Foreign Office secretary finds himself by an accident, at a full meeting of the Cabinet . . . .He is asked by the philosophical Prime Minister what he thinks is the most important thing in the world, and he replies without hesitation:—'Love—and Anglo-American relations'.
>
> I am glad to think that my department is popularly considered to have its fundamental policy so firmly based.

Gwatkin felt that the most that could be looked for from the United States in a war was pacific benevolence, a favourable adjustment of the neutrality act, and possibly eventual participation, as in 1917, if the war were prolonged. It was here that Gwatkin felt that the attitude of Canada was important. Canada, in his view, was trying to avoid having a foreign policy and was 'hesitating between imperial obligations and American abstentianism'. If Canada decided not to fight with Britain in a war, the United States would probably ask why it should participate.[107]

The Anglo-American trade treaty was seen as another means of achieving co-operation with the United States. Sir A. Sinclair asked questions about the progress of the trade treaty negotiations in the house of commons at the end of July. The prime minister explained that he regarded the trade

[105] *Cab 23*, 94, pp. 12–6, Cab 31 (38) 6, Secret, 6.7.1938.
[106] Ibid., pp. 10–4, Cab 32 (38) 8, Secret, 13.7.1938.
[107] *Cab 24*, 277, pp. 1–7, C P 161 (38), Annexed Memorandum by F. Ashton-Gwatkin.

treaty not merely as a commercial arrangement, but as 'a forerunner of a policy of wider application'. The reason for the delay was that the treaty covered so wide a field.[108]

The state department also made threatening sounds. Hull let it be known that the United States had contributed its share but this was 'in marked contrast to the attitude thus far displayed by the British'. He warned that if the opportunity were lost, the United States would move towards political and economic isolation.[109]

The British cabinet discussed the matter on 27 July. Oliver Stanley said that the British would have to make concessions on certain goods or there would be no agreement. Chamberlain also referred to his discussions with Kennedy who had done much behind the scenes to work out a compromise. He noted with satisfaction the ambassador's attitude that although the practical results of the agreement might not be very great, the psychological effect was of great importance.[110]

In August British cultivation of the United States had some reward. There was a public and positive demonstration from the state department that the United States was not neutral, that it did take sides. On 16 August Hull speaking implicitly to the dictators said:

> All nations have a primary interest in peace with justice, in economic well-being with stability, and in conditions of order under law. There are constant objectives of this country. Each of these objectives is today seriously jeopardized in many parts of the world. All governments and all peoples should therefore be on guard against certain dangerous developments which imperil them, and be alive to the issues involved.[111]

Chamberlain welcomed the speech as a frank expression of the degree to which the interests of the United States were linked with those of Europe.[112] The British were aware, however, that this did not mark any swing away from isolationism in the United States.[113] Roosevelt, on 18 August, reinforced Hull's speech by declaring at Kingston, Canada, that

> The Dominion of Canada is part of the sisterhood of the British Empire. I give to you assurance that the people of the United States will not stand idly by if domination of Canadian soil is threatened by any other empire.[114]

---

[108] *U K Parl Deb H of C* 338, col. 2939, 26.7.1938; cols. 2960–1, 26.7.1938.
[109] *FRUS* 1938(2), pp. 39–41, 611.4131/1681, Hull to Kennedy, Telegram No. 387, 25.7.1938.
[110] *Cab 23*, 94, pp. 5–9, Cab 36 (38) 3, Secret, 28.7.1938; Whalen, pp. 323–3.
[111] Cordell Hull, *The Memoirs of Cordell Hull*, 1 (London, 1948), p. 587.
[112] *Times*, 18.8.1938.
[113] Ibid., *loc. cit.*
[114] Hull 1, p. 587.

Halifax suggested that if Hull or Roosevelt spoke again of the dangers in central Europe before the nazi rally at Nuremburg in September, it might have a restraining influence on Hitler.[115]

These utterances by Hull and Roosevelt were, however, probably ahead of United States public opinion, and the British reaction was rightly cautious.[116] A key to the president's personal attitude, and the extent of the action that he was prepared to take is outlined in a personal letter that Roosevelt wrote on 15 September:

> Today I think ninety per cent. of our people are definitely anti-German and anti-Italian in sentiment—and incidently, I would not propose to ask them to be neutral in thought. I would strongly encourage their natural sympathy while at the same time avoding any thought of sending troops to Europe.[117]

With Runciman assessing the position in Prague, and Hitler touring Germany's fortifications on the Czechoslovakian border, the situation worsened towards the end of August. Britain, however, was still limited by the consideration of United States and dominion opinion. On 25 August the French were menaced by a German communication that unless the Czechoslovakian problem were settled by the end of September the German government would take appropriate measures to resolve it. Halifax explained to M. Cambon, the French *chargé d'affaires*, that the limit to British action had been set by Chamberlain's statement on 24 March. This was maintained not because of the European situation, but rather because a more specific commitment would evoke 'violent opposition' from certain quarters in Britain, and probably also in the dominions.[118] From Berlin Henderson used the same arguments as Halifax. On 22 August he wrote:

> We are on the worst of wickets and to go into battle, without having our Empire behind us—and we surely won't have it wholeheartedly on such an issue—seems to me inconceivable. I think, in spite of the humiliation, that I would rather almost anything than that.[119]

By the end of August United States sympathy too was not as forthcoming as might have been supposed from the speeches that Hull and Roosevelt had made earlier that month. The British information sent to the United States painted a grim and fatal situation. Halifax told Johnson that Hitler was 'for all practical purposes' a 'madman'. Lasting peace in

[115] *DBFP* 2, p. 149, No. 679, C8694/1941/18, Halifax to Lindsay, Telegram No. 701, 24.8.1938.

[116] *New York Times*, 17.8.1938, 20.8.1938, Ed.

[117] Elliott Roosevelt, Ed., *F.D.R. His Personal Letters. 1928–1945*, 2 (New York, 1950), pp. 810–11, Roosevelt to William Phillips in Rome, 15.9.1938.

[118] *DBFP* 2, pp. 158–9, No. 691, C8727/1941/18, Halifax to Campbell, No. 1915, 25.8.1938.

[119] Ibid., pp. 131–2, No. 665, C11048/1941/18, Henderson to Halifax, 22.8.1938.

Europe was impossible until the spirit of nazism had been killed in Germany. The British government had not then decided on a definite policy, but the contingency of a war lasting a few years was being entertained.[120]

On 30 August Kennedy saw Chamberlain and the ambassador said that he believed that if France and Britain were involved in war, the United States would follow before long. Kennedy also asked if there were anything that the United States or Roosevelt could do. The ambassador said further that he was convinced that Roosevelt had decided 'to go in with Chamberlain: whatever course Chamberlain decides to adopt I would think right'.[121]

But when Halifax saw Kennedy on 31 August the ambassador spoke in a different vein. Kennedy basing his opinions on information from Bullitt said that United States opinion did not think it necessary to plunge Europe into general war on account of German economic penetration. Halifax enquired what United States reaction would be to Europe standing aloof from a German invasion of Czechoslovakia. He hoped for United States silence on the subject. Faced with this predicament Kennedy asked Hull for advice as to how he should handle the British attitude.[122] The state department sent a rebuke: the public statements of Roosevelt and Hull 'accurately' reflected the United States attitude to the European and the world situation. It would 'not be practicable to be more specific as to our reaction in hypothetical circumstances'.[123]

On 30 August British policy was discussed at a meeting of ministers. Oliver Stanley and Duff Cooper were anxious to force the issue with Halifax. Halifax pointed out that the only effective deterrent against Hitler would be to declare that if Germany invaded Czechoslovakia Britain would declare war: such a move would only divide opinion in Britain and in the commonwealth. The foreign secretary did cede that Britain was concerned with the wider issue of dictator countries attaining their ends by force, but he doubted whether it was justifiable to fight a certain war then to forestall a possible war later.

Chamberlain supported his foreign secretary: if war were forced on Britain, Britain should do its best, but the strategic position seemed worse than it had been in May, as France was weaker and relations with Italy

120 *FRUS* 1938(1), pp. 549–51, 760F.62/597, Johnson to Hull, Telegram No. 815, 24.8.1938.
121 *F O 371*, 21734, pp. 357–62, C9158/1941/18, Minute by Wilson, 30.8.1938.
122 Ibid., pp 216–9, C9008/1941/18, Memorandum recording between Halifax and Kennedy, 31.8.1938; *FRUS* 1938(1), pp. 365–6, 760F 62/634, Kennedy to Hull, Telegram No. 846, 31.8.1938.
123 *FRUS* 1938(1), pp. 568–9, Kennedy Joseph P/109, Hull to Kennedy, Telegram No. 492, 1.9.1938.

had deteriorated. The prime minister was also worried about South Africa's reaction. He concluded:

> The policy of an immediate declaration or threat might well result in disunity, in this country, and in the Empire.

Warnings were also forthcoming from Lord Maugham, the lord chancellor. He pointed to the difficult situation in the far east, the likelihood of Italy's entry, and the uncertainty of reaction in India.

> He thought that the other members of the Commonwealth would be placed in a very difficult position and the position might lead to the break up of the Empire.

MacDonald, as secretary of state for colonies, was asked by Chamberlain to deal with the situation with regard to the dominions, as Lord Stanley was away in Canada. MacDonald considered the question of whether Britain should go to war if Czechoslovakia were invaded by Germany:

> Looking at the matter first solely from the point of view of the United Kingdom we should not go to war. Apart from considerations of military strength, we should be hampered by the opposition of a very large minority in this country. Indeed, before long it might be a majority and not a minority. It was also necessary to consider the point of view of the Dominions. It was extremely doubtful whether we had the *political* right (as contrasted with the constitutional right) to make a threat that in certain circumstances we should go to war, without consulting the other units of the British Commonwealth. This threat would in actual practice commit not only us, but at least certain of the Dominions. Australia and New Zealand would certainly follow our lead in declaring war. Constitutionally the other Dominions were bound to go to war if we did, but it was rather doubtful whether in fact they would do so in the case now envisaged.
>
> The result of consultation with the Dominions would probably, therefore, be that we should not be in a position to utter the threat. If, nevertheless, we made the threat, we should put a great strain on the loyalty of the Dominions and might break up the Commonwealth. The British Commonwealth of Nations and the United States of America together were the only force which could eventually check the progress of dictatorship; one day this combination might have to fight to defeat the growing evil. His Majesty's Government should not take a step now which would break the Commonwealth.

MacDonald further explained that the dominions had been informed of the events, but, until then, none had reacted. He did not doubt, however, that the dominions would be 'in favour of holding this country back'.

It is doubtful whether constitutional lawyers in South Africa and Canada would have agreed with MacDonald's view that, constitutionally, if Britain were at war, the commonwealth was at war, but his analysis of dominion reaction seems perceptive in the light of the views of the statesmen at the time.

Duff Cooper, in contrast, argued that the United States would be encouraged to keep out of further entanglements if Britain took no action in the face of aggression against Czechoslovakia.

Henderson, back from Berlin, told the meeting of ministers that he felt Hitler had not decided what steps he should take to settle the Sudeten German question. The ambassador warned that if Benes had not made his revised offers by the time of the Nuremburg meeting which was to take place between 5 and 12 September, Hitler would take the initiative and the Runciman mission would be 'left in the air'.

In the end the arguments of Chamberlain, Halifax and MacDonald were conceded, and the meeting of ministers decided that British policy should be based on Chamberlain's speech of 24 March, restated on 27 August by the chancellor of the exchequer at Lanark. Nothing was to be done to exacerbate German feeling and the usual manoeuvres were not to be brought forward. The French were to be urged to consult with the British before taking any action which might involve them in war. The dominions, however, were to be kept in the dark about the decisions reached at the meeting.[124]

At the time of the breakdown of the Runciman negotiations the British cabinet in making any decision on the Czechoslovakian situation had to take into account the reluctance, or refusal, of Canada, South Africa, and Australia to take part in European ventures. Practical support from the United States could also be discounted: it was probable that Roosevelt's Kingston address had meant as little as his Chicago speech ten months previously. United States opinion was isolationist. Roosevelt and Hull might want to educate the public away from isolationism, but the British had no assurance how far United States statesmen were prepared to go in this matter. As MacDonald had repeatedly warned the cabinet, the commonwealth and the United States were the only forces which could eventually check the dictators, and one day that combination might have to fight. It would have been unwise for the British government to guarantee Czechoslovakia at that time, as such a step might have broken up the commonwealth.

---

[124] *Cab 23*, 94, pp. 1–33, Notes of a Meeting of Ministers, Secret, 30.8.1938.

VI

BERCHTESGADEN, GODESBERG, AND MUNICH

Berchtesgaden, Godesberg, and Munich

APOLOGISTS writing about Munich cite dominion opinion as a decisive factor influencing British policy.[1] Critics discount this.[2] It should not be forgotten that Britain had responsibilities outside Europe. If Britain were to go to war, it first had to consider the attitude of the dominions, and even opinion in the United States.

On 1 September Hertzog composed a declaration of South African policy. It was neutrality. No one, however, would be allowed to use South African territory to infringe obligations, both with Britain and the commonwealth such as those arising from the Simonstown agreements, and those arising from membership of the league. At a meeting of the inner cabinet Smuts asked for time to consider the matter. He had Hertzog's assurance that this statement would only be used for a war fought over disputes in central and eastern Europe. The next day Smuts agreed to support Hertzog's policy.[3]

Mackenzie King anticipated war and was preparing for the possible summoning of parliament. Whether he was willing to advise a declaration of war is not clear.[4]

On 6 September the Australian government was cheered when Lyons spoke of his government doing all it could to support British efforts for peace.[5]

Information of the crisis was cabled to the dominions. By 6 September Australia was the only one that had expressed an official attitude. On 31 August the acting high commissioner in Australia wired that Lyons had summoned a cabinet meeting for 1 September. Lyons was conscious that a war involving Britain would, in fact, see Australia committed to active participation, but felt that the British government should not over-estimate the moral support in Australia for a conflict over Czechoslovakia:

---

[1] See, for example, Earl of Halifax, *Fullness of Days* (London, 1957), pp. 198, 204; Earl of Birkenhead, *Halifax* (London, 1965), p. 425; Lord Templewood, *Nine Troubled Years* (London, 1954), p. 323.

[2] Anthony Eden, *The Reckoning* (London, 1965), p. 24.

[3] Oswald Pirow, *James Barry Munnik Hertzog* (Cape Town, 1958), p. 226.

[4] *Mackenzie King Papers*, Mackenzie King to Tweedsmuir, 6.9.1938; Mackenzie King to Charles Dunning, 3.9.1938. Quoted by James Eayrs, *In Defence of Canada. Appeasement and Rearmament* (Toronto, 1965), p. 64.

[5] *Times*, 7.9.1938.

The Czechoslovakian problem is not a question on which war for the British Empire can justifiably be contemplated. . . . The present threat, if it should materialize, is better justified by a history of Czech repression, is not one obviously directed against British interests, and is likely to put the United Kingdom in a position where she strikes the first blow. . . . The oppression of the Roman Catholics [Lyons, a Roman Catholic, had strong views on this] and the barbarities of Germany to the Jews are horrifying, but they do not outweigh the fact that it would be a mistaken policy to treat the Sudeten issue as a *casus belli* heralding havoc for the British peoples. Mr. Lyons is aware of the clear language used towards France, . . . but still feels that he has reason to fear that the United Kingdom and with her the Commonwealth may awaken to find themselves involved in a war arising out of what might be viewed as a second-hand commitment via France's treaty obligations. The Labour Party here, in spite of all their open antagonism to dictator States would, he considers, wholly share these views.[6]

At the cabinet meeting Lyons's views prevailed. The cabinet disapproved of Benes:

In our opinion the Czechoslovak Government have not shown sufficient conciliation or offered concessions likely to satisfy the aspirations of the Sudeten Germans.[7]

Chamberlain assured Lyons that the British were giving the Australian views the most careful consideration.[8]

Kennedy, passing this information on to the state department, commented cynically that it would 'prove a useful lever in the hands of the British both internationally and in due course nationally *vis-à-vis* the opposition'.[9] On 7 September Mallet explained to Pierrepont Moffat his government's dilemma: if Britain stayed out of a war Germany would increase its strength. But even if there were a war the mistake of placing the Sudetens under the Czechs could not be repeated. Mallet's final argument was the one that Kennedy had anticipated:

It was becoming clearer that the Dominions were isolationist, and there could be no sense in fighting a war which would break the British Empire while trying to assure the safety of the United Kingdom.[10]

The British presented much the same point of view to the French. On 7 September Corbin told Halifax that Bonnet was anxious that Britain should make its position clear to Hitler. Halifax's excuse had not changed:

[6] *D O 114*, 94, pp. 44–5, Appendix II, No. 4, F82/95, Acting High Commissioner in Australia to Dominions Office, Telegram No. 165 Pts. 1 and 2, Secret, 31.8.1938 (paraphrase).

[7] Ibid., p. 45, No. 5, F82/100, Australian Government to British Government, Telegram No. 84, Secret, 1.9.1938 (cypher).

[8] Ibid., p. 45, No. 6, F82/104, Chamberlain to Lyons, Telegram No. 84, Secret, 3.9.1938.

[9] *Foreign Relations of the United States* (hereafter cited as '*FRUS*') 1938(1), pp. 577–8, 760 f.62/666, Kennedy to Hull, Telegram No. 869, 6.9.1938.

[10] Ibid., pp. 580–1, 760 F62/719, Memorandum by Moffat, 7.9.1938.

his government was 'constantly obliged to have regard to public opinion in this country and in the Empire'.[11] On 12 September Halifax was more emphatic. Bonnet had approached Phipps to ascertain how the British would react in the event of a German attack on Czechoslovakia, to a French inquiry: 'We are going to March, will you march with us?' Halifax explained that no answer could be given. Any decision would commit the dominions, and dominion governments would want to judge the circumstances for themselves.[12]

Britain kept in close touch with the United States.[13] Public announcements from the state department were not encouraging. The influential press suggested that the United States would provide the democracies with food, and possibly arms, against the dictators.[14] Roosevelt was sensitive to isolationist opinion. He lessened the impact of his Kingston address by blaming the press for creating the impression that he would assume moral commitments to support the democracies if there were a war against the dictators.[15] The ambiguity in United States policy persisted. The state department, on 10 September, made public the theoretical and rather meaningless terms on which Hull had accepted the invitation to the Pan American conference. Agitated isolationists immediately decided that Hull was moving towards United States participation.[16]

When the British cabinet were considering whether or not to send a strongly worded warning to Hitler, Kennedy was briefed of the changing policy.[17] On 10 September Halifax asked Kennedy about the state of United States opinion. Their accounts differ. According to Halifax Kennedy favoured the sending of a strong note to Hitler. If there were war the immediate reaction of the United States would be to keep out. But an event like the bombing of London would cause a revulsion of feeling, culminating in United States intervention.[18] Kennedy wired Hull that he had told Halifax that he did not know what United States reaction would be, except that it would want to stay out of war.[19] According to Lindsay United States opinion thought that Britain should take a strong stand

[11] *Documents on British Foreign Policy* 3rd Series (hereafter cited as '*DBFP*') 2, pp. 262–4, No. 798, C9408/1941/18, Halifax to Phipps, No. 2032, 7.9.1938.
[12] Ibid., p. 303, No. 843, C9818/1941/18, Halifax to Phipps, Unnumbered, 12.9.1938.
[13] *F O 414*, 275 Pt L, pp. 22–3, No. 11, A6875/1/45, Halifax to Lindsay, Telegram No. 734, 5.9.1938.
[14] *News Chronicle*, 10.9.1938; *Daily Telegraph*, 2.9.1938; 3.9.1938.
[15] *New York Times*, 10.9.1938.
[16] Whitney H. Shephardson and William O. Scroggs, *The United States in World Affairs, 1938* (New York, 1938), p. 67.
[17] *FRUS* 1938(1), pp. 584–5, 76OF.62/715, Kennedy to Hull, Telegram No. 891, 9.9.1938.
[18] *DBFP* 2, pp. 284–5, No. 824, C9512/1941/18, Halifax to Lindsay, Telegram No. 619, 10.9.1938.
[19] *FRUS* 1938(1), pp. 585–6,/780F.62/723, Kennedy to Hull, Telegram No. 893, 10.9.1938.

against German aggression. Compromise might 'bring about a certain let-down of American friendliness'. But this was not all important: 'If accommodation is really wise, we should be able to recover any ground lost.'[20]

Consideration of United States and dominion opinion was a factor in British policy during those weeks. Concern for the United States was not decisive. It could be argued that the dominions acted as a scapegoat for British policy. This case, however, would seem cynical in the light of earlier cabinet decisions on Czechoslovakia.

The cabinet met on 12 September to discuss the Czechoslovakian crisis. Halifax gave his diagnosis: Hitler was probably mad, and might have decided to attack Czechoslovakia. If this were the case there was nothing Britain could do to stop him.

The attitude of the dominions was discussed: MacDonald mentioned that Australia was the only dominion which had sent any comment, but that generally the attitude of the dominions had been as forecast at the meeting of ministers on 30 August. Halifax had been warned by Massey that the majority of Canadians would be against any forward action, in the hope that Britain would not be involved in war. The position with regard to the French was awkward: MacDonald pointed out that there would only be a short time in which to decide what line to take should France mobilise and declare war.

> It was clear that the decision taken by H.M. Government committed the Empire. Difficulties would arise if we reached a decision without allowing time for what the Dominions would regard as reasonable consultation in the circumstances.[21]

From 12 September to 1 October care was taken to keep the dominions informed of British policy. MacDonald even said that the dominions had more information at their disposal than members of the cabinet. One hundred and forty telegrams were sent to dominion governments and 14 meetings were held with dominion representatives. The meetings in London were attended by the high commissioners for Canada (who was given special authority by his government to attend these meetings), South Africa, and Ireland. The high commissioner for Australia, Bruce, was attending the league assembly in Geneva, and was represented by the official secretary until he returned on 14 September. Jordan could not

[20] *DBFP* 2, p. 301, No. 841, C9711/1941/18, Lindsay to Halifax, Telegram No. 342, 12.9.1938 r. 13.9.1938; *F O 371*, 21737, pp. 259–61, C9711/1941/18, Lindsay to Halifax, Telegram No. 342, 12.9.1938 r. 13.9.1938 r. in r. 14.9.1938 (cypher).

[21] *Cab 23*, 95, pp. 9–35, Cab 37 (38), Secret, 12.9.1938.

leave Geneva as he was president of the council. New Zealand was represented by the secretary to the high commissioner's office, Sandford, until 27 September, and by Jordan after that. The minister who headed the British delegation at the assembly of the league, Lord de la Warr, also had three meetings with dominion delegates. The dominion high commissioners were supplied with copies of all the telegrams to their governments, and arrangements were also made for the delivery of these copies to the high commissioners' private addresses out of office hours and at week ends. Two copies were sent to Dulanty so that he could forward one to de Valera at Geneva by foreign office bag.[22]

MacDonald met the dominion representatives on 12 September before Hitler spoke at Nuremberg. MacDonald said that Germany might attack Czechoslovakia. Britain would be involved if France were, as British interests were affected by a threat to French security. Before taking action the French would consult the British. Britain would have to ascertain the views of the dominions. MacDonald suggested that the dominions might be informed of the cabinet's decision by telegram, and might be asked to reply by a certain time. He told te Water that the cabinet decision would be tentative, pending dominion reactions. Dulanty and te Water explained their governments' probable views. De Valera had said that Ireland should aim at 'friendly neutrality'. Dulanty thought that a German bombing of London might be considered as an attack on the security of Ireland. He doubted whether a threat to French security would be so regarded.[23] R. L. Speaight of the foreign office minuted, perhaps misguidedly: 'This really amounts to the same as saying that she wd. [*sic*] be with us all along'.[24]

Te Water said that his government would try to persuade Britain not to defend France until France was in danger of being overwhelmed, this being regarded as a threat to Britain.[25] R. L. Speaight noted that te Water made no mention of South Africa's support, but felt that it could be inferred that South Africa would participate in the circumstances outlined by te Water.[26] I. Mallet noted, however, that if te Water's conditions were fulfilled, Britain might be too late to save itself.[27]

[22] *D O 114*, 94, pp. 3–4, Memoranda General.

[23] Ibid., pp. 21–3, Appendix I, No. 7, F82/146, Note of Meeting between MacDonald and Dominion Representatives, Secret, 12.9.1938.

[24] *F O 371*, 21738, pp. 206–19, C10023/1941/18, Garner to Hoyer Millar, 14.9.1938; No. 5 at Flag A, Minute by R. L. Speaight, 19.9.1938.

[25] *D O 114*, 94, pp. 21–3, Appendix I, No. 7, F82/146, Note of Meeting between MacDonald and Dominion Representatives, Secret, 12.9.1938.

[26] *F O 371*, 21738, pp. 206–19, C10023/1941/18, Garner to Hoyer Millar, 14.9.1938; No. 5 at Flag A, Minute by R. L. Speaight, 19.9.1938.

[27] Ibid., Minute by I. Mallet, 20.9.1938.

Hitler's speech at Nuremberg, though 'brutal and bombastic' was not a declaration of war.[28]

The commonwealth press was vociferous in its comment. In Australia the Melbourne *Sun* noted that Hitler had thrown the onus for finding a way out of the difficulties onto the other powers. New Zealand press comment was depressed. The Canadian Ottawa *Journal* was thankful for a breathing space while the Toronto *Globe and Mail* was pessimistic. In South Africa Hitler's speech caused little comment and no questions.[29]

De la Warr met the dominion delegates at Geneva on 12 September. He explained that there were three brakes on British policy: British public opinion; the danger of any automatic commitment which might mean foreign governments controlling British policy; and public opinion in the commonwealth.

> If the United Kingdom should eventually be drawn into a war, they wished to make absolutely certain first that the action of the United Kingdom Government received the approval of public opinion throughout the Empire.

Should there be a major war in Europe de la Warr thought that Britain would inevitably be involved.

On this point the dominion representatives were not encouraging. Bruce of Australia and Lapointe of Canada approved the British role of peace maker. Bruce was anxious that Benes might step out of line. Only New Zealand gave unqualified support.[30]

After Hitler's Nuremberg speech the situation deteriorated rapidly On 13 September, about 3 p.m., 'things began rattling down to war'. There were reports of German troop movements and fighting in Czechoslovakia. Daladier tried to telephone Chamberlain, but the prime minister would not speak to him. Daladier told Phipps that Germany should be prevented from invading Czechoslovakia, because in that case France would be faced with its obligations.[31] Inskip recorded in his diary:

> This seemed to appal Daladier. Similar reports had come from other sources to me. Everything showed that the French didn't want to fight, were not fit to fight, and wouldn't fight.[32]

---

[28] William L. Shirer, *The Rise and Fall of the Third Reich* (London, 1964), p. 469.

[29] *Manchester Guardian*, 14.9.1938.

[30] *D O 114*, 94, pp. 56–8, Appendix III, No. 1, F82/168, Note of Meeting of de la Warr with Dominion and Indian Delegations at Geneva, 12.9.1938.

[31] *Inskip Papers* 1, pp. 8–10, Diary, 12.9.1938 (copy); *Cab 23*, 95, pp. 37–8, Cab 38 (38), Secret, 14.9.1938.

[32] *Inskip Papers* 1, pp. 9–10, Diary, 12.9.1938 (copy).

In the evening Konrad Henlein, the leader of the Sudeten Germans, informed Benes that unless he recalled his police negotiations would be Broken off. Benes refused, and Henlein stopped negotiations.[33]

In these circumstances Chamberlain, in consultation with Halifax, Simon, and Templewood, decided to put plan 'Z' into operation.[34] Chamberlain had conceived this idea during the last days of August.[35] He thought that he might offer to go to Germany to see Hitler. Inskip was tepid about the proposal. Vansittart fought the idea: 'it was Henry IV going to Canossa over again'. MacDonald and Kingsley Wood were also consulted before 8 September. Henderson thought that it might do some good.[36] Chamberlain did not consult the full cabinet on 13 September as there was no time.[37]

When Chamberlain explained the situation to the cabinet on 14 September MacDonald supported him. MacDonald had seen te Water who had said that all rested in Britain's hands: 'We alone could influence the Germans now, and we had the man to influence them—the Prime Minister.'[38] On 13 September te Water had argued for a plebiscite: in that case Britain should 'insist' that the Germans should not use force. The French should be held to Bonnet's statement that France would not fight against a plebiscite.[39] The next day, however, te Water had moderated his attitude: Britain need not make the threat to go to war with Germany clear at once.[40] MacDonald, at the cabinet meeting, argued that there would be 'tremendous support for a plebiscite now, if the only alternative was war'. He felt that opinion was almost certainly shared by the dominions and cited a telegram from the acting high commissioner in Australia which said that opinion in that country would prefer almost any course to war.[41]

Before flying to Berchtesgaden Chamberlain saw a report from the chiefs of staff which reaffirmed their view that no pressure that Britain or France could bring to bear could prevent Germany defeating Czechoslovakia. The war would be an unlimited war with Britain receiving between 500–600 tons of bombs a day for two months against being able

33 Ibid., *loc. cit.*; *Cab 23*, 95, p. 38, Cab 38 (38), Secret, 14.9.1938.

34 *Cab 23*, 95, p. 38, Cab 38 (38), Secret, 14.9.1938.

35 *Zetland Papers* 10, p. 56, Zetland to Brabourne, Private, 16–20.10.1938.

36 *Inskip Papers* 1, p. 5, Diary, 8.9.1938 (copy).

37 *Templewood Papers* XIX (C) 11, Chamberlain to Hilda Chamberlain, 13.9.1938. (copy); *Cab 23*, 95, p. 38, Cab 38 (38), Secret, 14.9.1938.

38 *Cab 23*, 95, p. 54, Cab 38 (38), Secret, 14.9.1938.

39 *D O 114*, 94, pp. 23–4, Appendix I, No. 8, F82/146, Note by MacDonald of a Conversation with te Water, Secret, 13.9.1938.

40 Ibid., p. 24, No. 9, F82/146, Note by MacDonald of a Conversation with te Water, 14.9.1938.

41 *Cab 23*, 95, p. 54, Cab 38 (38), Secret, 14.9.1938.

only to deliver 100 tons, and together with France, 200 tons.[42] Chamberlain knew that he had the support of some of the dominions.

The Canadian government, led by an enthusiastic Mackenzie King, approved. On 13 September the Canadian cabinet refused to indicate an attitude.[43] That day Massey, for the first time since his posting in 1935, telephoned Ottawa, to say how seriously the British government regarded the Sudeten disturbances.[44] Mackenzie King not only sent a personal message to Chamberlain expressing his 'admiration for the vision and courage shown in your decision to have a personal interview with Hitler'[45] and his cabinet's 'deep satisfaction' with this move,[46] but also took the unprecedented step of publicising his views.[47] This was, however, support for the appeasement of Europe. On 8 September, Loring Christie, second only to Skelton in the Canadian department of external affairs, had written a memorandum suggesting only a 'qualified' Canadian participation in a war over the Sudetenland. The Canadian government should 'give no lead to take the people into Europe'.[48] On 15 September Massey saw MacDonald and told him that Canadians would support te Water's views on a plebiscite.[49] Barrington-Ward of *The Times*, lunching with Massey on 16 September, found the high commissioner opposed to a world war fought to keep dissident minorities under Czech rule. The next day Massey spoke of the 'timid and isolationist Canadian Government' and the 'inert Mackenzie King'.[50]

The acting high commissioner in Canada, however, did report on 16 September that there were no signs that the Canadian government was trying to shelter behind Roosevelt's Kingston declaration, and to press for a policy of neutrality and isolation from European affairs in collaboration with the United States.[51]

Mackenzie King also contacted Ribbentrop in the hope that the German minister would let Hitler know that the Canadian prime minister believed

---

[42] *Inskip Papers* 1, p. 11, Diary, 14.9.1938 (copy).

[43] *Times*, 15.9.1938.

[44] Vincent Massey, *What's Past is Prologue* (London, 1963), p. 258.

[45] Eayrs, p. 65; *D O 114*, 94, p. 46, Appendix III, No. 8, F82/130, Mackenzie King to Chamberlain, Telegram No. 43, 14.9.1938 r. 15.9.1938.

[46] *Times*, 15.9.1938.

[47] Ibid., 16.9.1938.

[48] *Christie Papers*, Notes on the Canadian Position in the Event of a German-Czech Conflict involving Great Britain, 8.9.1938. Quoted by Eayrs, p. 72.

[49] *D O 114*, 94, p. 24, Appendix I, No. 10, F82/147, Note by MacDonald of an Interview with Massey, 15.9.1938.

[50] Anonymous, *The History of the Times. The 150th Anniversary and Beyond 1219–1948*, 4 Pt 2, (London, 1952), p. 759.

[51] *F O 371*, 21778, pp. 362–6, C11285/5302/18, F82/218, Dominions Office to Foreign Office, 28.9.1938 r. 1.10.1938; Transmitting Mason to Devonshire, 16.9.1938.

that the efforts of the führer would 'serve to preserve and further the peace of the world'.[52] Henderson delivered the message, and reported to Mackenzie King that it had been 'most useful and timely'.[53]

The Australian government supported the British moves for peace, but did not offer to help in case of war. On 11 September Menzies returned from his European trip. He urged Australians not to take sides too hastily over Czechoslovakia, and spoke sympathetically about Germany's feeling of injustice.[54] Menzies's views presumably carried weight in the cabinet, as he was the only leading Australian to have had contact with Germany. Lyons welcomed the Berchtesgaden flight, and personally telegrammed his commendation to Chamberlain. Curtin also commended Chamberlain's gesture.[55] The tenor of Australian press comment was that if this pilgrimage of peace failed the nazis could be branded for the war.[56] The labour executive carried a resolution reaffirming the party's principle to resist any attempt to involve Australia in a European war, and appointed an emergency committee.[57] Labour's fears had no foundation. On 5 October Menzies assured the opposition that Australia had made no commitment to Britain.[58]

New Zealand was fully behind Britain. Savage praised Chamberlain for 'an outstanding appreciation of the responsibilities of his high office'.[59] On 16 September Mr. A. Hamilton, the leader of the opposition, assured the government of the opposition's co-operation if the commonwealth were involved in war.[60] Press comment in the dominion was in favour of Chamberlain taking a firm stand against Hitler.[61]

Hertzog maintained his silence. There was some agitation in the lobbies of the houses of parliament but the tone of the South African press was one of relief, and in some cases of pessimism. The nationalists argued that South Africa was not concerned.[62]

---

[52] *Mackenzie King Papers*, Mackenzie King to Ribbentrop, Telegram, 14.9.1938. Quoted by Eayrs p. 65.
[53] Eayrs, p. 65.
[54] *West Australian*, 13.9.1938; *Times*, 15.9.1938.
[55] *Times*, 16.9.1938; *D O 114*, 94, p. 46, Appendix II, No. 7, F82/133, Acting High Commissioner in Australia to British Government, Telegram Most Secret, 15.9.1938 r. 14.9.1938 (cypher).
[56] *Manchester Guardian*, 16.9.1938; *West Australian*, 16.9.1938, Ed.; *Sydney Morning Herald*, 16.9.1938, Ed.; Anonymous, 'Overseas Reactions to the Crisis: Australia', *Round Table*, XXIX (1938–9), pp. 44–9.
[57] *Sydney Morning Herald*, 17.9.1938; *Times*, 17.9.1938.
[58] *Aust Parl Deb* 1938–9 157, H of R, cols. 430–1, 5.10.1938.
[59] *Times*, 16.9.1938.
[60] *Manchester Guardian*, 17.9.1938.
[61] Ibid., 16.9.1938.
[62] *Times*, 16.9.1938; *Daily Telegraph*, 14.9.1938; 16.9.1938; *Manchester Guardian*, 15.9.1938; 16.9.1938.

Hitler eventually did send a telegram to Chamberlain on 17 September saying that South Africa 'very sincerely appreciates and admires the step which you have taken, convinced as we are that it will be more material contribution towards general appeasement.'[63]

De Valera was enthusiastic.[64] He wrote to Chamberlain that he was 'completely satisfied that you are doing the right thing'.[65]

Opinion in the United States reacted favourably to Chamberlain's mission. The *Sunday Times* correspondent concluded that the Berchtesgaden flight had brought United States public opinion 'into accord with Britain at the time which counts'.[66] United States officialdom was silent.[67] Kennedy, however, arranged for United States warships on a visit to Britain to move up to London.[68] He was also happy to read the evening paper at 10 Downing Street if Chamberlain were too busy to see him to give the impression that the United States was in full sympathy with Britain.[69] On 12 September J. Balfour of the foreign office suggested that with the friendly disposition of Roosevelt, Britain might address a general appeal to the United States when there was no further hope of averting war.[70] Lindsay was instructed that upon receipt of emergency instructions, he should use his discretion as to whether Roosevelt should be asked not to apply the neutrality act.[71]

Chamberlain met Hitler in his mountain lair on 15 September, and told the cabinet on 17 September: 'it was impossible not to be impressed with the power of the man'.[72] The führer was assured that Chamberlain accepted the principal of self determination for the Sudeten Germans. Chamberlain, however, saw practical difficulties on the way of a plebiscite, and suggested that he return to England for further consultations.[73]

When Chamberlain returned to London on 16 September, the dominions were told that the situation was 'enigmatical and must be so treated'. The British cabinet then met. After the meeting the dominion prime ministers

[63] *D O 114*, 94, p. 46, Appendix II, No. 9, F82/148, Hertzog to Chamberlain, Telegram No. 18, Secret, 17.9.1938 (paraphrase).
[64] Duff Cooper, *Old Men Forget* (London, 1953), p. 229.
[65] *Chamberlain Papers*, De Valera to Chamberlain, 15.9.1938. Quoted by Keith Feiling, *The Life of Neville Chamberlain* (London, 1946), p. 364.
[66] *Sunday Times*, 18.9.1938.
[67] *New York Times*, 18.9.1938; 19.9.1938.
[68] *Cab 23*, 95, p. 9, Cab 37 (38), Secret, 12.9.1938; *Inskip Papers* 1, Diary, 12.9.1938 (copy).
[69] *Zetland Papers* 10, pp. 50–3, Zetland to Brabourne, Private, 13.9.1938.
[70] *F O 371*, 21543, pp. 227–31, A7125/7125/45, Foreign Office Minute by J. Balfour, 12.9.1938.
[71] Ibid., pp. 230–1, Foreign Office to Lindsay, Telegram No. 10 Saving by Bag, Secret, 13.9.1938.
[72] *Cab 23*, 95, p. 72, Cab 39 (38), Secret, 17.9.1938.
[73] *DBFP* 2, pp. 338–41, No. 895, C10084/1941/18, Notes by Chamberlain of his Conversation with Hitler, 15.9.1938.

were sent fuller information: Chamberlain felt that Hitler was prepared to use force to incorporate the Sudeten territories; the British cabinet had decided to support self determination for the Sudeten Germans.[74]

At this cabinet meeting on the afternoon of 17 September Duff Cooper argued against Chamberlain: he said that it was in the British interest to resist German domination of Europe.

> At the present time, the country was singularly united, and the dominions would probably be more attracted by the idea of supporting the democratic countries in a fight against the dictators than they were by the issues with which we were faced in 1914. . . . He was afraid that Germany might make some attempt on our Colonial Empire, and that on such an issue neither France nor the United States would rally to our help.

In contrast Viscount Hailsham, the lord chancellor, felt that the position of the empire had to be considered: the congress party in India might take advantage of the position; there might be an Arab revolt in Asia; and armed neutrality, if not war, on the part of Japan. Zetland also pointed out that Britain should not overplay the issue of self determination as the congress party might take advantage of such a declaration.[75]

MacDonald told the dominion high commissioners the same day that there was a chance that something less than a plebiscite or an immediate transfer of territory might be accepted. The representatives did not express any decisive opinions.[76]

Chamberlain asked Kennedy on 17 September if agreement were reached on the principle of self determination and orderly elections, whether the United States would join with other countries in protecting peace and order. No immediate reply was expected.[77]

The question of a British guarantee to Czechoslovakia became important. At the Anglo-French conversations held in London on 18 September Halifax used the usual argument about limitations on British policy. The direction of British policy could not be placed in the hands of another country. This had added force in that 'although this was not the strict legal position, we also spoke in fact for the Dominions in undertaking any commitments'.[78] At these conversations the British and French agreed

---

[74] *Cab 23*, 95, p. 76, Cab 39 (38), Secret, 17.9.1938; Eayrs, pp. 66–7.

[75] *Cab 23*, 95, pp. 87–111, Cab 39 (38), Secret, 17.9.1938.

[76] *D O 114*, 94, pp. 25–6, Appendix I, No. 12, F82/171, Note of a Discussion between MacDonald and Dominion Representatives, Most Secret, 17.9.1938.

[77] *FRUS* 1938(1), pp. 609–12, 760F.62/891, Kennedy to Hull, Telegram No. 960, 17.9.1938.

[78] *DBFP* 2, pp. 373–400 at p. 394, No. 928, C10729/1941/18, Record of Anglo-French Conversations on 18 September 1938.

that the Czechoslovaks disliked the idea of a plebiscite. Chamberlain suggested it might be preferable to make it appear that Czechoslovakia had had the choice, and had opted for territorial cession. As a concession he agreed to an international guarantee of the new Czechoslovakia.[79]

MacDonald told the cabinet on 19 September that normally 'a guarantee of this kind should not be undertaken, even on behalf of the United Kingdom alone, without a prior consultation with the Dominions'. The dominions would have to be informed, but he thought they could raise no objection. The lord president of the council thought that the guarantee would be impossible to carry out' and might make a wedge between us and the Dominions, who would not accept such an obligation'.[80]

MacDonald saw the dominion high commissioners the same day and explained that the idea of a plebiscite had fallen into the background. Normally Britain would not have made a firm offer of a guarantee in central Europe without informing the dominions in advance, and giving them adequate time to consent. Because of the attitude of the French there had been no time. The dominion representatives did not criticise this. Bruce urged that the dominions should participate in the proposed guarantee, though he ceded that this was unlikely. Te Water made it clear that South Africa would not participate. MacDonald suggested that South Africa might want assistance from European countries if Germany were to attack South West Africa. It might be a wise policy for South Africa to show more interest in opposing aggression in Europe.[81]

MacDonald saw Bruce afterwards and said that he recognised that none of the dominions would be likely to bind themselves beforehand to support Britain if it were forced to carry out a guarantee to a reconstituted Czechoslovakia. Even if Lyons were to do this MacDonald anticipated that the labour opposition in Australia would agitate and split the country. In the next general election labour might well become the government and repudiate the obligation. Bruce agreed that this was the position. MacDonald, however, hoped for an approving speech by Lyons and Savage to avoid the suggestion of commonwealth disapproval.[82]

---

[79] Ibid., pp. 373–400.

[80] *Cab 23*, 95, pp. 124–5, Cab 40 (38), Secret, 19.9.1938.

[81] *D O 114*, 94, pp. 27–8, Appendix I, No. 13, F82/171, Note of Discussion between MacDonald and Dominion Representatives, Most Secret, 17.9.1938.

[82] Ibid., pp. 28–9, No. 14, F82/166, Note by MacDonald of a Conversation with Bruce, Secret and Important, 19.9.1938.

On 20 September dominion delegates at Geneva did not criticise British policy either.[83]

A guarantee to Czechoslavakia was given without dominion consultation, because of pressure from the French. The dominions did not disapprove. They were not bound by the British guarantee. The dominions were not used by Chamberlain as a scapegoat for British policy.

The United States administration maintained its silence. But on 19 September Roosevelt had a secret meeting with Lindsay, so secret that not even the state department were to know of it. The president described the Anglo-French note to Czechoslovakia as 'the most terrible remorseless sacrifice that had ever been demanded of a state'. He predicted that it would cause 'a highly unfavourable reaction' in the United States. Roosevelt did not blame the British or French governments for the stand that they had taken, and if Chamberlain's policy were successful he would be 'the first to cheer'. The president did not know what he could do to help: he dare not publicly approve the recommendations put to the Czechoslovak government; if he condemned German aggression it might encourage Czechoslovakia to make a vain resistance. Considerations such as these were responsible for his public attitude of 'no comment'.

Roosevelt was not hopeful about the immediate future: if there were war he anticipated that the allies might be defeated. He did suggest a possible alternative, but it should never be known where the idea had originated as that might lead to his impeachment. Assuming that expedients would only delay the crisis, the western powers might call a world conference to reorganise unsatisfactory frontiers on rational lines. Heads of states, including Hitler, should be invited. Roosevelt said that he would attend provided that the conference did not sit in Europe.

If the western powers did go to war Roosevelt had a scheme for carrying it on purely by blockade and in a defensive manner. Overtones of sanctions should be avoided:

> Blockade must be based on loftiest humanitarian grounds and on the desire to wage hostilities with minimum of suffering and the least possible loss of life and property, and yet to bring the enemy to his knees.

War by blockade would meet with approval in the United States if the humanitarian purpose were emphasised. He could not take the initiative but it was the constitutional prerogative of the president to declare a

---

[83] Ibid., p. 59, Appendix III, No. 2, F302/13, Note of a Meeting of de la Warr with Dominion and Indian Delegations at Geneva, 20.9.1938.

blockade effective, and he could then, under the neutrality act, forbid United States vessels to enter a danger zone except at their own risk. Roosevelt was hesitant about the possibility of the United States government turning a blind eye to any evasion of the prohibition of exports of arms and ammunition in Britain's favour. He did, however, suggest that the western powers could overcome this difficulty by not declaring war on Germany. They could call their action defensive measures or something plausible. Even if Germany declared war on Britain, provided Britain did not reciprocate, he might then be able to find that Britain was not at war, and so avoid applying the arms prohibition.

Throughout the conversation Roosevelt was dubious about the likelihood of the United States taking any action. The president was alive to the possibility that in indefinable circumstances the United States might again find itself involved in a European war. So strong was isolationist opinion that even in such a case he thought it 'almost inconceivable' that he would be able to send United States troops across the Atlantic. If Britain were invaded, however, it was possible that a wave of emotion would send the United States army overseas.[84]

Just before Godesberg Halifax and Chamberlain knew how far Roosevelt would go if there were war. The most the British could hope for was a benevolent neutrality.[85] On 23 September Halifax wired Lindsay that he anticipated if there were a war, Britain's main role would be the enforcement of a blockade, along the lines that the president had suggested. In this the position of Italy would be crucial: it might be necessary to choose between a neutral Italy with an ineffective blockade and a hostile Italy with an effective blockade.[86] Duff Cooper was probably over optimistic in his assessment of United States support when, at a cabinet meeting on 21 September he urged Chamberlain to go to war. If the war were to stop Hitler from dominating Europe the United States 'would come in on our side'.[87] Newton urged from Prague on 21 September that the United States be approached to help 'sweeten the pill' for the Benes government by making it clear that they thought acceptance of the terms in Czechoslovakia's best interests.[88]

[84] *F O 371*, 21527, pp. 346ff., A7504/64/45, No. 349, Lindsay to Foreign Office, Telegram, Most Secret and Important, 19.9.1938.

[85] Ibid., Minute by Foreign Office Official, 3.10.1938.

[86] *DBFP* 7, p. 629, Appendix IV(vi), A7504/64/45, Lindsay to Halifax, Telegram No. 351, 21.9.1938 r. 22.9.1938; p. 630, Appendix IV(vii), Halifax to Lindsay, Telegram No. 640, 23.9.1938.

[87] *Cab 23*, 95, p. 160, Cab 40 (39), Secret, 21.9.1938.

[88] *DBFP* 2, p. 439, No. 994, C10288/1941/18, Newton to Halifax, Telegram No. 671, 21.9.1938.

In the United States the press from Atlantic to Pacific denounced the reported British and French decision to hand over the Sudetenland to Hitler.[89]

Press opinion in the dominions was not much more favourable, but it did not divide along predictable lines. In South Africa the *Cape Argus*, and the Johannesburg *Star* and *Rand Daily Mail*, were hostile to the idea of proposals. In Australia the *Sydney Morning Herald* found itself in company with the socialist *Labor Daily*, which no longer reflected the official attitude of the labour party, in its criticism.[90] The acting high commissioner in Australia reported that public opinion was ready to support Britain over the session of the Sudeten areas, but there was a growing apprehension that unless it was clear that Germany would be halted, the plan 'will certainly fail to save us from a war on which we shall have to embark after suffering "a staggering blow to British prestige" '.[91]

Comment in the New Zealand press was consistent with the government's policy: it was restrained, or damnatory, but never enthusiastic.[92]

The Canadian English language press varied. The Canadian government approved the cession of the Sudetenland to Germany, and relied on Chamberlain's methods and motives: 'They are regarded as designed to promote world peace and merit support, even though the terms may be considered very high.'[93]

In India Jawaharlal Nehru, the former president of the Indian congress, announced: 'The people of India have no intention of submitting to any foreign decision on war'. Some of the princes, however, offered their services to the British in case of war.[94]

After Berchtesgaden opinion in the dominions was clearly divided. Judging from press comment it would seem that in each dominion there were people who were prepared to fight. The dominion governments, however, were more likely to be sensitive to those sections opposed to foreign commitments.

By 21 September the Czechs had been browbeaten into accepting the British and French proposals. But, as MacDonald explained to the high

---

[89] *Daily Telegraph*, 20–23.9.1938; *News Chronicle*, 20.9.1938; *Manchester Guardian*, 22.9.1938.

[90] *Daily Telegraph*, 20–23.9.1938; *News Chronicle*, 22.9.1938; *Manchester Guardian*, 20.9.1938; *Sydney Morning Herald*, 20.9.2938, Ed.; *Labor Daily*, 16.9.1938, Ed; 20.9.1938, Ed.

[91] *D O 114*, 94, pp. 47–8, Appendix II, No. 11, F82/173, Acting High Commissioner in Australia to Dominions Office, Telegram No. 184, 21.9.1938 (cypher).

[92] *Daily Telegraph*, 22–3.9.1938.

[93] Ibid., *loc. cit.*; *News Chronicle*, 22.9.1938.

[94] *Manchester Guardian*, 20.9.1938; 23.9.1938.

commissioners on that day, it was likely that Poland and Hungary would put forward claims on behalf of their minorities in Czechoslovakia. Bruce pointed to the need for a wider settlement and safeguards against further aggression by Germany.[95]

De la Warr explained to the dominion delegates at Geneva on 22 September that the cabinet had felt it necessary to 'ride the horse' of peace to the last moment. Lapointe of Canada liked this reference. Jordan was cynical: the proposals merely attempted to show that Chamberlain had been successful.[96]

Chamberlain flew to Godesberg on 22 September. The prime minister had anticipated a cession of the Sudetenland in line with the agreed formula. Hitler conceded only that German troops could be withdrawn from the mixed areas in Czechoslovakia, after a plebiscite in these areas. A new frontier would be established by Germany on 1 October. A plebiscite would take place by 25 November at latest. Chamberlain met Hitler again at 11 p.m. on 23 September to discuss the proposal.[97]

Reports of the Godesberg proceedings caused a reaction in London.[98] The role of the dominion high commissioners assumed new importance: they tried to determine British policy. It could be said that the high commissioners in London formulated what was closest to a common commonwealth foreign policy, and were more effective collectively in influencing British policy than the individual dominion leaders.

On the night of 22 September Massey was woken with the news that a telegram had been circulated to the dominion capitals that Hitler's attitude had been unsatisfactory.[99] MacDonald explained this to the dominion high commissioners the next day: Hitler's insistence upon the occupation of the Sudetenland by German troops was 'a challenge to the whole principle of peaceful negotiations'. This aroused speculation that the führer was a man of wider and more dangerous ambitions than he had admitted to Chamberlain at Berchtesgaden.

Only Bruce supported a stand on the basis of the principle of negotiation against force being the method of settling international questions. Te Water doubted whether the occupation of the Sudeten areas by

95 *D O 114*, 94, p. 29, Appendix I, No. 15, F82/208, Note of a Discussion between MacDonald and Dominion Representatives, Most Secret, 21.9.1938.

96 Ibid., pp. 59–61, Appendix III, No. 3, F82/250, Note of a Meeting of de la Warr with the Dominion and Indian Delegations at Geneva, 22.9.1938.

97 Keith Robbins, *Munich 1938* (London, 1968), pp. 281–5.

98 Ibid., p. 285.

99 Massey, p. 259.

German troops should be regarded as a question of principle, and suggested a compromise on methods.[100] Chamberlain afterwards took special note of te Water's view.[101] Dulanty and Massey agreed with te Water. MacDonald said that he shared Bruce's views, but that there was still the possibility of compromise. The New Zealand representative did not speak.[102]

At a meeting at 3.00 p.m. of the inner cabinet of Halifax, Simon and, Templewood—which for the previous week had discussed policy though not necessarily decided it—MacDonald explained the high commissioners' views. Commonwealth support would be less likely over Czechoslovakia than if the issue were French security.[103]

When Chamberlain met Hitler at 11 p.m. on 23 September the führer did make minor concessions: the supervisory commission was to be international, and the dateline advanced to 1 October.[104] Hitler's Godesberg memorandum was circulated to the high commissioners at noon on 24 September.[105] Bruce and Massey found it vaguely encouraging, and te Water asked whether it would be possible to restrain Czechoslovakia. MacDonald pointed out that much depended on Hitler's map, not then available, and on Chamberlain's opinion of Hitler's intentions.[106]

Chamberlain gave his account to the cabinet at 5.30 p.m. on 24 September. He was sure that Hitler was anxious to secure the friendship of Britain and was not aiming for the domination of Europe, but only racial unity. The colonial question was outstanding, but was no cause for war. Chamberlain saw no chance of getting a peaceful solution on any lines other than those proposed.

> That morning he had flown up the river over London. He had imagined a German bomber flying the same course. He had asked himself what degree of protection we could afford to the thousands of homes which he had seen stretched out below him, and he had felt that we were in no position to justify waging a war to-day in order to prevent a war hereafter.

Duff Cooper was not impressed: he favoured general mobilisation.[107]

[100] *D O 114*, 94, pp. 30–1, Appendix I, No. 16, F82/208, Note of a Discussion between MacDonald and Dominion Representatives, Most Secret, 23.9.1938.
[101] *Premier 1*, 242, p. 47, Meeting of MacDonald and Dominion High Commissioners, 23.9.1938. The Relevant Paragraph is marked.
[102] *D O 114*, 94, pp. 30–1, Appendix I, No. 16, F82/208, Note of a Discussion between MacDonald and Dominion Representatives, Most Secret, 23.9.1938.
[103] *Cab 27*, 646, pp. 81–2, C S (38) 11, Meeting of Ministers, Secret Lock and Key, 23.9.1938.
[104] Robbins, pp. 286–7.
[105] *D O 114*, 94, pp. 31–2, Appendix I, No. 17, F82/220, Note of a Discussion between MacDonald and Dominion Representatives, Most Secret, 24.9.1938.
[106] Ibid., *loc. cit.*
[107] *Cab 23*, 95, pp. 179–84, Cab 42 (38), 24.9.1938.

The dominion high commissioners were told at 8.30 p.m. of Chamberlain's report to the cabinet. According to the official minutes MacDonald asked the high commissioners how opinion in their dominions would react to an acceptance of the German proposals. Te Water forecast some division of opinion in South Africa, but said that Chamberlain's prestige was so high that it would carry public opinion in support of the proposals. Massey and Dulanty did not foresee difficulties in their countries. Bruce suggested that the dominant consideration in Australia would be fear of the aftermath. Sandford referred to Savage's speech saying that New Zealand would be involved in war if Britain were at war:

> New Zealand was generally in favour of protecting small nations. If the principle of cession were accepted New Zealand would not be greatly concerned as to the method of giving effect to it.

According to the official minutes the high commissioners personally were in favour of the proposals being accepted.[108] Massey's diary suggests that the high commissioners took a rather different view from MacDonald:

> We are all prepared to pay a higher price for peace than he. [MacDonald] The difference is because the Dominions are removed further away from Europe not because our sense of honour is less acute. Bruce, whose government uses him (unlike mine in relation to their H.C.) feels very strongly that the German proposals *can't* be allowed to be a *casus belli* and says so on behalf of his Govt. Te Water and Dulanty speak with great vehemence as well. I take the same line but of course as an individual.[109]

At 10.30 a.m. on 25 September MacDonald explained to the cabinet that te Water, Dulanty, and Massey all felt that Britain had accepted the principle of a transfer a week previously. Britain ought to accept proposals which would make it clear that Britain would guarantee the new Czechoslovakia, so as to retain the confidence of Rumania, Yugoslavia, and other countries whose support might be needed in a future war. Bruce agreed that the guarantee should be given in such a form as to make it clear that Britain would fight if Germany went any further. MacDonald argued that Britain should declare that if the German army crossed the frontier it would go to war with Germany. He was not as hopeful about Hitler's intentions as was Chamberlain.[110] The discussion was continued after 3 p.m. Templewood felt a final decision should not be taken until it was known how Britain stood with the dominions. He had information that

[108] *D O 114*, 94, pp. 32–3, Appendix I, No. 18, F82/220, Note of a Discussion between MacDonald and Dominion Representatives, Most Secret, 24.9.1938.

[109] Massey, pp. 259–61.

[110] *Cab 23*, 95, pp. 210–4, Cab 43 (38), Secret, 25.9.1938.

there was a possibility that if Britain entered the war to help Czecho-slovakia, Mackenzie King would hold a referendum. Canada was likely to reject any proposal for joining a war. If war broke out 'it might not be in the interests not merely of ourselves but of our allies, that we should delay joining in'.

In contrast Halifax wondered whether Hitler had not gained power by words in the present instance, 'and that if he was not driven to war the result might be to help bring down the Nazi regime'. The foreign secretary said that he had worked closely with Chamberlain but he was no longer sure whether 'their minds were still altogether at one'.

Chamberlain when he spoke again seems to have changed his position slightly. Probably he was shaken by Halifax's attitude. The prime minister realised that war was likely, and MacDonald's warnings seem to have counted for something. He told the cabinet:

> It was clear that a position had arisen in which we might before long be involved in war. If that happened, it was essential that we should enter war united, both as a country and as an Empire. It was of the utmost importance, therefore, that whatever steps we took, we should try to bring the whole country and Empire along with us, and should allow public opinion to realise that all possible steps had been taken to avoid a conflict.[111]

Chamberlain was to discuss the matter with Daladier and Bonnet after the cabinet meeting, and it was decided that Britain could not undertake either to declare or not to declare war on Germany. Daladier later told Chamberlain that Hitler planned aggression and France would do its duty. The prime minister refused to say what Britain's attitude would be.[112]

At 11.30 p.m. the cabinet met again. Chamberlain felt that since Czechoslovakia had decided to reject Hitler's proposals, Hitler would march into Czechoslovakia and it would be up to France. The prime minsiter, however, was 'unwilling to leave unexplored any possible chance of avoiding war'. He planned to send Sir Horace Wilson to Hitler the next day with a message suggesting an international commission to put into effect proposals already accepted by the Czechoslovak government. If Hitler did not respond suitably Wilson would be authorised to say that France would go to war, 'and that if that happened it seemed certain that we should be drawn in'. Chamberlain told the cabinet that this move 'might also help to rally the Dominions to our side'. MacDonald agreed: such procedure was essential to secure the co-operation of the dominions.

111 Ibid., p. 227.
112 Ibid., pp. 219–27.

He cited a telegram from Gie in Berlin which said that the South African government could not regard 'war on the present issue as in any way justified'. The possible effect on the commonwealth had to be carefully watched.[113]

That day Massey was 'greatly perturbed' by the papers, generally the British press wanted a firm stand. He was horrified that there might be war over the method of transfer of the Sudeten territory which was already ceded. He saw Dawson of *The Times*, and the two agreed to act. Massey suggested that Dawson see Halifax, and persuade Bruce who had influence with the high commissioners as he had at one time been prime minister.[114] Dawson apparently saw most of the high commissioners on 25 September and on the morning of 26th.[115] Bruce telephoned MacDonald between the first two cabinet meetings and said that he still felt inclined to accept the German memorandum. MacDonald saw Bruce after the afternoon cabinet meeting and the high commissioner maintained that attitude.[116]

On Monday 26 September MacDonald met the high commissioners: Massey's tactics had worked. Bruce said that he had telephoned Lyons, who subject to the confirmation of the Australian cabinet, had said that Britain should not get involved in war on the present issue. Dulanty had not received his government's views but felt that they would incline towards those of Bruce. Te Water and Massey concurred. Te Water emphatically said that failure to improve on the terms of the German memorandum should on no account involve the commonwealth in war. The high commissioners agreed, however, that if if did come to war 'the Dominions would, however reluctantly, be in sooner or later on the side of the United Kingdom'.[117]

The cabinet met at 12 noon. Chamberlain mentioned that he had had a message from Roosevelt urging him to continue negotiations. It was decided to institute the precautionary stage of mobilisation the following day. MacDonald also reported that all the high commissioners had taken the view that the acceptance of Hitler's proposals was better than war. If there were war MacDonald felt that Australia and New Zealand might join after a short delay. In the case of Ireland and South Africa the delay might be considerable. MacDonald did not speculate about Canada's

---

[113] Ibid., pp. 240–5, Cab 44 (38), Secret, 25.9.1938.

[114] Massey, 259–61.

[115] Ibid., *loc. cit.*

[116] *F O 371*, 21777, p. 251, C10938/5302/18, Hankinson to Harvey, 21–6.9.1938; Enclosing Memorandum by MacDonald of Conversation with Bruce, Most Secret, 25.9.1938.

[117] *D O 114*, 94, pp. 33–4, Appendix I, No. 19, F82/252, Note of a Discussion between MacDonald and Dominion Representatives, Most Secret, 26.9.1938.

reaction. Chamberlain, in support of this mentioned a telephone message that he had from Lyons that morning. Lyons had approved of the British attitude and said that he regarded the present issue as a 'method of procedure rather than principle'.[118]

A telegram was received from the Australian government at 12.57 p.m· saying that the method of cession of the Sudeten areas was not 'a matter of sufficient importance to warrant a dispute leading to war'. Speaight of the foreign office minuted on 27 September that this showed 'considerable uneasiness' on the part of the Australian government.[119] The acting high commissioner in Australia, however, telegrammed that the message was primarily the work of Menzies and Casey and 'as such is obviously entitled to all the respect due to authoritive views which can only be expressed by Ministers'. Lyons's message was 'very far from representing the core of Australian majority opinion'.[120]

On 26 September at 3.45 p.m. a telegram was also received from the high commissioner in South Africa. He had spent some time with Hertzog and Havenga the previous day and had concluded that 'Hertzog steadfastly refuses to believe that war will be the outcome of the present crisis and I doubt whether he lets his mind dwell at all on the possibility of other alternatives'.[121]

At 7 p.m. that evening Chamberlain, Halifax, MacDonald and Amery met the dominion representatives at Downing Street. According to Massey's diary Chamberlain 'had reluctantly come to the conclusion that Hitler's profession of limited objectives was not sincere and that his ambitions were far wider than the boundaries of Sudetenland'. The prime minister also referred to having doubts as to whether the French would fulfill their pledge to Czechoslovakia. Massey's impression was that Chamberlain was 'as anxious as any of us not to allow a matter of method to be the cause of a world war but he had an inflexible sense of principle and a principle he feels is now at stake'.[122] This account conflicts with that which Chamberlain gave to the cabinet on his return from Godesberg.

---

[118] *Cab 23*, 95, pp. 247–56, Cab 45 (38) 1, 5, 7, Secret, 26.9.1938; *Premier 1*, 266A, p.110, Roosevelt to Chamberlain, Telegram, 26.9.1938.

[119] *F O 371*, 21777, pp. 181–5, C10852/5302/18, Dominions Office to Foreign Office, Secret, 26.9.1938 r. in r. 27.9.1938; Transmitting Copy of Telegram No. 96 of 26.9.1938 from Australian Government; Foreign Office Minute by Speaight, 27.9.1938.

[120] Ibid., pp. 261–3, C10972/5302/18, Dominions Office to Foreign Office, Secret, 27.9.1938 r. in r. 28.9.1938; Transmitting Acting High Commissioner in Australia to Dominions Office, Telegram No. 186, Immediate Secret and Personal, 27.9.1938 r. 26.9.1938.

[121] Ibid., pp. 152–7, C10734/5302/18, High Commissioner in South Africa to Dominions Office, Telegram No. 138 Pts 1, 2, and 3, 26.9.1938.

[122] Massey, pp. 259–61. I can find no record of this Meeting in Cabinet, Foreign Office, Dominions Office or Premier 1 Files.

Perhaps Chamberlain had been convinced by the cabinet discussions, or else he was testing dominion reaction to the prospect of war.

The dominion high commissioners were disturbed. Te Water saw Mac-Donald on the morning of 27 September. Lyons's message to Chamberlain had been communicated to Hertzog, and Hertzog had asked that the British be informed that he and his colleagues felt that the German proposals should be accepted. Hertzog emphasised that South Africa was less likely than ever to go to war over a matter of procedure.[123] In a further message Hertzog said that he had studied Hitler's speech at *Sportpalast* in Berlin the previous evening.[124] Hitler had assured Chamberlain that when the Czechs had come to terms with their other minorities he had 'no further interest in the Czech state'.[125] Hertzog felt that if a European war were still to take place after Hitler's speech 'the responsibility for that will not be placed upon the shoulders of Germany'.[126] Gie had also cabled te Water from Berlin that there was much to be said for Hitler's case.[127] Te Water said that Hertzog probably had not considered South Africa's position if war broke out as war seemed incredible. MacDonald understood, without any foundation, that Hertzog would be anxious to bring South Africa into the war at Britain's side, against parliamentary opposition.[128]

MacDonald met the high commissioners at 11.30 a.m. on 27 September and told them of Wilson's interview with Hitler the previous day. Hitler had agreed to a meeting between Czech and German representatives provided his memorandum were accepted by 28 September. Hitler was excited: it was no use talking any further. Wilson had decided not to deliver Chamberlain's ultimatum on that day because of Hitler's emotion and the forthcoming *Sportpalast* speech. MacDonald, in reply to a question by Bruce, said that he believed that Chamberlain intended to 'preserve his attitude as mediator until the last possible moment'. Bruce, Massey and te Water concurred that the adoption of any other course would be 'quite disastrous'.[129]

The high commissioners were perturbed by a telegram from Henderson which said that unless Britain advised Czechoslovakia to make peace with

[123] *D O 114*, 94, pp. 34–5, Appendix I, No. 20, Note by MacDonald of a Conversation with te Water, 27.9.1938; p. 35, Enclosure 1 in No. 20, Aide Memoire, 27.9.1938.

[124] Ibid., *loc. cit.*

[125] N. H. Baynes, Ed., *The Speeches of Adolf Hitler* (London, 1942), pp. 1508–27.

[126] *D O 114*, 94, p. 35, Appendix I, Enclosure 1 in No. 20, Aide Memoire, 27.9.1938.

[127] Ibid., Enclosure 2 in No. 20, Decode of Cable from Gie to te Water, 27.9.1938.

[128] Ibid., pp. 34–5, No. 20, Note by MacDonald of a Conversation with te Water, 27.9.1938.

[129] Ibid., p. 36, No. 21, Note by MacDonald of a Discussion with Dominion Representatives, Most Secret, 27.9.1938.

Berlin 'we should be exposing Czechoslovakia to the fate of Abyssinia'. MacDonald wrote to Chamberlain that they urged since 'the decision which is being taken by our Government today is so far-reaching and may commit them to so much that they feel their views must be represented to the Ministers who are now considering the policy'.[130]

Bruce addressed a meeting of the inner cabinet at 4.30 p.m. The high commissioners were reluctant to commit themselves in writing as their attitude would be that 'the terms of the German Memorandum were not a sufficient cause for a world war'. Bruce's own view was that Britain had either to take the line that the matters in dispute were relatively small and should at all costs be settled by negotiation, or that they were a challenge between force and peaceful negotiation which had to be met. Any written statement from the dominions would be that the former view of the situation was correct.[131]

The cabinet met at 9.30 p.m. Chamberlain read the telegram from Henderson. The prime minister had also seen the military attaché from Berlin who had visited Czechoslovakia and reported that the Czechoslovaks would offer a feeble resistance. But 'more disturbing than this was the fact that the Dominions were far from happy about the situation'. Chamberlain read the messages from Lyons and Hertzog. The high commissioners also all had visited Downing Street that afternoon and made representations that pressure should be put upon the Czechoslovak government to accept Hitler's terms. 'The situation *vis-à-vis* the Dominions was thus very delicate'. MacDonald elaborated the position: in his view 'all the Dominions would sooner or later come in with us, but it was clear that they would come in only after making a number of reservations half-heartedly and with mental reservations about our policy'. MacDonald ceded that it was difficult to be certain about public opinion in the dominions, and mentioned the telegram from the acting high commissioner in Australia which had contradicted Lyons's message. There was no doubt, however, about the unanimity of the high commissioners.

Duff Cooper argued against this case: he referred to the message from Roosevelt, and to reports from Phipps in Paris which showed 'a much firmer spirit in France'. Cooper did not think that much importance could be attached to the opinions of the high commissioners:

After all, our position in regard to the co-operation of the Dominions was much more favourable than it had been in 1914, when there had been a revolution in

130 *Premier 1*, 242, p. 25, MacDonald to Chamberlain, 27.9.1938.
131 *Cab 27*, 646, pp. 102–3, C S (38) 15, Meeting of Ministers, Secret Lock and Key, 27.9.1938.

South Africa. He thought that if we waited until there was complete unanimity with the Dominion Governments on issues of peace and war in Europe, that would mean that we should never go to war.

Halifax spoke strongly against capitulating to Germany and putting pressure on Czechoslovakia. Simon supported him.

Chamberlain told the cabinet that at a meeting held that afternoon he had authorised Duff Cooper to proceed with the mobilisation of the navy. This did not involve general mobilisation of the army or airforce, or the institution of the 'preliminary stage'.[132]

MacDonald met the high commissioners immediately after the cabinet meeting. Massey, te Water, and Bruce had been discussing the position, and they asked for further consultation with MacDonald after the foreign office officials had left. The dominion representatives, with the exception of Sandford, all laboured the dangerous reaction in the commonwealth if Britain went to war over the issue of how Hitler was to take possession of territory already ceded to him in principle. Chamberlain's fears were confirmed. Bruce and te Water urged these views on behalf of their governments and warned that the effect of war in such circumstances 'must be most seriously to endanger the future unity and cohesion of the Commonwealth'. Massey feared that 'the minority of Canadians who were not favourably disposed towards the British connexion would, long after the war was over, continue to use the fact that Canada had become involved in it to reinforce their view'. Te Water similarly agreed that 'South Africa would be most unwilling to fight on this issue and that the result of becoming involved in war would be to strengthen enormously the position of those hostile to the British connexion'. Dulanty took the same view.

The high commissioners also wondered whether they could make it easier for Chamberlain by sending him messages which he could refer to in the house of commons, and thus make it easier for Britain to keep out of war. It was agreed that MacDonald had done his best to keep the cabinet aware of the dominions point of view, and that no further action by the dominion governments was possible at that time.

MacDonald pointed out to the high commissioners that if war came it would not be fought on a question of principle. The British government felt that Hitler's objectives were wider than he had admitted. Britain 'must be entitled to take the view that its vital interests were at stake'.[133]

---

[132] *Cab 23*, 95, pp. 261–76, Cab 46 (38) 1, Secret, 27.9.1938.
[133] *D O 114*, 94, pp. 36–7, Appendix I, No. 22, F82/288, Note by the Duke of Devonshire of a Talk between MacDonald and the Dominion High Commissioners on 27 September 1938, 28.9.1938.

An examination of opinion in the dominions at this time does not altogether support the views of the high commissioners expressed on the night of 27 September. But then the high commissioners were speaking of the long term consequences of becoming involved in war.

In South Africa on 28 September, at Hertzog's instigation, the full cabinet accepted the declaration of benevolent neutrality agreed on earlier by the inner cabinet.[134] That section of the press which had attacked Chamberlain's so called 'appeasement' policy adopted a more conciliatory line.[135] But the South African government was pledged to a policy of neutrality, and even though the British government did not know of the decision of 28 September, te Water had warned repeatedly that this would be the attitude.

On 27 September the high commissioner in South Africa warned the British government that the French minister had called on Hertzog that morning and had been told by the prime minister that he proposed to keep out of war if he could. South Africa would discharge its obligations in respect of Simonstown. Hertzog said that he would not prevent South African nationals from joining the British army, but that recruiting in South Africa would not be permitted. The high commissioner hoped that this referred only to the interim period before parliament could re-assemble.[136] In this assessment the high commissioner proved to be wrong.

T. K. Roberts of the foreign office, however, minuted on 28 September that perhaps Hertzog might have hoped to have a restraining effect on the French:

> He is surely a little naïve in supposing that the use of Simonstown by the British fleet would be regarded by Germany as compatible with Union neutrality. Nor does he appear to have considered the probable reactions of this attitude among the British in the Cape.[137]

South Africans, however, did not know what their government's policy was likely to be: Hertzog merely reiterated his pledge to submit the issue of peace or war to parliament.[138] Pirow said that South Africa would keep South Africa 'at any price to the extent of using force of arms'.[139] Foreign

---

134 C. M. van den Heever, *Generaal J. B. M. Hertzog* (Johannesburg, 1944), p. 275; Pirow, pp. 226–7.

135 *Daily Telegraph*, 27.9.1938; 28.9.1938; *Times*, 29.9.1938.

136 *F O 371*, 21777, pp. 219–22, C10886/5302/18, Transmitting D28/7B, High Commissioner in South Africa to Dominions Office, Telegram No. 139, 27.9.1938 (cypher).

137 Ibid., Minute by T. K. Roberts, 28.9.1938.

138 *F O 371*, 21777, pp. 283–8, C10989/5302/18, Dominions Office to Foreign Office, 26.9.1938 r. in r. 29.9.1938; Transmitting High Commissioner in South Africa to Dominions Office, Telegram No. 137, Immediate, 26.9.1938.

139 Ibid., pp. 292–5, C10991/5302/18, Dominions Office to Foreign Office, 27.9.1938; Transmitting same Telegraph as cited above; Minute by T. K. Roberts, 1.10.1938.

office officials formed the impression that the predominant feeling in South Africa was a fear that it might be 'dragged in' to a war.[140]

In Australia, after Godesberg, comment shifted to Australia's role in the likely event of war. Probably as a consequence of the government's policy of avoiding discussion, a large group of Australians had no formulated attitude. Labour was divided. Curtin told the house of representatives on 27 September that the labour movement would oppose sending troops overseas. A claim by Hitler in excess of the territory ceded would not justify war. In Sydney and Adelaide the industrial wing demanded an Australian declaration of support for Czechoslovak independence.[141] Lyons, after a telephone call from Bruce postponed making a statement on 27 September. Lyons finally spoke at 11 p.m. on 28 September (Australian time). The acting high commissioner in Australia reported that Lyons's historical account of the events was 'colourless and neutral in tone betraying little or no sign of national leadership to match the crisis'.

> What the Government of Great Britain has been doing with the support of the Government of Australia has been to make every effort to preserve the world's peace.

Curtin justly voiced the disgust and disappointment of the house at the government's failure to define its own attitude.[142] Newspaper comment the next day was that Australia could not be at peace if Britain were at war.[143]

Probably the observation of F. H. Cleobury of the foreign office on 30 September is a fair assessment:

> Things have moved so quickly that Australian opinion has doubtless found it difficult to keep up with them. My own impression is that *before* an outbreak of war Australia would be for peace at almost any price—but after the outbreak she would do all that we could reasonably expect.[144]

---

[140] Ibid., pp. 70–5, C12465/5302/18, Dominions Office to Foreign Office, 17.10.1938 r. in r. 18.10.1938; Transmitting F82/324, Clark to Stanley, No. 409, 5.10.1938; Minute by R. J. E. Thorington Smith, 21.10.1938.

[141] Anonymous, 'Overseas Reactions to the Crisis: Australia', *Round Table*, XXIX (1938–9), pp. 44–9. *Observer*, 25.9.1938; *Sydney Morning Herald*, 26.9.1938; *Daily Telegraph*, 26–8.9.1938; *Manchester Guardian*, 28.9.1938; *Labor Daily*, 28.9.1938, Ed., *West Australian*, 28.9.1938, Ed.; *F O 371*, 21777, pp. 351–3, C11267/5302/18, Dominions Office to Foreign Office, 29.9.1938 r. in r. 1.10.1938; Transmitting F82/268, Acting High Commissioner in Australia to Dominions Office, Telegram No. 192, 29.9.1938.

[142] *F O 371*, 21777, pp. 320–2, C11113/5302/18, Dominions Office to Foreign Office, 28.9.1938 r. in r. 30.9.1938; Transmitting F82/217, Acting High Commissioner in Australia to Dominions Office, Telegram No. 190, Important, 28.9.1938; pp. 340–2, C11210/5302/18, Dominions Office to Foreign Office, 29.9.1938 r. in r. 30.9.1938; Transmitting F82, Acting High Commissioner in Australia to Dominions Office, Telegram No. 191, Important, 28.9.1938.

[143] *Age*, 29.9.1938.

[144] *F O 371*, 21777, p. 261, C10972/5302/18, Minute by F. H. Cleobury, 30.9.1938.

The New Zealand government was sufficiently moved by the news of the Munich flight to cable to Chamberlain 'that they most earnestly support his continued and determined efforts for the peace of Europe and the world which they sincerely trust will be crowned with success'.[145]

It seems that Mackenzie King was prepared to recommend that Canada fight. Massey did not know of this decision. Mackenzie King was in touch with his chief lieutenant in the cabinet, Ernest Lapointe, who was in Geneva. On 24 September Lapointe wired Mackenzie King advising him that the immediate cause of a war would be minority problems in central Europe, a matter which was not likely to enthuse Canadians. Lapointe urged that the declared policy of leaving the Canadian parliament to decide should be maintained, and no statement made before the outbreak or war. Following Lapointe's advice Mackenzie King decided against any definite Canadian declaration of support, but he planned, in the event of war, to summon parliament within two weeks, and to submit to it a policy of Canadian participation. Five years later Mackenzie King wrote:

> I had . . . made up my mind to advocate Canada's immediate participation, but I know I should have had at that time, instead of a unanimous parliament at my back, a House of Commons and a Senate each of which would have been wholly divided.[146]

London did not know what Mackenzie King was prepared to do. Massey was the most active of the high commissioners in the campaign against a forceful policy.

Judging from reports of the press, and of observers, English speaking Canada was prepared, if necessary, to go to war behind the mother country.[147]

Chamberlain's speech on 27 September made 'the deepest impression' in Canada. He said:

> How horrible, fantastic, incredible it is that we should be digging trenches and trying on gas-masks here because of a quarrel in a far-away country between people of whom we know nothing.

Canadian opinion was likely to be in agreement with these views, but the following statement was contentious:

[145] Galway to MacDonald, 29.9.1938. Quoted by F. L. W. Wood, *The New Zealand People at War. Political and External Affairs* (Wellington, 1958), p. 91; *Times*, 30.9.1938.
[146] *Mackenzie King Papers*, Lapointe to Mackenzie King, 24.9.1938; Mackenzie King to Greenwood, 1.11.1943. Quoted by Eayrs, p. 71.
[147] Anonymous, 'Overseas Reactions to the Crisis: Canada', *Round Table*, XXIX (1938–9), pp. 42–3; F. H. Soward, *Canada in World Affairs. The Pre-War Years* (Oxford, 1941), p. 115; *Sunday Times*, 25.9.1938; *Observer*, 25.9.1938; *Daily Telegraph*, 28.9.1938.

However much we may sympathise with a small nation confronted by a big and powerful neighbour we cannot in all circumstances undertake to involve the whole British Empire in war simply on her account.

It was generally felt in Canada that Britain had no right to involve the dominions in any war, and as Stephen L. Holmes, the acting high commissioner, wrote:

It is to the credit of the strict academic constitutionalists that they do not yet seem to have commented on this.[148]

What French Canada thought it difficult to assess: its newspapers denounced Germany but did not say much about foreign entanglements for Canada.[149] Holmes reported on 26 September that there was evidence that French Canadian opinion was showing signs of abandoning its isolationist tendency. Provided there was no conscription it was felt that French Canada would not oppose a policy of active support of Britain.[150]

On 27 September the Canadian cabinet issued a statement that the government was ready for the immediate summoning of parliament should efforts to preserve the peace fail.[151]

During these weeks Holmes did not have much contact with the government. Skelton said that Mackenzie King would only see Holmes in an emergency. Mackenzie King was anxious to be free of contacts so that he could face parliament 'with a clean sheet'.[152]

On balance it does seem that Canada, though possibly divided, would have gone to war. But at the time of Munich the British government did not know this. Massey implied that Canada would participate, but with consequences that would mean a break in the commonwealth.

The British government did consider the issue of dominion neutrality. On 26 September a telegram was sent to the acting high commissioners in Canada and Australia, and to the high commissioner in South Africa. The telegram argued that with the constitutional position of the king no dominion could remain neutral in international law. It was hoped that dominion governments would accept the doctrine of common belligerency.

[148] Neville Chamberlain, *The Struggle for Peace* (London, 1939), pp. 274–6; *F O 371*, 21777, pp. 46–53. C12253/5302/18, Dominions Office to Hadow, 11.10.1938 r. in r. 11.10.1938; Transmitting F82/320, 734/154, Holmes to Harding, Secret, 29.9.1938.

[149] *Daily Telegraph*, 27.9.1938.

[150] *D O 114*, 94, pp. 51–2, Appendix II, No. 15, F82/228, Acting High Commissioner in Canada to MacDonald, Telegram No. 213, Most Secret, 26.9.1938 r. 27.9.1938 (cypher).

[151] Ibid., p. 53, No. 17, F82/254, Acting High Commissioner in Canada to MacDonald, Telegram No. 216, 27.9.1938 r. 28.9.1938.

[152] *F O 371*, 21777, pp. 46–53, C12253/5302/18, Dominions Office to Hadow, 11.10.1938 r. in r. 11.10.1938; Transmitting F82/320, 743/154, Holmes to Harding, Secret, 29.9.1938.

Britain wanted the dominions to take such measures of co-operation as were envisaged in the war book scheme, even though a particular dominion might wish to make it clear that active participation was a matter for parliament to decide.

Difficulties were anticipated if any dominion wished to declare an attitude of neutrality in connection with war book plans, and also constitutional controversies which could extend to the question of continued membership of the commonwealth. Opinion could regard the continued dominion diplomatic representation in enemy countries as a crucial test. It was felt that Britain should make every effort to see that no dominion made a declaration of neutrality. The acting high commissioner in Australia was advised that neutrality was 'not in the least likely to arise in the case of Australia'.[153]

Before the telegram was despatched a report was received from the high commissioner in South Africa, W. H. Clark, which suggested that South Africa as well as Ireland might wish to adopt an attitude of neutrality.[154] The prepared telegram was sent, but not with a view to the high commissioners taking immediate action.[155]

On 29 September Clark reported that he feared South Africa might make a formal declaration of neutrality as soon as Britain declared war.[156]

The dominions were implicated in war book measures. Since the precautionary stage was likely to be instituted a telegram was sent on 23 September to the British representatives in the dominions asking them to arrange with the respective prime ministers to be able to contact them at any hour. A telegram that the position had eased, however, was sent on 28 September.

On 28 September steps were taken in Britain to mobilise the fleet and to call up naval personnel. The war book arrangements provided for the despatch of prepared telegrams to the dominions relating to this matter, but it was decided, particularly in view of the doubts as to South Africa's position in the event of war, and since these prepared telegrams included an invitation to dominion governments to co-operate on prepared lines, not to send them.

---

[153] *D O 114*, 94, pp. 62–4, Appendix IV, No. 2, D28/8, Telegrams to Acting High Commissioners in Canada and Australia and High Commissioner in South Africa, Secret and Personal, 26.9.1938.

[154] Ibid., p. 8, Memoranda; p. 62, Appendix IV, No. 1, D28/7B, High Commissioner in South Africa to British Government, Telegram No. 139, 27.9.1938 (cypher).

[155] Ibid., p. 8, Memoranda.

[156] Ibid., p. 64, Appendix IV no. 3, D28/9, High Commissioner in South Africa to British Government, Telegram No. 140, Secret and Personal, 29.9.1938 (cypher).

There was trouble in South Africa: the commander in chief Africa station telegraphed all royal naval personnel in South Africa summoning them for duty and pressed for action by the South African government as was provided for in the Africa station war organisation book. Pirow objected. With the improvement in the international situation the commander in chief and the high commissioner agreed that no further action should be taken.

There were also difficulties in Canada: an admiralty telegram instructing commands to establish naval control service staffs was addressed as a circular to the chief of naval staff, Ottawa. The Canadian government felt that any action on their part should be taken only on a formal request from the British government, and not on an admiralty message, but eventually they decided that necessary arrangements should be made to the extent of those representing only precautionary measures.

Australia and New Zealand, however, took full naval measures, as well as various army and air force preparations. Canada also took steps to improve the defence of Halifax, and it was reported that Mackenzie King authorised the expenditure of Can.$6,000,000 for defence purposes. No action was taken in South Africa, nor as far as was known in Ireland.[157]

The preparations taken for war at the end of September suggest that Britain anticipated that Australia and New Zealand would fight. South Africa and Ireland were likely to remain neutral. Canada was less predictable, would likely take an independent line, and be reluctant to fight.

While the dominion governments were preparing for the contingency of war the United States administration put out peace feelers in a way which could be seen as bolstering Chamberlain's efforts. On 26 September Roosevelt sent messages to Chamberlain, Benes, Daladier and Hitler urging settlement by resort to reason. An appeal was made to Mussolini and on 27 September Roosevelt reiterated his appeal for peaceful methods with the significant proviso that:

> The Government of the United States has no political involvements in Europe, and will assume no obligations in the conduct of the present negotiations.

There is slight, if any, evidence that the president's appeal motivated Hitler to call the Munich conference. The British, afterwards, publicly credited Roosevelt for this, but such action can be understood in the light of a British attempt to involve the United States in Europe.[158]

---

[157] Ibid., pp. 8–12, Memoranda War Book Measures.

[158] William L. Langer and S. Everett Gleason, *The Challenge to Isolation* (London, 1952), pp. 33–4; *FRUS* 1938(1), p. 663, 760F62/1101, Chamberlain to Hull, Telegram, Undated; pp. 678–9, 760F.62/117 6/10, Telephone Conversation between Kennedy and Welles, 27.9.1938; pp. 679–80, 27.9.2938; pp. 692–2. 760F.62/1248, Kennedy to Hull, Telegram No. 1073, 28.9.1938.

On 27 September, following Roosevelt's appeal, Chamberlain instructed Perth to call on Ciano to urge Mussolini to restrain Hitler. Roosevelt's appeal confirmed the French desire for a fresh diplomatic initiative.[159]

In the early hours of 28 September Chamberlain received a message from Lyons suggesting that the Australian high commissioner should fly to Rome with a personal message for Mussolini. This seemed to confirm that Chamberlain's initiative to Mussolini was correct.[160]

Perth saw Ciano at 10.20 a.m. and Ciano. alarmed by the warning about the extent of the impending conflict saw Mussolini at once. The duce telephoned his ambassador in Berlin and instructed him to see Hitler.

In London at 11.30 a.m. messages were sent to Berlin and Rome. Henderson was told to say that Chamberlain was ready to go to Berlin for discussions on the transfer of populations with Hitler and Czechoslovak representatives, together with French and Italian delegates if Hitler thought they were necessary. Mussolini was asked to be represented at such a conference.[161]

MacDonald told the dominion high commissioners of these developments at 11.50 a.m. The representatives expressed warm appreciation of Chamberlain's messages to Hitler and Mussolini. MacDonald also explained that the French had suggested 'that neither Government should take any offensive measures, including a declaration of war, without previous consultation with and agreement by the other'. Massey remarked that the British government was 'once more in control'. Both he and Bruce were anxious lest bellicose statements in parliament should prejudice the negotiations.[162]

The duce's ambassador saw Hitler and the führer agreed to meet Chamberlain provided Mussolini were present. Mussolini accepted, and a conference was arranged for 11 a.m. the following morning at Munich. Daladier was also invited.

While Hitler and Mussolini were finalising details Chamberlain was gravely addressing the house of commons. When Hitler's invitation to Munich was passed on to him he dramatically read it to the house.[163]

159 Robbins, pp. 308–9.
160 Ibid., p. 310; *Premier 1*, 242, p. 18, Note by C. G. L. Syers, 28.9.1938; pp. 19–21, Lyons to Chamberlain, Telegram, Most Immediate, 28.9.1938.
161 Robbins, pp. 311–2.
162 *D O 114*, 94, pp. 37–8, Appendix I, No. 23, F87/270, Note of Discussion between MacDonald and Dominion Representatives, Most Secret, 28.9.1938.
163 Robbins, pp. 312–3.

Roosevelt sent a telegram to Chamberlain: 'good man'.[164] Hostility to Chamberlain noticeably diminished in the United States press. He became the man who perhaps had prevented another war.[165]

In Australia Lyons, on 29 September, took credit for suggesting the association of Mussolini in mediatory efforts, and he and Curtin paid cordial tribute to Chamberlain's services to the cause of peace, amid the acclamations of the whole house.[166]

The acting high commissioner in Canada wired that there was 'considerable relief amounting perhaps to undue optimism' at the news of the Munich meeting.[167]

When Chamberlain left for Munich he knew that the dominions were totally opposed to war over Czechoslovakia. The prime minister disliked war, and feared the suffering that air raids would bring to Britain. But it was the attitude of the dominions which had weighed most heavily in the account that Chamberlain had given of the situation to the cabinet on 27 September. Chamberlain and most of the cabinet still believed in the commonwealth. It seemed clear that a war over Czechoslovakia would endanger the continued existence of that body: Ireland and South Africa would be most likely to be neutral; Canada was reluctant to become involved in a war over a European question; the Australian government was not enthusiastic and felt that the Czechs should be told what to do; only New Zealand was behind Britain 'right or wrong'. If war had to come, as Chamberlain had often said, it would be best if Britain and the empire could face it with a united front. On 29 September 1938 this did not seem probable, and even if all the dominions did eventually join in, it seemed that internal repercussions in those countries, in the long run might lead to the dissolution of the commonwealth. Even the United States whom it was hoped might eventually help to stop the dictators, supported a negotiated peace.

While the future of Czechoslovakia was being settled at Munich, MacDonald met the dominion high commissioners at 6.50 p.m. When he read the Czechoslovak government's objections to the British plan Bruce said that the time had come to take a firm line with Benes. Any reluctance to bring pressure to bear on the Czechoslovak government would be a

---

164 *FRUS* 1938(1), p. 688, 760F.62/1358 a Hull to Kennedy, Telegram No. 572, 28.9.1938.

165 *Manchester Guardian*, 28.9.1938, 30.9.1938; *Daily Telegraph*, 28–9.9.1938.

166 *D O 114*, 94, p. 54, Appendix II, No. 19, F82/268, Acting High Commissioner in Australia to British Government, Telegram No. 192, 29.9.1938.

167 Ibid., p. 53, No. 18, F82/272, Acting High Commissioner in Canada to MacDonald, Telegram No. 217, Most Secret, 28.9.1938 r. 29.9.1938 (cypher).

mistake 'particularly in view of the attitude of the Dominion Govern-ments'. Bruce was supported in this by Massey and te Water. Bruce then suggested, with the support of Massey and te Water that a telegram be sent making it clear to the Czechoslovak ministers and officials that 'the obstructive tactics of the Czech Government were unwelcome to the United Kingdom and Dominion Governments'. MacDonald thought that this would be premature until it was known what Chamberlain had achieved.[168]

In thirteen hours at Munich Chamberlain achieved a bargain which seemed better than the terms offered at Godesberg: military occupation was to take place in stages; the frontier was to be fixed by an international commission and not by Germany; there would be some international supervision; and a common guarantee was also given in principle to the remainder of Czechoslovakia.[169]

Chamberlain's reception in England was tumultuous[170] but MacDonald told the dominion high commissioners on 30 September that the prime minister was likely to be attacked in parliament. MacDonald suggested that the dominions might help there. The high commissioners agreed, despite the possibility of political difficulties in certain of the dominions, to suggest to their governments that they send messages supporting the agreement. But while the meeting was in progress such messages arrived from Lyons and Mackenzie King.[171]

The next day MacDonald saw the high commissioners and assured them that no reference had been made at Munich to the ex-German colonies, The important point was that Chamberlain 'had reached the conclusion that Herr Hitler was a man with whom it would be possible to negotiate a general settlement'. Jordan suggested privately that the high com-missioners might unite in a message to Chamberlain expressing their appreciation for what the prime minister had done. Dulanty, however, pointed to the difficulties inherent in the suggestion.[172]

The Munich settlement was enthusiastically received in the dominions and by dominion statesmen. Significantly it was Jordan who had taken

---

[168] Ibid., p. 38, Appendix I, No. 24, F82/295, Note of a Discussion between MacDonald and Dominion High Commissioners, Most Secret, 29.9.1938.

[169] Robbins, p. 319.

[170] Ibid., *loc. cit.*

[171] *D O 114*, 94, p. 39, Appendix I, No. 25, F82/295, Note of a Discussion between MacDonald and Dominion High Commissioners, Most Secret, 30.9.1938.

[172] Ibid., pp. 39–40, Appendix I, No. 26, F82/315, Note of a Discussion between MacDonald and Dominion High Commissioners, Most Secret, 1.10.1938.

such a moral line at the league over Abyssinia, that suggested the message to Chamberlain from the high commissioners.

Hertzog sent a congratulary cable to Chamberlain.[173] Smuts saw the conference as a triumph for all concerned.[174] Te Water wrote to Simon on 6 October that if Britain had 'the moral strength to take the high road of understanding, then its leadership will continue to be accepted by us of the Commonwealth'. Otherwise it would be 'the end'.[175] The press in South Africa was laudatory.[176] The editor of the *Cape Argus* who on 22 September had criticised the idea of a compromise settlement had been dismissed.[177]

Tribute, too, was paid in Australia to Chamberlain for his 'triumph of diplomacy'.[178] Lyons cabled Chamberlain: 'Australians in common with all other peoples of the British Empire owe a deep debt of gratitude to you for your unceasing efforts to preserve peace'.[179] The *Sydney Morning Herald* and the *Labor Daily* were exceptional with warning and critical editorials.[180]

The New Zealand cabinet did not join the chorus of praise when they cabled their relief: they earnestly trusted 'that the basis of settlement is such as will prove to be a lasting safeguard of world peace, founded on justice and order between nations'.[181] New Zealand newspapers also conveyed this feeling.

Mackenzie King was relieved[182] and sent a congratulatory cable to Chamberlain.[183] The Canadian conservative leader and the press also welcomed the agreement.[184] A dissentient voice, however, came from J. W. Dafoe, who in an editorial on 3 October in the *Winnipeg Free Press* enquired 'What's the Cheering for?'.

---

173 *Manchester Guardian*, 3.10.1938.

174 *Daily Telegraph*, 1.10.1938.

175 *Simon Papers*, 1938–9, te Water to Simon, 6.10.1938.

176 *Daily Telegraph*, 3.10.1938.

177 H. Lindsay Smith, *Behind the Press in South Africa* (Cape Town, 1946), pp. 92–4.

178 *Daily Telegraph*, 30.9.1938; 1.10.1938.

179 *D O 114*, 94, p. 55, Appendix II, No. 21, F82/299, Lyons to Chamberlain, Telegram, 30.8.1938.

180 *Sydney Morning Herald*, 3.10.1938, Ed.; *Labor Daily*, 1.10.1938.

181 Galway to MacDonald, 30.9.1938. Quoted by Wood, p. 91. *Daily Telegraph*, 3.10.1938; 1.10.1938.

182 *Mackenzie King Papers*, Mackenzie King to MacDonald, 1.10.1938. Quoted by Eayrs, p. 72. See also *Documents on Canadian External Relations* 6, pp. 1100–3, No. 903, Memorandum by O. D. Skelton After the Munich Agreement, 3.10.1938.

183 *D O 114*, 94, p. 54, Appendix II, No. 20, F82/299, Mackenzie King to Chamberlain, Telegram, 30.9.1938.

184 *Times*, 30.9.1938; *Manchester Guardian*, 1.10.1938; *Daily Telegraph*, 1.10.1938; *Sunday Times*, 2.10.1938.

Chamberlain became the 'man of the hour' in the United States.[185] This only lasted a few days before the questioning of the durability of the settlement changed the mood.[186] The administration was cautious from the outset and declined to comment on the merits of the pact.[187] There is evidence that Roosevelt temporarily shared the general enthusiasm. The president wrote on 5 October 1938 to Chamberlain suggesting that the British prime minister use his personal influence with Hitler to try to alleviate anti Semitism in Germany.[188]

When Chamberlain spoke to the house of commons on 3 October he said that he wished to place on record

> how greatly I was encouraged on each of the journeys I made to Germany by the knowledge that I went with the good wishes of the governments of the Dominions. They shared all our anxieties and all our hopes. They rejoiced with us that peace was preserved.[189]

Perhaps the dominions had played an even more significant role than Chamberlain admitted to the house. Throughout the crisis the cabinet had been conscious that war over Czechoslovakia might have meant the dissolution of the commonwealth. On the crucial day of 27 September Chamberlain and the majority of the cabinet seem to have been swayed by this consideration. At the very least Chamberlain used it to reinforce a policy which he had already decided upon. But Chamberlain made it clear to the cabinet that if the majority thought otherwise he was prepared to abandon conciliation. The majority had not. The commonwealth still counted.

---

[185] *Winnipeg Free Press*, 3.10.1938, Ed.

[186] *Daily Telegraph*, 1.10.1938; *Observer*, 2.10.1938; *Sunday Times*, 2.10.1938; *New York Times*, 2.10.1938.

[187] *Daily Telegraph*, 3.10.1938.

[188] Langer and Gleason, p. 35.

[189] Roosevelt to Kennedy, 5.10.1938, Telegram. Quoted by Langer and Gleason, p. 35.

VII

CONCILIATION AND REARMAMENT

Conciliation and Rearmament

CHAMBERLAIN returned from Munich with a certain confidence in Hitler and Mussolini. But this was not a blind trust. He told the cabinet on 3 October that although the position was 'more hopeful' in that contact had been established with the dictator powers, it would be madness to stop rearming until Britain's deficiencies had been made good.[1]

The cabinet drew the fine distinction between accelerating defence programmes which had already been approved, and starting on fresh ones. From 6 October the cabinet, the committee of imperial defence, and the service chiefs began to investigate ways of 'acceleration'.[2] Various recommendations were approved by the cabinet on 7 November. Twenty new naval escort vessels were to be laid. The air force was to be expanded by a considerable increase of the reserve strength as well as being re-equipped with the latest type of machines. There was to be concentration on fighter production and a bomber force was envisaged as 'the best deterrent to avoid war'.[3]

Presentation of defence policy was a problem. British foreign policy was that of the appeasement of Europe. Germany and Italy suspected that British rearmament was directed against them, and, as Chamberlain told the cabinet, it was important not to encourage such suspicions.[4] The defensive aspect of the new air programme had to be emphasised: Chamberlain felt that it was difficult to represent bombers in this light and that aspect should not be stressed. As the prime minister said: 'In our foreign policy we were doing our best to drive two horses abreast: conciliation and rearmament'.[5]

Increased production capacity was necessary, and some of the dominions assisted. On 19 October the cabinet considered the report of the air mission to Canada and decided to place an 'educational' order for eighty Hampden aircraft. This was to be done without any attempt to get from the Canadian government an assurance that the production capacity would be available to Britain in time of war. Orders were also placed for

1 *Cab 23*, 95, p. 304, Cab 48 (38) 5, Secret, 3.10.1938.
2 Ibid., 96, pp. 29–30, Cab 49 (38) 11, Secret, 19.10.1938.
3 Ibid., pp. 142–6, Cab 53 (3) 2, Secret, 7.11.1938.
4 Ibid., pp. 92–3, Cab 51 (38) 3, Secret, 31.10.1938.
5 Ibid., p. 164, Cab 53 (38) 2, Secret, 7.11.1938.

a maximum of forty fighter and twenty general reconnaissance aircraft. An air ministry expert was to be sent to explore the possibility of a group scheme for producing aeroplane engines in Canada.[6]

Wood, in his memorandum on the air mission, had warned of the seriousness of the political issue in Canada: Mackenzie King had only agreed to a communique on the mission after an amendment had been inserted which emphasised that the Canadian government was in no way involved in the arrangements which were to be concluded directly between the British government and Canadian industry. The Canadian prime minister feared that a reference to the delivery of big bombers across the Atlantic would suggest a restriction on the Canadian parliament's freedom to chose what stand to take in the event of war. The Canadian government was also embarrassed by the mission which was discussing the training of pilots in Canda for the royal air force.[7]

On 21 December a proposal initiated by Bruce, and supported by Lyons, for the creation of war potential to produce aircraft in Australia that could be used by the British and Australian air forces, came before the cabinet.[8] Lyons implied that Australia should be rewarded for its good behaviour over defence preparations:

Some scheme of this nature is a vital gesture at this juncture, particularly in view of prominence given in the press to favourable conditions under which factories are apparently being established in Canada.[9]

Even though this scheme was expensive the cabinet decided to pursue it as the advantage of having war potential away from possible trouble, 'and in a place where the capacity could be used to reinforce Singapore and perhaps commands further West' would justify the cost. The desirability of sending a similar mission to New Zealand was to be investigated.[10]

Alongside rearmament the other 'horse' of British foreign policy was conciliation. As Chamberlain told the cabinet on 31 October:

Our Foreign Policy was one of appeasement: we must aim at establishing relations with the Dictator Powers which will lead to a settlement in Europe and to a sense of stability.

Chamberlain hoped to follow up Munich and to achieve better relations with Hitler and Mussolini. An 'improvement in confidence' was necessary

[6] Ibid., pp. 31–2, Cab 49 (38) 12, Secret, 19.10.1938.

[7] *Cab 24*, 270, pp. 175–6, C P 224 (38), Memorandum by Wood on Creation of a War Production Potential for Aircraft Production in Canada, Secret, 13.10.1938.

[8] *Cab 23*, 96, pp. 454–5, Cab 60 (38) 12, Secret, 21.12.1938.

[9] *Cab 24*, 281, C P 294 (38), Memorandum by Wood on Manufacture of Aircraft in Australia, Secret, 15.12.1938; Appendix, Lyons to Bruce, Telegram, Most Secret, 9.12.1938.

[10] *Cab 23*, 96, pp. 454–5, Cab 60 (38) 12, Secret, 21.12.1938.

before there could be a limitation of armaments. The bringing into effect of the Anglo-Italian agreement was seen as a step in this direction.[11]

Since May the only obstacle in the way of the Italian agreement had been the Spanish question. After Munich Mussolini withdrew half of the Italian infantry from Spain, and Halifax recommended to the cabinet on 26 October that the agreement should be brought into force since, if the opportunity were not grasped, it might not recur. Halifax felt that every effort should be made to liberate Mussolini from Berlin.[12]

Although dominion views on this subject were not mentioned to the cabinet, Chamberlain, when he faced the house of commons on 2 November, used the argument of Australian pressure and South African approval of the *de jure* recognition of the conquest of Abyssinia.[13]

According to a memorandum prepared by the dominions office of the views of the dominion governments on the Anglo-Italian agreement, dated 6 October, the only government to have made recent moves on this matter had been South Africa. In August the Italian *chargé d'affaires* in South Africa had raised the question of recognition of the king of Italy as emperor of Abyssinia. On 16 August South Africa let Britain know that it was prepared to act accordingly but it did not wish to do so if this would prove awkward for the British. The reply was that naturally the British would prefer the commonwealth to follow a common course of action in this matter. South Africa took no further action. The Czecho-slovakian crisis probably accounts for South Africa's concern at this time.[14] On 31 October Hertzog welcomed the bringing into effect of the Anglo-Italian agreement as 'wise and necessary' and as contributing 'materially' to appeasement in Europe.[15]

The Australian government, as Lyons later explained publicly, had been consistently of the opinion that the maintenance of harmonious relations with Italy should be a cardinal aim of British foreign policy owing to contiguous British and Italian interests in the Mediterranean, the Suez canal, the Red sea, and in east Africa. Because of its geographical position this was of particular importance to Australia: Lyons on 17 April had welcomed the clause establishing liberty of transit through the Suez canal as being 'particularly gratifying to Australia as the Suez Canal is such an

11 Ibid., pp. 92–3, Cab 51 (38) 3, Secret, 31.10.1938.

12 Ibid., pp. 46–52, Cab 50 (38) 2, Secret, 26.10.1938.

13 *U.K. Parl Deb H of C*, 340, col. 211, 2.11.1938.

14 *D O 114*, 88, No. 104, F43/162, Note Prepared in Dominions Office on the Views of Dominion Governments on Anglo-Italian Agrrement, 6.10.1938 (proof).

15 Ibid., No. 106, F43/116, te Water to MacDonald, 31.10.1938.

essential factor in her communications with United Kingdon and European markets'. In July Lyons's government had telegraphed Sir Earle Page, the Australian deputy prime minister who was then in London, requesting him to urge the British government that the bringing into effect of the Anglo-Italian agreement was of paramount importance. Then on 26 October Australia had sent a further message to the effect that the Anglo-Italian agreement should be brought into effect immediately.[16]

Mackenzie King was careful to emphasise that Canada had not been consulted, but had only been informed of the Anglo-Italian agreement.[17] But Canadian recognition of Abyssinia followed shortly,[18] and there was general approval from the rest of the commonwealth, even though the opposition in Australia objected on moral grounds.[19] New Zealand did not express any opinion.

This was an instance in which the dominions were informed rather than consulted. There is little evidence of dominion views having a decisive influence on British statesmen, but the stand by Lyons and Hertzog bolstered Chamberlain's case, and probably helped the prime minister to secure a favourable reception for his policy. On the whole the dominions favoured the British policy of conciliation and rearmament and assisted the British government where they could, but were careful to maintain freedom of choice in their hands.

The extent to which the British were prepared to conciliate the dictators at this time can be guaged from reaction to the issue of colonial compensation for Germany. The issue had been dormant for six months and by October the Germans still had not sent the promised written reply to the proposals that Henderson had made to Hitler on 3 March 1938.[20] Seemingly the British were not anxious to reopen negotiations, but Hertzog, and Pirow, spoke of settling the issue as far so South Africa was concerned, by offering Germany monetary compensation for South West Africa.[21] In mid October Pirow's statements to the press on this subject caused the British some concern, especially as Pirow was scheduled to

---

[16] *Times*, 3.11.1938; *F O 800*, 310, p. 25, H/IX/112, Lyons to British Government, Telegram, Personal Secret, 6.7.1938.

[17] *D O 114*, 88, No. 107, F43/167, High Commissioner in Canada to Dominions Office, Telegram No. 241, 2.11.1938 r. 3.11.1938.

[18] P.N.S. Mansergh, *Survey of British Commonwealth Affairs. Problems of External Policy 1931–1939* (Oxford, 1952), p. 131.

[19] *Aust. Parl Deb*, 1938 157, H of R, cols. 1484–5, 16.11.1938.

[20] *F O 371*, 21682, pp. 265–9, C13657/184/18, Foreign Office Memorandum on Action taken with regard to German Colonial Claims since the beginning of 1938, 21.10.1938.

[21] Ibid., 21681, pp. 81–5, C12550/184/18, Colonial Office to Foreign Office, Secret, 15.10.1938 r. in r. 19.10.1938; Transmitting High Commissioner in South Africa to Dominions Office, Telegram No. 149, 14.10.1938 (copy).

visit various European capitals.[22] Settlers in Tanganyika were uneasy too.[23] On 19 October the high commissioner in South Africa impressed upon Pirow the undesirability of making statements on the colonial question in case they should prejudice possible discussions with Germany on a general settlement.[24] When the high commissioner spoke to Smuts the following day he ascertained that Pirow did not have a mandate to discuss the colonial question in London. But the South African government would be glad if the British did discuss the matter with Pirow. Smuts felt that the South West African issue still could be settled by monetary payment, and wondered whether the British could not do the same with Tanganyika.[25] Foreign office officials were surprised that Smuts did not have a higher opinion of the strategic value of Tanganyika. R. L. Speaight was sceptical:

> It seems to me fantastic to suggest that at this stage Hitler wd [*sic*] accept money payments as an equivalent of any of Germany's former African colonies; although he has said that he wd. [*sic*] accept equivalent territory elsewhere in Africa in place of Tanganyika.[26]

Consequently a foreign office memorandum on action taken over Germany's colonial claims was drawn up on 21 October. Cadogan did not see it, but Sir O. Sargent wrote a long minute on 22 October suggesting that at Munich Hitler and Chamberlain had stated that they were determined to remove all possible sources of difference between their countries. Sargent felt that the colonial question was the chief source of difference. If the question were to be reopened in the spirit of the Munich declaration it would be best for the British to keep the initiative as they could then discuss their proposals rather than those of Hitler. Britain would have to decide what territories it would be prepared to hand back: in the interview of 3 March Hitler had noticed this omission. The other mandatory powers also would have to be consulted. Germany could be asked for a *quid pro quo* in the interests of European appeasement generally. Another advantage would be that a conference of mandatories

> would have the effect of bringing the South African government into the open and would force General Hertzog to explain how he proposes to harmonise his

22 Ibid., p. 82, Foreign Office Minute by I. Mallet, 18.10.1938.

23 Ibid., pp. 96–7, C12652/184/18, Dixon to Strang, Secret, 19.10.1938 r. in r. 21.10.1938; Transmitting F24/174, Dominions Office to High Commissioner in South Africa, Telegram No. 120, Important Secret, 17.10.1938 (cypher).

24 Ibid., p. 98, F25/174, Dominions Office to High Commissioner in South Africa, Telegram No. 122, Immediate Secret, 18.10.1938; pp. 119–21, C12717/184/18, Dominions Office to Foreign Office, 20.10.1938 r. in r. 22.10.1938; Transmitting High Commissioner in South Africa to Dominions Office, Telegram No. 154, Secret, 19.10.1938 (paraphrase).

25 Ibid., pp. 154–8, C12908/184/18, Cockram to Strang, 21.10.1938 r. in r. 26.10.1938; Transmitting F25/177, High Commissioner in South Africa to Dominions Office, Telegram No. 157, Secret, 20.10.1938 (paraphrase).

26 Ibid., Foreign Office Minutes by Creswell, 26.10.1938; R. L. Speaight, Undated. See also *Premier 1*, 289.

policy of reconciliation with Germany with his refusal to hand back German South West Africa and with the veto which he placed on H.M.G. handing back Tanganyika.[27]

Pirow broached the matter in London on 3 November at a meeting with MacDonald. South Africa was prepared only to make 'sunstantial financial sacrifices'. For political and military reasons South Africa was opposed to Germany receiving Tanganyika. Militarily, such a move would mean the end of Kenya and would bring Pretoria and the Witwatersrand into effective bombing range. Politically, Smuts had cleared the Germans out of Tanganyika and South African lives had been lost in the campaign. Pirow explained that South West Africa was a different matter as it concerned South Africa alone, but South Africa's position on that territory was substantially the same.[28]

Pirow was more expansive in an interview on 7 November. He thought that the German claim could be settled by the handing over of territory on the west coast of Africa. Germany could be given Togoland, the Cameroons and French Equatorial Africa. France could be compensated elsewhere. If Germany were not satisfied perhaps the Belgians and the Portuguese would make a contribution in that part of Africa. Britain could compensate the Belgians and Portuguese with a part of Tanganyika.

As was usual this involved other countries making the sacrifices. Mac-Donald delicately enquired whether South Africa would help by giving Portugal a piece of South West Africa. Pirow doubted whether Portugal would want the northern part of that territory as it was desert and worthless.

Pirow learned that the British had had a plan to settle the colonial issue, but that the *Anschluss* had intervened. The British were beginning to examine the question again, but no conclusions had been reached. Pirow was relieved as he had been afraid that Britain had decided to return Tanganyika.[29]

Gie told Sir E. T. Harding of the dominions office on 4 November that German intent was concentrated on Africa.[30] Harding spoke also to Sir Pierre van Ryneveld, the South African chief of the general staff, on

[27] Ibid., pp. 262–9, C13657/184/18, Foreign Office Memorandum on Action taken with regard to German Colonial Claims since the beginning of 1938, 21.10.1938; Foreign Office Minute by O. E. Sargent, 22.10.1938.

[28] Ibid., pp. 242–9, C13625/184/18, Hankinson to Harvey, 4.11.1938; Transmitting Conversation between MacDonald, Inskip, Pirow and te Water, 3.11.1938.

[29] Ibid., pp. 300–3, C13874/184/18, Dixon to Foreign Office, 14.11.1938; Transmitting Conversation between MacDonald and Pirow, 7.11.1938.

[30] Ibid., pp. 304–5, Transmitting Conversation between Sir E. J. Harding and Gie, 4.11.1938.

8 November and learned that Herr Dewitz had said that the Germans would lay stress on the return of Tanganyika.[31]

The foreign office remained unimpressed by the case made by the various South Africans. T. K. Roberts minuted:

> I cannot help feeling that the Union Govt. is living in a fool's paradise if it imagines that German colonial claims can be permanently satisfied without German S.W. Africa or Tanganyika.[32]

Henderson saw Pirow in London on 11 November. The ambassador to Germany found Pirow 'very German in his mentality', and suggested that being a German himself 'Pirow wants Germany as far away as possible from the Union'. Pirow was told of the British Congo basin offer to Hitler of 3 March and Henderson suggested to Pirow that he might try to sound Hitler as it would be useful to know if the führer had any views beyond the restoration of all Germany's old colonies. Pirow, however, should make it clear that he was 'speaking without authority and personally'.[33]

Chamberlain did explain to the cabinet that the colonial question could be discussed only as part of a general settlement: 'such a settlement was clearly impossible in the circumstances'. Halifax thought that Pirow would make it clear to Berlin that for the present no progress could be made.[34]

In Germany Pirow saw Ribbentrop on 18 November and learnt that the colonial question was not acute. When Pirow met Hitler at Berchtesgaden on 24 November the führer seemed disinterested in this subject. Pirow, however, told Hitler that Chamberlain had mentioned to te Water a few months previously that Hitler's claim to African colonies would have to be sympathetically considered. The führer learnt that South Africa was opposed to the return of South West Africa for political and military reasons, but was prepared to pay £50,000,000 compensation and to give Germany certain trading advantages. The South African government was equally implacable over east Africa. Pirow explained that:

> East Africa was a country which was already integrated as a result of its internal relations, in the great stretch of territory of the whites in Africa, which extended in a chain from Abyssinia to the Cape. This was a community of a white master race as opposed to the Negroes.

Germany could hardly become a member of this since they would stand outside the community being Germans first and Africans second. Hitler

---

[31] Ibid., p. 306, Transmitting Conversation between Sir E. J. Harding and Sir Pierre van Ryneveld, 8.11.1938.

[32] Ibid., p. 300, Foreign Office Minute by T.K. Roberts, 18.11.1938.

[33] Ibid., pp. 291–4, C13874/184/18, Henderson (London) to Halifax 11.11.1938.

[34] *Cab 23*, 96, p. 218, Cab 55 (38) 2, Secret, 16.11.1938.

seemed disinterested: the colonial question 'must be brought up again in 5 or 6 years'.[35] According to MacDonald, however, Pirow apparently told Hitler and Goering that if it were essential 'for world peace that South West Africa should go back to Germany, then Germany could have it'.[36] T. K. Roberts minuted that this was dangerous and that Pirow might regret it later.[37] Perhaps Pirow spoke in a moment of despair: his impressions of Germany made him pessimistic about the future, and he returned to South Africa expecting war.[38]

Because of the attitude of South African statesmen the British government had to reconsider the colonial question. Despite the 'spirit of Munich' this was thought possible only as part of a general settlement. By November that was not likely. As Halifax told the cabinet on 16 November British policy was to 'press on with the acceleration of our defence measures and with administrative arrangements in connection with air raid precautions, and with a view to encouraging the moderate opinion and discouraging the extremists in Germany'.[39] Pirow also, after his visit to Europe, was so pessimistic that South Africa was not likely to believe any more that Germany could be bought off on the South West Africa question.

The principal object of Pirow's visit, however, was to discuss defence matters. The committee for imperial defence considered preparations in this regard, and co-operation with South African forces, on 27 October. MacDonald pointed out that Britain needed South African help for the defence of the east African colonies. For instance, during the Munich crisis, the air ministry had asked the dominions office to approach the South African government for the assistance of two squadrons, but the crisis had passed before any definite approach had been made. MacDonald felt that it would be better to have joint plans drawn up beforehand. Pirow would not commit himself. South Africa was likely to have the same attitude as Canada and Ireland. But the same procedure should be followed as was intended with Ireland: two sets of plans should be drawn up, one on the assumption of the event of war, the other not. There were fears that South Africa might demand a say in the governing of the east African colonies, but if the plans were conditional only it would be reasonable for

[35] *Documents on German Foreign Policy* D IV (hereafter cited as '*DGFP*'), p. 335, No. 270, 1585/382908–9 R M No. 257, Memorandum by Ribbentrop, 18.11.1938; pp.33–41, No. 271, 217/147842–54, Memorandum by Hewel, 24.11.1938; Oswald Pirow, *James Barry Munnik Hertzog* (Cape Town, 1958), pp. 233–8.

[36] *F O 371*, 21791, pp. 358–66, C15125/13564/18, Hankinson to Harvey, 6.12.1938; Transmitting Conversation between MacDonald and Pirow, 5.12.1938.

[37] Ibid., p. 358, Foreign Office Minute by T. K. Roberts, 9.12.1938.

[38] Ibid., pp. 337–43, C1465/13564/18, Harding to Clark, Secret and Personal, 2.12.1938; Transmitting Sir O. Forbes to Dominions Office, Telegram No. 729, 26.11.1938.

[39] *Cab 23*, 96, p. 218, Cab 55 (38) 2, Secret, 16.11.1938.

Britain to retain complete control in this area. Halifax pointed out that Pirow 'would no doubt be ready to recognise the close analogy afforded by the fact that although the British Navy gave protection to South Africa, we did not claim on that account to have any control over the policy of the Union Government'.

Pirow's main concern, however, was for the defence of Cape Town. And MacDonald warned the committee that it would be difficult to negotiate with Pirow. Pirow, to carry out the £6,000,000 scheme to put the defences of South Africa in order, required a large amount of material and equipment from Britain. If Pirow failed, his reputation in South Africa would suffer.

The committee's interest was in the protection of Simonstown. MacDonald warned that if Britain did not meet Pirow's demands South Africa might go elsewhere and would not be forthcoming over the defence of Simonstown. Every effort was made to meet 'the personal peculiarities of Mr. Pirow and the rather tortuous methods of negotiation which he employed'.[40]

MacDonald saw Pirow on 2 November. Pirow said that he intended to put the guns into position for the defence of Simonstown 'straight away' and hoped that in return Britain would supply South Africa with Bren guns and a monitor for Durban. MacDonald delicately broached the matter of defence co-operation in Africa while making it clear that Britain understood that South Africa could not undertake any commitment automatically to be at war if Britain were at war. Pirow saw no difficulty in this, and added, perhaps surprisingly:

> The possibility of the Union remaining neutral in a war in which Great Britain was involved was becoming more and more theoretical. In practice war was no respecter of persons or countries, and we should be in together.[41]

The next day Pirow spoke generally about South Africa's position: it was possible that the time would come when South Africa, as the only white nation in those parts, would be responsible for the peace of southern Africa, even including the Belgian Congo. There was the difficulty of Belgian and Portuguese suspicions of South African expansionist tendencies, as well as nationalist opposition suspicion that military preparations meant that South Africa was becoming 'a pawn or puppet in imperial policy'. These difficulties could be overcome, but if South Africa were,

---

[40] *Cab 2*, 8, pp. 69–72, C I D Minutes of 336th Mtg, Secret Lock and Key, 27.10.1938.
[41] *F O 371*, 21682, pp. 36–41, C13624/184/18, Hankinson to Harvey, 3.11.1938; Transmitting Conversation between MacDonald and Pirow, 2.11.1938.

say to defend Kenya, it would need help from Britain, particularly in regard to tank corps and aircraft equipment. Inskip protested that this would throw a double burden on Britain: 'that of providing equipment for a South African army, and, at the same time, of being herself equipped to undertake the tasks which Mr. Pirow envisaged in the event of South Africa's non-intervention'. It turned out that Pirow, if anything, wanted more: the co-operation of equipped units, such as tank corps, anti aircraft batteries and artillery. For this an exchange of information between staffs was desirable, but he would need the authority of the South African cabinet before there could be progress with the preparation of a joint defence plan. South Africa would have to know what the future of Tanganyika was to be.

Generally Pirow seemed prepared to fall in with British plans for South Africa's naval defence: Pirow felt that South Africa would be overinsured —as did the British but it was considered useless to impress Pirow with the technical arguments—but South Africa was 'prepared to incur this expense in view of the vital importance of Cape Town to the security of the trade routes of the Empire'. In most directions the British were able to supply Pirow with the equipment he wanted 'as soon as, or nearly as soon as, he could make use of it'. There was minor disagreement on the Bren gun issue, probably as a result of Pirow's confusion between the old machine gun and the Bren gun, but Pirow undertook to consult his chief of staff on this question.[42]

On the instructions of the committee for imperial defence the chiefs of staff sub committee drew up a list of suggestions for closer potential co-operation in imperial defence between South Africa and Britain. The paper pointed out:

> If we [Britain] became engaged in war with Germany and Italy at the same time the military resources of the United Kingdom would be strained to the utmost, and it would be to the interest of the Union Government themselves to assist our local forces in Africa to hold out wherever they may be attacked, even as far north as the shores of the Mediterranean.

Suggestions were made for South Africa to increase certain naval precautions, and to prepare units for garrisoning important points in other parts of Africa which might be of strategic importance in war, especially if the Mediterranean route were closed. Lourenço Marques, in allied Portuguese hands, was also only lightly garrisoned and should be a matter

---

[42] Ibid., pp. 242–9, C13625/184/18, Hankinson to Harvey, 4.11.1938; Transmitting Conversation between MacDonald, Inskip, Pirow and te Water, 3.11.1938.

of concern to South Africa. Mention was made also of the maintenance of field units for use outside South Africa in the event, for instance, of an Italian raid on Mombasa, assistance in the defence of the Sudan, or to meet the advance by an enemy from Lourenço Marques. Air assistance could be given also by the despatch on the outbreak of war, of reinforcing squadrons to north east Africa or Aden, and the provision of maintenance personnel for British depots in Egypt, Iraq, and possibly also in Kenya.[43]

Pirow was told of the existence of this memorandum on 11 November by Harding. For political reasons Pirow did not want a copy to be on view in South Africa, but agreed that Lieutenant Colonel R. A. O. Brooks, royal marines, who was attached to him as a liaison officer could inform van Ryneveld of the contents of the paper.[44]

Most of the defence measures were fairly satisfactory concluded. South Africa accepted the offer, made in 1936, of the loan of H.M.S. *Erebus* as a temporary addition to the coast defences of South Africa pending the installation of shore batteries. South Africa was also contemplating provisions of 'a very secret nature' for the defence of Lourenço Marques.[45]

Pirow, after his visits to London and Europe, seems to have been left without illusions. When asked by Hitler and Goering about the attitude of the dominions in general and South Africa in particular, he had replied:

> In the case of the last crisis South Africa would not have entered the war at once. But a Government which had not taken South Africa into the war would not have lived very long, and within six months the Union would have been fighting on the side of Britain. He had told both the German leaders that South Africa was definitely in the Empire, and that she would remain in the Empire for the next hundred years or so.[46]

Pirow, when in Italy, told leading Italians the same story.[47] The impression that Pirow left on the Italians was that of being 'an outstanding example of the rapidity with which a race living in another latitude could deteriorate'.[48]

---

[43] *Cab 5*, 9, 488C, C I D South Africa Co-operation in Imperial Defence Visit of Pirow to England, Secret, Jan. 1939; Enclosure C O S 794, Chiefs of Staff Sub Committee Memorandum on South Africa Co-operation in Imperial Defence Visit of Pirow to England, 14.11.1938.

[44] Ibid., 488C, C I D South Africa Co-operation in Imperial Defence Visit of Pirow to England, Secret, Jan. 1939.

[45] *Cab 5*, 9, 4870, South African Coast Defences Note by Ismay, Secret, 7.12.1938.

[46] *F O 371*, 21791, pp. 358–66, C15125/13564/18, Hankinson to Harvey, 6.12.1938; Transmitting Conversation between MacDonald and Pirow, 5.12.1938.

[47] Ibid., pp. 347–55, C15021/13564/18, Perth to Halifax, 28.11.1938.

[48] *DGFP*, p. 342, No. 272, 2129/464890–1, Mackenson to German Foreign Ministry, Telegram No. 313, Most Secret, 28.11.1938.

Conciliation and Rearmament

From the Britsh point of view, with regard to defence and Pirow's education, the mission of the South African minister was satisfactory. The British policy of not trying to secure automatic South African commitment in the event of war had resulted in Pirow taking a fairly co-operative stand. Personally Pirow did not believe that South Africa could stay out of war indefinitely. Pirow seemed to feel that war was inevitable, and as T. K. Roberts minuted, Pirow's impressions 'although extremely pessimistic, are not very wide of the mark . . . Mr. Pirow's remarks about South Africa's attitude to the Empire and the necessity for some gesture from the German side should have done good coming from him'.[49]

On his visit to Germany Pirow also acted as a messenger of the British government: he undertook to gauge Hitler's reaction to certain proposals for the settlement of refugees. In the months after Munich the cabinet was concerned with this question especially as it was one on which United States opinion was sensitive.

Chamberlain was conscious of United States opinion, and its significance for his policy. According to Lord Home it was this awareness that led Chamberlain to secure Hitler's signature to the Munich declaration as being 'symbolic of the desire of our two peoples never to go to war with one another again'. Chamberlain told Home just before Hitler signed the document:

If he [Hitler] signs it and sticks to it that will be fine, but if he breaks it that will convince the Americans of the kind of man he is.[50]

Britain kept the United States informed of its policy. On 12 October Halifax, according to Kennedy, spoke of Hitler not wanting war with Britain, and of their being no sense in fighting Germany unless the dominions were threatened. Britain should concentrate on its air defences and allow Hitler free reign in central Europe. Britain's future role was a limited one: the maintenance of friendly relations with Portugal, hopefully Spain, Greece, Turkey, Egypt, and Palestine; the connections in the Red sea and with the dominions; and of friendly relations with the United States.[51] Later, on 28 October, Halifax hinted that Roosevelt was the only suitable arbitrator for the colonial question.[52]

---

[49] *F O 371*, 21791, p. 358, C15125/13564/18, Hankinson to Harvey, 6.12.1938; Foreign Office Minute by T. K. Roberts, 9.12.1938.

[50] Iain Macleod, *Neville Chamberlain* (London, 1961), pp. 255–6.

[51] *Foreign Relations of the United States* (hereafter cited as 'FRUS') 1938(1), pp. 85–6, 741.00/202, Kennedy to Hull, Telegram No. 1167, 12.10.1938.

[52] Ibid., pp. 95–7, 740.00/501, Kennedy to Hull, Telegram No. 1260, 28.10.1938.

Roosevelt was soon disillusioned with the Munich agreement: on 11 October the president announced that the United States defence budget would be increased by $3,000,000.[53] During October United States press reaction also changed. By the end of the month a tone of isolationist revulsion was discernible.[54]

It was the refugee question that in the end roused United States opinion. As early as 6 October Roosevelt sent a personal message to Chamberlain hoping that the prime minister would find a suitable opportunity to take this matter up with Hitler. Chamberlain wrote to Roosevelt that he shared the president's concern; the chairman of the inter governmental committee on refugees was considering the possibility of the director visiting Berlin.[55]

The dominions did not co-operate wholeheartedly on this issue. MacDonald met dominion representatives on 5 October to discuss the question of Sudeten refugees. He emphasised that Britain and the dominion governments had a greater 'moral responsibility in this case than in the case of Jewish and other refugees from Germany proper or Austria'. The dominion representatives argued that their governments were already taking Jewish refugees, could not consider any mass settlement, and would be prepared only to consider individual applications on their merits. The only concession came from Bruce and Massey: if the refugees were farming stock they might be welcomed in Australia and Canada.[56]

When Winterton, as chairman of the inter governmental committee dealing with the refugee question, brought the matter to the cabinet's attention on 19 October, he mentioned the danger that Britain would find itself 'in controversy' with the United States government on this issue. The director of the committee was a personal friend of Roosevelt. The United States representatives were saying that the United States had offered to take 27,000 refugees, not a generous response considering that there were over 600,000, and that Britain had not agreed to receive any definite number.[57]

[53] William L. Langer and S. Everett Gleason, *The Challenge to Isolation* (London, 1952), p. 37.

[54] Anonymous, 'Overseas Reactions to the Crisis: The United States of America', *Round Table*, XXIX (1938–9), pp. 28–31; *Daily Telegraph*, 3.10.1938, 11.10.1938, 19.10.1938; *New York Times*, 5.10.1938, 8.10.1938; *Observer*, 9.10.1938; *Evening Standard*, 10.10.1938; *Daily Herald*, 14.10.1938; *Sunday Times*, 16.10.1938; *Manchester Guardian*, 20.10.1938, 21.10.1938.

[55] *F O 414*, 275 L, p. 32, No. 19, W13303/104/98, Halifax to Lindsay, Telegram No. 683, 7.10.1938.

[56] *F O 371*, 21745, pp. 289–302, C11684/1914/18, Foreign Office Minute by T. K. Roberts on Conversation between MacDonald and Dominion Representatives about possible Emigration of Sudeten Refugees to the Dominions, 5.10.1938 r. in r. 6.11.1938.

[57] *Cab 23*, 96, pp. 8–23, Cab 49 (38) 3, Secret, 19.10.1938.

The repercussions of Hitler's pogrom against the Jews made the matter more acute, Kennedy told Halifax that the German action had produced a 'strong anti-British atmosphere' in the United States. United States opinion did not reason: presumably it argued that Britain was 'near at hand and that it was supposed that it should have been able to take effective steps to stop the persecution of the Jews'. Halifax said that he was 'at a complete loss to understand by what process American opinion could properly blame us because the German Government chose to persecute Jews, especially as they did not seem very forward in willingness to do anything very substantial themselves'.[58]

The foreign secretary explained to the cabinet on 16 November that public opinion in the United States was about as critical as it could be. He hoped that if Britain could take a lead which would force the United States to take some positive action, the position might be restored, the way to do this was to help the Jews. Possibly some part of the empire could be found for Jewish settlement. MacDonald, however, explained that the likelihood of such settlement should not be exaggerated. Winterton reported that the state department felt that Britain was not doing enough. This Winterton felt was untrue: Australia, under British pressure, was taking 5,000 a year; New Zealand accepted a few; and Winterton had had satisfactory talks with Massey who felt that Canada should take some action. Britain was accepting a large number but the figure could not be published in case of anti Semitic reaction. The United States, however, would accept no more refugees than their normal immigration quota. Even Australia's action compared favourably with that of the United States: Bruce had told MacDonald that the Australian quota might be raised to 6,000 or even 7,000.[59]

Winterton also saw Pirow on 16 November about the refugee question. Pirow explained that South Africa was not unsympathetic, but that it had a serious Jewish problem and refugees could not be allowed to settle there.[60]

It was Pirow who sounded Hitler on the refugee question, acting as the British government's unofficial emissary. Chamberlain told Pirow of a scheme which had been drawn up by a British member of parliament,

[58] *F O 414*, 275 L, pp. 46–7, C13900/1667/62, Halifax to Lindsay, Telegram No. 905, 15.11.1938.

[59] *Cab 23*, 96, pp. 221–9, Cab 55 (38) 5, Secret, 16.11.1938. See also *F O 371*, 22537, pp. 62–113, W15343/104/98, Hobbert to Makins, 20.11.1938 r. in r. 23.11.1938; Transmitting Information on Settlement of German Refugees in the Colonial Empire.

[60] *F O 371*, 22537, pp. 337–44, W15214/104/98, Foreign Office Minute by Mr. Reilly recording Discussion between Winterton, Rublee and Pell, 17.11.1938 r. in r. 21.11.1938.

Captain Victor Cazalet. If the Jews in Germany could leave half their property their fellows in Britain and the United States would make up the difference. It might then be possible to set up a national home for the Jews in Tanganyika, Madagascar or British Guiana. Chamberlain said that if Hitler were to release half of the property Britain would guarantee a loan.[61] In substance this scheme was not very different from that suggested by Kennedy to Halifax on 15 November. Kennedy had said that while there was no hope of getting direct financial contributions from the United States government he thought that private sources in the United States could put up 100 or 200 million dollars, if a large scheme of land settlement could be proposed.[62]

Hitler was not enthusiastic about Chamberlain's scheme. The führer expostulated to Pirow against Jewish settlement of Tanganyika on the ground that he would never agree to hand over to Germany's arch enemy a country in which so much German blood had been sacrificed. And Hitler was sceptical about French willingness to sacrifice Madagascar.[63] Pirow was no more successful in Italy. He saw Ciano and suggested 'among other similar stupidities . . . that Mussolini should negotiate between Hitler and the Jews'.[64]

Pirow reported to Chamberlain on 7 December that Goering had spoken of giving up claims to Tanganyika if it could be used for settlement of Jews, but Hitler had repudiated the idea. The South African minister of defence was under the impression that no further move towards the appeasement of Europe could be expected from Hitler.[65]

British policy on the refugee question was influenced by a concern for United States opinion, a rather irrational opinion which seemed to blame Britain more than Germany, and to expect Britain to act in a case where the United States was not prepared to do anything.

Another move in the direction of consolidating Anglo-American co-operation was the signing of the trade treaties between the United States and Britain, and the United States and Canada, on 17 November.[66] In September the British felt that the United States was taking advantage of

61 Pirow, pp. 233–8.
62 *F O 414*, 275L, pp. 46–7, No. 27, C13900/1667/62, Halifax to Lindsay, Telegram No. 905, 15.11.1938.
63 Pirow, pp. 233–8; *DGFP*, pp. 336–41, No. 271, 217/147842–54, Memorandum by Hewel, 24.11.1938.
64 *DGFP*, p. 342, No. 272, 2129/464890–1, Mackensen to German Foreign Ministry, Telegram No. 313, Most Secret, 28.11.1938.
65 *F O 371*, 21791, pp. 375–8, C15270/13564/18, Chamberlain to Foreign Office, 7.12.1938 r. in r. 10.12.1938.
66 Richard N. Kottman, *Reciprocity and the North Atlantic Triangle, 1932–1938* (Ithaca New York, 1968), pp. 265–6.

the European situation to 'force an unfair agreement down . . . their throats'. Lindsay was reassured on this issue, but warned that the state department considered the United States proposals fair to both parties.[67] On 9 October Lindsay advised the British government that it would be unwise to face a breakdown of the negotiations on these demands.[68]

The cabinet debated the matter on 19 October. Simon doubted whether the treaty would be approved by the commercial community in Britain, Stanley, the president of the board of trade, felt that 'we should make up our minds now as how far we should go and should refuse to make any further concessions'. Discussions with Kennedy had confirmed Stanley in this view.[69] Kennedy certainly reported to his government that Chamberlain headed a cabinet opposed to the treaty, and that Stanley was concerned about accusations in parliament of a 'complete sell out'. Chamberlain wanted an agreement:

> He had never hoped that we should obtain any great economic or political support from the United States as a result of making this Agreement. The advantages to be derived were of a somewhat negative kind. It was clear that if after months of negotiations no Agreement was reached, hard things would be said.[70]

Lindsay delivered the British proposals on 25 October with the warning that they were 'virtually the last word'. Although Hull did not like the ultimatum, he accepted the British scheme rather than risk the economic and political consequences that might result from the collapse of negotiations.[71]

Throughout these negotiations Canada played a significant role. Mackenzie King wanted an Anglo-American agreement, but he faced divisions in his cabinet. Canada, for political reasons, had to be compensated for its losses by concessions in the United States market.[72] On 30 September Mackenzie King urged Chamberlain to conclude the trade negotiations in the interests of world peace and economic appeasement. The Canadian government had agreed to modify all margins of preference enjoyed by Canada in Britain necessary to facilitate an agreement between Britain and the United States.[73] Mackenzie King even urged Chamberlain to travel to the United States to sign the trade agreement. The Canadian

---

[67] Ibid., p. 259.
[68] *Cab 23*, 96, p. 17, Cab 49 (38), 9, 19.10.1938.
[69] Ibid., pp. 18–23.
[70] Kottman, pp. 260–1; *Cab 23*, 96, pp. 18–23, Cab 49 (38) 9, Secret, 19.10.1938.
[71] Kottman, pp. 262–3.
[72] Ibid., p. 243.
[73] *F O 371*, 21506, pp. 86–9, A7627/1/45, Hankinson to Caccia, 4.10.1938 r. in r. 8.10.1938; Transmitting T766/449, Chamberlain to Mackenzie King, Telegram No. 56, Immediate Confidential, 4.10.1938.

prime minister had mentioned the possibility to Roosevelt who had appeared delighted.[74] A foreign office official minuted:

> The idea was not doubt Mr. Mackenzie King's and the President could hardly have done other than welcome it when it was put to him in this way.[75]

The Canadian prime minister wrote to Chamberlain, a man whom he admired:

> I cannot urge too strongly upon yourself and your colleagues the wisdom of this trip from the point of view of your own health, the significance and importance of the trade agreement and the effect at this time upon the world of the evident friendship between Great Britain and America.

Chamberlain replied warmly, but pointed out that it would be difficult for him to travel to the United States as there were 'so many exceptionally important and pressing questions' requiring his attention in Britain.[76] On 14 November Chamberlain finally excused himself on the grounds of time: the United States wanted the agreement signed the following week.[77] Mackenzie King accepted this in a congratulatory telegram on the signing of the agreement in Washington.[78]

The press in Britain and the United States welcomed the agreement as strengthening the ties of friendship between the two countries. The co-operation of the dominions, and especially of Canada, in matching the British concessions to the United States was seen also as proof of commonwealth solidarity, and the desire of the member states for closer friendship with the United States.[79] Mackenzie King stated that he hoped that the arrangements would strengthen 'the friendly relations between the two countries with whose fortunes those of Canada are so closely associated'.[80]

By November 1938 the British cabinet was not as enthusiastic about the trade treaty as it had been in 1937. It was seen as offering political rather than economic advantages. And by that time Chamberlain felt that the advantages were negative. Concessions, however, had to be made on all

---

[74] Ibid., pp. 145–9, A7759/1/45, Hankinson to Harvey, Secret, 11.10.1938 r. in r. 13.10.1938; Transmitting Mackenzie King to Chamberlain, Unnumbered, Telegram, Strictly Personal, 10.10.1938 r. 11.10.1938.

[75] Ibid., pp. 145–6, Foreign Office Minute, 14.10.1938.

[76] Ibid., pp. 148–9, Mackenzie King to Chamberlain, Unnumbered, Telegram, Strictly Personal, 10.10.1938 r. 11.10.1938; 21507, pp. 118–21, A7964/1/45, Hankinson to Harvey, 21.10.1938 r. in r. 24.10.1938; Transmitting Chamberlain to Mackenzie King, Telegram Undated (cypher, draft), Action taken see 77977/A8556.

[77] Ibid., 21508, pp. 210–3, A8556/1/45, Hankinson to Harvey, 10.11.1938 r. in r. 14.11.1938; Transmitting T766/4608, Chamberlain to Mackenzie King, Telegram, Personal, Undated (cypher, draft).

[78] *F O 371*, 21509, pp. 164–6, A8509/1/45, Hankinson to Harvey, 23.11.1938 r. in r. 25.11.1938; Transmitting Mackenzie King to Chamberlain, Telegram, Personal, 18.11.1938 (copy). See also *Premier 1*, 291.

[79] *Times*, 19.11.1938; *New York Times*, 19.11.1938. See also Kottman, pp. 267–71.

[80] *Can Parl Deb H of C* 1939(1), p. 59, 16.1.1939.

sides, and treaties could be seen as marking a growing association between the United States and the commonwealth.

Another effort was made to win over United States public opinion with Eden's visit to that country in December 1938. Eden's opposition to Chamberlain's policy was well known. Kennedy felt that Eden might help to mollify opinion in the United States which had been critical of Munich and consequently anti British. Halifax was in favour of the visit, and Kennedy persuaded Eden to accept an invitation to address the national association of manufacturers in New York.[81]

Eden's visit had the desired effect. Mallet reported that the press comment was generally favourable, and singled out Eden's address to the national press club at Washington. There Eden

> made a special point of assuring his audience that nobody of the slightest importance in English public life was inclined either towards fascism or communism. This was a good point to make before an audience of journalists, many of whom are somewhat distressed by gossip about the 'Cliveden set', and tales that the Prime Minister has Fascist tendencies.[82]

Eden saw Sumner Welles and Roosevelt on 13 December. Roosevelt avoided the delicate topic of foreign policy, but kept insisting that Britain should increase its air strength. The president, however, 'gave no glimpse of any positive American policy either in the Far East or in Europe'.[83]

Another indication of the wish of the British government to do what it could to foster better feeling in the United States was the appointment of Lord Lothian as ambassador to Washington in succession to Lindsay. In the end Lothian did not take up the appointment until August, 1939, but the reasons for the appointment are significant. One of Lothian's correspondents in the United States had complained that the aloof and arrogant atmosphere of the British embassy in Washington offended United States journalists and congressmen alike. The building itself was known as 'the British compound'. The state department, too, did not react favourably to the formal notes from the British embassy, and the foreign relations committee characterised British *précis* as 'the British commands'.[84] Lothian agreed with many of these criticisms, and attributed their source to the fact that the embassy staff usually consisted of old

---

[81] Anthony Eden, *The Reckoning* (London, 1964), pp. 39–41.

[82] *F O 414*, 275L, pp. 70–2, No. 48, A9584/9029/45, Mallet to Halifax, No. 1107, 15.12.1938 r. 22.12.1938.

[83] Eden, pp. 39–41.

[84] *Lothian Papers* 358, pp. 666–70, James M. Witherow to Lothian, 5.11.1937; pp. 677–9, Witherow to Lothian, 26.2.1938.

public school boys 'many of whom manifest a constitutional inhibition when dealing with the average politician either in the Senate or the House of Representatives'. Lothian decided to take the matter up with Halifax,[85] and in August, 1938, Lothian himself agreed to go as ambassador to Washington.[86] Because of the delicate international situation it was considered inopportune to recall Lindsay, and in November 1938 a 'gentleman's agreement' was reached by which Lothian could be called upon to accept the post.[87] In December Lothian sailed for the United States under the guise of doing Rhodes scholarship business, to guage opinion.[88] He wrote to one of his correspondents: 'America really holds the key to the whole future'.[89]

Although at this time British efforts to secure the support of the United States in Europe came to little, in the far east there was some Anglo-American co-operation. When the Japanese closed the Yangtse river the United States initiated the protest even though it was British interests that were mainly affected.[90] On 3 November the United States decided to make representations to Japan as to the freedom of navigation on the Yangtse up to Hankow. The United States asked the British and French to make parallel representations. Only Britain was approached by the United States as to what action it would be prepared to take if the reply were unfavourable.[91]

Halifax raised this question in the cabinet on 10 November. He explained the significance of the action: until then the United States representations to the Japanese had been made independently. For the British, however, retaliation was difficult: a year previously the cabinet had decided that there was nothing that could be done. On that occasion action by Britain alone had been envisaged. If the United States were to co-operate the position might be different. Chamberlain warned that a United States proposal that relied on economic pressure only might not be effective. A possible consequence would be a Japanese attack on Hong Kong. The cabinet did not decide on action.[92]

At the end of November Britain proposed a currency loan to China as this was the only concrete action that it could take. It was decided that

85 Ibid., 367, p. 884, Lothian to Stamp, 10.5.1938 (copy).
86 Ibid., 369, pp. 4–6, Halifax to Lothian, Private and Confidential, 11.8.1938.
87 Ibid., p. 16, Halifax to Lothian, 22.11.1938.
88 Ibid., p. 40, Lothian to Frank Aydelotte, 2.12.1938 (copy).
89 Ibid., pp. 74–5, Lothian to Miss Butler, 13.12.1938 (copy).
90 Nicholas Clifford, *Retreat from China* (London, 1967), p. 89.
91 *Cab 23*, 96, pp. 181–2, Cab 54 (38) 3, Secret, 10.11.1938.
92 Ibid., *loc. cit.*

the United States should be approached for its support on this issue,[93] and on 21 December the cabinet agreed on a guarantee loan for currency purposes of up to £3,000,000 if the United States were prepared to take parallel action.[94] The United States replied on 11 January that it was prepared to take parallel and simultaneous, but not identical action. The difficulty of parallel action was that Japan could retaliate against Britain alone, without bringing in the United States. Chamberlain suggested that Britain might act on its own. He explained to the cabinet that the United States was 'anxious that we should come in and that if we took no action they would feel that we had done less than they in the matter'. The cabinet resolved on 18 January to ask the United States for details of the parallel action that it proposed.[95] But by 1 February it was obvious that the United States was 'backsliding'. The state department were alarmed at a suggestion that there might be a statement in the British parliament that the United States was proposing to take simultaneous and parallel action with Britain on the currency loan, and was worried about difficulties with the isolationists. The United States took the view that if Britain gave the loan it would be doing only as much for China as the United States had already done.[96]

What initially seemed like a change in the United States attitude in the far east did not materialise. The United States was still wary of becoming involved alongside Britain in a situation which could lead to war. Isolationist sentiment was strong.

Chamberlain, however, in December, did have Roosevelt's assurance that the president would try to see that the prime minister had 'the industrial resources of the American nation behind him in the event of war with the dictatorships'.[97] Colonel Arthur Murray, a close personal friend of Roosevelt, had visited the president at Hyde Park in October. Roosevelt told Murray that he hoped to provide Britain, if it were at war with the dictators, with basic materials such as aluminium plates, steel casings for engines and cylinder blocks, not covered by the neutrality acts, to enable the building of an extra 20,000 to 30,000 planes, to give superiority over Germany and Italy in the air.[98] Roosevelt was glad that this plan

93 Ibid., pp. 296–302, Cab 57 (38) 9, Secret, 30.11.1938.
94 Ibid., pp. 421–4, Cab 60 (38) 2, Secret, 21.12.1938.
95 Ibid., 97, pp. 13–6, Cab 1 (39) 3, Secret, 18.1.1939.
96 Ibid., pp. 105–6, Cab 3 (39) 3, Secret, 1.2.1939.
97 *Premier 1*, 367, Note of a Conversation between Roosevelt and Murray, Confidential, 16.10.1938. Left with Chamberlain by Murray, 14.12.1938.
98 *Elibank Papers* 8809, pp. 105–8, Murray to Halifax, October 1938 (copy).

helped the prime minister to realise his 'real friendship' for him.[99] Murray also, through Tweedsmuir, passed a suggestion of Roosevelt to Mackenzie King for the appointment of liaison officers between Canada and the United States so that information on aspects of aircraft design, engines and manufacture could pass confidentially between the Canadian, United States and British governments. Roosevelt was opposed to using existing official channels.[100]

In May 1939 Murray sent a message from Kingsley Wood to Roosevelt that the air ministry's chief needs would be light alloys and instruments used in aircraft. Britain would have adequate manufacturing facilities for any basic materials supplied from the United States.[101] Wood suggested that Kennedy might be informed of the arrangement. Murray opposed this: the president valued the unorthodox form of contact.[102] Roosevelt acknowledged the request on 10 July: 'Things along that line are going much better both in England and the United States'.[103] Although the cash and carry amendemnts to the neutrality legislation made the operation of the plan unnecessary, it did show the extent to which Roosevelt was prepared to help Britain, and the high regard he had for Chamberlain.[104]

By the end of 1938 conciliation and rearmament was still the policy of the British government. The general impression of this policy was given, perhaps, by Jordan at a meeting of dominion high commissioners on 1 December 1938. When told by MacDonald that the French had asked for additional assistance should a war break out Jordan protested that since Munich the 'assumption had seemed to be that war was inevitable and that it was necessary to increase armaments at once'.[105] Chamberlain, in pursuing this policy did his best to secure dominion co-operation on matters of defence, even though he had to work on the assumption that in the event of war South Africa, Ireland, Canada and even possibly Australia would not fight alongside Britain. At the same time Chamberlain made every effort to conciliate United States opinion, which after Munich and the Jewish pogrom verged on being anti British. The policy of conciliation,

[99] Ibid., pp. 162–3, Roosevelt to Col. and Mrs. Murray, 19.1.1939; p. 164, Murray to Chamberlain, 1.2.1939 (copy).

[100] Ibid., pp. 109–10, Note of Conversation between Roosevelt and Murray at Hyde Park, Confidential, 23.10.1938; p. 127, Murray to Roosevelt, 30.10.1938 (copy).

[101] Ibid., pp. 173–4, Wood to Murray, Secret, 10.5.1939; pp. 178–9, Murray to Roosevelt, Secret, 20.5.1939 (copy).

[102] Ibid., pp. 173–4, Wood to Murray, Secret, 10.5.1939; pp. 175–6, Murray to Wood, 12.5.1939 (copy).

[103] Ibid., pp. 182–3, Roosevelt to Murray, 10.7.1939.

[104] Ibid., p. 200, Murray to Wood, 12.9.1939 (copy); p. 201, Wood to Murray, 14.9.1939. See also Donald Watt, 'Roosevelt and Neville Chamberlain: Two Appeasers', *International Journal*, XXVIII (1973), pp. 185–204.

[105] *D O 114*, 88, No. 103, F62/1/9, Meeting between MacDonald and Dominion High Commissioners, 1.12.1938 (proof).

in practical terms, seemed to consist of an attempt to detach Italy from Germany. This was reflected by the bringing into operation of the Anglo-Italian agreement and Chamberlain's proposed visit to Mussolini. But, as Halifax assured the cabinet on 21 December, the discussions between Chamberlain and Mussolini would be on the principle 'nothing for nothing'.[106] Pirow's visit to Hitler had shown that no further steps in the direction of the appeasement of Europe could be expected from Germany. In any case the reaction of public opinion to Hitler's treatment of the Jews meant that any handling of territory to Germany as colonial compensation was out of the question. As MacDonald told the high commissioners on 1 December:

> There was . . . a large and important section in Germany who were clearly determined on an aggressive policy. We had to take the existence of this section into account and to make our preparations accordingly.[107]

Britain had to prepare itself for the likelihood of war. As well as rearmament it was necessary to secure the support of the dominions for co-operation in defence, and to try to lead the United States out of isolationism.

[106] *Cab 23*, 95, p. 428, Cab 60 (38) 4, Secret, 21.12.1938.
[107] *D O 114*, 88, No. 103, F62/1/9, Meeting between MacDonald and Dominion High Commissioners, 1.12.1938 (proof).

VIII

PRAGUE AND THE GUARANTEES

Prague and the Guarantees

FROM January to March 1939 British policy towards Europe vacillated between pessimism and optimism. In the middle of January Chamberlain was hopeful about the prospects for peace. He visited Mussolini. He told the cabinet that Mussolini had appeared sincere and had stressed that peace was essential for Italy's development. The prime minister ceded that Mussolini had remained loyal to Hitler.[1]

The mood soon changed. On 25 January Halifax presented a paper to the cabinet on the situation as revealed in telegrams from Berlin. The cabinet and foreign affairs committee were divided on the significance of these 'sensational reports produced by Vansittart'.[2]

The report outlined four possible contingencies: Hitler could urge Italy to advance its claims by force; attack Holland; make impossible demands for colonies; and there was also the likelihood of a sudden German air attack on Britain. Reports suggested that there were orders for German mobilisation for the middle of February. A foreign adventure would distract attention from German domestic difficulties and provide the desperately needed natural resources.[3]

Chamberlain told the cabinet that he 'was a long way from accepting all this information'. If Germany attacked Holland, Britain would have to intervene, but Chamberlain doubted whether that should be stated. The cabinet agreed to place the defence services in a state of readiness.[4] It had been decided to inform the dominions and the United States of these apprehensions before the cabinet met.[5]

On 24 January Halifax asked Roosevelt for some indication of the United States's attitude: possibly Roosevelt might make a public statement before Hitler's speech on 30 January.[6] The impact of the message on the state department was probably lessened by Kennedy's suggestion that the

---

[1] *Templewood Papers* XIX (C) 12, Chamberlain to Hilda Chamberlain, 15.1.1939 (copy); *Cab 23*, 97, pp. 4–5, Cab 1 (39) 1, Secret, 18.1.1939.

[2] *Inskip Papers* 2, p. 9, Diary, 23.1.1939 (copy); *Cab 23*, 97, pp. 53–64, Cab 2 (39) 1, Secret, 25.1.1939.

[3] *Documents on British Foreign Policy* 3rd Series (hereafter cited as '*DBFP*') 4, pp. 4–7, No. 5, C939/15/18, Halifax to Mallet, Telegram No. 37, 21.4.1939.

[4] *Cab 23*, 97, pp. 53–64, Cab 2 (39) 1, Secret, 25.1.1939.

[5] *Cab 27*, 624, F P (36) 35th Mtg, Secret, 23.1.1939.

[6] *Foreign Relations of the United States* (hereafter cited as '*FRUS*') 1939(1), pp. 2–6, 740.00/548, Johnson to Hull, Telegram No. 94, 24.1.1939.

British anxiety could be attributed to the awareness that the combined forces of Britain and France were not equal to those of Germany and Italy.[7] Roosevelt was discreetly cautious: the United States had its national defence programme, and if aspects were singled out they would be misinterpreted. Mallet's analysis was that Roosevelt and Hull were 'only too anxious to do what they can to help but are obsessed by the risk of going too far ahead of public opinion and thus losing control of Congress which could be so essential if the crisis arises'. The situation had not been improved by the discovery that the French government had been authorised to test, with a view to purchase, some of the most recent secret United States aeroplanes. Roosevelt probably felt that he should not give 'a handle to the isolationists'. His speech on 4 January which had hinted at positive United States action against the dictators had possibly done just this.[8] This position was carefully explained to the dominions.[9]

Dominion reaction was equally cautious.

The high commissioner in Canada reported on 29 January that although Mackenzie King had initially summoned his minister of national defence and chiefs of staff, by 28 January the prime minister was inclined 'to discount the gravity of the immediate situation'.[10] On 1 February, after Hitler's moderate speech, the high commissioner in Canada warned that the Canadian government had 'swung to the opposite extreme.' He suggested an 'appropriate message' to 'prevent the Canadian Government from relapsing into possibly unjustified state of confidence'.[11]

Hertzog, according to the high commissioner in South Africa, was not likely 'to be converted to the belief that war may really be near'.[12]

The New Zealand government maintained its silence.[13] Reports from the dominion suggested that the public were unprepared for any emergency involving the commonwealth.[14]

---

[7] Ibid., *loc. cit.*

[8] Ibid., pp. 6–7, 740.00/548, Hull to Johnson, Telegram No. 76, 29.1.1939; *DBFP* 4, p. 27, No. 26, C1093/15/18, Mallet to Halifax, Telegram No. 43, 27.1.1939 r. 28.1.1939; p. 29, No. 28, C1094/15/18, Mallet to Halifax, Telegram No. 44, 27.1.1939 r. 28.1.1939.

[9] *F O 372*, 3315, pp. 110–1, Dominions Office to Dominions, Telegram Circular B No. 34, Most Secret, 1.2.1939.

[10] Ibid., pp. 97–8, T1462/436/384, High Commissioner in Canada to Dominions Office, Telegram No. 31, Important, 29.1.1939 (cypher).

[11] Ibid., p. 99, T1462/436/384, High Commissioner in Canada to Dominions Office, Telegram No. 32, Secret, 1.2.1939 r. 2.2.1939 (cypher).

[12] Ibid., p. 101, T1499/436/384, High Commissioner in South Africa to Dominions Office, Telegram No. 11, Most Secret, 31.1.1939 r. 1.2.1939 (cypher).

[13] Ibid., pp. 113–4, T15101/436/384, Foreign Office Minute by Hadow, 1.2.1939.

[14] Ibid., Boyd Shannon to Dominions Office, Telegram No. 9, 31.1.1939.

Absence of official dominion comment could be attributed to their being informed rather than consulted on British policy. The decision that a German attack on Switzerland or Holland would necessitate British intervention, for instance, was taken without consulting the dominions.[15] The cabinet committee on foreign policy did consider the attitude of the dominions on 26 January. MacDonald argued that if Holland were attacked, and Britain did not act, the effect on the dominions would be adverse:

> Australia and New Zealand were very sensitive to any threat to the Dutch East Indies. South Africa would certainly be greatly affected; in fact an invasion of Holland might bring South Africa into a war in which we had intervened on Holland's behalf more quickly than possibly any other circumstance. Even Eire might be expected to show strong sympathy for the misfortunes of another small country. If an invasion of Holland evoked no response from this country the Dominions would conclude that our sun had set.[16]

The cabinet considered the question on 1 February. The French had suggested that a German attack on Holland or Switzerland should be considered as a cause for war by Britain and France. The cabinet agreed. It also endorsed a report of the chiefs of staff sub committee dated 25 January 1939. The report said that if Britain were to fight in the near future the outcome might depend on the intervention of other powers, and in particular the United States. Failure to intervene, however, 'would have such moral and other repercussions as would seriously undermine our position in the eyes of the Dominions and the world in general'.[17]

The foreign office was concerned about sceptical dominion reaction. Hadow minuted that dominion attitude might be important in case of a sudden attack. He suggested this reticence could be a consequence of an underlying feeling that as Britain was only informing and not consulting the dominions, the dominions felt under no obligation to disclose their attitude. Australia and New Zealand, if not also South Africa, were, in Hadow's view, affected by the British decision over Holland. If the dominions were defenceless they would pose a temptation which the Japanese could not resist. Hadow wondered whether the dominion governments were satisfied with co-ordination and staff talks on a basis of a decision in the taking of which the dominions might claim that they had had no say. Perhaps the British government should allow the dominions to see its sources of information.[18] Cadogan thought that this suggestion

15 Ibid., p. 167, T2299/436/384, Foreign Office Minute by Hadow, 9.2.1939.

16 *Cab 27*, 624, F P (36) 36th Mtg, Secret, 26.1.1939.

17 *Cab 23*, 97, pp. 109–17, Cab 3 (39) 5, Secret, 1.2.1939; *F O 372*, 3315, p. 167, T2299/436/384, Foreign Office Minute by Hadow, 9.2.1939.

18 *F O 372*, 3315, p. 167, T2299/436/384, Foreign Office Minute by Hadow, 9.2.1939.

would further complicate the issue. He pointed out on 11 February that the dominion high commissioners could not see all the reports, and that it would be difficult to make a balanced selection. The dominions had to trust Britain. Cadogan suggested that Inskip, the new secretary of state for dominion affairs, should be asked whether he had any reason to feel that British procedure had caused 'offence or misgiving in the Dominions'.[19]

At the time when dominion consultation was being debated, there was a new man in the post of secretary of state for dominion affairs. Lord Stanley had died in October 1938, and MacDonald had taken over the dominions again, as well as handling the colonies.[20] The cabinet, however, possibly thought that someone with more of a military background than Inskip should take over the portfolio of co-ordination of defence. On 17 January Chamberlain had seen Inskip and suggested that he move to the dominions instead:

> It isn't a very absorbing Dept. and I regard that as important. You will be available for committees.[21]

Halifax took up the matter of information for the dominions with Inskip on 2 March: 'we must expect the Dominions to trust us to draw a just conclusion from the reports which we receive'.[22]

In February 1939 the committee of imperial defence faced with the question whether to consult or to inform the dominions had the same approach as the foreign office. On 9 February the committee considered denouncing the general act for the pacific settlement of international disputes. The three dominions which adhered to the act, Canada, Australia, and New Zealand, did not wish to denounce the act in peace time. The committee decided to send a letter to the league revising Britain's position. New Zealand followed Britain's lead, but Canada, Australia and Ireland did not.[23] This was consultation of a sort in that the dominions were asked for their views. But, in the end, Britain acted on its own, and risked the appearance of division in the commonwealth.

The attitude of the dominions was given further consideration when the committee of imperial defence discussed the European appreciation of the defence plans for 1939–40 on 24 February. If Japan intervened in the war there was the prospect of the Mediterranean being denuded of capital

19 Ibid., pp. 167–8, Foreign Office Minute by Cadogan, 11.2.1939.

20 *Cab 23*, 96, p. 4, Cab 49 (38) 1, Secret, 19.10.1938.

21 *Inskip Papers* 2, pp. 4–8, 17.1.1939 (copy).

22 *F O 372*, 3315, pp. 170–1, T2299/436/384, Halifax to Inskip, Secret, 2.3.1939.

23 *Cab 2*, 8, pp. 142–4, Committee of Imperial Defence Minutes of 346th Meeting, Secret Lock and Key, 9.2.1939; p. 144, Annex 1.

ships as the dominions had been assured that a fleet would be sent to the far east in these circumstances. Chamberlain said that the committee should consider whether the dominions should be informed that the strength of the fleet that could be sent might not be adequate. Chatfield suggested:

> It appeared quite out of the question to put forward a satisfactory argument to the Dominions for weakening the assurance which we had given them. In fact, in his opinion, it would be dangerous to do so and would have an extremely bad effect on Dominion opinion. Even if we only sent a force of 7 or 8 capital ships to the Far East, we could trust to our superior efficiency to hold the position and to contain the Japanese fleet.

This procedure was approved. Stanhope also envisaged the possibility of assistance from the United States: if one or two capital ships were sent to Singapore they would be a deterrent to Japan, especially if the United States fleet moved to Honolulu. But this contingency was not included in the contingency plans.[24]

Australia was also concerned about the situation in Palestine, Egypt and the near east, as it could affect imperial communications. Lyons telegrammed Chamberlain on 14 February about his government's concern that a settlement 'unduly favourable to the Jews' in Palestine might estrange the Moslem world. Partition schemes were politically unwise, and a settlement maintaining the present situation, and preventing Jewish predominance might be best.[25]

The dominions, however, were neither consulted nor informed about the changed defence plans which affected their interests directly. The committee of imperial defence even controlled some cabinet information that went to the dominions,[26] such as the conclusion that Japan could embarrass Britain 'by making a strategic disposition of her forces which would constitute a severe threat to Australia and India'.[27]

The information circulated to the dominions deliberately presented a serious picture of the situation in Europe.[28] The cabinet agreed on 22 February that the dominions should be told of developments by

[24] Ibid., pp. 154–6, Committee of Imperial Defence Minutes of 348th Meeting, Secret Lock and Key, 24.2.1939.

[25] *Premier 1*, 353, Lyons to Chamberlain, Telegram, 14.2.1939 (paraphrase).

[26] *F O 372*, 3316, pp. 184–7, T2301/436/384, Foreign Office Minute by Hadow, 18.2.1939.

[27] *Cab 23*, 97, p. 211, Cab 6 (39), Secret, 8.2.1939.

[28] *F O 371*, 23053, pp. 293–5, C2298/691/18, Hadow to Sir O. Sargent, 22.2.1939 r. in r. 24.2.1939; Foreign Office Minute by O. E. Sargent, 22.2.1939; pp. 305–7, Dominions Office to Dominions, Telegram Circular B No. 63, Secret, 23.2.1939 (cypher).

summaries telegraphed every three or four days, 'but that care should be taken not to incorporate into such messages unsubstantial rumours'.[29]

By the time of Hitler's occupation of Prague education of opinion in the dominions had progressed considerably. Hitler, with his anti Semitic purges and broken promises probably played as a large a part in this as any efforts by Chamberlain or the dominion leaders. The euphoria of Munich did not last, and from December 1938 the dominions made decisive moves towards rearmament, military preparedness, and even conscription.

The split in the governing party in South Africa became more noticeable. In October 1938 both Hertzog and Smuts believed that a lasting peace was possible.[30] Duncan wrote on 22 November 1938: 'Britain simply cannot afford to be tied up to France even to the extent of saving her from a military defeat'.[31] As early as 3 November Smuts spoke of the spirit of lawlessness that prevailed in the world, and of the need for South Africa to prepare.[32] On 11 December he warned of the danger of ignorant people in South Africa who spoke of 'neutrality in all circumstances and in all cases'.[33] Hertzog refused to be drawn. Parliamentary debate on international affairs was avoided. Pirow explained in February 1939 that he knew of no common scheme for commonwealth defence.[34] At the nationalist party congress in November 1938 Malan advocated neutrality, and the settlement of the German colonial question as far as it concerned South Africa by friendly negotiations and co-operation with Germany.[35] Sections of the English press urged a commonwealth foreign policy.[36] F. H. Cleobury, surveying the position in South Africa for the foreign office, minuted on 26 January 1939:

> Fortunately the republican Afrikaners are only a small minority in the Union as a whole. Their attitude is a refusal to face realities they would antagonise the natives and the English at the same time while ignoring the existence of an aggressive Germany. Hertzog is probaly at heart one of them, but he is usually (with occasional lapses) clearheaded enough to see the folly of it all.[37]

In Australia the months following Munich were notable for attempts to achieve a reassuring defence policy. Opinion in the dominion, according

[29] *Cab 23*, 97, p. 293, Cab 8 (39) 2, Secret, 22.2.1939.
[30] *Manchester Guardian*, 21.10.1938; *Daily Telegraph*, 31.10.1938.
[31] *Lothian Papers* 371, pp. 253–4, Duncan to Lothian, 22.11.1938.
[32] *Times*, 4.11.1938.
[33] Ibid., 12.12.1938.
[34] *S A Parl Deb H of A* 33, col. 33, 7.2.1939.
[35] *Burger*, 7.11.1938, Ed.; 13.1.1939, Ed.
[36] *Natal Witness*, 3.11.1938, Ed.
[37] *F O 372*, 3314, p. 322, T1157/90/384, Dominions Office to Foreign Office, No. G/91/203, 17.1.1939 r. in r. 25.2.1939; Minute by F. H. Cleobury, 26.1.1939.

to contemporary observers, tended to be moulded by telegrams from Britain. Press comment, on the whole, formally supported Chamberlain. Australian opinion hardened with the wave of anti Semitism in Germany,[38] and appeasement in Europe seemed less attractive when New Guinea was reported to be under consideration as part of Germany's colonial compensation.[39] Australians did not doubt Britain's wish to help in time of danger, but they questioned that country's ability to send troops to the Pacific.[40] On 5 October Curtin suggested that Australia could not depend on Britain and needed to prepare its own defence: Australia could not afford to dissipate its strength in the struggles of Europe.[41] Hughes designated this attitude as 'nothing more than isolation and non-co-operation'.[42] Menzies rejected the suggestion of an independent Australian foreign policy: division in the commonwealth would please the dictators.[43]

At the beginning of November the cabinet deadlocked on the conscription issue.[44] Menzies challenged Lyons and demanded the defence portfolio. The prime minister obtained a vote of confidence from his party, and the cabinet decided to try the voluntary system before resorting to conscription.[45]

By December 1938 many in Australia saw the likelihood of war. On 6 December Streit, the new minister of defence, announced plans to increase defence expenditure over the following three years from the proposed £49,000,000 to £63,000,000.[46] Co-operation with Britain on rearmament was continued.[47] On 14 December Lyons made his first recruiting address in Adelaide: Australia preferred to stand with the empire rather than to fall into isolation.[48]

The seriousness of the international situation was presumably confirmed by Bruce when he addressed the defence council in Melbourne on 25 January 1939. After the meeting Lyons issued a statement that Australians should realise quickly that European events might precipitate a world conflict with 'tragic suddeness', and that Australia almost certainly would

---

[38] Anonymous, 'Australia', *Round Table*, XXIX (1938–9), pp. 412–23 at pp. 412–6; Paul Hasluck, *The Governmnt and the People 1939–1941* (Canberra, 1952), pp. 97–8.

[39] *Aust Parl Deb* 182, H of R, cols. 1844–5, 22.11.1938.

[40] Anonymous, 'Australia', *Round Table*, XXIX (1938–9), pp. 412–23 at pp. 412–6; Hasluck, pp. 97–8.

[41] *Aust Parl Deb* 181, H of R, Col. 395, 5.10.1938.

[42] Ibid., cols. 397–9.

[43] Ibid., col. 429, 5.10.1938.

[44] *Times*, 1.11.1938.

[45] Ibid., 3.11.1938; 4.11.1938.

[46] *Journal of Parliamentary Debates of the Empire* 20, p. 20, 6.12.1938; Anonymous, 'Australia', *Round Table*, XXIX (1938–9), p. 417.

[47] *Times*, 31.12.1938.

[48] Ibid., 15.12.1938.

be involved.[49] The public remained disatisfied with the measures taken: the recruiting drive, despite labour's assurance that it would support the government's defence measures, was not making headway.[50]

In October 1938 a labour government was returned in New Zealand. It concentrated on the defence question. By March 1939 the territorial force had reached a level of efficiency which could be surpassed only by compulsory training. The navy and air squadrons were developed. Neutrality was not an issue. The minister of defence, Mr. F. James, said early in February 1939 that New Zealand would do its share in any crisis.[51]

Ireland's position was given by de Valera in a press interview in October 1938: Ireland would not be used as a base for enemy attacks on Britain, but there was little chance of co-operation in a European war so long as Ireland remained partitioned.[52]

In Canada the public was becoming more interested in defence, and there were conversations between Canada and the United States on this subject in November 1938. These discussions were to be private, and held on condition that Canada would not disclose their nature to Britain. The British high commissioner was assured that these conversations had been 'of a relatively trivial nature'.[53] He also reported that the department of national defence in Canada was in a bad position, largely because it was headed by a minister 'whose competence, weight with his colleagues and interest in his work are so small as Mackenzie's'.[54]

Some, in Canada, still had faith in the appeasement of Europe. This attitude was reflected in the governor general's speech from the throne on 12 January 1939. But, with the 'possibility of further tensions in the meantime' the government was strengthening Canada's defences.[55] Professor F. R. Scott, in discussing a policy of neutrality for Canada, suggested that after Munich Canadian opinion divided into those who were isolationist, and those who were imperialist.[56]

[49] Ibid., 29.1.1939.
[50] Ibid., 3.2.1939.
[51] Ibid., 10.2.1939; Anonymous, 'New Zealand', *Round Table*, XXIX (1938–9), pp. 649–63 at p. 663; pp. 323–37 at p. 323.
[52] P. N. S. Mansergh, *Survey of British Commonwealth Affairs, Problems of External Policy 1931–1939* (Oxford, 1952), p. 331.
[53] *F O 371*, 22821, pp. 1–5, Dominions Office to Foreign Office, No. D185/41, Secret, 11.1.1939; Transmitting Extract from Letter from S. Holmes to N. Archer, 9.12.1938; pp. 12–4, A875/300/45, Dominions Office to Foreign Office, No. D180/48, Secret, 1.2.1939; Foreign Office Minute, 8.2.1939.
[54] Ibid., pp. 6–11, A689/300/45, Dominions Office to Foreign Office, No. D180/43, Secret, 11.1.1939; Transmitting Holmes to Archer, Secret, 3.1.1939.
[55] *Can Parl Deb H of C* 1939(1), col. 3, 12.1.1939.
[56] F. R. Scott, 'A Policy of Neutrality for Canada', *Foreign Affairs*, XVII (1938–9), pp. 403–16 at p. 413.

On 12 January 1939 Mackenzie King did hint as to his government's attitude. He quoted approvingly a statement made by Sir Wilfred Laurier in 1910:

> If England is at war, we are at war and liable to attack. I do not say that we will always be attacked; neither do I say that we should take part in all the wars of England. That is a matter that must be guided by circumstances upon which the Canadian parliament will have to pronounce, and will have to decide in its own best judgement.

The isolationists in the liberal party objected.[57] Conservatives agitated for recognition that there was co-operation with Britain on defence. But the government denied any such co-operation.[58] The bickerings in parliament over the possibility of Bren guns being manufactured in Canada, and the hesitations over the training of pilots for the royal air force, were indicative of the government's difficult position, even if it did want closer co-operation with Britain on defence. Mackenzie King, personally, was still a disciple of the policy of the appeasement of Europe.[59]

By early March, however, the rapid progress of British rearmament, and the firm ministerial statements from London on solidarity with France, had helped to mitigate isolationist sentiments in Canada. This mood was noted in the Montreal *Gazette* and other newspapers. There was still strong criticism of Chamberlain in the *Winnipeg Free Press*, and French Canadian journals remained isolationist in tone.[60]

The position of the dominions by March 1939 was as satisfactory as could be expected: defence preparations were being accelerated, and there was a degree of awareness of the international situation.

Education of opinion in the United States was more difficult for there was little that Britain could do in this direction except keep quiet. On 2 February Kennedy, back in the United States for a visit, sent a message to Chamberlain: 'Everything going fine on this side. Do not discuss anything over here,' Halifax took this to mean that 'the less said in this country about Roosevelt the better'.[61] The central department of the foreign office informed the United States on the same lines as it did the

---

[57] Anonymous, 'Canada and the War Danger', *Round Table*, XXIX (1938–9), pp. 570–83 at pp. 571–2.

[58] *Times*, 20.1.1939.

[59] See James Eayrs, *In Defence of Canada. Appeasement and Rearmament* (Toronto, 1965), pp. 91–7; pp. 119–22.

[60] *Times*, 8.3.1939.

[61] *F O 371*, 22827, pp. 141–4, A1090/1090/45, Foreign Office Minute by Halifax, 3.2.1939 r. in r. 9.2.1939; Minute by Chamberlain, 7.2.1939.

dominion prime ministers, on all major aspects of foreign policy. Britain did consult the United States on certain aspects of far eastern policy.[62]

At this time Britain had a bad press in the United States. Mallet reported on 26 January that Americans felt that British defence efforts were 'rather feeble and half-hearted'.[63] The foreign office had another reliable report that Roosevelt was tired of this *'morituri te salutamus* attitude of the British'. Roosevelt was reported to have said:

'I got so wild with Lothian who came to see me and spoke like this that I could hardly listen to him.' If the British wanted co-operation what they ought to make America belive was that they had enough backbone to retain their position by their own efforts and lick the other going on their own as they had done before. 'What the British need is a good stiff grog.'[64]

The foreign office attitude was that the British case had to be kept on a high moral plane for United States consumption.[65]

There was little that Britain could do to help Roosevelt modify the neutrality legislation. Foreign office officials were not confident of the outcome. Cadogan minuted on 2 February:

I am afraid that, taught by experience, I have little faith in America. We shall want quick starters in the next war, and I doubt whether even Pres. R [*sic*] can be quick enough off the mark. I think at least he wont [*sic*] hinder us, with the Neutrality Act. But I doubt whether non-Neutrality (if he can get it) will be enough. I am not blaming him.[66]

The impression that the state department had of British policy was confused. Kennedy reported that on the one hand there was the foreign office which did not trust Hitler and expected an explosion, while on the other there was Chamberlain who assumed that it was possible to do business with Hitler. The situation was complicated by Chamberlain's two points of view:

His hope that appeasement will still be worked out and his fear that Hitler has in his hands, and is quite likely to use them, the means of causing a world war.[67]

Lindsay confirmed Kennedy's impression when he saw Welles on 20 February.[68]

---

[62] Ibid., 22812, pp. 194–6, A1274/98/45, Foreign Office Minutes by W. Strang, 9.2.1939; E. M. B. Ingram, 9.2.1939; R. S. Howe, 10.2.1939 r. in r. 16.2.1939.

[63] Ibid., 22827, pp. 169–80, A1143/1143/45, Mallet to David Scott, Private, 26.1.1939 r. in r. 11.2.1939.

[64] Ibid., pp. 179–80, Michael Vyvyan (Cambridge) to Strang, 4.3.1939 (copy); John Harvey, Ed., *The Diplomatic Diaries of Oliver Harvey 1937–1940* (London, 1970), pp. 258–9, Diary, 3.3.1939.

[65] Ibid., p. 174, Foreign Office Minute by Vansittart, 16.2.1939.

[66] Ibid., 22812, p. 51, A660/98/45, Foreign Office Minute by Cadogan, 2.2.1939.

[67] *FRUS* 1939(1), pp. 14–7, 740.00/588, Kennedy to Hull, Telegram No. 246, 17.2.1939.

[68] Ibid., pp. 18–20, 740/00/595½, Memorandum of Conversation with Lindsay by Welles, 20.2.1939.

The only initiative that came from the United States was a suggestion that Kennedy made to Halifax on 17 February. The ambassador asked whether action on ecomomic lines might not divert Germany from war:

> He was sure that, if this was so, the President would try to do whatever could be done to give economic help and open up economic opportunity.

Chamberlain felt that economic appeasement was realistic given the state of the German economy.[69] Moves in this direction were made.[70] Hull responded: he let Lindsay know of the 'strong American interest' in both the political and economic implications of any possible agreement between Britain and Germany.[71] The discussions continued, however, and towards the end of March the *Reichsgruppe* industries and the federation of British industries drew up a joint declaration.[72] Halifax had to mollify the state department's suspicions with the assurance that the Anglo-German trade talks would not be resumed until a political settlement were reached.[73]

On 15 March German troops entered Prague. By a law of 22 November 1938 the Czechoslovak government had granted autonomy to Slovakia. On 9 March Prague learned that Slovak separatists were planning to overthrow the government. On 16 March Hitler proclaimed Bohemia and Moravia a protectorate within the German reich, and accepted the protection of the Slovak state. Hungary invaded Ruthenia on 14 March, and on 16 March incorporated Ruthenia in Hungary.[74]

Until this time Chamberlain still hoped for European appeasement, although the hope was fading and he was gambling for time. Chamberlain wrote to his sister from Cliveden on 26 February:

> If Anthony Eden were in the Cabinet it would be like it was before + I should have him objecting to every proposal to get better understanding with the Dictators. Indeed the mere announcement that he had been taken back would be enough to convince them that we had changed our policy + might tempt them to break out now before the democracies had further strengthened their position.[75]

The cabinet met on 15 March. Halifax explained the French agreed that there was 'no possibility of effectively influencing the position' in

---

69 *FRUS* 1939(1), pp. 14–7, 740.00/588, Kennedy to Hull, Telegram No. 246, 17.2.1939.
70 Ibid., pp. 21–2, 740.00/592, Kennedy to Hull, Telegram No. 259, 23.2.1939.
71 Ibid., pp. 28–9, 641.6231/167, Hull to Kennedy, Telegram No. 169, 1.3.1939.
72 Ibid., p. 76, 641.6231/178, Welles to Kennedy, Telegram No. 201, 20.3.1939.
73 Ibid., p. 81, 641.6231/182, Kennedy to Hull, Telegram No. 376, 20.3.1939.
74 H. H. E. Craster, Ed., *Speeches on Foreign Policy by Viscount Halifax* (Oxford, 1940), pp. 233, 238.
75 *Templewood Papers* XIX (C) 12, Chamberlain to Hilda Chamberlain, 26.2.1939 (copy).

Czechoslovakia. Chamberlain argued: 'our guarantee was not a guarantee against the exercise of moral pressure'.[76]

On 17 March Chamberlain spoke at Birmingham. He avoided making specific pledges but the gist of what he said was that Germany's expansionist aims were clear and had to be countered. Britain looked to the commonwealth and France for assistance in this.[77] Chamberlain explained the reasons for this speech to the cabinet on 18 March:

> Up till a week ago we had proceeded on the assumption that we should be able to continue with our policy of getting on to better terms with the Dictator Powers, and that although these powers had aims, those aims were limited. We had all along had at the back of our minds the reservation that this might not prove to be the case but we had felt that it was right to try out the possibility of this course.

But Chamberlain had concluded that Hitler's attitude made 'it impossible to continue to negotiate on the old basis with the Nazi regime'.

The cabinet also considered a message from M. Tilea, the Rumanian minister in London, that the German government had asked for a monopoly of Rumanian exports and measures of industrial restriction inside Rumania in German interests, in return for a German guarantee of frontiers. Halifax felt that the cabinet should consider Britain's likely position. He mentioned, as a reason for this, that he had seen Kennedy that morning: the ambassador had warmly approved Chamberlain's speech, 'but had added that it carried with it the consolation that this country would not submit to further aggressive action on Germany's part'. Chamberlain said that Britain had to ascertain what friends it had that would join in resisting aggression: at least the co-operation of the French could be relied upon. He did not mention the dominions. Maugham suggested that it would make a great difference to public opinion, particularly in the dominions 'if Roumania were to put up a real fight'. He was worried that the congress party in India would seize the chance to break with Britain if there were war: 'if we could put off the evil day, our position would be improved'. Zetland said that Moslem opinion in India would be reassured by British proposals for Palestine. Zetland did not anticipate more than 'a certain degree of embarrassment for a short time at the outbreak of war'.

Inskip reported the views of the dominion high commissioners whom he had seen that afternoon. With the exception of Jordan they had all approve the Birmingham speech. Massey was worried, however, that the

[76] *Cab 23*, 98, pp. 6–17, Cab 11 (39) 2, Secret, 15.3.1939.
[77] *Times*, 18.3.1939.

Canadian people might ask why, if Britain did not want to go to war over Czechoslovakia, it would do so over Rumania. If Germany attacked Rumania, and Britain then declared war on Germany, it might be alleged that Britain was attacking Germany in the west. Te Water thought that opinion in South Africa was likely to support Britain in resisting German aggression: anti German feeling was running high in the Cape, and 150 Germans had been refused permission to land.

Chamberlain felt that the real issue was whether Britain could obtain sufficient assurances from other countries to justify a 'public pronouncement that we should resist any further act of aggression on the part of Germany'. Such an announcement might deter Germany for a while and Britain could take full advantage of the breathing space it offered. Poland was the key to the situation.

The cabinet approved Chamberlain's new policy and it was decided to make approaches to Russia, Poland, Yugoslavia, Turkey, Greece and Rumania. to obtain assurances from them that they would join with Britain in resisting 'any act of German aggression aimed at obtaining domination in South-Eastern Europe'. The French government would be informed, and action concerted with them. If these assurances were forthcoming there would be a public pronouncement.[78]

The dominions were not consulted on this decision, except that the procedure adopted at the imperial conferences of 1926 and 1930 was followed: the British government informed the dominion governments of the action it was taking or contemplating, and, in the absence of adverse comment assumed that no objection was seen to its policy.[79] The opinions of the high commissioners were considered by the cabinet, but these did not differ markedly from those of Chamberlain.

Chamberlain wrote to his sister on 19 March: 'As always I want to gain time for I never accept the view that war is inevitable'.[80] A week later he was not so optimistic. On 21 March there were reports that Germany had mobilised twenty divisions on the western frontier. Chamberlain alerted the forces and had patrols out in the channel looking for submarines. He wrote to his sister: 'I cannot feel safe with Hitler'. This convinced Chamberlain that defence plans were inadequate, and he set experts to devise a scheme whereby defences could be manned, or partially manned, night and day all the year round. The situation improved, but Chamberlain

[78] *Cab 23*, 98, pp. 43–63, Cab 12 (39) 1, Secret, 18.3.1939.
[79] *D O 114*, 98, p. 1, Introduction.
[80] *Templewood Papers* XIX (C) 12, Chamberlain to Hilda Chamberlain, 19.3.1939 (copy).

feared that it would be only a lull. The declaration of powers did not materialise: 'It soon became evident that Poland would find great difficulty in signing it. . . . if she now joins with Russia + Western democracies in a declaration which aims at curbing German ambitions, will not the Germans say to her Aha! now we see where you stand.' After this Chamberlain considered whether it would be worthwhile to continue with Russia. He wrote:

> I must confess the most profound distrust of Russia. I have no belief whatever in her ability to maintain an effective offensive even if she wanted to. And I distrust her motives, which seem to me to have little connection with our ideas of liberty + to be concerned only with getting everyone else by the ears. Moreover she is both hated + suspected by many of the smaller States notably by Poland, Roumania + Finland, so that our close association with her might easily cost us the sympathy of those who would much more effectively help us if we can get them on our side.

Chamberlain had another possibility in mind. If Rumania would fight Poland might agree to come to its assistance. Then Britain and France would join to resist aggression.[81]

Reaction in the dominions to British policy at this time was, on the whole, favourable. But the dominions were still informed rather than consulted. The issue of consultation with the dominions was raised once again by Inskip on 22 March. The dominions were satisfied with the information that they received, but were now beginning to think in terms of specific consultation. According to Inskip 'both Canada and New Zealand had made considerable advances on what they had previously undertaken to do in the way of co-operation'.[82]

In South Africa the English press deplored the invasion of Czechoslovakia and commented that Chamberlain, at Birmingham, was speaking for the commonwealth.[83] The nationalist organ, the *Burger*, demanded a policy of rigid neutrality.[84] The *Suiderstem*, the official government newspaper, commented that Chamberlain had not lost prestige, and supported the British prime minister's declaration that not everything should be sacrificed for peace.[85]

Hertzog again refused to be drawn on foreign affairs. Addressing the house of representatives on 21 March 1939 he stressed that the British

---

[81] Ibid., Chamberlain to Hilda Chamberlain, 26.3.1939 (copy).
[82] *Cab 23*, 98, p. 96, Cab 14 (39) 2, Secret, 22.3.1939.
[83] *Sunday Times*, 19.3.1939.
[84] *Burger*, 21.3.1939, Ed.
[85] *Suiderstem*, 17.3.1939, Ed.

government had not asked South Africa to support its policy. Hertzog was not prepared to declare a policy on a matter in which the interests of South Africa were not more closely involved than they were at that time. Later in the month Hertzog outlined the circumstances in which European affairs might be discussed:

> When and where the activities of a European country are of such a nature or extent that it can be inferred therefrom that its object and endeavour is the domination of other free countries and peoples, and that the liberty and interests of the Union are also threatened thereby, the time will then also come for this Government to warn the people of the Union and to ask this House to occupy itself with European affairs, even where the Union would otherwise have no interests or would take no interest in them.[86]

South Africa would only become involved when its own interests were threatened. Many united party supporters, however, understood that this meant South Africa would be at Britain's side if Hitler advanced again.[87]

Hertzog did warn the British government on 23 March that the consequences of German encirclement could only be war, for which the British would be responsible. He hoped the appeasement of Europe would be pursued. A revival of the policy of German encirclement would have 'most regrettable' results in South Africa.[88]

The high commissioner in South Africa interviewed Hertzog on 23 March. Hertzog did not believe that there would be war: in the last resort Germany would not challenge the democratic powers that had made their position clear. The high commissioner found this 'illogical' in the light of Hertzog's views on encirclement. Hertzog had told the French minister that if Britain were attacked South Africa would have to come in. This rather surprised the high commissioner. But then Hertzog had said that the seizure of Czechoslovakia had 'undoubetdly affected opinion in South Africa about Germany'.[89]

Hitler's moves in March took Smuts by surprise.[90] Smuts wrote to Lothian that the Munich agreement had been destroyed, and Chamberlain's policy exploded. Smuts criticised Chamberlain for dealing a final blow to the league over Abyssinia, and consequently destroying the 'most successful effort ever made to build up a system of public law against the

86 *S A Parl Deb H of A* 33, col. 2089, 21.3.1939; *Journal of Parliamentary Debates of the Empire* 20, p. 736.

87 Mansergh, p. 265.

88 *D O 114*, 98, p. 7, No. 7, F706/113, Aide Memoire from Hertzog, 23.3.1939.

89 Ibid., pp. 8–9, No. 9, F706/116, High Commissioner in South Africa to Dominions Office, Telegram No. 31, Secret, 24.3.1939.

90 W. K. Hancock, *Smuts. The Fields of Force, 1919–1950* (Cambridge, 1968), pp. 309–11.

menace of public violence'.[91] Perhaps Smuts had misunderstand Chamberlain's role in British policy over Abyssinia. Smuts made no effort to lead South African opinion: he did not speak in the limited discussions in parliament; nor, it seems, did he come out with any firm statements in public.

Various precautionary measures were taken in South Africa. Leave was cancelled for the South African police, and steps were taken to guard the barrage on the Vaal river which supplied the water for the Witwatersrand and the mines. In the Iscor steel works the authorities took steps to get rid of a number of German employees. Members of the South African royal naval reserve were warned to be available if required in the near future. Action was taken on Smuts's authority, without cabinet sanction, though it was felt that this would be forthcoming if necessary.

When asked why this crisis had led to so much more definite action than the previous one Colonel de Villiers, the chief of police, offered two reasons:

> The first was that public opinion, not excluding Nationalist opinion, had gradually changed during the last six months and had certainly had a great shock in the last few days; but the principal reason for thinking that it was desirable to take these precautions was the growth of an organisation called the 'Ossewa Brandwag' (Ox Wagon Guard). . . . It had definite Nazi ideals. . . . He believes that van Rensburg, the Administrator of the Free State, and Pirow are somewhat deeply implicated in this movement.[92]

F. H. Cleobury minuted on 6 April that the information was 'a little mysterious':

> Mr. Pirow's general attitude for some time has been quite satisfactory from our point of view.[93]

The foreign office did not appreciate local conditions in South Africa, and the strength of German sympathy of people like Pirow.

Hitler's invasion shocked opinion in South Africa. But with the ruling party divided on the issue of participation in a European war there was no stated policy.

The events of March helped to unify Australia. The press saw Chamberlain's speech at Birmingham as marking a departure from the policy of the appeasement of Europe. Generally the move was welcomed. The press did

[91] *Lothian Papers* 375, pp. 829–30, Smuts to Lothian, 27.3.1939.
[92] *F O 372*, 3314, pp. 344–8, T4490/90/384, Dixon to Cleobury, Confidential, 1.4.1939 r. in r. 4.4.1939; Transmitting Clark to Harding, Confidential, 21.3.1939 (copy).
[93] Ibid., Foreign Office Minute by F. H. Cleobury, 6.4.1939.

not, however, vilify what Chamberlain had achieved at Munich.[94] On 19 March Lyons spoke to Chamberlain on the telephone, and, afterwards, announced that 'there can be no doubt about Australia supporting Britain in any development that might occur'. A cabinet meeting was called, and Bruce delayed his departure for London to be available for consultation.[95] On 21 March, after the meeting of the federal cabinet, a statement was issued giving Australia's position:

> The Commonwealth Government has assured the British Government of its readiness to co-operate with it in its endeavours to deal with the international situation, and has expressed its wholehearted support of the efforts which the British government is now making to ensure the peace and security of the world from further encroachments by force on the freedom and independence of other nations.[96]

This assurance was enthusiastically received by the Australian press.[97]

When Mussolini supported Hitler, W. M. Hughes, the minister for external affairs, broadcast threatening words about Italy.[98] Menzies was cautious. On 27 March the former attorney general stressed that there was no reason for war. He did not see a conflict of interests between Britain, Germany and Italy.[99]

Considering the attitude of Lyons and part of the Australian press at the time of Munich, it seems that Chamberlain had succeeded in educating Australian opinion. The newspaper editorials were careful to stress that the policy of appeasement had been tried, and that Hitler's intentions were now clear. There was hardly any criticism of Chamberlain, and the Australian government placed itself in a position where it was prepared to follow the British prime minister's lead. The only apparent consultation on this matter had been Lyons's telephone conversation with Chamberlain.

After March New Zealand was committed to support British policy psychologically, if not legally. The New Zealand press was not surprised by Hitler's invasion of Czechoslovakia. British policy was supported. But press comment disliked the idea of commitments in the Balkans, or of an agreement with Russia.[100]

94 *Sydney Morning Herald*, 16.3.1939, Ed.; 18.3.1939, Ed.; 20.3.1939, Ed.; *Argus*, 20.3.1939, Ed.; *Age*, 20.3.1939, Ed.

95 *Times*, 20.3.1939; *Sydney Morning Herald*, 21.3.1939; *Argus*, 21.3.1939; *Daily Telegraph*, 21.3.1939; 22.3.1939; *Manchester Guardian*, 22.3.1939.

96 *Sydney Morning Herald*, 22.3.1939.

97 *Age*, 22.3.1939, Ed.; *Sydney Morning Herald*, 23.3.1939, Ed.; *Times*, 24.3.1939.

98 *Daily Telegraph*, 27.3.1939.

99 *Sydney Morning Herald*, 28.3.1939.

100 F. L. W. Wood, *The New Zealand People at War. Political and External Affairs* (Wellington, 1958) p. 95.

The New Zealand government, however, maintained a consistent policy. On 21 March a message was sent to the British government suggesting a conference of nations, summoned by the commonwealth, to discuss the defence of principles of international decency. The message also urged Britain to achieve closer collaboration with the United States. New Zealand pledged itself to play its 'full part should the occasion unhappily arise, in defence of the fight against the brutalities and the naked power policies of aggressor states'.[101] This message was made public.[102] The leader of the opposition pledged his party's support for any government action supporting Britain's defences.[103]

Britain kept the New Zealand government informed of developments. On 28 March the British government feared that Hitler planned to strike westwards before striking at Russia. There was, Britain explained on 31 March, real difficulty in trying to arrange any general conference: certain governments wished to maintain a strict neutrality, while others feared provoking German retaliation.[104]

New Zealand was united: the government supported Chamberlain; the opposition was, if anything, more loyal. Although there was disquiet in the press about Britain's Balkan policy, this did not result in protest from the New Zealand government.

Mackenzie King continued to favour the appeasement of Europe.[105] He supported Chamberlain's new policy even though he disapproved of it. But perhaps Mackenzie King was not fully conscious of the change in British policy. Skelton warned Mackenzie King against giving Chamberlain 'a blank cheque'.[106]

On 20 March Mackenzie King spoke to the Canadian house of commons. A statement of Canada's position at the outbreak of war was expected. Canadian opinion was roused on this issue.[107] Astutely the prime minister showed himself to be preparing for war but still hoping for peace. He stressed that Chamberlain had repeatedly spoken of the need for consultation amongst the powers before any commitments were made. Canada

[101] *D O 114*, 98, p. 4, No. 2, F706/106, New Zealand Government to Dominions Office, Telegram No. 36, Secret, 21.3.1939.

[102] Wood, p. 95.

[103] *Daily Telegraph*, 23.3.1939.

[104] Wood, p. 94; *D O 114*, 98, pp. 11–2, No. 13, F706/106, Dominions Office to New Zealand Government, Telegram No. 47, Secret, 31.3.1939.

[105] Eayrs, p. 73.

[106] *Mackenzie King Papers*, Skelton to Mackenzie King, 20.3.1939. Quoted by Eayrs, p. 73.

[107] *Lothian Papers* 388, pp. 48–67, Memorandum on 'Some Observations on the present Political Situation in Canada, April 1939', J. Bunyon Beckersteld to Lothian, 4.4.1939.

approved this. If the Canadian cabinet knew what policies were envisaged, it would be able to recommend appropriate action to parliament. Mackenzie King did speculate that:

> If there were a prospect of an aggressor launching an attack on Britain, with bombers raining death on London, I have no doubt what the decision of the Canadian people and parliament would be. We would regard it as an act of aggression, menacing freedom in all parts of the British commonwealth. If it were a case, on the other hand, of a dispute over trade or prestige in some far corner of the world, that would raise quite different considerations.

He would say nothing more. He had not received information as to what British policy was likely to be.[108]

Manion issued a press statement that the conservative opposition would support the government.[109] The CCF leader suggested an embargo on the export of war material to Germany.[110]

Canadian press comments on the party leaders' cautious statements varied from the observation that the Laurier thesis on Canadian participation had not been restated, to accusations that the pronouncements could have come from the leaders of a non British democracy. The French Canadian press was critical.

Quebec was uneasy. The St. Jean Baptiste society organised a meeting in Montreal. Delegates unanimously warned that French Canada was opposed to Canadian participation in foreign wars. The mayor of Montreal promised to head any anti conscription movement.

In Ontario the premier, Mr. Mitchell Hepburn, moved a resolution pledging the co-operation of the government and the people of Ontario with Britain, and urged the federal government to introduce legislation enabling the man power and natural resources of Canada to be mobilised immediately in case of war. In the debate most members spoke of their ardent loyalty to Britain, and the resolution was carried without a hostile vote.[111]

The high commissioner in Canada reported that Mackenzie King had been under pressure to take a definite stand on the side of the democracies, if only to 'cut the ground from under the feet of the Premier of Ontario'.[112]

---

[108] *Can Parl Deb H of C* 1939(2), cols. 2042–3, 20.3.1939.

[109] *Times*, 21.3.1939.

[110] *Can Parl Deb H of C* 1939(2), col. 2046, 20.3.1939.

[111] Anonymous, 'Canada and the War Danger', *Round Table*, XXIX (1938–9), pp. 570–83 at pp. 574–7; *Times*, 20.3.1939.

[112] *D O 114*, 98, p. 6, No. 5, F706/110, High Commissioner in Canada to Dominions Office, Telegram No. 5, Secret, 21.3.1939.

Following the British cabinet discussion on 22 March a telegram was sent to the high commissioner in Canada about Mackenzie King's statement that the Canadian government was prepared to take part in consultation.[113] Mackenzie King, however, protested that attendance of Massey at the meetings with the dominion high commissioners in London should not be 'regarded or represented as constituting consultation of Canada'. Mackenzie King professed to be disturbed by the 'manifold inaccurate references' to consultation with the dominions. The high commissioner was under the impression that Mackenzie King was satisfied with the procedure adopted during the recent events: the Canadian government had been informed direct, and he appreciated that had he wished to comment on British plans he would have been able to do so.[114]

The high commissioner reported further on Mackenzie King on 25 March:

It is abundantly evident that he hopes to be able to maintain until the last possible moment a position of detachment from Europe and indeed the rest of the Empire and that he is if anything less disposed to co-operate with other countries in the defence of democracy than are the Government of the United States.

Mackenzie King was worried that Canada was going to be invited to join some form of military alliance between Britain and other European countries. This would cause him 'grave embarrassment'. An alliance between Britain and Russia would be especially regrettable:

From the Canadian point of view particularly that of French Canadians and other Roman Catholic communities that association would still be regarded as very unfortunate.

Generally the high commissioner was left with the impression that Canada would not be brought into any war which appeared to have been due to a Balkan dispute or a dispute between what Mackenzie King called 'African countries', such as one between France and Italy over North African territories.[115]

Britain was careful to take Mackenzie King's views into account. At the cabinet committee on foreign policy meeting on 27 March Inskip mentioned that Mackenzie King had indicated his dislike of Russian participation in the pact.[116] It was subsequently pointed out to Mackenzie King that it

113 Ibid., pp. 6–7, No. 6, F706/110, Dominions Office to High Commissioner in Canada, Telegram No. 55, Secret, 22.3.1939.
114 Ibid., p. 9, No. 10, F706/117, High Commissioner in Canada to Dominions Office, Telegram No. 79, Secret, 24.3.1939 r. 25.3.1939.
115 Ibid., p. 10, No. 11, F706/118, High Commissioner in Canada to Dominions Office, Telegram No. 80, Secret, 24.3.1939 r. 25.3.1939.
116 *Cab 27*, 624, p. 21, F P (36) 38th Mtg, Secret, 27.3.1939.

was no longer proposed to invite Russia to play such a predominant part in the scheme. The British government apologised informally to Mackenzie King for using 'consultation' in a way open to misunderstanding.[117]

As a result of the explosive situation in Canada Mackenzie King made another statement. This resulted in one of the longest debates on foreign affairs in the Canadian parliament. Altogether 33 members participated, but the intentions of the government were still obscure at the end of it.[118]

Mackenzie King spoke on 30 March. He revealed his admiration for Chamberlain by a survey of the month of Munich and of the stand taken by the various members of the commonwealth. Mackenzie King reiterated that it was for the Canadian parliament to decide the issue of peace or war.[119] Lapointe spoke of the difficulties of neutrality, and referred to it as a 'hazardous policy'.[120] There were hints of a policy of limited liability on Canada's part in the event of a European war.[121]

Hitler's action did not unify the Canadian nation, but rather emphasised sectional interests. Canada's liability in the case of a European war was limited, and with the divisions in the dominion it could not be anything else.

By 29 March British hopes for a joint declaration had faded. Russia was prepared to sign provided that Poland would do so. Poland's answer was hesitant. Association with Russia was also causing difficulties with countries like Portugal, Spain, Japan, Italy and Canada. The cabinet did not decide what action to take.[122]

Overnight the situation changed. Chamberlain saw Ian Colvin, the journalist who had sent back accurate reports on German intentions during the Munich crisis. Colvin convinced Chamberlain that Hitler was ready to attack and absorb Poland. The fall of Lithuania would follow and other states would then be exposed. Following this there would be the possibility of a Russian-German alliance, and ultimately the British empire would be swallowed up by Hitler. Chamberlain decided at once that Poland would have to be guaranteed.[123]

---

[117] *D O 114*, 98, p. 12, No. 14, F706/118, Dominions Office to High Commissioner in Canada, Telegram No. 69, Secret, 1.3.1939.

[118] Anonymous 'Canada and the War Danger', *Round Table*, XXIX (1938–9), pp. 570–83 at p. 582.

[119] *Can Parl Deb H of C* 1939(3), cols. 2408–63, 30.3.1939.

[120] Ibid., cols. 2467–8, 31.3.1939.

[121] Anonymous, 'Canada and the War Danger', *Round Table*, XXIX (1938–9), pp. 570–83 at p. 582.

[122] *Cab 23*, 98, pp. 120–6, Cab 15 (39) 2, Secret, 29.3.1939.

[123] *Templewood Papers* XIX (C) 12, Chamberlain to Hilda Chamberlain, 3.4.1939 (copy).

Halifax presented the case to the cabinet the next day. He mentioned the interview with Colvin. Kennedy had also reported that the United States ambassador in Warsaw had heard that Ribbentrop was anxious to bring off another *coup* while Britain and France were still discussing what action to take. Halifax wanted a draft statement agreed to by Britain and France, of which the dominions were to be informed. The cabinet did discuss whether the statement should argue that Britain had a vital interest in Poland. It was thought, however, that given the state of public opinion in the United States, this would not be the best approach. The form agreed upon was that 'in the event of action which clearly threatened Polish independence, and which Poland felt obliged to resist, His Majesty's Government would lend Poland all the support in their power'.

The cabinet was given a review of the attitude of the dominions. Halifax said that Lyons had telephoned him that morning, and had intimated that if 'we became involved in a war, Australia would be with us'. Lyons, however, was worried about commitments to 'certain rather weak countries', and 'he seemed to have no very high opinion of Russia'. Halifax had told Lyons that Britain might at any time find itself faced with a threat of war, and that 'the best plan was probably to meet it at once'. Inskip mentioned that anti German feeling was increasing in South Africa. He also pointed to the issue raised by Mackenzie King who 'drew a distinction between a communication sent to a Dominion Prime Minister for purposes of consultation, in which he was specifically asked for his consent to a line of action, and a communication sent to him for his information, which merely gave him an opportunity of objecting if he so desired'. Chamberlain decided that in this instance the telegrams sent to the dominions should be informatory and not consultative. A telegram was to be sent to the dominions that day giving an account of the information received, but the terms of the draft statement would not be telegraphed until later.[124]

After the cabinet Inskip saw the dominion high commissioners. Massey, speaking for himself and not the Canadian government, was concerned about possible German action against Danzig: defence of the Polish position in Danzig would be 'an extremely bad reason for which to go to war with Germany'. Te Water supported him: the Germans had a genuine claim to Danzig. Public opinion in South Africa would find it difficult to realise why Britain felt it necessary to draw the line at Danzig'.

Inskip realised that the dominions 'would have to satisfy themselves as to what was the right course for them to take'. In the time available it had

---

[124] *Cab 23*, 98, pp. 156–75, Cab 16 16 (39) 1, Secret, 30.3.1939.

only been possible to inform the dominion governments. Inskip felt sure that the dominions 'would not have wished that the United Kingdom should invite them to share responsibility for the decision'. Massey and te Water agreed. The other high commissioners did not comment.[125]

Chamberlain wrote to his sister:

> But, of course, I can never forget that the ultimate decision the Yes or No which may decide the fate not only of all this generation but of the British Empire itself, rests with me.[126]

He called an unexpected cabinet meeting on 31 March so that the whole cabinet could agree on the wording of the statement. Maugham did suggest an amendment as he had been told that public opinion in Canada was 'very ignorant in regard to Poland, and might be surprised that we should enter into so binding a commitment in regard to that country'. If the statement linked British and French action more closely, the criticism could be met. The suggestion was rejected as this was specifically a statement by the British government. Chamberlain said that he would give the statement to Kennedy so that Roosevelt could have it before publication. The cabinet was also informed of the 'somewhat delicate relations' with Russia.[127]

None of the dominion governments replied directly about the information sent them about the Polish guarantee. The British high commissioner in New Zealand, however, did report that Savage had agreed that the time had come to make a stand: Savage only thought it regrettable that this had not been done over Czechoslovakia.[128]

Chamberlain went ahead with implementing proposals for east European guarantees. Beck arrived from Poland on 3 April. Rumania was hesitant and insisted on consulting with its partners in the Balkan *entente*. Russia was annoyed at being left out: Litvinoff protested to Seeds, the British ambassador in Moscow, that Russia was being isolated. Oliver Harvey probably expressed the thinking of many British officials when he noted in his diary:

> If we want to keep the Poles in, we cannot have the Russians in too. And the Poles are better military material immediately than the Russians.[129]

Chamberlain found the talks with Beck satisfactory. Beck did not want any closer association with Russia as that could cause Hitler to launch an

125 *F O 371*, 22969, pp. 13–5, C5265/15/18, Hankinson to Harvey, 6.4.1939; Transmitting Notes of Meeting between Inskip and Dominion High Commissioners, 30.3.1939.

126 *Templewood Papers* XIX (C) 12, Chamberlain to Hilda Chamberlain, 3.4.1939 (copy).

127 *Cab 23*, 98, pp. 187–94, Cab 17 (39), Secret, 31.3.1939.

128 *D O 114*, 98, p. 1, Introduction.

129 Harvey, p. 272, Diary, 3.4.1939.

attack which might otherwise be avoided. Chamberlain agreed: he thought Russia unreliable as a friend, a country with little capacity to help anyway, and felt that an association with Russia could annoy other countries.[130] Halifax explained to the cabinet on 5 April that Beck had warned that if Britain and France entered into any closer relationship with Russia, Beck would have to declare publicly that Poland was unaffected.[131]

Inskip met the dominion high commissioners on 6 April and explained this position to them. Both te Water and Massey thought that Russia would stand out of a war between the capitalist states. Massey specifically asked whether it would be possible to pursue British policy without Russian co-operation. Inskip reassured Massey that Britain proposed to do this: British experts felt that Russia had great defensive but little offensive power.

Te Water was concerned, too, that according to the South African minister in Berlin, Gie, the official view in Germany was that British policy was one of encirclement. Moderate German opinion was inclined to believe that Britain was threatening a preventive war. Te Water and Massey urged that steps be taken to minimise this. Te Water had already suggested to Chamberlain that a practical step would be to offer Germany a non aggression agreement at the right moment. Inskip felt that this might be possible, but only if Hitler were to change his policy.

Jordan was surprised that the league had not been brought into any of the discussions. Inskip had to point out that the idea of collective security was unrealisable under present conditions.[132]

Sir G. Ogilvie-Forbes in Berlin reported Gie's view on 6 April. Gie was reporting to the South African government that Chamberlain's speech on 31 March had been calamitous: it had irritated nazi circles; and it meant that Britain was committing itself to an uncertain ally, Poland. Ogilvie-Forbes explained that Gie felt that Germany's natural *lebensraum* was in the east: if Britain were drawn into a war to impede Germany's expansion in that area, Gie 'would not consider that South Africa would, from the moral or practical point of view, be justified in involving herself in such a war'. T. K. Roberts minuted that it was a pity that Gie should confirm Hertzog and te Water in their similar views.[133]

---

[130] *Templewood Papers* XIX (C) 12, Chamberlain to Hilda Chamberlain, 9.4.1939 (copy).
[131] *Cab 23*, 98, p. 209, Cab 18 (39) 4, Secret, 5.4.1939.
[132] *F O 372*, 3317, pp. 179–84, T6064/436/384, Dominions Office to Foreign Office, 7.4.1939 r. in r. 9.4.1939; Enclosing Notes of a Meeting between Inskip and Dominion High Commissioners, 6.4.1939.
[133] *F O 371*, 22969, pp. 185–7, C5093/15/18, Ogilvie-Forbes to Strang, 462/68/39, Secret, 6.4.1939 r. in r. 12.4.1939; Minute by T. K. Roberts, 14.4.1939.

The British government, however, did have information which suggested that South Africa might not remain neutral if war came. In the middle of April R. H. Hadow of the foreign office discussed this issue informally with the political secretary of the high commissioner for South Africa, Mr. Parmenter. Parmenter was considered a patriot in the South African sense, and was not an enthusiast for either war, or Britain. He felt that South Africa would come in if Britain were involved in war, and did not believe in even a short period of neutrality. The British element would volunteer for service in Europe, while the Afrikaners could be counted on to furnish 10,000 men for home service.[134]

A similar hopeful report came from the high commissioner in South Africa on 13 April. Hertzog had told him that if Hitler launched another attack 'conversion of public opinion in South Africa would be complete and people would realise that they would have no option but to range themselves on our side in the event of war'.[135]

At this time te Water and Massey were paying increasing attention to the development of affairs. They requested that they should see the various telegrams received and sent by the foreign office which were of particular interest to them.[136] Cadogan agreed to send 'political distribution' telegrams to the two high commissioners.[137]

In early April there were rumours of Italian moves against Albania. Chamberlain was away fishing in Scotland when a conference of ministers was held in Albania.[138] Halifax felt that it was impossible to send a fleet to the Adriatic even though public opinion in certain countries like the United States would take the view that while Britain 'used brave words, our action was less heroic'. It would be wrong to start a European war by sending Mussolini an ultimatum on this matter which he could not accept. Rather Britain should reach agreement with Greece and Turkey which would show that Britain would not tolerate interference with those countries.[139] Templewood was concerned about United States public opinion on this issue: the considerable Albanian community there might make it particularly sensitive.[140] Kennedy, however, co-operated, and

134 *F O 372*, 3314, p. 356, T5054/90/384, Minute by R. H. Hadow, 19.4.1939.
135 *D O 114*, 98, p. 14, No. 17, F1706/137, High Commissioner in South Africa to Dominions Office, Telegram No. 39, Confidential, 134.1939.
136 *F O 372*, 3317, pp. 42–6, T5424/436/384, Harding to Cadogan, 13.4.1939 r. in r. 26.4.1939.
137 Ibid., p. 46, Cadogan to Harding, 21.4.1939 (copy).
138 Harvey, p. 275, Diary, 8.4.1939.
139 *Cab 23*, 98, p. 242, Conference of Ministers, Secret, 8.4.1939.
140 Ibid., p. 251.

agreed to keep the press in the United States 'as steady as possible', and to see that criticism was not directed against Britain.[141]

Chamberlain had hoped that Mussolini would present his *coup* as an agreed arrangement, and so 'raise as little as possible questions of European significance'. This Mussolini failed to do. Chamberlain wrote on 15 April:

> Any chance of further *rapprochement* with Italy has been blocked by Musso. [*sic*] just as Hitler has blocked my German *rapprochement*. That does not show that I have been wrong as my partisan critics declare. The fruits can be seen in the consolidation of world opinion + in the improvement of the military position of ourselves + France.[142]

The anti axis front with Poland at one end and Turkey at the other with Rumania and Greece in between, was furthered on 10 April by the British unilateral pledge to Greece and Rumania that if aggression took place against either of those countries, and they resisted, Britain would come to their aid.[143]

Britain had stood firm. The defensive agreements could be seen as an encirclement of Germany, or, alternatively, as an attempt to deter Germany from making further annexations by a threat of strength. Britain was committed and the dominions made little direct comment officially. Within the dominions opinion varied in its reaction to the guarantees.

In South Africa the guarantee to Poland had a mixed reception. A reason for this was the fear that a new system of alliances would include Russia. This view had been expressed as early as 22 March by Malan.[144] It was widely held, and shared even by Duncan: 'I thought Chamberlain had come to Munich to get France free of these lunacies and now we have caught the disease ourselves'.[145]

Press reaction, however, did not harp on the Russian fear. More concern was shown about Chamberlain's speech, and whether he had committed the commonwealth to the Polish pledge. The press was divided in its interpretation of this.[146] Mr. Fourie, the minister of railways, however, argued that Chamberlain's policy was to get nations to join in a 'peace pact' against aggression.[147]

[141] Ibid., p. 256, Cab 19 (39) 1, Secret, 10.4.1939.
[142] *Templewood Papers* XIX (C) 12, Chamberlain to Hilda Chamberlain, 15.4.1939 (copy).
[143] *Cab 23*, 98, p. 297, Cab 19 (39), Secret, 10.4.1939.
[144] *S A Parl Deb H of A* 33, col. 2142, 22.3.1939.
[145] *Lothian Papers* 381, pp. 251–3, Duncan to Lothian, 25.3.1939.
[146] *Daily Telegraph*, 5.4.1939; *Suiderstem*, 4.4.1939; 5.4.1939, Ed.; 10.4.1939, Ed.; *Burger*, 3.4.1939, Ed.
[147] *Times*, 6.4.1939.

In the house of assembly, on 12 April, Hertzog again reiterated that South Africa was not concerned 'in any single respect' with the situation in Europe.[148] The relationship between Britain and South Africa was one of friendship and not of alliance.[149] Hertzog did not consider South Africa bound by the Polish guarantee, or by any other guarantee that Britain might give.

Smuts's understanding of the situation was similar to that of Hertzog. Smuts wrote on 6 April:

> Chamberlain's Polish guarantee has simply made us gasp—from the Commonwealth point of view. I cannot see the Dominions following Great Britain in this sort of Imperial policy the dangers of which to the Commonwealth are obvious. We still remember Lloyd George's Chanak escapade.[150]

Lothian did try to reassure both Smuts and Duncan on this issue. On 5 April Lothian wrote explaining that the decision to guarantee Poland had been taken because it had been felt that unless a firm stand were made Europe would capitulate, and the United States would lose all faith in Britain and France and 'retire into isolation'. Lothian elaborated the further need for a military alliance with Russia, Rumania and Turkey.[151] This mention of Russia could hardly have quietened Duncan's qualms.

The Polish guarantee did not change South Africa's policy: Hertzog argued that it did not concern South Africa; Smuts did not contradict his leader.

The Australian government and most of the Australian press were firm in their support of Chamberlain's guarantee to Poland.[152] On 2 April Mr. Hughes, the minister for external affairs, spoke of the empire being the same as it was thirty years previously: Australia would not be intimidated.[153] The labour view was stated by Mr. Lang, the leader of the opposition, at a party conference on 9 April: it was isolationism. Lang saw no reason why Australia should be drawn into any European political quarrel.[154] The labour party, however, was still divided. On 10 April, Mr. J. R. Hughes, president of the trades and labour council, managed to

[148] *S A Parl Deb H of A* 34, col. 2714, 12.4.1939.

[149] Ibid., col. 2779. See also *D O 114*, 98, p. 13, No. 16, F706/137, High Commissioner in South Africa to Dominions Office, Telegram No. 38, Secret, 13.4.1939.

[150] *Smuts Papers* 60, No. 196, Smuts to M. C. Gillet, 17.3.1939. Quoted by Hancock, p. 311.

[151] *Lothian Papers* 381, pp. 254–6, Lothian to Duncan, 5.4.1939 (copy); 382, p. 667, Lothian to Smuts, 5.4.1939 (copy).

[152] *Argus*, 1.4.1939, Ed.; *Daily Telegraph*, 1.4.1939; *Daily News*, 5.4.1939, Ed.; *Age*, 5.4.1939, Ed.

[153] *Sydney Morning Herald*, 3.4.1939.

[154] Ibid., 10.4.1939.

carry a resolution unanimously calling for labour to fight against international fascism.[155]

The death of Lyons further complicated the situation. After disputes Menzies was elected and there were doubts whether the coalition government could continue under his leadership. Menzies was not popular. But he was known to favour conscription, and to be determined to improve Australian defences. Despite internal uncertainty there seemed little doubt that Australia would fight with Britain.[156]

The Polish guarantee confirmed a policy that the New Zealand government had been urging for several years, The fact that Chamberlain, the apostle of peace had taken this step, merely showed the urgency of the situation. At the labour party conference in April Savage spoke of steps to prepare the country's peacetime economy to meet any emergency.[157]

In Canada the guarantee to Poland did not noticeably change opinion: English language newspapers such as the Toronto *Star* spoke of British sentiment being 'solidified'; French Canadian reaction was predictable; Mackenzie King did not comment. The high commissioner in Canada pointed to the cross currents of opinion to which Mackenzie King was subjected as possibly being responsible for what appeared to be Mackenzie King's inability to make a clear statement of the Canadian government's attitude.[158]

Reaction in the United States to the new British policy was favourable. Roosevelt considered Chamberlain's statement to the house on 31 March 'excellent': the United States would believe that 'war was imminent' but the president did not think 'that this would do any harm'.[159] But Roosevelt was in a difficult position. The mood was such that he avoided being linked with any modifications of the neutrality legislation. Proposals for amendments which favoured the allies met with a stormy reception in congress, even against the background of the worsening situation in Europe.

First mooted in February 1939 the Thomas amendment, sponsored by a loyal member of the administration, was introduced in both houses, and

[155] Ibid., 11.4.1939.

[156] Anonymous, 'Australia', *Round Table* XXIX (1938–9), pp. 622–33 at pp. 624–8. See also Earle Page, *Truant Surgeon* (Sydney, 1963), pp. 262–78.

[157] Wood, pp. 90, 96–7; *Daily Telegraph*, 11.4.1939; *Sydney Morning Herald*, 11.4.1939.

[158] *Manchester Guardian*, 1.4.1939; 3.4.1939; *Times*, 3.4.1939; *F O 371*, 22971, pp. 271–28, C6106/15/18, Dominions Office to Foreign Office, Confidential, 25.4.1939 r. in r. 28.4.1939; Enclosing High Commissioner in Canada to Dominions Office, No. 107, 28.3.1939. See also *Documents on Canadian External Relations* 6, 1936–9, pp. 1155–64, No. 946, Memorandum by L. C. Christie The New British Policy in Europe, 12.4.1939.

[159] *F O 414*, 276 LI, p. 76, No. 34, C4529/54/18, Halifax to Lindsay, Telegram No. 156, 31.3.1939.

did not muster much support.[160] On 20 March senator Pittman introduced a resolution to the senate which was referred to the foreign relations committee. Sumner Welles pointed out that this proposal did not emanate from the executive branch. Pittman's proposal extended the 'cash and carry' provisions of the 1937 legislation. The foreign relations committee was divided. In a broadcast speech of 25 March senator Borah criticised the democracies and said that the United States's first responsibility was to put its 'own house in order'.[161]

At a time when Hitler's intentions in Europe were becoming obvious, isolationism in congress was rampant.[162]

Public opinion, as distinct from congress, was becoming more alive to the worsening situation. By the middle of March *Mein Kampf* headed the best seller list in Washington, and was second in New York and Philadelphia. It was not listed in Los Angeles.[163] The east coast, with its more traditional links with Europe, was more aware than the west.

The press in the United States followed the events of March closely. Hitler's march into Prague was noted by the United States newspapers with gloom, and, almost all stressed, in the words of the *New York Times* London correspondent, that Britain and France were 'resolutely looking the other way'.[164] Chamberlain's pledge to Poland had a cordial reception: it was seen by most editors as a courageous stand.[165] Sections of the United States press reinforced their advocacy of the repeal of the neutrality legislation.[166] After the Italian invasion of Albania there was bitter comment in the United States press.[167] According to opinion polls at this time events in Europe had educated the public, though not congress.[168]

While Chamberlain's statement on the British pledges to Greece and Rumania was well received in the United States, Roosevelt's endorsement of a *Washington Post* editorial aroused the isolationists. The editorial argued that the United States would be involved inevitably in any European war. The best way to prevent such a war was to make it clear in

[160] Francis O. Wilcox, 'American Government and Politics. The Neutrality Fight in Congress, 1939', *The American Political Science Review*, XXXIII (1939), pp. 811–25 at pp. 811–2; *New York Times*, 15.2.1939, Ed.
[161] *Times*, 21.3.1939; 27.3.1939.
[162] *New York Times*, 2.3.1939, Ed.
[163] Ibid., 13.3.1939.
[164] *News Chronicle*, 15.3.1939; *Daily Telegraph*, 16.3.1939.
[165] *Sunday Times*, 2.4.1939; *Daily Telegraph*, 4.4.1939; 5.4.1939.
[166] *Daily Telegraph*, 8.4.1939; *New York Times*, 9.4.1939.
[167] *Sunday Times*, 9.4.1939; *New York Times*, 9.4.1939.
[168] *News Chronicle*, 10.4.1939.

advance that the United States would be found alongside the democratic powers.[169]

On 14 April Kennedy informed the British of the developing situation in the United States. The ambassador gave a realistic picture. Under the United States system members of congress had the power to declare war, and they were inclined to be obedient to the sectional interests that they represented. Consequently their attitude was swayed by the developments of public opinion. At that time there was widespread hatred of the totalitarian states whose methods were 'deeply repugnant to the moral standards on which the average American bases his judgments of the outside world'. Because of this the extensive arms programme had been approved. But it was designed to enable the United States to protect its own interests against aggression. There was a growing realisation amongst the more thoughtful elements of the community that the United States could not dissociate itself from the consequences of nazi expansion. Kennedy warned, however, that it would be 'altogether mistaken to conclude that this development in the direction of realism has progressed to a point which would overcome the intense reluctance of the American people to become involved in a war'. The British government should expect no more from the United States in wartime 'than the maximum degree of assistance compatible with the preservation of U.S. neutrality'. Kennedy was hopeful that the neutrality legislation would be amended to enable Britain and France to obtain goods on a cash and carry basis. Roosevelt could be counted on to do everything possible to aid Britain and France, but the president's loss of prestige in congress was a difficulty. This information was incorporated in a paper for the chiefs of staff.[170]

Despite his difficult position in congress Roosevelt did make a stand against the dictators. He sent a message which was made public on 15 April, and of which the British were informed only a few hours before its release,[171] to Hitler and Mussolini. The president told the dictators that the constant fear of war was 'of definite concern to the people of the United States'. Roosevelt asked for a statement of policy from Hitler and Mussolini. The president wanted an assurance that the dictators would not attack the countries surrounding them. Then it might be possible to readjust differences around the conference table. The United States would be prepared to take part in such discussions.[172]

---

[169] *Daily Telegraph*, 14.4.1939.

[170] *F O 371*, 22829, pp. 281–3, A1358/1292/45, Foreign Office Minute by Balfour of Conversation with Kennedy, 14.4.1939 r. in r. 19.4.1939; Minute by W. Strang, 17.4.1939.

[171] *DBFP* 5, p. 218, No. 188, C5431/15/18, Text of a Communique issued to the Press, 15.4.1939.

[172] Ibid., pp. 212–4, No. 180, C5339/15/18, Lindsay to Halifax, Telegram No. 179, 15.4.1939 r. 16.4.1939.

This could be seen as an attempt by Roosevelt to capitalise on a public opinion aroused by Italy's occupation of Albania, and a growing disenchantment with the dictators, and particularly United States opinion against the dictators.[173]

The response in the United States to Roosevelt's appeal was favourable. Most newspaper editors saw it as a timely attempt to assist Britain and France in preserving world peace. Some were concerned that Roosevelt had committed the United States to armed intervention in any conflict that might arise.[174] But Roosevelt's opinion was invidious: his foreign policy was a political issue in a country markedly divided, and lacking the common front that Roosevelt had asked for in his message to congress in January.

Chamberlain tried to assist Roosevelt to consolidate United States public opinion by introducing conscription in Britain. At the cabinet meeting on 24 April the prime minister explained that there was great pressure on Britain to introduce some form of compulsory training, not only from France, but also from the United States.[175] Presumably Chamberlain hoped that this would help to win over United States public opinion, and help the passage of the amended neutrality laws through congress.

Chamberlain was reluctant to take this step, and felt that it could be done only with the support of the trade unions. Halifax, however, told Kennedy 'in great confidence' on 18 April that he personally favoured conscription.[176] Bullitt had told Phipps that he was certain that Roosevelt believed that it was of 'the highest importance' for Britain to introduce conscription'.[177] Roosevelt maintained, however, that this was a matter of British internal policy, and it was not possible for him to express any views on it.[178] But Phipps told the British government on 20 April that he had learnt from Bullitt that Roosevelt felt strongly that it was absolutely essential for Britain to introduce compulsory national service at once and before 28 April.[179]

The east European guarantees marked the decisive shift in British foreign policy. An analysis of the cabinet discussions shows Chamberlain in

[173] *Templewood Papers* XIX (C) 12, Chamberlain to Hilda Chamberlain, 15.4.1939 (copy).

[174] *New York Times*, 17.4.1939; 18.4.1939; *Daily Telegraph*, 17.4.1939, 18.4.1939; *New York Tribune*, 20.4.1939.

[175] *Cab 23*, 99, p. 8, Cab 22 (39) 3, Secret, 24.3.1939.

[176] *FRUS* 1939(1), pp. 141–2, 740.00/940, Kennedy to Hull, Telegram No. 512, 18.4.1939.

[177] Ibid., pp. 169–70, 841.2222/39, Bullitt to Hull, Telegram No. 785, 19.4.1939 r. 20.4.1939.

[178] Ibid., p. 170, 841.2222/39, Hull to Bullitt, Telegram No. 283, 20.4.1939.

[179] *DBFP* 5, pp. 251–2, No. 227, C5610/15/18, Phipps to Halifax, Telegram No. 178, 20.4.1939.

control. No step was taken, or policy implemented until the prime minister had decided that it should be.

Throughout the views of the dominions were considered, but they did not decisively influence policy. Possibly the dominions would not have wished that: they were informed rather than consulted, and thus Canada and South Africa could feel that they were not committed by British policy. It was the views of the dominion high commissioners in London that probably had most influence on the cabinet.

The dominions did not always receive full information. Care was taken to avoid sending them optimistic reports.

After Hitler's occupation of Prague Australia and New Zealand were, in reality, committed to British policy. In South Africa Hertzog would not be drawn, and Smuts offered no lead. Mackenzie King, from internal considerations, and possibly personal convictions, would try to stand outside European affairs till the last moment.

The United States was sent much the same information as went to the dominions. Probably the United States public had been educated to the realities of the European situation but the same was not so of congress. Roosevelt could be relied upon to do what he could, but he had lost prestige in congress. All that Britain could do was to maintain silence in the hope of not arousing sensitive congressional opinion over the amendment of the neutrality legislation, or introduce measures like conscription with an eye to winning United States support.

The commonwealth was not united after Prague, nor was support from the United States any more likely than it had been during the Munich crisis.

IX

CONTINGENCY PLANNING FOR WAR IN TIIE FAR EAST AND UNITED STATES OPINION

Contingency Planning for War in the Far East and United States Opinion

WITH the Russian negotiations in progress attention shifted to the far east in June. Japanese intransigence and maltreatment of British subjects in the Tientsin concession meant that for a time it seemed as if war would start in the far east and not in Europe. This meant a serious rethinking of British contingency planning. If war did start in the east, it was unlikely that Germany and Italy would be able to resist the temptation to move in Europe. Britain might have to fight on three fronts simultaneously. The despatch of a fleet to the far east had to be questioned seriously, with obvious ramifications for Australia and New Zealand. In previous years the United States had consistently refused to be embroiled with Britain in the far east, possibly with an eye on entanglement in Europe. But it seemed that there was little that Britain could do in the far east without United States assistance, or at least, co-operation. British plans, however did assume that the United States would be friendly.[1]

After Hitler's invasion of Prague Halifax had suggested to Kennedy on 21 March that if trouble started it would be a great help to Britain with regard to Japan if part of the United States fleet could be sent to Honolulu. Initially Kennedy was enthusiastic, and promised to suggest it to Roosevelt. But when Chatfield, the minister for co-ordination of defence, mentioned the matter to the ambassador in the evening, the enthusiasm had waned somewhat, and Kennedy would only pass on the proposal that the United States fleet should be brought to 'a state of preparedness'.[2]

Roosevelt did take some action: on 16 April he announced that the United States fleet would be moved from the Atlantic to its 'normal operating areas' in the Pacific. But the president would not act on Daladier's suggestion that ships of the United States Atlantic fleet might visit European ports.[3]

Kennedy also let the British government know on 14 April that if Japan arraigned itself as a belligerent with Germany and Italy 'the United States

---

[1] *Cab 2*, 8, p. 156, Committee of Imperial Defence Minutes of 349th Meeting, Secret Lock and Key, 3.3.1939.

[2] *Cab 23*, 98, p. 97, Cab 14 (39) 2, Secret, 22.3.1939.

[3] *Documents on British Foreign Policy* 3rd Series (hereinafter cited as '*DBFP*') 5, pp. 251–2, No. 227, C5610/15/18, Phipps to Halifax, Telegram No. 178, 20.4.1939.

might well feel compelled in the opening phases of hostilities to resort to common naval action with France and Great Britain':

> In particular any Japanese threat to Australia and New Zealand, whether by way of a direct descent upon them or indirectly in the form of an expedition against Singapore, would be a matter to which the U.S.A. could hardly remain for long indifferent.

The whole western Pacific and even western Canada might be menaced by invasion.[4]

Early in 1939 Britain and the United States were hoping that Japan could be restrained from joining a threatened triple alliance with the axis powers. Consequently no very firm action was taken, and the United States's insistence on parallel action meant that Tokyo was little affected by United States and British protests. Japan seriously threatened the western position in China with attacks on the international settlements at Shanghai and Amoy. But the main concentration fell on the British concession at Tientsin.[5]

Japanese motivations in choosing Tientsin for a showdown were probably partially influenced by a desire to drive a wedge between the United States and British governments. The United States had no direct interest in Tientsin. Craigie warned the British government of this late in May.[6] Halifax agreed with Craigie that the position would be improved if the United States took a strong line defending its interests in China:

> But if they do, it must be of their own volition and when they judge the proper time has come. Rather than put any pressure on them to work with us, I think we must accustom ourselves to having to take an isolated step forward. And it may well be that this will in the end prove to be the most effective means of encouraging the United States of America to follow, for they have always in the past shown a marked disposition to help those that help themselves.[7]

On 5 June Craigie warned of the changed Japanese policy that no longer dealt with Britain and the United States on simultaneous and identical lines. The ambassador, however, doubted the wisdom of taking any step in advance of the United States at that time.[8]

---

[4] *F O 371*, 22829, pp. 281–3, A2865/1292/45, Foreign Office Minute by Balfour, 14.4.1939 r. in r. 19.4.1939.

[5] Nicholas R. Clifford, 'Britain, America and the Far East, 1937–1940: a Failure in Co-operation', *Journal of British Studies*, III (1963–4), pp. 137–54 at pp. 146–7.

[6] *DBFP* 9, pp. 102–3, No. 107, F4981/1236/23, Craigie to Cadogan, Telegram No. 464, 23.5.1939; pp. 107–8, No. 116, F5037/1236/23, Craigie to Halifax, Telegram No. 483, 26.5.1939.

[7] Ibid., p. 120. No. 5, F4981/1236/23, Halifax to Craigie, Telegram No. 254, 1.6.1939.

[8] Ibid., pp. 134–5, No. 150, F537/12368/1236/23, Craigie to Halifax, Telegram No. 573, 5.6.1939 r. 6.6.1939.

In Tientsin the arrest of a number of suspected terrorists in the British concession, followed by what seemed to be a break of the British promise to surrender them to the Japanese, made Tokyo obstructive. The Japanese demanded negotiations on issues wider than Tientsin, on British relations to Japan in occupied China.[9] On 15 June Britain asked for United States assistance in the form of mediation.[10] The immediate reply was that though the proposals were receiving 'careful and friendly consideration' it was 'felt necessary to proceed with some deliberation'.[11]

There had been no reply from the United States when the cabinet committee on foreign policy met to discuss the situation on 19 June. Halifax explained that he had told Kennedy that there was little that Britain could do in the far east 'unless the United States joined in with us'. Kennedy merely reported that the wider issues raised by the Japanese military spokesmen at Tientsin had put both the United States and Britain on a 'tough spot'.

In the absence of any intimations from the United States the committee was left to discuss Craigie's suggestion that he urge independently upon the Japanese the following terms: blockade measures to be withdrawn, Britain being prepared to discuss all outstanding questions relating to Tientsin on the basis that British authority in the concession be maintained intact, and that 'all possible steps consistent with the maintenance of neutrality be taken by us to ensure that the concession is not used for any purposes demonstrably prejudicial to military international political interests of occupying Powers'.

Halifax felt that such terms would place Britain in a humiliating position. But, as the chiefs of staff pointed out the strategic situation was grave, even if the optimistic view were taken that the United States would side with Britain. The foreign secretary thought that bearing in mind the dangers in the European situation, and provided that there were United States diplomatic support in Tokyo, it might be best to authorise Craigie to negotiate on the lines he suggested. Chamberlain agreed. He was impressed by the time factor: if there were any delay it might prove impossible to evacuate British personnel and ships from Tientsin, and possibly other blockaded concessions. Chamberlain overrode the suggestion of Cadogan that it might be advisable to wait for definite reactions from the United States. Seemingly the prime minister was not optimistic

9 Clifford, pp. 144–5.
10 *DBFP* 9, pp. 183–4, No. 210, F5893/1/10, Halifax to Lindsay, Telegram No. 270, 15.6.1939.
11 Ibid., p. 189, No. 218, F5970/1/10, Lindsay to Halifax, Telegram No. 267, 16.6.1939 r. 17.6.1939.

about United States co-operation. Concern was expressed about the effect on the United States if Britain undertook direct negotiations with the Japanese so soon after an appeal for United States intervention. Chamberlain retorted that he thought 'the United States Government would be likely to be greatly relieved, if the Tientsin trouble could be settled without American intervention'. Halifax thought that if the United States refused the British request 'a *fortiori* would they refuse to participate in military action against Japan such as was contemplated in the Report of the Chiefs of Staff Sub-Committee'?[12]

On 19 June Hull made a statement which from the British point of view did not amount to much. Halifax told Kennedy that Craigie was being instructed to make certain suggestions to the Japanese government. It would be helpful if the United States made some previous approach to the Japanese. Kennedy felt that the United States government would not take further action at that time. After Craigie's approach Britain could enquire again. Following this message from Kennedy it was decided that there was nothing to gain from further delay, and Craigie was instructed to go ahead with his proposals. The committee had decided to wait for United States reaction, and Kennedy's telephone message was considered the key to it.[13]

Because of the seriousness of the situation in the far east, and the independent action that Britain was taking, the committee paid particular attention to the strategic situation. If a fleet of sufficient size, namely seven capital ships, were sent to the far east, there was the danger that the naval position in home waters and in the Mediterranean would be insecure. Chamberlain felt that this was a decisive argument for reaching an early settlement of the Tientsin dispute, provided that the Japanese did not make the British position intolerable. Halifax agreed, but pointed out that if the United States co-operated this choice would not have to be faced. The minister for co-ordination of defence said that United States co-operation would be most likely if Britain had in mind the sending of a substantial fleet to the far east. A possible alternative was to concentrate the fleet at Alexandria: it would then not be known whether Britain intended to hold the Mediterranean in force, or to send the fleet to the far east. Inskip warned that if Britain were at war with Japan and it was decided to keep the fleet in the Mediterranean rather than send it to the far east, 'the

12 *Cab 27*, 625, pp. 7–14, F P (36) 52nd Mtg, Lock and Key, 19.6.1939.
13 Ibid., pp. 1–2, F P (36) 53rd Mtg, Lock and Key, 20.6.1939.

position would give rise to profound dismay in Australia and New Zealand.' It was decided to remit the issues to the defence plans committee.[14]

The committee of imperial defence had last considered the despatch of a fleet to the far east on 2 May 1939. Then it had been pointed out that the chiefs of staff had repeatedly emphasised that British present and potential naval strength was insufficient and was not designed to engage three naval powers simultaneously without grave risks. Chatfield explained that the stationing of the United States navy in the Pacific was an important factor in the issue of whether Britain could knock out Italy before the Japanese caused irreparable damage. The United States was informed of this. The guarantees to Greece, Rumania and Turkey, and the alliances with Egypt and Iraq had changed the position: if British ships were moved from the Mediterranean, as Lord Stanhope pointed out, there would be serious repercussions in those countries. With these difficulties in mind the committee decided:

> That there are so many variable factors which cannot at present be assessed, that it is not possible to state definitely how soon after Japanese intervention a Fleet could be despatched to the Far East. Neither is it possible to ennumerate precisely the size of the Fleet that we could afford to send.[15]

This decision had considerable ramifications for the dominions, particularly Australia and New Zealand who were most open to Japanese attack. Australia had shown concern about this earlier.

On 8 March 1938 Chamberlain had spoken to the house of commons outlining British defence policy. The prime minister explained that the cornerstone of British defence policy was the security of the United Kingdom:

> Our first main efforts must have two main objectives: we must protect this country and we must preserve the trade routes upon which we depend for our food and raw materials.
>
> Our third objective is the defence of British territories overseas from attack. . . . They are not as vital as the defence of our own country, because as long as we are undefeated at home, although we sustained losses ourselves we might have an opportunity of making them good hereafter.[16]

This statement caused misgivings in Australia, the inference being that in the event of war Britain might not be able to defend its overseas

---

[14] Ibid., pp. 6–8.

[15] *Cab 2*, 8, pp. 207–8, Committee of Imperial Defence Minutes of 355th Meeting D P (P), Secret Lock and Key, 2.5.1939.

[16] Ibid., 9, p. 32, Annex II to Appendix I, Chamberlain to Lyons, Telegram, Secret and Personal, 11.3.1938 (copy).

possessions. Lyons asked Chamberlain for a reassuring statement. Chamberlain replied that because it appeared third on his list, it would be wrong to deduce that the protection of overseas possessions was not regarded as of 'first-rate importance'.[17]

Chamberlain was more specific after a telephone call from Lyons following Hitler's occupation of Prague. He sent a telegram to the Australian prime minister on 20 March stating that should Japan join Germany and Italy in a war against Britain, it would still be the British government's 'full intention' to despatch a fleet to Singapore. Such a combination had not been envisaged in earlier plans, and the size of the fleet would be dependent on the moment Japan entered the war, as well as what losses previously had been sustained.[18] This satisfied Lyons. He was, however, concerned about delays in the delivery of Australian defence orders. Menzies had to be reassured by Chamberlain that Australian 'requirements shall be given substantially equal priority with our own'.[19]

But at the meeting of the committee of imperial defence on 2 May Inskip pointed out that there had been 'a considerable scaling down' of the British undertaking to the dominions to send a fleet to the far east in all circumstances. Bruce and Nash would be arriving in Britain shortly and would be likely to attempt to obtain more definite assurances. Chamberlain, however, felt that the position had been stated clearly in his telegram of 20 March to Lyons. The prime minister argued that if Britain were defeated 'the fate of the Dominions would be sealed':

> While, therefore, we should do all we could for the protection of the Dominions, the important thing was to defeat the enemy. He thought that the position should be frankly put before Mr. Bruce, who, he was sure, would fully appreciate and endorse the reasons for the modification of policy.[20]

The committee of imperial defence considered this matter further on 22 June. But it was decided to wait until the chiefs of staff had decided what action to take in the event of a war starting in the east.[21]

The cabinet considered the situation in the far east on 21 June. Chamberlain explained that measures against the Japanese could be effective only

---

[17] Ibid., Lyons to Chamberlain, Telegram, Secret and Personal, 10.3.1938 (copy); Chamberlain to Lyons, Telegram, Secret and Personal, 11.3.1938 (copy).

[18] Ibid., 8, p. 210, Appendix, Chamberlain to Lyons, Telegram, Immediate Personal Most Secret, 20.3.1939 (copy, cypher).

[19] *Premier 1*, 310, Lyons to Chamberlain, Telegram No. 33, Secret, 29.3.1939; Chamberlain to Menzies, Telegram No. 29, Secret, 6.4.1939.

[20] *Cab 2*, 8, pp. 207–8, Committee of Imperial Defence Minutes of 355th Meeting D P (P), Secret Lock and Key, 2.5.1939; See also *Premier 1*, 309.

[21] *Cab 2*, 8, p. 230, Committee of Imperial Defence Minutes of 360th Meeting D P (P), Secret Lock and Key, 22.6.1939. For an account of British strategy during the Tientsin crisis see W. R. Louis, *British Strategy in the Far East 1919–39* (Oxford, 1971), pp. 261–7.

with the co-operation of the United States. It was useless to embark upon a policy of retaliation unless Britain were prepared to impose sanctions. Japan might react, and it was important, therefore, before imposing sanctions, to examine the strategic situation. Mention was made of the Russian assistance in the far east, but Chamberlain felt that the position of the United States was more important. It was represented, however, that the United States could not afford Britain much assistance there 'without jeopardising the prospects of the passage of the Bill amending their neutrality legislation'.[22]

In a way Britain was impotent. On the one hand British prestige was being seriously challenged by the Japanese. To retaliate significantly might mean the weakening of home defences and of the Mediterranean, thus providing the dictators with their chance in Europe. Little help could be expected from the United States: traditionally that country had refused to be involved with Britain in the far east. And, in any event, at this time any mention of such assistance might jeopardise seriously any amendment to the neutrality legislation. Britain needed such modification if war were to be carried on for long. Furthermore, if a significant fleet were not sent to the far east in the event of war, the security of Australia and New Zealand might be threatened, and the dominions were anxious for reassurance on this point. On 24 June Menzies asked for confirmation that Australia be entitled to assume 'that in the event of war with Japan the United Kingdom Government would send a fleet to Singapore within appropriate time capable of containing Japanese fleet to a degree sufficient to prevent a major act of aggression against Australia'.[23] The situation in the far east was so serious that contingency plans had to be changed to meet the eventuality of the outbreak of war in the far east rather than in Europe. The committee of imperial defence met on 26 June to consider this point.

Chamberlain pointed to the need to establish priorities: Britain could not be as strong as it would like in all three parts of the world where its interests were threatened. Halifax on this point, was worried that the despatch of a fleet to Singapore 'might avail us nothing in the Far East, while involving us in considerable risk elsewhere'. The prime minister mentioned the disadvantage of withdrawal from the Mediterranean. He felt that unless Japan forced war upon Britain, Britain should not take retaliatory action which could lead to war against Japan and the axis powers. Warnings came from MacDonald of the deplorable effect on

---

[22] *Cab 23*, 100, pp. 8–14, Cab 33 (39) 3, Secret, 21.6.1939.
[23] *Cab 2*, 9, p. 32, Annex I to Appendix I, Menzies to Chamberlain, Telegram, Secret Personal, 24.6.1939 (copy).

British prestige not only in the far east but in India and the colonies generally. Zetland supported him by mentioning the possible encouragement to disaffected interests in India. They hoped for some retaliatory action short of actual war. Hore-Belisha then raised the question of economic pressure but agreed that this was governed by the attitude of the United States. On this point Chamberlain thought that 'experience showed the best way of obtaining anything from America was not to ask for it'. With these factors in mind the committee agreed that nothing should be done to jeopardise the success of the impending negotiations at Tokyo. It further accepted the view of the chiefs of staff that six capital ships was the minimum that should be retained in home waters. If capital ships were withdrawn from the eastern Mediterranean the French should be 'strongly pressed not to withdraw their two Battle Cruisers from the Atlantic so long as they have the three Lorraine class ships available in the Mediterranean to deal with the Italian capital ships in those waters'. Further the chiefs of staff were requested to consider if a situation arose which looked as though it might lead to hostilities with Japan, whether it would be 'practicable and advisable for whatever fleet might be destined for despatch to the Far east to be concentrated initially in the Eastern Mediterranean'.[24]

It was also decided that Chamberlain and Inskip should see Bruce and Nash to explain the position of the Tientsin affair, and the despatch of a fleet to the far east. The chiefs of staff were requested to draft a reply to Menzies's enquiry about the latter aspect.[25] Accordingly a telegram repeating Chamberlain's assurance of 20 March 1939 to Lyons was sent to Menzies on 29 June.

On 28 June Chamberlain and Inskip met Bruce and Nash and explained the situation. The reply to Menzies's enquiry of 24 June was also discussed. Chamberlain put it that if the British fleet were sent to Singapore to deal with Japan the axis powers might take advantage of the situation. The British position with the recent commitments to certain European countries would then be difficult. It was necessary to retain sufficient ships in home waters, and it was useless sending a fleet to Singapore unless it were strong enough to achieve the objects set out in the telegram to Menzies. The inference was that sending a fleet to Singapore might not be a top priority in the new situation. Chamberlain was hopeful of the negotiations at

[24] Ibid., pp. 28–30, Committee of Imperial Defence Minutes of 362nd Meeting D P (P), Secret Lock and Key, 26.6.1939.
[25] Ibid., pp. 30–2, Appendix II, Chamberlain to Menzies, Telegram, Secret and Personal, 29.6.1939 (copy).

Tientsin, but it might be impossible to avoid hostilities. He mentioned, perhaps optimistically, the attitude of the United States as a limiting factor on Japan. The British government was keeping in touch with the United States: the latter country was 'wary but helpful'. This assessment contrasted with that given by Chamberlain to the committee of imperial defence.

Bruce offered his personal estimate of Australia's reaction to the present situation. His government felt that the foreign office had taken 'a somewhat too precise and exacting view of the technicalities'. They would favour a settlement in Japan 'short of accepting intolerable humiliation'. The Australian government would co-operate if Britain decided that sanctions were the only way of maintaining the position. In the case of armed conflict Australia would want to know the size of the fleet to be sent to Singapore, and when it would be despatched. During his recent visit to the United States Bruce had gained the impression that opinion there was 'not disinclined to take an interest in Far Eastern Affairs'. Chamberlain put this in perspective by saying that 'the United States was more forthcoming as regards Far Eastern Affairs than anything else'.

Bruce mentioned that as far back as 1938 he had doubted whether it would be possible for the British government to send a fleet to Singapore, if there were war with Germany, Italy and Japan simultaneously. The admiralty, however, in November 1938, had assured him that it was the firm intention to send seven battleships. Consequently Chamberlain's telegram to Lyons of 20 March came as a surprise.

These points raised by Bruce were not answered, and the high commissioner brought them up again at a further meeting on 11 July. He mentioned what a bombshell Chamberlain's telegram of 20 March had been. It was pointed out to him that the situation had changed. Whereas previously it had been hoped that with a war starting in Europe Japan might not intervene on the side of the axis for some time, and it might have been sounder strategy to knock out Italy first and then to release the bulk of the naval forces to proceed to the far east should Japan intervene. The prevailing situation was that a war might start with Japan and then spread to Europe. Bruce insisted on knowing the British government's intentions in such a contingency. All that Inskip could tell him was that the position was indeterminate, and that Chamberlain's earlier assurances to Menzies still held good. Chatfield mentioned a possible plan: the fleet destined for the far east could be concentrated at Alexandria. Such a scheme would keep the country guessing, and postpone a decision till it could be seen how matters developed. But there was no question of Britain abdicating its position in the far east without fighting. No definite decision had been taken, however, as to what action would be taken if war started in the far east.[26]

Nearly on the verge of war with Japan, Britain, for strategic reasons of the difficulty of fighting on three fronts simultaneously, was in the position of having to accommodate Japan provided the humiliation was not too extreme. The United States was not obliging. The lack of Anglo-American co-operation in the far east was especially obvious at this time.

The United States response to the British request in mid June merely was to deliver a strong note to Japan. Even that was not sent. Grew, and the *chargé d'affaires*, Eugene Dooman, opposed it. All that was forthcoming was an expression of United States concern at the spread of anti British outbreaks in occupied China from Dooman, and a mention from Hull to the press that Washington was concerned with the 'broader aspects' of the Tientsin crisis.[27]

Britain, however, had to be wary of United States opinion lest it be offended at a crucial time. Not much could be expected from the United States and the pretext of jeopardising the amendments to the neutrality legislation always could be used. The United States, though not prepared to do anything itself, felt that Britain should take a firm stand. Lindsay telegrammed on 26 June that feeling in the United States supported Britain taking a stand against Japan. The ambassador mentioned that the United States was always less isolationist towards the far east than Europe. He warned of the bad consequences of anything that could be construed as a return to the policy of appeasement, and the effect that this might have on the neutrality legislation: the press and the public were behind Britain and the difficulties were congressional.[28]

From the time of the occupation of Prague Britain, and Chamberlain in particular, had taken great care not to offend United States sensibilities. Britain hoped for a repeal of the neutrality laws, and Roosevelt probably did too, to coincide with the royal visit. Such a move would tie in with the British policy of alliances in acting as a deterrent to Germany. If this policy did not succeed the repeal would be of obvious advantage to Britain if it came to a shooting war. British concern for United States

---

[26] Ibid., pp. 33–9, 14/13/72, Record of Meeting between Chamberlain, Inskip, Nash and Bruce, Secret, 28.6.1939; pp. 40–5, Record of Meeting with Bruce, Secret, 11.7.1939.

[27] Clifford, p. 147.

[28] *DBFP* 9, pp. 227–8, No. 264, F6423/1/10, Lindsay to Halifax, Telegram No. 283, 26.6.1939 r. 27.6.1939.

public and congressional opinion was shown in every aspect of policy. Britain refrained from making any comment, official or public, on the neutrality debates. Even Lothian, the newly appointed ambassador, was warned by Lindsay that he should not comment on the situation in the United States before he arrived.[29] The Palestine white paper was tied in with a report on the settlement of refugees in British Guiana to keep opinion favourable in the United States. Concern was felt over the financial position and possible help from the United States. But only naval conversations along the lines of the Ingersoll mission and correspondence over obtaining a secret gunsight were immediate practical results.

In the middle of June foreign office officials were hopeful that the neutrality legislation might be amended in Britain's favour: Hull's statement that there should be a drastic revision eliminating the embargo[30] was well received, and welcomed by the chairmen of the senate and house committees on foreign affairs. Another favourable sign was taken to be the drafting of two new bills by senator Gillette and representative Bloom. These bills did not provide any form of embargo on the export of materials to belligerents. The Bloom bill still insisted on the cash and carry requirement. It was thought by the foreign office that both these bills might have been drafted with administration approval.[31]

Hull hoped that if the house passed a bill dropping the arms embargo the senate might be induced to do likewise. On 29 May Bloom introduced his bill along the lines generally recommended by Hull. The house, however, on 30 June, inserted an amendment by a majority of two votes, containing a modified arms embargo. Hull issued a statement on 1 July to which the president gave his enthusiastic approval:

> Its failure to pass the house by a narrow margin is a matter of regret and disappointment from the standpoint of peace and the best interests of this country in international relations.[32]

Butler saw Winant, director of the ILO, on 4 July, and explained that British officials all understood what the administration had wished. Winant said how careful he thought the British had been 'in saying nothing which could offend America'. Butler minuted, somewhat disillusioned:

> I cannot tell you what a deplorable impression this news makes on my mind. In my political life I have always been privately convinced that we can no more

29 *Lothian Papers* 392, pp. 402–4, Lindsay to Lothian, 16.5.1939; pp. 405–6, Lothian to Lindsay, 25.5.1939 (copy).

30 *Times*, 3.7.1939.

31 *F O 371*, 22814, pp. 236–7, Foreign Office Minute by B. E. T. Gage, 19.6.1939.

32 Cordell Hull, *The Memoirs of Cordell Hull* (London, 1948), 1, pp. 645–7.

count on America than on Brazil, but I had been led myself to hope that this legislation might at least be passed.[33]

The position was that if congress did not insert any further legislation when war started there would be an embargo on the export of arms, ammunition and implements of war, but that it would not be necessary for Britain to purchase any other materials on the cash and carry basis. But, in any case, the British government was in default under the Johnson act in that it had not repaid its war debts, and so could not raise loans in the United States.[34]

Foreign office officials thought that the defeat of the administration's 'amended neutrality legislation' was caused by a combination of a dislike of Roosevelt's dictatorial methods and a desire to keep clear of European quarrels.[35] Britain had to proceed on the assumption that United States help would not be forthcoming.

On 11 July Pittman, at Hull's suggestion, placed the amended neutrality legislation before the senate committee. At a press conference Hull publicly stated his approval and Roosevelt backed him. The committee did not respond: it voted 12 to 11 to postpone all consideration of neutrality legislation to the next session of congress in January 1940.[36]

Halifax told the cabinet on 12 July that the neutrality amendment had been unfavourable. This was 'unfortunate, especially in view of the fact that the United States Government had given as their reason for being unable to help us in several matters that to do so would prejudice the passage of the amending legislation'.[37]

This was galling to Britain: the repeal failed despite the attention that had been paid to United States congressional and public opinion.

United States opinion had been a primary concern in the handling of the refugee question. At the cabinet committee on foreign policy on 14 November 1938 Halifax had pointed out that Kennedy had been told by a prominent United States journalist that United States public opinion was becoming anti British because it felt that Britain was doing nothing to relieve the situation of the refugees. MacDonald mentioned a suggestion

[33] *F O 371*, 22814, pp. 294–9, A4583/28/45, Lindsay to Foreign Office, Telegram No. 295(R), 2.7.1939 r. in r. 3.7.1939; Foreign Office Minutes by R. Butler, 4.7.1939; 3.7.1939.
[34] Ibid., 22815, pp. 10–2, A4701/98/45, Foreign Office Minute by Balfour, 29.6.1939 r. in r. 7.7.1939.
[35] Ibid., pp. 15–22, A4794/98/45, Lindsay to Foreign Office, Telegram No. 741E, 3.7.1939 r. in r. 11.7.1939; Foreign Office Minutes by B. E. T. Gage, 14.7.1939; J. V. Perowne, 14.7.1939.
[36] Hull 1, pp. 647–8.
[37] *Cab 23*, 100, p. 155, Cab 37 (39) 5, Secret, 12.7.1937.

that British Guiana might be suitable for large scale Jewish settlement, or something might be done in Western Australia.[38]

The matter became before the cabinet at the time of the United States neutrality debates, when the matter was considered with the British white paper limiting the entry of refugees into Palestine, and the possible consequences of that on sensitive United States public opinion at the time of the visit of the king and queen. Kennedy thought that the publication of the white paper in the near future would not affect the visit, but that the application of conscription in Ulster might have resulted in the working up of Irish agitation in the United States. Chamberlain, always sensitive to United States opinion, stressed that the government's statement on settling refugees in British Guiana should be published well in advance of the publication of the white paper on Palestine. The cabinet agreed to this. MacDonald outlined the British statement: settlement could be started in October; Britain would provide facilities for an industrial development survey; if the scheme were a success Britain would be prepared to make practically the whole country available except for the coastal belt; Britain would accept financial responsibility for arterial communications to the coast. MacDonald's information was that United States opinion would be impressed favourably by the scheme.[39]

The tactic was successful: MacDonald was able to report on 23 May to the cabinet that the position of public opinion in the United States over the publication of the Palestine white paper was 'not unsatisfactory'.[40]

The cabinet again discussed a further report of the cabinet committee on 12 July. Unless British Guiana were developed the colonial empire could take comparatively few refugees. The prospect of dominion co-operation was slight: at one time it had been suggested that Australia take 30,000 refugees over three years but its government had reduced this figure to 15,000, and Inskip felt that Australia should not be pressed on the matter. Chamberlain stressed that it was necessary to secure the co-operation of the United States before doing anything further.[41]

The royal visit in June 1939 to the United States was 'an unqualified success'.[42] The psychological aspects of the visit were those that were

[38] *Cab 27*, 624, pp. 6–12, F P (36) 32nd Mtg, Lock and Key, 14.11.1938.
[39] *Cab 24*, 286, pp. 73–82, C P 105 (39), Memorandum by MacDonald on Possibilities of Refugee Settlement in British G iana, Secret, 4.5.1939; *Cab 23*, 99, pp. 168–73, Cab 27 (39) 7, Secret, 10.5.1939.
[40] *Cab 23*, 99, p. 251, Cab 29 (39) 5, Secret, 23.5.1939.
[41] Ibid., 100, pp. 163–75, Cab 37 (39) 11, Secret, 12.7.1939.
[42] William L. Langer and S. Everett Gleason, *The Challenge to Isolation* (London, 1952), p. 129.

thought to be important.[43] As Roosevelt had written to King George: 'to the American people, the essential democracy of yourself and the Queen makes the greatest appeal of all'.[44] Roosevelt had no misgivings about the proposed visit even though some critics had implied that it might be taken as evidence of an Anglo-American alliance or an attempt to lure the United States into one.[45] In the privacy of Hyde Park Roosevelt apparently told the king in confidence that he approved the new firm British policy.[46] He formed a 'really deep and affectionate regard' for the king.[47]

In the short term the tangible results of these efforts were slight but of some military significance.

At the time of Hitler's move into Prague the British government approached the United States about the possibility of resuming the naval exchange of views which had been initiated by the Ingersoll mission in 1938. If Britain were involved in a European conflict it might be unable to enforce on a large scale its naval forces in the far east, and this could affect the United States naval dispositions.[48] Roosevelt was prepared to reopen the conversations but the procedure adopted the previous year was not suitable. Secrecy was essential as such an exchange could seriously compromise the pending neutrality legislation. An officer might be sent to the United States to conduct conversations along the lines of those carried out by Gaunt in 1915.[49] This meant that Roosevelt probably had something wide in scope in mind.[50]

The British were not sure what they intended,[51] but the admiralty preferred that the conversations should follow the 1938 pattern.[52] Commander T. C. Hampton was chosen to travel as a private individual to Baltimore and Washington, ostensibly on business.[53] At the request of the committee of imperial defence Hampton was to inform the United

---

[43] *F O 371*, 21584, pp. 261–8, A8061/7673/45, Lindsay to Cadogan, Confidential, 1.11.1938 r. in r. 23.11.1938.

[44] Elliott Roosevelt, Ed., *F.D.R. His Personal Letters. 1928–1945* (New York, 1950), 2, p. 824, Roosevelt to George VI, 2.11.1938.

[45] *F O 371*, 21584, pp. 261–8, A8061/7376/45, Lindsay to Foreign Office, Telegram No. 389, Confidential, 25.10.1938 r. 26.10.1938.

[46] Langer and Gleason, p. 129.

[47] *Elibank Papers* 8809, pp. 182–3, Roosevelt to Murray, 10.7.1939.

[48] *F O 371*, 23560, pp. 71–3, F2879/456/23, Halifax to Lindsay, Telegram No. 131, Important Most Secret, 19.3.1939 (cypher).

[49] Ibid., pp. 74–5, F2880/456/23, Lindsay to Halifax, Telegram No. 124, Important Most Secret 21.3.1939 (cypher).

[50] Ibid., pp. 76–7, F2881/456/23, Halifax to Lindsay, Telegram No. 126, Most Secret, 22.3.1939 (cypher).

[51] Ibid., p. 90, F2943/456/23, Minute by Ronald, 28.4.1939; pp. 90–1, F2943/456/23, Foreign Office Minute, 1.5.1939.

[52] Ibid., p. 92. F2943/G, Halifax to Lindsay, Telegram Most Secret, 5.5.1939 (cypher).

[53] Ibid., 23561, p. 282, F21519/G, Halifax to Lindsay, Telegram No. 237, Most Secret, 22.5.1939 (draft cypher).

States of the general considerations affecting the despatch of a fleet to the far east in the event of a war with Japan.[54] The initiative for suggesting any combined form of strategy had to rest with the United States.[55]

Hampton met Admiral W. D. Leahy, the United States chief of naval operations and Admiral R. L. Chormley, the director of plans, on 12 June. Leahy confined his remarks to the situation where Britain and France were engaged with Germany and Italy, and the United States was neutral. In such a case the United States fleet would be moved to Hawaii as a deterrent to Japan. It was unlikely that the Japanese would then embark upon large scale operations against either Australia or New Zealand. There would be United States patrols in the Atlantic, and it was possible that the information they obtained might be passed to British naval forces in the Atlantic through the navy department in Washington. Leahy was reluctant to commit himself to any naval plans in the event of the United States becoming allied to Britain. It was decided to attempt to invite Leahy to discuss the question of co-operation in war and on 14 June the arrangements for the distribution of books to the United States fleet was broached. The United States representatives were satisfied that the arrangements would enable all the United States units to co-operate with British units 'throughout the world in case of necessity'. Public opinion in the United States would be adverse to sending a fleet to assist Britain unless Britain could despatch an adequate token force. Some capital ships would be expected, but Leahy would not define in detail what he considered to be an adequate token force. The United States naval staff had no detailed plans about the passage to Singapore, though the question was being examined. Leahy was unwilling to discuss plans for co-operation in detail. British convoy operations in the Atlantic in the event of a European war were outlined in broad terms. Leahy 'expressed the opinion that in the event of the United States entering the war, arrangements for co-operation in the organisation of convoys and all other detailed arrangements for mutual support in the Atlantic could readily be co-ordinated at the time, working on the basis of the arrangements made in 1917–8'. Technical questions as to co-operation in HFD/F (high frequency direction finding), and the location of United States LFD/F (low frequency direction finding) stations were not pursued, and were to be followed up by the naval attaché.

---

54 Ibid., p. 271, Minute by Ashley Clarke, 10.5.1939; Minute by Ronald, 12.5.1939; pp. 321–2, F4962/456/23, V. H. Dancwerts (Admiralty) to Ronald, Most Secret Orders for Commander T. C. Hampton, 24.5.1939.
55 Ibid., *loc. cit.*

In assessing the results of his visit Hampton warned that Roosevelt was probably far ahead of the majority of his people in 'his championship of the democracies'. Hampton felt that it was evident that the United States navy had no detailed plans for active co-operation with the British fleet in war. Ashley Clarke minuted that the visit had been worthwhile:

It was hardly to be expected that the Americans could go further in what they said in view of the internal political difficulties.[56]

That these talks took place at all suggests that leading officials in Britain and the United States felt that there was a special relationship between the two countries. Given the state of isolationist opinion in the United States, and the need for secrecy it would be considered a considerable gesture on the part of the United States even to discuss the potential relief of Singapore, or convoying operations. Moves like these would imply at least a state of passive belligerency. On the other hand there was little that the British could calculate on with certainty in their defence preparations.

The possibility of purchasing arms from the United States and Canada was carefully investigated. Lord Riverdale visited those countries with that in mind and drew up a memorandum on 17 August for the cabinet.[57] Britain, however, was anxious for more than ordinary purchases.

In the middle of August the air ministry suggested that the United States authorities be approached for details of the Norden bomb sight, the most effective instrument of its kind. Efforts to effect a suitable exchange of information had been unsuccessful. There were difficulties in that the existence of the sight was well known in the United States and the release of details might cause political troubles. But Kingsley Wood wrote to Halifax that 'we should spare no effort to persuade the Americans to help us in this matter which would have such a far-reaching effect on the efficiency of the Royal Air Force'.[58] Kennedy felt sure that the best way was for Chamberlain to approach Roosevelt. This personal approach should not introduce the question of exchange but should be based on the certainty that Britain and the United States would never fight each other, and that Britain was 'likely to be engaged in a front-rank struggle for all the values and ways of life that the Americans and we shared'.[59]

---

[56] Ibid., pp. 103–18, F7010/456/23, Seal to Harvey, 3.7.1939; Enclosing Reports of Meetings between Hampton and United States Naval Officials, 12.6.1939, 14.6.1939; Minute by Ashley Clarke, 10.7.1939.
[57] *Cab 24*, 288, pp. 202–10, Memorandum by Lord Riverdale, Lock and Key, 17.8.1939.
[58] *F O 371*, 22797, pp. 60–5, A5835/26/45, Wood to Halifax, Secret, 17.8.1939.
[59] Ibid., Halifax to Wood, 23.8.1939 (copy).

Chamberlain did write to Roosevelt but the president's initial survey led him to conclude that Chamberlain's request could not be granted unless the sight were made available simultaneously to all other governments which was obviously not in Britain or the United State's interests.[60]

Aid in other forms from the United States was discussed by the cabinet on 5 July when it considered the financial position in the event of war. This was worse than in 1919 unless the United States were prepared to help. The primary need would be for the United States to give Britain a share of its production without paying for it.[61]

In July 1939 despite repeated efforts to win over the United States Britain was not in a position where it could count on much more than that country's sympathy. When Halifax saw Kennedy on 27 June the ambassador recognised how different the position would be if the United States were able to promise naval co-operation with Britain. But that 'in present circumstances was out of the question'. Kennedy agreed it would be unwise for Britain to weaken its position in Europe by sending a fleet to the far east.[62]

Britain did ask the United States on 12 July whether it could send a representative to the Tokyo talks if they included the currency issue as that involved the interests of all the powers in China.[63] The United States refused, and merely expressed its concern.[64] Lindsay opined:

> I hardly think United States Government will be prepared to take open action at present. They might be more disposed when congress has adjourned, but even that may be problematical.[65]

Chamberlain considered the ineptitude of the foreign office responsible for the British predicament. Because of it Britain was alone and being attacked for a policy equally essential for the United States, France, and Germany. Chamberlain did hope that Craigie's good relations with Arita could save Britain, but felt that with the foreign office's anti Japanese bias the ambassador had never had much of a chance.[66]

---

[60] Ibid., p. 68, Rucker to Mallet, Secret and Very Urgent, 25.8.1939; pp. 105–12, Enclosing A6301/26/45, Chamberlain to Roosevelt; From Rucker, Secret, 14.9.1939; Enclosing Roosevelt to Chamberlain 31.8.1939 (copy); pp. 100–2, A6178/26/45, Lothian to Halifax, No. 447, Secret, 7.9.1939 d. 8.9.1939.

[61] *Cab 23*, 100, pp. 110–40, Cab 36 (39) 2, Secret, 5.7.1939. For the general Cabinet Discussion of the Financial Situation see Ian Colvin, *The Chamberlain Cabinet* (London, 1971), pp. 229–30.

[62] *DBFP* 9, pp. 232–4, No. 270, F6469/1/10, Halifax to Lindsay, Telegram No. 647, 27.6.1939.

[63] Ibid., p. 258, No. 297, F7017/6457/10, Halifax to Lindsay, Telegram No. 297, 11.7.1939.

[64] Ibid., p. 283, No. 329, F7392/6457/10, Lindsay to Halifax, Telegram No. 313, 15.7.1939 r. 16.7.1939.

[65] Ibid., pp. 284–5, No. 330, F7394/6457/10, Lindsay to Halifax, Telegram No. 315, 16.7.1939 r. 15.7.1939.

[66] *Templewood Papers* XIX (C) 11, Chamberlain to Hilda Chamberlain, 15.7.1939 (copy).

The absence of United States co-operation was a factor behind the announcement of the acceptance of the Craigie-Arita formula for negotiating with Japan on 24 July.[67] The strategic considerations, however, were probably paramount. Then without warning the United States gave the required six months notice for the abrogation of its commercial treaty with Japan on 26 July. This meant that from 26 January 1940 United States trade with Japan would be on a day to day basis.[68] Roosevelt later explained that he had not contemplated this move. But when the president heard on 26 July that the senate had decided to shelve the resolutions on the neutrality act for the session, he and Hull had decided that they must act immediately 'in order that the dictators should not imagine that they could get away with it'. Accordingly the note was drafted and delivered to Japan that afternoon. Roosevelt hoped that the British did not think that he was going behind their backs, but there had been no time to inform them beforehand.[69] Initially Hull had told Lindsay on 27 July that the denunciation was merely a commercial step with no political implications. The ambassador doubted whether the United States would contemplate any further measures.[70]

Chamberlain had to face questions in the house on 31 July as to why Britain had not followed the example of the United States in denouncing its commercial treaty with Japan. The prime minister pointed out that Britain had to give twelve months notice of such intention and consultation with the dominions would be necessary.[71]

The committee of imperial defence considered what economic measures could be taken against Japan but came to no firm conclusion. The report by the advisory committee on trade questions in time of war suggested that an embargo on Japanese exports to the British commonwealth coupled with a deterioration of its gold reserves 'would have a damaging effect on the Japanese economic situation which would be greatly increased by the collaboration of the U.S.A'. To achieve this, co-operation of the dominions and India was essential. This was not likely to be forthcoming if action against Japan took the form of retaliation for damage to British interests in China. Inskip elaborated this point: the interests of Australia and New Zealand in China were so small that they could only be expected to act on a basis of loyalty to Britain. He doubted

67 Clifford, p. 148.
68 Ibid., *loc. cit.*
69 *DBFP* 9, pp. 370–1, No. 431, F8216/1236/23, Lindsay to Halifax, Telegram No. 338A, 31.7.1939 r. 1.8.1939.
70 Ibid., pp. 348–9, No. 405, Lindsay to Halifax, Telegram No. 344, 28.7.1939.
71 *U K Parl Deb H of C* 350, cols. 1925–6, 2002, 2054–5, 31.7.1939.

whether those dominions should be asked to act at all. If Britain did decide to act Inskip felt that 'there should be no question of an informatory telegram having to be sent to the Dominions at the last moment'. Zetland felt that these considerations applied with greater force to India as it would be particularly vulnerable to Japanese counter attack.

Aside from the difficult position of the dominions Halifax pointed to Craigie's anxiety in case there be legislation covering retaliatory action. Practical steps without legislation had to be considered, and the extent to which it was possible to secure the support of the United States for these. Without such support it might be imprudent to act. The position had been changed by the United States denunciation of the commercial treaty with Japan. Chatfield enquired whether this did not affect the following conclusion:

> The Foreign Office view is that the best procedure for securing U.S.A. co-operation in exercising economic pressure on Japan would be to decide upon some definite action and, if possible, put it into operation before the support of that country is sought.

Halifax agreed that the situation would have to be reviewed, but with the delicate negotiations that were being undertaken with Japan, he thought it inopportune to take provocative action against that country.[72]

The matter came before the cabinet on 2 August. It decided that copies of the report should be sent to the dominions and to India with an explanation that no decision had been taken and that Britain was not asking for the views of the other governments on the matter.[73] A telegram was sent accordingly on 8 August.[74]

The United States did inform Britain about its attitude to the negotiations over Tientsin. Hornbeck made it clear on 1 August that the United States did not feel entitled to offer Britain advice, but that the United States would prefer to see Britain resist Japanese demands.[75] Craigie, after seeing Dooman on 2 August telegraphed to Halifax: 'it is clear the State department has no intention yet of being drawn from their lair'.[76] The ambassador warned that Britain could not risk a breakdown of the negotiations at Tientsin without 'full assurance in advance of the United States's support'.[77]

---

[72] *Cab 2*, 9, pp. 81–2, Committee of Imperial Defence Minutes of 370th Meeting, Secret Lock and Key, 27.7.1939.

[73] *Cab 23*, 100, pp. 279–88, Cab 40 (39) 9, Secret, 2.8.1939.

[74] *D O 114*, 82, No. 51, F10/400, Circular B No. 267 Telegram to 5 Dominions, Secret, 8.8.1939 (cypher).

[75] *DBFP 9*, p. 381, No. 443, F8294/6457/10, Lindsay to Halifax, Telegram No. 342, 1.8.1939 r. 2.8.1939.

[76] Ibid., pp. 394–5, No. 457, F8389/6457/10, Craigie to Halifax, Telegram No. 928, 3.8.1939.

[77] Ibid., p. 395, No. 458, F8389/6457/10, Craigie to Halifax, Telegram No. 929, 3.9.1939.

United States expectations, however, were that Britain should take a firm stand against Japan. When Welles mentioned to Roosevelt that rumour had it that Britain might succumb to Japanese pressure and close the Burma road the president remarked:

> If this is true the position of United States would be that of a Government which is trying to lend its moral support to a Power which is deliberately intent on suicide.

Britain had to respond that there was no foundation for such a rumour.[78]

Craigie was also puzzled by Roosevelt's comments that he had denounced the commercial treaty 'in order that dictators should not imagine that they could get away with it.' The ambassador felt that the effect of this action had been to revive the pro German alliance movement in Tokyo.[79]

Halifax, however, told Craigie that he was less pessimistic than the ambassador about the United States's attitude to the far east. Halifax thought that the United States was preparing the way 'for more positive measures of pressure later if United States interests seem to require them'.[80]

Further considerations of the issues involved in a British denunciation of its commercial treaties with Japan was circulated to the dominions on 16 August. The matter had been discussed earlier in a foreign office memorandum of 18 March 1939.[81] The dominions were told on the question of the advisability of denouncing the treaty that it would be desirable to bring home to the Japanese government that it was British policy to move along parallel lines with the United States. The dominions were asked to comment on this by 22 August when a meeting of ministers would consider the matter further.[82]

The situation was complicated. There was not one treaty to be denounced. The United Kingdom-Japanese treaty of 1911 covered the crown colonies, and Canada and Ireland were still parties to this treaty. South Africa and New Zealand had their own treaties with Japan. The Australian treaty was being kept in force by periodic exchanges of notes to overcome Japanese infractions of the main treaty. India was negotiating

---

[78] Ibid., pp. 395–6, No. 459, F8416/6547/10, Lindsay to Halifax, Telegram No. 347, 3.8.1939.

[79] Ibid., p. 415, No. 477, F8524/126/23, Craigie to Halifax, Telegram No. 953, 5.8.1939.

[80] Ibid., p. 423, No. 488, F8245/6457/10, Halifax to Craigie, Telegram No. 468, 7.8.1939.

[81] *Cab 24*, 284, pp. 241–2b, C P 76 (39), Foreign Office Memorandum, 18.3.1939.

[82] *D O 114*, 82, pp. 35–6, No. 52, F10/401, Circular B No. 273 Telegram to 5 Dominions, Secret, 16.8.1939 (cypher); p. 36, No. 53, F10/401, Dixon to J. P. Walshe, Secret, 16.8.1939; No. 54, F10/401, Circular Z No. 20 Telegram to High Commissioners in 4 Dominions, Secret, 16.8.1939.

a new commercial treaty with Japan, and Burma would have to do so also in the new future.[83] Canada and Australia were in special positions: Canada concluded a separate exchange of notes with Japan dated 26 December 1935;[84] Australia had recently made a voluntary commercial arrangement with Japan.[85]

The dominions' interest in the Tientsin dispute, as was pointed out to the United States, was limited to the effects it had on 'white prestige', the Washington treaties, and the league of nations resolutions. The British government would 'not necessarily be guided entirely' by what the dominion governments said.[86]

Reaction of the dominion governments to the British enquiry was surprisingly favourable, particularly as in the case of Canada and New Zealand any such action would have affected them more immediately than Britain.

The Canadian government pointed out that Canadian exports to Japan ran from three or four times as great to China in a period when Britain's exports to China were from two to four times as great as to Japan. Canada's special interests in China were only connected with missionary activities. Furthermore, as a result of Canada's different tariff structure, Canada, while having 'less direct and distinctly national ground for action' might find itself, on the expiration of the twelve months' notice of the termination of the treaty, the only country applying severe restrictions on Japanese imports. The Canadian government, however, stated:

> While we consider that is is essential for full understanding of the situation to make clear the special considerations which affect Canada, we are far from wishing to imply that they would offset our desire to co-operate with the United Kingdom and the United States in any action taken, particularly so in view of the long-range interests involved. If the Government of the United Kingdom concludes that developments in the Far East require them to give notice of the denunciation of the Treaty of 1911, the Canadian Government would be quite prepared to concur in that decision. The termination of the Agreement by the United Kingdom would, we are advised, automatically terminate our own adherence.[87]

[83] *Foreign Relations of the United States* (hereafter cited as 'FRUS') 1939 (3), pp. 570–3, 711.942/243, Johnson to Hull, Telegram No. 1178, 17.8.1939.

[84] *D O 114*, 82, p. 37, No. 55, F10/401, Dominions Office to High Commissioner in Canada, Telegram No. 176, Secret, 16.8.1939 (paraphrase).

[85] Ibid., No. 56, F10/401, Dominions Office to High Commissioner in Australia, Telegram No. 162, Secret, 16.8.1939 (paraphrase).

[86] *FRUS* 1939(3), pp. 570–3, 711.942/243, Johnson to Hull, Telegram No. 1178, 17.8.1939.

[87] *D O 114*, 82, pp. 40–2, No. 62, F10/411, Canadian Government to British Government, Telegram No. 46, Secret, 21.8.1939 r. 22.8.1939 (cypher); pp. 38–9, No. 58, F10/407, High Commissioner in Canada to Dominions Office, Telegram No. 259, Secret, 18.8.1939 r. 19.8.1939 (paraphrase).

The deteriorating European situation, together with the consideration that this was a move made initially by the United States, might explain the Canadian reaction.

New Zealand pointed out that the period for denunciation of their treaty with Japan was three months, and that the result of a simultaneous notice would be that New Zealand's trade arrangements with Japan would conclude nine months earlier than those of Britain. Consequently New Zealand felt bound to make any action that it took contingent on the other dominions, and particularly Australia and Canada, taking a similar course.[88]

The high commissioner in Australia saw Menzies on 21 August and reported that the latter's view was that the treaty should be denounced 'and the sooner the better'.[89] The Australian government had not subscribed to the treaty and so were 'not directly concerned'. It offered no objection to the course proposed. Trade arrangements between Australia and Japan had expired on 30 June 1939. Japan had continued with certain voluntary arrangements, but the Australian government had made no reciprocal undertaking.[90]

No further action was taken, however, because of the outbreak of war with Germany.[91]

Halifax did prepare a memorandum for the cabinet on 21 August on the position in the far east. The foreign secretary pointed out that, in view of the European situation the only way that the British government could meet a Japanese attack was by non resistance and evacuation, or resistance, shown by denouncing the Anglo-Japanese commercial treaty 'and such economic reprisals as seem to be reasonably effective and prudent'. He felt that:

> In view of the 'lead' which the United States Government no doubt consider they have given, it may well prove necessary for us at some point to denounce our treaty, if we are to avoid the damaging accusation that His Majesty's Government have again let down the United States in their attempt to check Japanese belligerence.

Britain was in a difficult position in the far east because of the consideration that had to be given to United States opinion. As Halifax wrote:

[88] Ibid., pp. 39–40, No. 60, F10/409, New Zealand Government to British Government, Telegram No. 92, Secret, 21.8.1937 (cypher).

[89] Ibid., p. 39, No. 59, F10/408, High Commissioner in Australia to Dominions Office, Telegram No. 83, Secret, 22.8.1939 (cypher).

[90] Ibid., p. 40, No. 61, F10/413, Australian Government to British Government, Telegram No. 83, Secret, 22.8.1939 (cypher).

[91] Ibid., p. 42, Note.

> If it is cardinal to our general policy to promote in any way possible co-operation with the United States, or at least to do nothing that would make that co-operation more difficult, we have not really got much choice, and from this point of view . . . it is better to face the situation now.

A gradual surrender would alienate United States opinion.[92]

In Japan Craigie did make some headway over the Tientsin negotiations. On 22 August Halifax was able to report to the cabinet that in effect Craigie had reached agreement. The British had informed the Japanese that they could not conclude a bilateral agreement on the wider economic issues as other governments were concerned. The United States was pleased with this reply.[93] On the currency issue the United States said that it had no objection to the British proposal to bring the negotiations at Tokyo to a conclusion on the basis of the withdrawal of the currency demand and the sealing of silver in its present location 'until the end of hostilities or agreement between the parties concerned whichever is the shorter'.[94] Craigie was left to conclude the negotiations at his own discretion. He was warned, however, that it would be dangerous for Britain to invite any proposals recognising some of Japan's special interest in north China. Such a move could be constructed as Britain bargaining at China's expense: alienation of United States opinion by such a suspicion had to be avoided.[95]

Roosevelt told Lothian on 30 August that he felt that the German-Russian agreement would probably lead to Japan coming to terms with China with the assistance of Britain and the United States. Roosevelt had said that Britain's attitude should be 'friendly but that we should display no eagerness'. If Japan became hostile again he had two more methods of pressure 'in the locker': firstly to send aircraft carriers and bombers to the Aleutian islands, about 700 miles from the Japanese northern island; the second was to move the United States fleet to Hawaii.[96]

In the far east, after Hitler's occupation of Prague, Britain was in an impossible situation. War on three fronts was a real possibility and the likelihood of United States support was slight. Yet the United States favoured Britain's taking a firm stand against Japan which would probably lead to war, and any United States support was likely to be in proportion to the firmness of the stand. As far as was possible British policy was geared to winning United States sympathy.

92 *Cab 24*, 288, pp. 211–2, C P 178 (39), Memorandum by Halifax on the Situation in the Far East, Lock and Key, 21.8.1939.

93 *Cab 23*, 100, p. 322, Cab 41 (39) 4, Secret, 22.8.1939.

94 *DBFP* 9, p. 503, No. 592, F9397/6457/10, Halifax to Lindsay, Telegram No. 426, 27.8.1939.

95 Ibid., pp. 509–10, No. 599, F9421/87/10, Halifax to Craigie, Telegram No. 556, 29.9.1939.

96 *F O 371*, 22815, pp. 203–5, A5899/98/45, Lothian to Halifax, Telegram No. 391, Important, 30.8.1939.

The dominions, however, whether for strategic or racial reasons, or from a realisation of the seriousness of the situation, were surprisingly co-operative. Britain, when considering the despatch of a fleet to the far east, did give careful consideration to the position of Australia and New Zealand, even if those dominions were not always given the fullest information of British policy likely to affect them.

Britain did not have to face war on three fronts: Chamberlain's cautious policy in the far east, hampered by the attitude of the United States, succeeded. And, on the eve of war, Roosevelt did indicate his willingness to apply pressure on Japan if that country became hostile.

X

THE RUSSIAN NEGOTIATIONS AND THE OUTBREAK OF WAR

The Russian Negotiations and the Outbreak of War

AT the time of Munich Vansittart wrote a minute characterising Russia as a 'ramshackle shambles'. That was the view that most British officials had at the time. It was with the desperate situation in March 1939 that Britain began to be 'less particular' about its friends, and feelers were put out towards the Russians. The Poles resisted the idea of Russia being admitted as an ally, and were opposed to any idea of Russian troops on their territory. The labour party was restive at the 'cold-shouldering' of Russia: on 24 March Chamberlain explained to members of that party that Britain was not 'cold-shouldering' Russia, but that the difficulty was due to the misgivings of Poland and others.[1] Canada, for example, had expressed its discontent at this after the occupation of Prague. Inskip told the foreign policy committee on 27 March that Mackenzie King had indicated his dislike of Russian participation in the pact.[2]

Pressure of events, however, caused Halifax and a number of officials at the foreign office to decide that Britain would have to try 'to rope in Russia'.[3] Russia pre-empted the first move. Ivan Maisky, the Russian ambassador in London, told Halifax that Russia would help Rumania. Halifax explained that Britain was about to ask whether Russia would be prepared to help Rumania and Poland. The tenor of the Russian stand was changed slightly: the Russian foreign minister told the British ambassador in Moscow that Russian assistance to Rumania was contingent on Britain implementing its assurance to Rumania. Russia had asked how help should be given. Britain had replied that Russia might make a declaration, offering assistance, if desired, to any of its European neighbours. Russia had then proposed a comprehensive European plan of mutual assistance and staff conversations between Britain, France and Russia, and assurances to Russia's western neighbours. Halifax explained to the cabinet on 19 April the need for caution in replying to Russia.[4] But at the cabinet committee on foreign policy held the same day Cadogan did argue the case for Russian intervention on Britain's side with the far

1 *Templewood Papers* XIX (C) 12, Cadogan to Templewood, 26.10.1951.
2 *Cab 27*, F P (36) 38th Mtg, Lock and Key, 27.3.1939.
3 *Templewood Papers* XIX (C) 12, Cadogan to Templewood, 26.10.1951.
4 *Cab 23*, 98, pp. 314–8, Cab 21 (39) 2, Secret, 19.4.1939.

eastern situation in view. In such an event Japan might be deterred from entering the war. At least Japan's preoccupation in China, and the possibility of Russian action in Manchokuo would almost certainly prevent Japan from carrying out large scale seaborne expeditions against Singapore, or Australia and New Zealand.[5] At the cabinet meeting on 26 April the foreign secretary went further: he said that he had reached the general conclusion that the value of Russia as a potential ally was not as high as seemed to be believed by prominent members of the labour party. He used the report by the chiefs of staff as evidence for this. British policy would be ordered so that, if war broke out, Russia would be either neutral or else come into the war on Britain's side. But the effect of Britain's relations with Russia on Poland, Rumania and other countries had to be borne in mind. Britain should go no further than ask Russia for assurances on Rumania and Poland. Any further action might endanger the common front that was being established.[6]

The dominions reacted when they received information of British negotiations with Russia.[7]

Te Water conveyed the views of the South African cabinet on 22 April. South Africa felt that 'bilateral obligations with Russia should if possible be avoided as well as any engagements which may commit Great Britain irrevocably to Russia and are thus calculated to cause maximum friction with Dictator States'. The cabinet attached much importance to Roosevelt's suggestion of 15 April[8] and suggested that nothing should be entered into with Russia which might preclude consideration of future economic and other peaceful negotiations with the dictators, including territorial, colonial or counter proposals which they might make. South Africa advised that the strength of the British case lay in its appeal to the public opinion of the world, including the United States. This was an additional reason for avoiding obligations which might make settlement by negotiation difficult, or which could appear to be aimed at maintaining the *status quo* 'and cutting off Germany from reasonable economic expansion eastwards'. The British government was advised also of Gie's despatch of 18 April that Hitler was keeping back from irrevocable action. Gie felt that any conclusion of an Anglo-Soviet pact might cause Hitler to take a step leading to war.[9]

[5] *Cab 27*, 624, p. 20, F P (36) 43rd Mtg, Lock and Key, 19.4.1939.
[6] *Cab 23*, 99, pp. 58–61, Cab 24 (39) 2, Secret, 26.4.1939. For a general discussion of the Russian negotiations see Ian Colvin, *The Chamberlain Cabinet* (London, 1971), pp. 199–216, 224–33.
[7] See chapter eight for a discussion of dominion fears of Russia at the time of the Polish guarantee.
[8] See pp. 235–6.
[9] *D O 114*, 98, pp. 14–5, No. 18, F706/175, Aide Mémoire from te Water, Secret, 22.4.1939.

Hertzog was anxious that peace be preserved, almost at any cost. He seemed to feel that Germany had justifiable grievances and should be allowed to expand eastwards to satisfy these. The South African prime minister still hoped for the appeasement of Europe and felt that there was evidence in Germany to suggest that this might be achieved. Perhaps, at this time, Hertzog's estimation was not so very different from Chamberlain's hopes. Chamberlain told the foreign policy committee on 25 April, perhaps approvingly, that this 'demonstrated General Hertzog's insight into the German mind'. Inskip also pointed out to the committee that this was the first time that a dominion, of its own volition had offered Britain advice on an important question of international affairs.[10]

Further indications of dominion assessment of British policy, and of the Russian negotiations in particular, came in the responses to a British request at the end of April that dominion prime ministers might make a statement of 'general appreciation and support' for the policy that the British government was pursuing. The reason for this request was that German papers were reporting apathy, discontent and criticism of British policy in various parts of the commonwealth. This, together with Ribbentrop's advice to Hitler that Britain did not mean business, was causing concern.[11] Perhaps the German press had good foundation for making these estimates. Dominion reaction, with the exception of Australia, was not favourable.

The high commissioner in South Africa doubted the expediency of approaching Hertzog on this subject, and consulted Smuts instead. Smuts said that Hertzog had his difficulties: the request would be embarrassing and would be unlikely to produce the desired results.[12]

In this interview Smuts spoke of the changing opinion in South Africa over Germany's intentions. Even Hertzog had come to realise that Germany was aiming at world domination. Hertzog and others were now realising that they would not be able to come to an agreement with Germany over South Africa, and that that country would be in the forefront of Germany's colonial demands. Smuts surprised the high commissioner by saying that there might be an uprising in South Africa in the event of South Africa 'joining in a British war'. It was not the nationalists

---

[10] *Cab 27*, 624, p. 5, F P (36) 44th Mtg, Lock and Key, 25.4.1939.

[11] *D O 114*, 98, p. 15, No. 20, F706/174, Circular Z No. 7 Telegram to High Commissioners in 4 Dominions, Secret, 25.4.1939.

[12] Ibid., p. 16, No. 24, F706/159, High Commissioner in South Africa to Dominions Office, Telegram No. 54, Secret, 4.5.1939; p. 19, No. 28, F706/159, Dominions Office to High Commissioner in South Africa, Telegram No. 23, Secret, 8.5.1939.

that worried Smuts but the *Ossewa Brandwag*, a supposed cultural organisation which he was having carefully watched by the police.[13] R. L. Speaight of the foreign office minuted on 23 May:

General Hertzog's education in proceeding satisfactorily. One finds it difficult to believe in the rumours of a Nationalist uprising, and the prospects of South African co-operation in the event of war seem brighter.

This minute suggests that the foreign office failed to estimate the seriousness of the situation in South Africa, or the strength of nationalist movements.

Menzies was prepared to make statements in the debates on foreign affairs and enquired whether there were any points that the British government wanted emphasised in particular. He proposed to say that information from the British government was prompt, that the dominions were consulted, and that the primary danger to Australia and New Zealand lay in the Pacific.[15] Britain's only concern here was that difficulties might arise with the other dominions if it were suggested that the meetings of the high commissioners in London were for the purpose of consultation.[16] The high commissioner mentioned this to Menzies and in the speech made the point was avoided.[17] Chamberlain sent his personal thanks to Menzies:

The knowledge of Australia's solidarity with us is a great encouragement to us.[18]

Although Savage was in 'entire agreement' with the course being pursued by the British government he felt that it would be a different thing to express 'approval of the method'. The high commissioner had the impression that Savage, like Hertzog, was harping on the idea of a conference.[19] The adoption of conscription in Britain made it impossible for Savage to make any public statement expressing approval of British policy. Savage was a known opponent of conscription, and he had refused requests by the press for comments because 'he was determined to say nothing which might embarrass the United Kingdom Government at the present crisis or could be interpreted as taking part in United Kingdom

13 *F O 371*, 22972, pp. 70–2, C7351/15/18, F706/167, Dominions Office to Foreign Office, 18.5.1939; Enclosing W. H. Clark to Sir E. Harding, Secret and Personal, 5.5.1939 (copy).

14 Ibid., p. 70, Minute by R. L. Speaight, 23.5.1939.

15 *D O 114*, 98, pp. 17–8, No. 25, F706/160, High Commissioner in Australia to Dominions Office, Telegram No. 84, Secret, 5.5.1939 (paraphrase).

16 Ibid., p. 19, No. 27, F706/161, Dominions Office to High Commissioner in Australia, Telegram No. 105, Secret, 8.5.1939 (paraphrase).

17 Ibid., p. 21, No. 31, F706/161, High Commissioner in Australia to Dominions Office, Telegram No. 93, Secret, 10.5.1939 (paraphrase).

18 Ibid., No. 32, F706/163, Chamberlain to Menzies, Telegram No. 40, Personal, 10.5.1939.

19 Ibid., p. 16, No. 22, F706/157, High Commissioner in New Zealand to Dominions Office, Telegram No. 112, Secret, 27.4.1939.

politics'. Savage stressed, however, that if Britain were in trouble New Zealand would be in too.[20]

On 27 April Mackenzie King explained to the high commissioner in Canada that he could not 'conscientiously' make such a statement: there was considerable opposition in Canada to the manner in which Britain appeared to be becoming entangled with Balkan and east European countries, and above all with Russia. The high commissioner had the impression that many ministers, including Mackenzie King opposed such entanglements. The prime minister could not forecast in advance of parliament, what line Canada would take if Britain were to help one of these countries, and as a result be attacked itself. Parliament had to be free to decide. Mackenzie King felt that a British policy guaranteeing eastern and south eastern Europe would split Canada: he had to try to see that there should be unity of feeling within Canada at the moment when a decision might have to be taken on participation in a conflict. The high commissioner tried unsuccessfully to ally Mackenzie King's fears by explaining that British policy was to preserve peace: he concluded that Mackenzie King had a 'temperamental and rooted dislike of becoming associated by means of any public statement in any European system of guarantees or alliances and particularly where Russia is concerned'.[21]

After these exchanges Inskip reported to the cabinet on 3 May that Canada was strongly opposed to any alliance with Russia, and that Hertzog had volunteered a statement on the same lines. The other dominions had, as then, not indicated any views. Halifax still thought that a tripartite pact between France, Britain and Russia would make war inevitable. But a refusal of Russia's offer might throw that country 'into Germany's arms'. The secretary of state for war agreed with this: 'although the idea might seem fantastic at the moment, the natural orientation suggested an arrangement between Germany and Russia'.[22]

On 5 May Inskip told the foreign policy committee that Canada and South Africa had already deprecated any alliance with Russia, and that New Zealand had recently decided upon the same attitude.[23]

[20] Ibid., p. 17, No. 23, F706/158, High Commissioner in New Zealand to Dominions Office, Telegram No. 117, Secret, 29.4.1939.

[21] Ibid., p. 16, No. 21, F706/155, High Commissioner in Canada to Dominions Office, Telegram No. 148, Secret, 26.4.1939 r. 27.4.1939.

[22] *Cab 23*, 99, pp. 128–30, Cab 26 (39) 4, Secret, 3.5.1939. See also *Documents on Canadian External Relations* 6, 1936–9, pp. 1175–9, High Commissioner to Canadian Secretary of State for Extrenal Affairs, Despatch A 114, 12.5.1939.

[23] *Cab 27*, 624, p. 10, F P (36) 45th Mtg, Lock and Key, 5.5.1939.

Halifax mentioned on 10 May to the cabinet that there seemed to be some element of misunderstanding between Britain and Russia: the Russians thought that they might be involved in war with Germany in circumstances in which we would not be involved. Halifax had tried to explain to the Russians that if war arose out of an attack on Poland and Rumania, if Russia were involved, Britain would almost certainly be involved as well. The foreign secretary explained that he had no information about a secret agreement between Hitler and Stalin.[24]

Then on 16 May at a foreign policy committee meeting the chiefs of staff swung around to favour an alliance with Russia.[25] Inskip was told to explain the position frankly to the dominion high commissioners.[26] The foreign policy committee decided that it was undesirable to delay an agreement with Russia any further and were unwilling to contemplate a breakdown in the negotiations. Halifax told the cabinet on 17 May that such an agreement should be reached at the earliest opportunity: the precise form of British assistance in such an agreement would involve staff conversations.[27] It was on this day that Vansittart minuted on the reported negotiations for a German-Russian alliance. The report came from the German general staff that Hitler was negotiating with Stalin through General Sirorg.[28] Russia, however, did not accede to the British proposals, and it was clear to the foreign policy committee on 19 May that Britain would face a choice between a Russian alliance, or pact of mutual assistance, and a breakdown in negotiations with all the consequences that that might entail. Chamberlain 'hated' the former aspect. Stanley, Templewood, MacDonald, Chatfield, E. L. Burgin, the minister of transport, and possibly Inskip favoured it. Morrison and Simon were in agreement with Chamberlain. But it was concluded that it had to be a cabinet decision.[29] Inskip consented to circulate to the cabinet the views of the dominions on these proposals.[30]

With the exception of New Zealand the dominions were opposed to any conclusion of an alliance with Russia.

Te Water gave the British government Hertzog's elaborated views on 19 May. Hertzog and his colleagues felt that an alliance with Russia would make war inevitable:

24 *Cab 23*, 99, pp. 155–8, Cab 27 (39) 1, Secret, 10.5.1939.
25 *Templewood Papers* XIX (C) 12, Cadogan to Templewood, 26.10.1951.
26 *Cab 27*, 625, F P (36) 47th Mtg, Lock and Key, 16.5.1939.
27 *Cab 23*, 99, pp. 185–92, Cab 28 (39) 1, Secret, 17.5.1939.
28 *F O 371*, 22972, pp. 45–8, C7553/15/18, Foreign Office Minute by Vansittart, 17.5.1939.
29 *Templewood Papers* XIX (C) 12, Cadogan to Templewood, 26.10.1951.
30 *Cab 27*, 625, p. 10, F P (36) 48th Mtg, Lock and Key, 19.5.1939.

The persistence with which resists any action by Western Europe calculated to interfere with the extension of her interests toward the east cannot be overlooked.[31]

Australia, with its strategic position, was unhappy about any agreement with Russia which applied to the far east. But it agreed that 'the opportunity should not be lost to make effective agreement between Great Britain and U.S.S.R. which would reinforce anti-aggression pact with Poland and which would strengthen in particular Turkey and Roumania. Short of a positive demand to expand agreement to Far East we think Russian negotiations should not be allowed to fail.'[32]

On 12 May the New Zealand government let Britain know that it would regard it as deplorable 'if Russian assistance in the prevention of aggression were not secured and in their view no reasonable opportunity should be lost of obtaining Russian collaboration in this essential policy'.[33] Since New Zealand was of its own volition committed by any British decision it would be reasonable to suppose that its views should carry some weight. On 22 May Savage broadcast:

> Let no one imagine that if Britain were involved in a general war this country could or would stand aloof enjoying undistrubed neutrality.[34]

On 23 May the high commissioner in New Zealand reported that Savage was disturbed by the delay in reaching agreement with the Russian government and felt that every effort should be made to resolve the apparent deadlock.[35]

The opposition of Canada had been expressed in the high commissioner's telegrams of 25 March[36] and 27 April.[37]

It was these views which Inskip circulated to the cabinet.[38]

The high commissioners in London then banded together as they had done during the Munich crisis. Inskip explained to the cabinet on 24 May that their suggestion had a good deal in common with that which Halifax had recently made to the German ambassador. The high commissioners

---

[31] *D O 114*, 98, p. 15, No. 19, F706/175, Aide Mémoire by te Water of a Message from Hertzog, 19.5.1939.

[32] *Cab 24*, 287, p. 73, C P (123), 39, No. 6, Menzies to Bruce, Telegram No. 35, Most Secret and Personal, 22.5.1939 (copy).

[33] *D O 114*, 98, p. 21, No. 33, F706/166, New Zealand Government to Dominions Office, Telegram No. 52, Secret, 12.5.1939.

[34] Ibid., p. 22, No. 35, F706/170, High Commissioner in New Zealand to Dominions Office, Telegram No. 145, 23.5.1939 d. 22.5.1939 r. 23.5.1939.

[35] Ibid., No. 36, F706/179, High Commissioner in New Zealand to Dominions Office, Telegram No. 146, Secret, 22.5.1939 r. 23.5.1939.

[36] See p. 225.

[37] Cab 24, 287, pp. 64–73, C P (123) 39, High Commissioner in Canada to Dominions Office, Telegram, 27.4.1939.

[38] Ibid., Memorandum by Inskip, Secret, 22.5.1939.

thought that when Britain had strengthened its position by making an agreement with the Russian government, it should 'take the position of strength, and Germany might be likely to listen'. Britain might indicate to Germany that it had no intention to encircle it economically, and that it was ready to discuss any matters in dispute. When Halifax had spoken to the German ambassador he had suggested that Hitler might take the initiative. It was Chamberlain who squashed this suggestion by the high commissioners. The prime minister thought it premature:

> It was necessary not merely that we should be strong, but that others should realise the fact. Further, public opinion in this country was not ready for such a move at this juncture.[39]

Chamberlain did not like the recent moves. Strang noted in his diary on 20 May: 'P.M. says he will resign rather than sign an alliance with the Soviet'. But Chamberlain was prevailed upon by his colleagues and by 24 May was resigned to the idea.[40] Chamberlain wrote to his sister:

> But worse . . . was my feeling that the lining up of opposition blocs + an association which would make any negotiation or discussion with the Totalitarians difficult, if not impossible. The only supporter I could get for my view was Rab Butler + he was not a very influential ally. In these circs. [*sic*] I sent for Horace Wilson to see if I could get any light from discussion with him + gradually there emerged an idea which has since been adopted. In substance it gives the Russians what they want, but in form + presentation it avoids the idea of an Alliance + substitutes a declaration of *intentions* in certain circumstances in fulfilment of our obligations under Art. XVI of the Covenant.[41]

The prime minister told the cabinet that day that he viewed an alliance with Russia with 'considerable misgiving'. He distrusted Russia's reliability, its capacity to help, and was worried about the opposition that the move would cause both in the dominions and certain other countries. Chamberlain did recognise, however, that if the Russian proposals were rejected, there would be a breakdown in negotiations which would be unfortunate coming so soon after the conclusion of the German Italian pact. This would have a bad effect on public opinion in Europe and discourage France and Turkey. Chamberlain was anxious that this should be presented as an arrangement with Russia under the covenant of the league of nations: this would make the move easier to accept by those who opposed it.

---

[39] *Cab 23*, 99, pp. 286–7, Cab 30 (39) 2, Secret, 24.5.1939. I have not been able to trace the minutes of the meeting of Inskip with the dominion high commissioners on 22.5.1939.

[40] *Templewood Papers* XIX (C) 12, Cadogan to Templewood, 26.10.1951.

[41] Ibid., XIX (C) 11, Chamberlain to Miss Chamberlain, 28.5.1939 (copy).

Inskip reassured the prime minister about the position of the dominions. The previous day the high commissioners for both Canada and South Africa had said that if Britain were faced with a choice between a breakdown of negotiations and the conclusion of an agreement on the terms proposed by the Russian government they had no doubt that 'their Governments would take the view that we should conclude an agreement':

> Broadly speaking, apart from New Zealand, all the Dominions appeared to dislike the idea of an agreement with Russia but recognised, nevertheless, that having gone so far it would be right to make an agreement rather than risk a complete breakdown.[42]

Australia had decided that the negotiations should not be delayed through fear of blame if war resulted through a breakdown in the talks.[43]

The cabinet collectively approved the Russian alliance. Chamberlain and Halifax decided that Seeds should be sent for from Moscow to lead the mission, but Seeds was ill.[44] Eden offered to go.[45] There being no one else Strang was sent. Not much effort was made to find a high powered personality. Probably Halifax did not go in case of embarrassment if the mission failed.[46]

It had taken almost two months to make a definite decision on whether to pursue the Russian negotiations. From the outset the dominions, and particularly Canada and South Africa had been uneasy about, if not opposed to, such a move. For the first time South Africa had volunteered advice on what British policy should be. The dominions were given the complete information on the subject, and every effort was made by the British government to secure their views. These opinions were mentioned both in the cabinet and in the foreign policy committee, but were not decisive in influencing the British government as to what steps it should take. The dominions were one factor that had to be considered, and, if possible, their reluctant acquiescence had to be obtained. Clearly the dominions, with the possible exception of New Zealand, were still anxious to pursue the appeasement of Europe. If there were to be a war, and Canada and South Africa were to fight on Britain's side, they would have to be convinced that every possible step had been taken to keep the peace first.

---

[42] *Cab 23*, 99, pp. 275–80, Cab 30 (39) 1, Secret, 24.5.1939.
[43] *F O 800*, 310, pp. 67–74, H/IX/129, Inskip to Halifax, 26.5.1939; Enclosing Memorandum by Bruce.
[44] *Templewood Papers* XIX (C) 12, Cadogan to Templewood, 26.10.1951.
[45] John Harvey, Ed., *The Diplomatic Diaries of Oliver Harvey* (London, 1970), p. 295, Diary, 5.6.1939.
[46] *Templewood Papers* XIX (C) 12, Cadogan to Templewood, 26.10.1951.

The British government, consequently, had to make preparations for the contingency that, in the event of war, some of the dominions might remain neutral.

R. H. Hadow drafted a minute on this subject on 24 May. This only reached the central department of the foreign office in August. J. M. Troutbeck felt 'fairly sure' that it had originally appeared as a co-ordination paper and had been 'turned down'.

Hadow considered that if an Anglo-Soviet agreement were concluded Britain would run the risk of South African neutrality at the outset of a war 'possibly only for a while but with dangerous possibilities'. Public opinion in Canada would probably bring that country into a war without much delay. Both the public and the government in Australia were likely at that time to follow the British lead whatever was decided. But Hadow was worried that unless Australia were assured that a fleet would eventually be sent to Singapore there would be a reaction in favour of neutrality 'or, at best, Pan-Pacific self-help only, under the aegis of America'. He feared a similar reaction in New Zealand. Working on this supposition Hadow urged a clear statement of the position to the dominions 'sugared' with the proposal that every effort should be made to swing United States public opinion in favour of a 'hands off the Pacific' attitude.[47]

A memorandum which Inskip prepared in collaboration with the foreign office and the service departments was more optimistic. This was printed for the committee of imperial defence in June. It was thought that the adoption of an attitude of neutrality on the part of Australia and New Zealand was 'most improbable'. This was not true of South Africa and Canada. The British high commissioners in the various dominions were circulated with this memorandum for guidance in the event of the eventuality arising but they were instructed to do nothing that might suggest to the dominion governments that 'the possibility has been contemplated of their non-participation in a war in which the United Kingdom is engaged'.

The British war book was drawn up on the hypothesis that a war would demand the whole resources of the commonwealth, and that the dominion governments would associate themselves with British action. Certain pre-arranged schemes of action by the British government presupposed some form of assistance from the dominions. But there were indications that in the case of South Africa, Canada and Ireland these assumptions were not immediately justified.

[47] *F O 371*, 22975, pp. 127–30, C10767/15/18, Minute by R. H. Hadow, 24.5.1939 r, in r. 3.8.1939; Minutes by T. K. Roberts, 18.8.1939; J. M. Troutbeck, 18.8.1939; *F O 800*, 310, pp. 64–6, H/IX/128, Minute by R. H. Hadow, 24.5.1939.

In South Africa's case it would seem from the despatches from the high commissioner there that force of circumstances would probably compel the government to participate, but it was committed to prior consultation with parliament. The inclination of the South African government would be to postpone a decision, and if parliament were in recess it might defer summoning it.

Canada, it was thought on the basis of despatches from the high commissioner, would participate in any circumstances then likely. But the Canadian parliament would have to be consulted: this might cause a week's delay.

It would appear from de Valera's statement in April 1939 that the Irish government was anxious to keep out of war. But he had recognised in a speech to the Dail on 16 February 1939 that Irish neutrality might not be respected and a belligerent power might try to interfere with trade between Ireland and Britain on which Ireland depended.

The conclusion of the memorandum was that every effort should be made to ensure that no constitutional issue of continued membership of the commonwealth be raised, and that the dominion did not take any action implying its intention to remain neutral. Care should be taken to avoid an unfavourable reaction in urging early consultation with the dominion parliament. The dominion should also be urged to offer Britain such facilities as it needed, and to deny them to the enemy, even if this meant a breach of formal neutrality. And if this attitude of non active participation were impossible to procure, efforts should be made to achieve at least sympathetic, or benevolent, aloofness. These measures could be covered as precautionary steps taken under the decision of the imperial conference of 1923 and subsequently confirmed, that each dominion was primarily responsible for its own local defence. It seemed, for example, that in September 1938 South Africa was counting on the protection of escort vessels of the royal navy on the outbreak of war.

The memorandum outlines contingency plans for the continuance of naval control, intelligence and contraband services in the dominions, and paid particular attention to the use of dominion ports by British warships. South Africa probably would be prepared to allow the royal navy the continued use of Simonstown. But before a decision by the South African parliament they would be unwilling to afford facilities at Cape Town or other ports. Pirow had indicated, however, in a conversation in April 1939 with the high commissioner, that South Africa might be prepared to search enemy ships for guns and ammunition before they left South African ports, and might also be prepared to remove the wireless apparatus. In Canada's case it was felt that the high commissioner there could argue that if ships of the royal navy had to use alternative ports they would not be able to afford Canadian territory and shipping protection against an enemy. Further, there should be no risk of closing down arrangements existing in the dominions for the training of personnel destined for British forces. This was especially so in the case of training pilots for the royal air force. Full facilities for volunteers to enlist in British combatant forces 'would be a matter of great importance for the Air Ministry, particularly in the case of the Union of South Africa, which could be in a strong strategic position for providing reinforcement personnel'. It was thought inadvisable to raise any of these issues with any dominion government unless an emergency arose.

The severance of diplomatic relations between the dominion government and the enemy was important from 'the point of view of the appearance of the position to the outside world'. South Africa, in particular, would be reluctant to take any such action before its parliament met. It was thought that it could be pointed out by the dominion high commissioners that the severance of diplomatic relations was not in any way inconsistent with an attitude of full neutrality.[48]

In any case Ireland was considered a bad security risk. On 9 February 1939 the committee for imperial defence had decided not to inform the high commissioner for Ireland of the existence of RDF (radar) when the other high commissioners were told. This decision was applied again at the end of April when a group of Irish officers visited Britain.[49]

On the other hand the committee of imperial defence had decided on 27 April to include on the following air ministry progress reports estimates of production from the aircraft factories on Canada, Australia and New Zealand.[50]

While the negotiations were continuing with Russia a few points of minor concern arose in connection with the dominions. South Africa demanded further trade concessions for oranges: the British cabinet considered it so important not to risk a breakdown of the negotiations

[48] *Cab 16*, 183A, D P P (P) 54, Enclosure, Memorandum by Inskip on the Position of the Dominions in the Event of War, Lock and Key, 5.5.1939, Printed for the Committee of Imperial Defence, June 1939.
[49] *Cab 2*, 8, p. 202, Committee of Imperial Defence Minutes of 354th Meeting D P R, Secret Lock and Key, 27.4.1939; R. G. Casey, *Personal Experience 1939–1946* (London, 1962), p. 5.
[50] *Cab 2*, 8, pp. 201, 204, Committee of Imperial Defence Minutes of 354th Meeting D P R, Secret Lock and Key, 27.4.1939.

with South Africa that it was prepared to grant these.[51] Australia complained about not being informed in advance of the abrogation of the Anglo-German naval agreement.[52] New Zealand asked for money but had to be satisfied with the reply that Britain was only granting export credits and not loans.[53]

Throughout the Russian negotiations during June and July the dominions, and South Africa, Canada and Australia in particular, continued to urge the appeasement of Europe.

On 31 May te Water conveyed to the British government an *aide mémoire* from Hertzog. The South African government was concerned that 'unless something is done to show that the position taken up by Great Britain and her allies has as its chief object no other but that of frustrating any attempt at domination by Germany and Italy, and of maintaining peace of Europe in a spirit of international justice and equality, the new alliance may before long be cause for a general European conflagration'. The time had come for a renewed attempt 'at a peaceful settlement of all claims and grievances with the axis Powers'. Those obstacles 'placed in the way of European appeasement by the Treaty of Versailles' had been 'swept out of the way almost completely, but those which still remain can be removed by peaceful negotiation'.[54]

South Africa clearly thought that Germany had genuine grievances which should be redressed. Germany should be allowed to expand to the east. The implication was that South Africa would not regard any war fought as a result of German encirclement one in which it would participate. It was anxious that the appeasement of Europe should be pursued. If South Africa were to go to war it would have to be convinced that all means of accommodating Germany had been tried.

Immediate British reaction was to inform South Africa of a speech made by Halifax on 8 June much along the lines that Hertzog suggested.[55] Then on 26 June an analysis of the British government's policy over the previous month in the light of Hertzog's *aide mémoire* was sent to South

[51] *Cab 24*, 286, pp. 253–5, C P 113 (39), Memorandum by Inskip and Stanley on Trade Negotiations with South Africa, Secret, 12.5.1939; *Cab 23*, 99, pp. 201–4, Cab 28 (39) 6, Secret, 17.5.1939.

[52] *F O 371*, 23961, pp. 226–7, W10309/9831/68, Minute by Hadow, 30.6.1939; *Cab 27*, 625, p. 21, F P (36) 51st Mtg, Lock and Key, 13.6.1939.

[53] *Cab 23*, 100, p. 27, Cab 33 (39) 8, Secret, 21.6.1939; pp. 160–2, Cab 37 (39) 9, Secret, 12.7.1939; F O 371, 23965, pp. 4–6, W10223/9961/68, Dominions Office to Foreign Office, 4.7.1939 r. in r. 5.7.1939; Enclosing Record of Meeting between British Ministers and Nash, 26.6.1939; Minute by R. H. Hadow, Undated.

[54] *D O 114*, 98, p. 23, No. 38, F706/178, Aide Mémoire by te Water of a Message from Hertzog to the British Government, 31.5.1939.

[55] Ibid., p. 24, No. 39, F706/178, Inskip to te Water, Secret, 9.6.1939.

Africa. It was explained that although after Hitler's aggression in March Britain had had to concentrate its immediate efforts upon the conclusion of an anti aggression front it had not abandoned its policy of securing a lasting peace in Europe. Britain now doubted whether any constructive proposals would be received in the same spirit by Germany. The British government was, however, waiting for any sign that might enable it to put forward constructive proposals along the lines suggested by Hertzog. But there was ground for arguing that the determination of the European powers to resist aggression was more likely to contribute to the preservation of peace in present circumstances than anything else.[56]

Britain made it clear to South Africa that although it was prepared to take up any peaceful initiative from Germany for the settlement of differences, it was going to argue from strength this time. In any case it was not hopeful of such an initiative being made.

Te Water brought up this point again at a meeting between Inskip and the high commissioners on 11 July. On 1 July the dominions had been told that reports indicated that the situation in Danzig was delicate and that developments might occur at short notice. Further information discounted the likelihood of an immediate *coup*.[57] Halifax explained on 11 July that while Britain was careful 'to shut no doors to negotiations, prabably the best course now would be to observe a "silence menaçant"',: if Hitler were prepared to risk a European war, he would very likely have it. 'But he would only be prepared to risk it, if he thought that he would not have it.' Bruce also actively urged a settlement. He asked whether Britain would consider it reasonable that Danzig should go to Germany, subject to international guarantees on non fortification and non militarisation. This might come close to the suggestions from Mussolini. Inskip felt that this would be a possible settlement with any country not having Germany's record. But Bruce suggested that 'we should never stop searching for methods of resolving the present tension'. Te Water supported Bruce and asked whether it could be proposed at some appropriate moment that the issue be postponed for a period and the situation stabilised.

Bruce also took up the question of France's attitude to Italy. He mentioned that the Australian government objected to the line taken by France. Halifax reassured Bruce that he had used his name in this connection and had indicated that the Australian government were tired of

[56] Ibid., pp. 24–8, No. 41, F706/211, Inskip to te Water, Secret, 26.6.1939; Enclosure.

[57] *F O 371*, 23961, pp. 204–7, W10299/9831/68, N. E. Archer to Hadow, 3.7.1939 r, in r. 7.7.1939; Enclosing Circular Z No. 12 Telegram Most Secret to High Commissioners in 4 Dominions, 1.7.1939 and Draft for further Consideration of Foreign Office.

the French habit of missing opportunites.[58] The Australian government had protested about France's attitude in June.[59] Bruce was supported by Dulanty and te Water.[60]

Inskip did give further consideration to the suggestion from te Water and Bruce on 12 July that an effort should be made, using Mussolini as an intermediary, to arrange a definite postponement of any attempt to settle the Danzig issue.[61] Inskip discussed the matter with Chamberlain and both concluded that such action would give the impression that Britain was in a state of nervous apprehension over Danzig and wanted Mussolini to get out of a difficult position. The matter was brought before the cabinet on 26 July.[62]

Halifax explained this decision to Bruce and te Water on 28 July: Britain felt that if Mussolini wanted to avoid war there was little doubt he would be doing everything he could with Hitler. Any such move might be interpreted as weakness on Britain's part at a time when it was essential to 'get firmly into the heads of the dictators that this country meant business'. But Bruce and te Water felt uneasy that there was no positive action being taken to arrest what they considered to be a drift to war. To comfort them Halifax thought he could ask the British ambassador in Italy to throw out, in conversation with Ciano, the kind of argument for the *status quo* that the high commissioners had put forward.[63] The British ambassador in Italy doubted the wisdom of any such action at that time, and Halifax concurred in his judgment.[64]

The opinions of Bruce and te Water were taken seriously by Chamberlain on another matter at this time. In July there were attempts to get Churchill into the government. Bruce called on Chamberlain and expressed his consternation at the idea. Chamberlain wrote to his sister:

> It is evident that Australia and South Africa are rather alarmed at the bellicose tone in the country and they think as I do that if Winston got into the Government it would not be too long before it were at war.[65]

[58] Ibid., 22975, pp. 124–7, C10103/15/18, Hankinson to Harvey, 14.7.1939; Enclosing Notes of a Meeting between Inskip, Halifax and the Dominion High Commissioners, 11.7.1939.

[59] *Premier 1*, 324, Menzies to Chamberlain, Telegram, Secret and Personal, 15.6.1939 (paraphrase).

[60] *F O 371*, 22975, pp. 124–7, C10103/15/18, Hankinson to Harvey, 14.7.1939; Enclosing Notes of a Meeting between Inskip, Halifax and the Dominion High Commissioners. 11,7.1939.

[61] *F O 800*, 309, H/VII/96, Notes of a Meeting between Halifax, te Water and Bruce, 12.7.1939.

[62] *Cab 99*, 100, pp. 219–21, Cab 39 (39) 2, Secret, 26.7.1939.

[63] *F O 371*, 22975, pp. 132–3, C10103/15/18, Notes of a Meeting between Halifax, Bruce and te Water, 28.7.1939.

[64] *Documents on British Foreign Policy* 3rd Series (hereafter cited as '*DFBP*') 7, p. 49, No. 47, C11662/54/18, Halifax to Lorraine, 17.8.1939; 6, pp. 633–4, No. 593, C11662/54/18, Lorraine to Halifax, 8.8.1939.

[65] *Templewood Papers* XIX (C) 11, Chamberlain to Hilda Chamberlain, 8.7.1939 (copy).

Chamberlain was conscious of the need to make every possible effort to show the dominions that means of averting war had been tried.

Reports from the British high commissioners in the dominions during July showed the need for this.

In South Africa references were made to neutrality. On 24 June Pirow discussed this question in a speech at Lydenberg and said that the defence of South Africa included that of South West Africa, as it was an integral part of South Africa. Pirow said that no world peace was conceivable without an acknowledgement of German colonial demands. In the case of South West Africa and Tanganyika fair compensation had to be arranged.[66]

In July, however, events in the far east disturbed Hertzog. The prime minister thought the 'background agreement' over Tientsin a climb down, and viewed certain of the Japanese demands as 'impertinent'. Pirow considered war with Japan as likely and offered the high commissioner his personal opinion that in the event of war with Japan South Africa would have to join in. Pirow was convinced that Durban had to be defended. He proposed to move *Erebus* there as soon as he obtained it. *Erebus* was a royal navy ship on loan to the South African government and a foreign office notation on this point read: 'raise Hell?'. Pirow attached most importance to air coastal defence. He claimed that Goering had promised him, if asked, the necessary military equipment for the South African Junkers civil aircraft, but for political reasons, he would prefer not to make this request. An alternative would be for Britain to let him have seven Blenheim bombers on loan. The high commissioner commented:

> The whole business seemed to me quite fantastic but Pirow was entirely serious and had the Chief of Staff and Broeksma waiting outside to receive orders for defence of Durban. I fancy the main import of it is colour prejudice and he may well be right to this extent that colour prejudice might quite possibly dispose some classes of Afrikanders to wage war with Japan who would be against war with Germany. Probably the same feeling affects the Prime Minister's point: he is usually as you know all for conciliation.

The dominions office were anxious for some information to reassure Hertzog about the far east but the foreign office were at a loss to think of anything that could ally the fears Pirow had expressed.[67] South Africa did go ahead with negotiations for a new barter agreement with Germany, the

[66] *F O 371*, 23964, pp. 12–4, W10211/9906/68, Hadow to Foreign Office, 28.6.1939 r. in r. 5.7.1939; Transmitting High Commissioner in South Africa to Dominions Office, Telegram No. 82, 26.6.1939 (copy).

[67] Ibid., pp. 50–3, W11507/9906/68, Pitblado to Hadow, 1.8.1939 r. in r. 2.8.1939; Transmitting Dominions Office to High Commissioner in South Africa, Telegram No. 94, Secret, 31.7.1939 (cypher); Foreign Office Minutes by D. S. Fox, 3.8.1939; Ronald, 4.8.1939.

previous one being due to expire on 31 August. M. Hankey minuted that this was 'not very good news'. This agreement was concluded on 19 August.[68]

The high commissioner in New Zealand wrote on 24 July that there was little if any doubt that New Zealand would stand by Britain in war. He tried to assess the extent of enthusiasm in New Zealand for this and concluded that it would depend on the issue on which war broke out. If this came through the bombing of London he felt that 'the whole Dominion would be ready to spring to arms', but that the help for the first six months, except in untrained manpower would be very small. Enthusiasm, however, might be less in the early stages if war broke out on an issue which, at first sight, Britain's vital interests might not seem to be involved. Savage had told the high commissioner that he would 'greatly regret war breaking out over Danzig'. The high commissioner felt that he had convinced Savage of the reasons why Britain had decided to call a halt to Hitler, but 'it might not be so easy for the people of the Dominion generally to appreciate their force'.

> Where peace and war are involved, however, the people are more likely to be swayed by sentiment than by reason, and Imperial sentiment in New Zealand is as strong as anywhere in the world.

The part of the world in which war broke out would also influence the issue. The possibility that war might start in the far east had effected public opinion. New Zealanders, like Australians, dreaded Japan, and the outbreak of war with that power would be regarded as an immediate and vital threat to the safety of New Zealand. This could lead to popular pressure in favour of priority for local defence measures. The high commissioner concluded:

> I trust I have not given the impression that New Zealand would be in any way lukewarm in supporting the United Kingdom in a war. The sentiment of solidarity with People of the United Kingdom, the pride in British race and traditions and the love of freedom are nowhere stronger than in these islands, and far transcend any political divisions. It is largely political considerations which account for the emphasis at present placed here . . . on local defence. The very remoteness of New Zealand from . . . European fears and ambitions and from the possibility of devastation from the skies, has perhaps not yet brought home to New Zealand the destructiveness of modern warfare and the havoc which it can cause. The first shock of arms in which the Mother Country is involved is

[68] Ibid., 24039, pp. 13–4, C11479/458/18, Henderson to Halifax, No. 908E (648/2/39), 12.8.1939 r. in r. 17.8.1939; p. 13. Minute by M. Hankey, 21.8.1939; pp. 15–6, C11852/458/18, Henderson to Halifax, No. 939E (648/3/39) 22.8.1939 r. in r. 24.8.1939.

likely to reveal the strength of the bonds uniting her with this, the smallest and most distant of the Dominions.[69]

The high commissioner in Canada wrote on 7 July that there had been no radical change in Mackenzie King's views, despite conversations between the Canadian prime minister and the king during the royal visit. Mackenzie King was annoyed by the warning early in July that the situation in Danzig was delicate[70] which was subsequently declared to have been based on a 'journalistic report'. The high commissioner made a fairly serious observation on Mackenzie King's growing distrust of foreign office reports:

> He [Mackenzie King] has evidently received in the past few days a letter from the new Canadian Legation in Holland indicating that last winter, when the situation was dangerous, the Dutch Foreign Office knew more than our Foreign Office did. This is all quite pernickety, but I mention it because I rather feel that Mackenzie King is coming to mistrust the Foreign Office and our diplomatic representatives, which is an unfortunate thing to happen.

Mackenzie King did not understand Hitler. Influenced by the interview that he had had with the führer after the imperial conference and by his 'sentimental nature' Mackenzie King felt that Hitler could be won over by an appeal 'to his better nature'.[71]

The foreign office did not receive this paper immediately: it was apparently delayed for the same reason as Hadow's minute of 23 May.[72] When it was received in the middle of August, when the situation was deteriorating rapidly, T. K. Roberts minuted that he doubted whether it were worthwhile asking the dominions office to suggest that the high commissioner in Canada should explain the position to Mackenzie King. R. H. Hadow endorsed this conclusion:

> He [Mackenzie King] is a laissez-faire 'isolationist' and does not want to know 'uncomfortable' information, . . . but I wd. [*sic*] not want this said to the D.O.[73]

Indications suggested that Ireland would try, as far as possible, to maintain a policy of neutrality. The Irish government did not express any opinion on events during the summer of 1939, nor did the high commissioner volunteer a view as to the probable attitude of Ireland in the

[69] Ibid., 23091, pp. 247–52, C12018/12018/18, Dominions Office to Foreign Office, Confidential, 24.8.1939 r. in r. 26.8.1939; Enclosing H. F. Batterbee to Inskip, No. 135, 24.7.1939 (copy).

[70] Ibid., 22975, pp. 122–3, C10766/15/18, E. L. Sykes to Caccia, Secret, 26.7.1939 r. in r. 3.8.1939; Enclosing Campbell to Harding, 743/379, Secret and Private, 7.7.1939 (copy).

[71] Ibid., *loc. cit.*

[72] See p. 275.

[73] *F O 371*, 22975, pp. 122–3, C10766/15/18, E. L. Sykes to Caccia, Secret, 26.7.1939 r. in r. 3.8.1939; Enclosing Campbell to Harding, 743/379, Secret and Private, 7.7.1939 (copy); Minutes by T. K. Roberts, 18.8.1939; R. H. Hadow, 18.8.1939.

event of war.[74] Vansittart had a conversation with Neville Laski to the effect that de Valera had told Judge Golden, a Jewish lawyer in San Francisco, that Ireland would remain neutral in a European war but 'would want her Price'. If there were no war de Valera would visit the United States in September and October to mobilise the Irish vote to bring pressure on the British government to agree to the union of all Ireland. Gladwyn Jebb minuted on 2 August: 'I rather think we know all this already'.[75]

During July Chamberlain still could not believe that a real alliance between Russia and Germany was possible: he told the cabinet this on 19 July. Chamberlain hoped for a deterrent defensive alliance, and was disappointed by congress's refusal to repeal the neutrality laws. He wrote to his sister on 23 July:

> You don't need offensive forces sufficient to win a smashing victory. What you want are defensive forces sufficiently strong to make it impossible for the other side to win except at such a cost as to make it not worth while.[76]

On 29 July the dominions were told that there was no longer hope of an early agreement with Russia. As there was no danger of the negotiations breaking down a stiffer line would be taken with Russia.[77] Significantly when the dominion high commissioners were showing curiosity as to the stage of the negotiations in mid August it was suggested that the relevant information be communicated through the British high commissioners in the dominions to the various prime ministers. This meant that the risk of leakage through Ireland could be excluded. The usual means through the several departments of external affairs might entail this.[78]

By the middle of August German claims to Danzig and the Polish corridor made an international crisis likely. Britain was warned by the United States on 17 August that Russia and Germany were concluding a non aggression pact.[79] This telegram was not received in the foreign office central department until 22 August,[80] and the cabinet did not have time

---

[74] *D O 114*, 98, Introduction, p. 2.

[75] *F O 371*, 22820, pp. 151–5, A5317/254/45, Foreign Office Minute by Jebb, 2.8.1939 r. in r. 3.8.1939.

[76] *Templewood Papers* XIX (C) 11, Chamberlain to Hilda Chamberlain, 23.7.1939. (copy)

[77] *F O 371*, 23961, p. 278, W10897/9831/68, Dominions Office to Foreign Office, 20.7.1939 r. in r. 21.7.1939; Enclosing Circular B No. 260 Telegram to 5 Dominions, 29.7.1939 (cypher).

[78] Ibid., 23962, pp. 70–3, W12140/9831/68, Foreign Office Minute by Hadow, Most Secret, 18.8.1939.

[79] *DBFP* 7, pp. 41–2, No. 41, C11723/15/18, Lindsay to Halifax, Telegram No. 359, 17.8.1939 r. 18.8.1939.

[80] Ibid., Note. Inskip noted in his diary on 3 August that Lindsay had sent this information on 17 August. [*Inskip Papers* 2, p. 13, Diary, 23.8.1939 (copy)]. Zetland, however, wrote that the news came as 'a complete surprise, and the Foreign Office were able to throw no light upon it'. [*Zetland Papers* 11, pp. 210–5, Zetland to Linlithgow, 19–23.8.1939 (copy)]. The message was delayed by a communist in the code room of the foreign office. [Charles E. Bohlen, *Witness to History 1929–1969* (London, 1973), p. 82].

to consider it. Co-operation with the United States at least extended to a transmission of information of this nature. On 22 August the impending Russian German non aggression pact was announced. Negotiations between Britain and Russia broke down and it was evident that the crisis was imminent. Chamberlain told the cabinet on that day that it was 'unthinkable' that the obligations to Poland should not be carried out.[81]

The dominion governments were kept informed by telegraph of every development in the situation, and of the preparatory defence measures taken by Britain. In London there were daily meetings with the high commissioners. During the last few days of peace the telegrams were sent by telegraph and not by bag.[82]

Inskip saw the high commissioners on the night of 22 August. Both Bruce and Dulanty thought the reaffirmation of the British position over Poland most dangerous, as it would only encourage Beck to be intransigent. In their view Britain ought to find out Beck's position first, and then make a pronouncement to fit that position. Bruce went to see Halifax and Chamberlain about this and they agreed to make a slight change, 'scarcely more than verbal' in the press statement about the Moscow pact. When Inskip saw Bruce on 23 August, he was 'much calmer'.[83]

On 23 August the British ambassador in Italy reported that Ciano was not anxious for a war.[84] At the cabinet meeting on 24 August Halifax asked the cabinet members to 'forget' the information that Italy would not join Germany in the war and that British military plans could be made out on that basis. This was most secret, and it was vital that nothing was said about it. When Halifax saw the high commissioners on that day he merely said that the Italian government was doing what it could to ease the situation: the feeling in Italy was in favour of peace. He also reassured Jordan that the effect of the German-Russian agreement on opinion in Japan had been good from our point of view'.

At this meeting te Water renewed his arguments that there should be some broad explicit statement of the general aims of the 'peace front'. Such a statement was necessary 'unless our policy was to brand ourselves as powerless to do anything more to prevent war'. What te Water had in mind was an explicit statement by the powers of the peace front of how far they were prepared to discuss at the conference table all outstanding

81 *Cab 23*, 100, p. 327, Cab 41 (39) 5, Secret, 22.8.1939.
82 *D O 114*, 98, In roduction, pp. 2–4.
83 *Inskip Papers* 2, p. 15, Diary, 23.8.1939 (copy).
84 Ibid., *loc. cit.*; p. 16, Diary, 25.8.1939.

European problems: the economic, raw material and colonial questions with Germany: the Italian colonial claims; and the German Polish questions. Halifax, in reply, said that Britain had given many indications that it was prepared to do this. What was wrong was Hitler's philosophy. Te Water still felt the need for a 'big and striking gesture to public opinion in all countries, including Germany, and to posterity'. This would need to be based 'on broad moral grounds' and a possible way would be if Roosevelt were to enquire the attitude of the nations concerned to such a conference. Bruce also favoured such a broad statement.[85] Halifax was 'rather attracted by this idea' and promised to think it over.[86]

On 25 August the foreign policy committee met to discuss the Anglo-Polish agreement. As Inskip noted: 'perhaps we all felt the form of the agreement in present circumstances was not very important.'[87]

That night Henderson visited Hitler at Halifax's request and later news of the führer's proposals came through: the demand was that Poland should be reasonable; after the Polish and Danzig questions had been settled Hitler would make a 'big offer'.[88] Inskip met the high commissioners at noon. With the exception of Jordan they were all anxious to meet Hitler half way. Bruce hoped that the British reply would deal not only with the Polish question but that it would be clear that Britain was prepared to discuss all questions and desired a settlement on a basis of negotiation fair to all parties. Bruce hoped that the Poles who 'had undoubtedly been guilty of maltreatment of the German minority as probably the Germans had of the Polish minority' would be induced to adopt a reasonable attitude. Massey agreed that Hitler should be answered on broad grounds, and that the führer's statement be taken at 'face value'. Te Water was sure that the South African government would feel sure that a great effort should be made to secure a comprehensive settlement. Te Water, Massey, Bruce and Dulanty were anxious that the best construction be put on Hitler's words. Te Water even suggested that Roosevelt might be inclined to intervene, but it was generally thought that Roosevelt would not commend himself to Hitler. Only Jordan was more cautious: he agreed that there should be a generous interpretation of Hitler's statement but hoped that Germany would not be unreasonable. Hitler had referred to the colonial question. The New Zealand government thought that this was

85 *F O 371*, 23962, pp. 230–2, Note of a Meeting with Dominion High Commissioners, Most Secret, 24.8.1939.

86 *Inskip Papers* 2, p. 17, Diary, 25.8.1939 (copy).

87 Ibid., *loc. cit.*

88 Ibid., pp. 18–9, Diary, 26.8.1939 (copy).

a matter for the league, but it might be possible to consider the return of Samoa provided it were not used as a naval base.[89]

By the time the cabinet met to discuss the reply to Hitler messages had come from Australia, New Zealand and Canada that they would fight. South Africa was still uncertain.

The high commissioner in South Africa saw Hertzog on 26 August: Hertzog hoped that Hitler's propositions might provide an opening for a settlement, but he took a 'more realistic view of the difficulties than he used to'. The South African parliament might have to meet before 6 September to prolong the life of the senate. This had advantages for Britain: if there were war it was essential that parliament meet at once. On the afternoon of 26 August te Water presented a message from Hertzog to the British government. Hertzog wished 'to impress on Prime Minister very strongly opinion of myself and my colleagues that every legitimate means should be used to induce Poland to be helpful in arriving at solution of Danzig and Corridor questions'. Hertzog hoped for 'a coming together of Germany and Poland' with such other powers as was thought advisable, to settle the Danzig and corridor questions. This would be followed by wider European discussions between the powers concerned.[90] The high commissioner in South Africa reported that Smuts would press Hertzog to make up his mind between belligerency and neutrality. Smuts was fairly hopeful of the latter.[91]

On 18 August Menzies telegrammed Chamberlain that he knew Britain was prepared to take advantage of the reported peace moves in Europe. Menzies felt that particular efforts should be made to ensure that 'Poland adopts reasonable and fair attitude and that no nation should ignore real efforts at settlement because of false notion of extreme prestige'. He assured Chamberlain of his government's support in any efforts to resolve outstanding differences. But Menzies was anxious that the pressure on Poland should not be so as to arouse in Hitler any doubt that the Anglo-French guarantee would be fulfilled. He concluded:

> Your anti-aggression pact and policy have so far succeeded. I do not need to tell you how warmly you and your work are regarded by us.[92]

[89] *F O 371*, 23962, pp. 233–6, W12807/9831/68, Hankinson to Harvey, Secret, 29.8.1939 r. in r. 31.8.1939; Enclosing Note of a Meeting with Dominion High Commissioners, Secret, 26.8.1939.

[90] *D O 114*, 98, p. 34, No. 35, F706/268, H gh Commissioner in South Africa to Dominions Office, Telegram No. 117, Most Secret, 26.8.1939; p. 35, No. 57, F706/265, Dominions Office to High Commissioner in South Africa, Telegram No. 74, Secret, 26.8.1939.

[91] *Inskip Papers* 2, p. 19, Diary, 26.8.1939 (copy).

[92] *D O 114*, 98, p. 29, No. 42, F706/253, Menzies to Chamberlain, Telegram No. 81, 18.8.1939 r, 19.8.1939.

Chamberlain cabled his appreciation of this message.[93] Menzies told parliament that Australia would stand by Britain if war broke out.[94] But on 27 August Menzies suggested that Australia would not consider Danzig and the corridor worth a war.[95] He did not dismiss Hitler's proposals and suggested that Chamberlain invite Hitler to London or some neutral meeting place.[96] On 1 September Chamberlain telegrammed Menzies 'that there seems to be only one course open to us', war.[97]

In New Zealand the acting prime minister, Fraser, declared, with the support of the opposition: 'come what may, New Zealand will stand shoulder to shoulder with the Mother Country'.[98] On 25 August Fraser decided to take the opposition leaders into his confidence, to show them the telegrams about the international situation, and to inform them of the precautionary measures taken. The New Zealand government cordially agreed with the terms of Chamberlain's speech on Poland.[99]

The high commissioner in Canada saw Skelton on 23 August: Skelton thought that no one could accuse the British and French governments of not having done their utmost to secure the co-operation of Russia. Skelton and Mackenzie King, however, deplored that Britain had found it necessary to commit itself so far in eastern Europe that it could be embarrassed by the apparent decision of Russia not to co-operate. Skelton thought that 'one effect of the Russo-German agreement would be to disgust the United States with European politics and appreciably confirm many circles in that country in their determination not to be drawn into developments themselves'.[100] Mackenzie King told the high commissioner that day that he thought Chamberlain's reaffirmation of the guarantee to Poland 'clear and fair'. It was a pity, however, that Britain had committed itself to Poland without first making sure of Russia. He thought that Hitler might be willing to enter into a conference. But Mackenzie King said that he was making it clear to those around him that 'it was no longer a question of Danzig but a question of force'. The high commissioner felt that this was

[93] Ibid., p. 33, No. 51, F706/253, Chamberlain to Menzies, Telegram No. 84, Secret, 25.8.1939.
[94] See pp. 307–8.
[95] *Premier 1*, 300, Menzies to Chamberlain, Telegram, Personal, Undated.
[96] Ibid., Menzies to Chamberlain, Telegram, r. 27.8.1937.
[97] Ibid., Chamberlain to Menzies, Telegram, Personal, 1.9.1939.
[98] *D O 114*, 98, pp. 30–1, No. 46, F706/220, High Commissioner in New Zealand to Dominions Office Telegram No. 239, 23.8.1939.
[99] *F O 371*, 23965, pp. 27–8, W12701/9961/68, Dominions Office to Foreign Office, 26.8.1939 r, in r. 30.8.1939; Enclosing High Commissioner in New Zealand to Dominions Office, Telegram No. 264, 25.8.1939; pp. 24–5, W12700/9961/68, Dominions Office to Foreign Office, 26.8.1939 r, in r. 30.8.1939; Enclosing High Commissioner in New Zealand to Dominions Office, Telegram No. 245, Important, 25.8.1939.
[100] *D O 114*, 98, pp. 29–30, No. 44, F706/219, High Commissioner in Canada to Dominions Office, Telegram No. 264, Secret, 23.8.1939.

a 'considerable and encouraging advance in the Prime Minister's interpretation of the situation'. Skelton, in a later interview, said that like Mackenzie King he felt 'it unwise to go to war for countries which the United Kingdom could not assist effectively'. He felt that Poland could be destroyed or occupied and Hitler could then profess unwillingness to fight the western powers.[101] Stevenson minuted:

> There is an undoubted reluctance in the Dominions to go to war 'for countries which Great Britain cannot assist effectively' as Dr. Skelton put it.
>
> But we can I think rely upon all the Dominions to take up our cause: except S. Africa of whom I am not quite sure at the very beginning.[102]

By 25 August Mackenzie King had decided Canada's course. He told the British high commissioner that with the consent of his colleagues, he was drafting a telegram to Hitler and Mussolini reminding them that the only way to secure justice was through peaceful negotiation. He would then summon the German and Italian representatives to tell them that his cabinet was unanimous in its decision to 'fight whole-heartedly' should war break out.[103] The high commissioner was further authorised to tell the British government that while the cabinet was unanimous in its decision to fight this could not be put into effect until the country had agreed through parliament. This decision was to be kept secret:

> Canada must be allowed to make her own choice as a nation . . . it will cause harmful impression if anything is said suggesting that she should come in automatically as though she were a Colonial possession.[104]

Hadow minuted: 'Canada is all right'.[105]

The high commissioner in Canada reported unprecedented activity on the part of the government in organising measures of preparedness, and a remarkable desire to co-operate with Britain. The defence department was given practically a free hand with money for their preparations, and a governor general's warrant was signed for this without parliamentary sanction. Even Skelton had said that if there were war Canada would desire to play a worthy part.[106]

101 *F O 371*, 23962, pp. 157–8, W12376/9831/68, Dominions Office to Foreign Office, F706/221, 24.8.1939 r. in r. 25.8.1939; Enclosing High Commissioner in Canada to Dominions Office, Telegram No. 268, Immediate Most Secret, 23.8.1939 r. 24.8.1939 (cypher).

102 Ibid., p. 151, W12376/9831/68, Minute by Stevenson, 25.8.1939.

103 *D O 114*, 98, p. 31, No. 49, F706/225, High Commissioner in Canada to Dominions Office, Telegram No. 275, Most Secret, 25.8.1939.

104 *F O 371*, 23966, pp. 172–3, W12646/10478/68, Dominions Office to Foreign Office, Most Secret and Immediate, 26.8.1939 r. in r. 29.8.1939; Enclosing High Commissioner in Canada to Dominions Office, Telegram No. 276, Immediate Most Secret, 25.8.1939 (cypher); *Premier 1*, 300, Inskip to Chamberlain, Most Secret and Confidential, 1.9.1939.

105 *F O 371*, 23966, p. 172, W12646/10478/68, Minute by R. H. Hadow, 28.8.1939.

106 *D O 114*, 98, p. 33, No. 52, F706/263, High Commissioner in Canada to Dominions Office, Telegram, No. 278, Secret, 25.8.1939.

Although determined to fight if necessary Mackenzie King still tried for peace. At the request of the German representative in Ottawa he sent a telegram to the Polish government similar to those sent to Hitler and Mussolini, but omitting the Canadian decision to fight.[107] Mackenzie King further suggested that the king should make a direct appeal to Hitler.[108]

Mackenzie King was told how much Canada's 'most helpful attitude' was appreciated by Britain.[109]

When the cabinet met on 26 August Henderson explained that what Hitler wanted was a gesture from Britain that Poland would not be unreasonable, Halifax thought Hitler's offer was merely an attempt to divide Britain from Poland. Chamberlain considered it a propaganda technique, although there could be the thought at the back of the führer's mind that Britain might be persuaded and Hitler could 'get his own way without war'. Inskip gave a favourable account of the attitude of the dominions: Australia, New Zealand and Canada were behind Britain: Smuts hoped that he would be able to carry his colleagues with him in deciding for belligerency. Mention was made of Hertzog's telegram and that the general view of te Water was that an attempt should be made to get a discussion with Hitler on a reasonable settlement. Mackenzie King's suggestion that the king should send a letter to Hitler met with 'no favour'. The cabinet considered the opinions of the dominions but there is little evidence that it was decisively influenced by them. Probably there was no need: with the possible exception of South Africa all stood behind Britain. Ireland, not mentioned, was seemingly not considered a dominion. There had been indications that it would be neutral. It is true, however, that the proposed draft which Chamberlain agreed to review in the light of criticism was 'less rasping' than, for instance, Inskip expected.[110]

That evening Inskip reported to the high commissioners that the reply to Hitler 'could be described as leaving the door open for reasonable negotiations without giving the impression that we were ready to submit to any demands that Hitler might like to make'. Inskip thought that it treated the matter without being specific, on the broad grounds that te

[107] Ibid., No. 53, F706/257, High Commissioner in Canada to Dominions Office, Telegram No. 280, Most Secret, 25.8.1939 r. 26.8.1939.

[108] Ibid., pp. 34–5, No. 56, F706/259, Mackenzie King to Chamberlain, Telegram No. 48, 26.8.1939

[109] Ibid., p. 34, No. 54, F706/277, Dominions Office to High Commissioner in Canada, Telegram No. 192, Most Secret, 26.8.1939.

[110] *Cab* 23, 100, pp. 370–86, Cab 43 (39) 1, Secret, 26.8.1939; *Inskip Papers* 2, pp. 19–20, Diary, 26.8.1939 (copy).

Water and Bruce had advocated.[111] Inskip noted in his diary that he had told the high commissioners 'a good deal of Cabinet stuff' but that he could hardly avoid that.[112]

The next day the cabinet meeting was postponed as Daladier thought that Hitler's offer had to be considered seriously. Menzies sent a telegram as to how he would approach Hitler's message. Inskip sent it on to Chamberlain as he thought it 'firm + yet forth-coming'.[113] There was a further delay in sending a reply to Hitler because of the intervention of a Swedish intermediary. Halifax also had a telephone conversation with Ciano who said that Mussolini was in touch with Hitler. It was a pleasure for Ciano and Mussolini to be working with Britain. The intermediary was authorised to tell Hitler and Goering: firstly, that Britain was anxious for peace; secondly, that Britain had to hold fast to its obligations to Poland; and, thirdly, that Germany had to be willing to agree to talk to the Poles, and to guarantee the execution of any agreement that they might make. Ogilvie-Forbes reported from Berlin that Hitler accepted the second point, enquired about an alliance or treaty on the first, and on the third Hitler said that the Poles had to be willing to meet him. Hitler would expect the British to reply to contain an assurance that Beck would agree to this.

When Inskip met the high commissioners on 28 August to read them the British reply he mentioned the intermediary and the three points, though not in detail. The high commissioners assented to not being told who the intermediary was and Inskip noted in his diary that they were 'behaving very well'.

Hitler replied on 29 August: he was prepared to talk though thought it was hopeless. He wanted a Polish delegate in Berlin on 30 August and was told immediately that that was impossible. Before the cabinet met on 30 August the high commissioners came to offer their ideas on the draft. They thought it should be 'friendly' and should make a clear statement of the British position. At the cabinet Halifax produced a draft which was discussed disjointedly: some saw 'ghosts of Munich in every sentence that came from Germany'. Halifax was left to settle the draft. Chamberlain wrote a separate letter to Hitler: the cabinet was not told of this. The high commissioners thought Halifax's draft 'cold' and at one point 'abrupt'. Inskip went to Halifax who was prepared at first to accept some

[111] *F O 371*, 23962, p. 237, W12807/9831/68, Note of a Meeting of Inskip with Dominion High Commissioners at 10 p.m., 26.8.1939.

[112] *Inskip Papers* 2, pp. 20–1, Diary, 26.8.1939 (copy).

[113] Ibid., p. 21, Diary, 27.8.1939. See *Cab 24*, 288, pp. 281–4, Telegram from Menzies, Lock and Key, 27.8.1939 (copy) and pp. 308–9.

of the suggestions made by the high commissioners. Halifax suddenly decided that: 'the note was meant to be firm and even sharp'. He felt that the high commissioners only saw part of the picture. Inskip was told he could let the high commissioners know about Chamberlain's letter to Hitler, though this was not for their governments. On hearing this Bruce had an idea which te Water thought offered a way out: if Poland were too unbending, or there were a 'breakoff', Britain should propose to discuss with Germany those questions between the two countries and the other powers, and the German Polish dispute could be settled at that conference. Inskip noted in his diary:

> It did not appeal to me very much, + te Water asked me several times what alternative I suggested. I couldn't give him an answer!!

On 31 August Ribbentrop gave Henderson the German terms. But Lipski, the Polish ambassador in Berlin, refused to see Ribbentrop. Britain suggested 'rather mildly' to Kennard that he should concert with his French colleague and approach the Poles suggesting contacts with Germany. The high commissioners were angry at the Polish attitude, but Inskip saw the objection to putting pressure on Poland to go blind into a conference. Then the news came that Poland was making contact with Berlin about the subject of conversations. At 9.30 p.m. Inskip had to explain to the high commissioners that Lipski would not meet Ribbentrop without orders, and even then would not accept the document containing the Danzig terms as he feared that an ultimatum would be given as well. Beck would not go to Berlin in case he were treated like Schuschnigg. But Beck was prepared to send someone to talk about procedure. He also wanted a *modus vivendi* for Danzig and proper guarantees. The high commissioners felt that Britain ought to urge him to go, or to send someone. Inskip noted: 'they naturally think of the consequences to their Dominions of a war'. Accordingly Inskip went to No. 10, but saw only Horace Wilson and the secretaries. While he was there the news came of Hitler's broadcast of his sixteen points. This was followed by reports of German troops crossing into Poland.

Chamberlain had written to his sister on 27 August:

> I think we may be fairly certain now that thanks to the policy we have pursued Italy will not come in if Hitler goes to war over Poland. And Japan has been so deeply shocked that we may find our anxieties in that quarter greatly relieved if not removed.[114]

---

[114] *Inskip Papers* 2, pp. 29–31, Diary, 31.8.1939 (copy); *Templewood Papers* XIX (C) 11, Chamberlain to Hilda Chamberlain, 27.8.1939 (copy).

The fear of war on three fronts had lessened. The situation in the dominions was favourable. Hadow minuted on 29 August that he expected Smuts's opposition to neutrality to prevail. The high commissioner, however, warned that even though Smuts might be prepared to face the 'wreckage' of the united party, Hertzog might ask for a dissolution of parliament 'so that the issue could be put to the people and everything would depend upon whether Duncan would be strong enough to refuse so disastrous a request'.[115] Ireland, as had been anticipated, opted for neutrality. On the evening of 31 August Dulanty delivered a message that de Valera had accepted that Germany intended to respect Ireland's neutrality.[116] The New Zealand government 'warmly' approved of the British reply to Hitler.[117] The high commissioner in Canada reported that he had seen the conservative opposition leader on 27 August. The leader had repeatedly stressed the need for Britain to be firm in resisting 'all offers to negotiate under threat of force'. The chief justice of Canada expressed similar sentiments on 28 August while the minister for national defence stressed the moral aspect: Britain 'if forced to take up arms in support of Poland would be fighting in an even loftier cause than she had in 1914'.[118]

The position with regard to the United States was fairly favourable. Britain had kept the United States informed of developments throughout the Russian negotiations. J. Balfour minuted on 1 September:

> The President can be relied upon to give the right lead to U.S. public opinion and he is also ready if need be, to assist in holding the ring in the Far East. The neutrality position is uncertain.[119]

After the conclusion of the German Russian agreement the United States press argued that the case for the repeal of the neutrality legislation had been strengthened.[120] On 26 August Roosevelt signed a declaration that all foreign merchant vessels were to be searched for arms before being given clearance. The president did tell Lindsay 'with impish glee' that while the search might delay German ships for two days, British ships

115 *F O 371*, 23964, pp. 86–8, W12645/9906/68, Dominions Office to Foreign Office, Most Secret Immediate, 26.8.1939 r. in r. 29.8.1939; Minute by Hadow, 29.8.1939; pp. 92–6, W12705/9906/68, Dominions Office to Foreign Office, 27.8.1939 r. in r. 30.8.1939; Enclosing High Commissioner in South Africa to Dominions Office, Telegram No. 124, Important Secret, 29.8.1939 (cypher).

116 *D O 114*, 98, Introduction, p. 3.

117 *F O 371*, 23965, pp. 28–30, W12855/9961/68, Dominions Office to Foreign Office, Secret, 29.8.1939 r. in r. 1.9.39; Enclosing New Zealand Government to Dominions Office, Telegram No. 106, Secret, 29.8.1939.

118 Ibid., 23091, pp. 253–5, C12579/12018/18, Archer to Hadow, Secret, 29.8.1939 r. in r. 1.9.1939; Enclosing High Commissioner in Canada to Dominions Office, Telegram No. 287, Important Secret, 28.8.1939 r. 29.8.1939.

119 *F O 371*, 22815, pp. 203–5, A5899/98/45, Lothian to Halifax, Telegram No. 391, 30.8.1939 r. in r. 31.8.1939; Minute by J. Balfour, 1.9.1939.

120 Ibid., pp. 182–4, A5788/98/45, Lindsay to Halifax, Telegram No. 367, 24.8.1939 r. in r. 25.8.1939; Minute by B. E. T. Gage.

would be cleared in half an hour.[121] Lothian presented his credentials as the new ambassador to Roosevelt on 30 August. The president 'could not have been more friendly'. He 'hoped and expected' that if war broke out congress would revoke the neutrality act. If hostilities were represented as police action, or some equivalent interpretation, he might be able to avoid applying the act altogether. In any event he would not declare aluminium sheets or engine blocks as aeroplane parts.[122] He had told Lindsay on 26 August that if war came he would delay the signature of the neutrality proclamation for probably five days during which time 'it would be open to the British authorities to crowd on any ship or transport into Canada all possible arms and ammunition on manufacture here that could be expected'.[123]

Roosevelt even developed ideas with Lothian about arranging for the American republics to combine to patrol half the distance to the African and European coasts to prevent entry by 'belligerent vessels or acts of war'. This could relieve the strain on the British and French navies, as well as making possible the transport of food and war materials from the Pan American coast to Halifax where they could be taken to Europe on allied ships.[124]

Roosevelt was prepared to favour Britain and to lead United States public and congressional opinion as far as he could.

The cabinet met at 11.30 p.m. on 1 September. Chamberlain said that the event against which they had fought so long had come upon them: 'But our consciences were clear, and there should be no possible question now where our duty lay'. The cabinet considered whether to avoid a formal declaration of war in view of the United States's neutrality acts, but it was generally held that a declaration of war was the right course.[125] Inskip mentioned that it had been thought that Ireland might be asked to break off diplomatic relations with Germany. The lord chancellor told of a talk that he had had with Mackenzie King on his visit to Canada in which the prime minister had said that Canada would be in with Britain. The lord chancellor also had the impression from people in the United States that that country would be in sooner or later.[126] The committee of

---

[121] Ibid., pp. 187–90, A5802/98/45, Lindsay to Halifax, Telegram No. 376, Important, 23.8.1939; p. 190, Lindsay to Halifax, Telegram, Important Secret No Distribution, 25.8.1939 d. 26.8.1939.

[122] Ibid., pp. 203–5, A5899/98/45, Lothian to Halifax, Telegram No. 391, Important, 30.8.1939 r. 31.8.1939.

[123] *DBFP* 7, p. 262, No. 317, A5801/98/45, Telegram No. 375, Lindsay to Halifax, 26.8.1939.

[124] Ibid., p. 429, No. 569, W12829/9805/49, Lothian to Halifax, Telegram No. 392, 31.8.1939.

[125] *Cab 23*, 100, pp. 443–50, Cab 47 (39) 1, Secret, 1.9.1939.

[126] Ibid., p. 456, Cab 47 (39) 3, Secret, 1.9.1939.

imperial defence met in the afternoon and decided on a policy of not bombing civilians to comply with an appeal by Roosevelt.[127]

The prearranged warning telegram, notifying the adoption of the precautionary stage of defence preparations against Germany and Italy was sent to the dominion governments at 2 p.m. On receipt of this certain preparatory measures were taken in Australia, New Zealand and Canada. At 2.30 p.m. a further telegram was sent to the dominions notifying them that the cabinet had decided, subject to consultation with the French government, to inform Germany that unless assurances were received that German forces were being withdrawn from Poland, Britain would fulfil its obligations to Poland.[128] The dominions were also warned on 2 September that the position of Italy had not been stated publicly, and that no action should be taken which could be considered provocative by Italy.[129]

Inskip saw Dulanty on the afternoon of 1 September and suggested that Ireland, if it decided to be neutral, might sever diplomatic relations with Germany. Such action might be taken as de Valera's real opinion about the war. Ireland did nothing.[130]

Chamberlain, as was expected, asked for the resignation of the cabinet, so that the war cabinet could be formed. He told Inskip that he wanted a change at the dominions office, without offering any reasons. Inskip accepted the lord chancellorship and noted in his diary:

> I dont [*sic*] like the P.M.'s. methods. He is a 'faux ami', and I think I shall be glad to get out of his inner circle.

Inskip felt that Chamberlain was conducting foreign policy, and wondered whether Halifax would stand it. Chamberlain was a 'man of peace'.[131]

The cabinet met after midnight on 3 September. It decided that Henderson should deliver a message to Ribbentrop at 9 a.m. If Hitler's reply were not received by 11 a.m. Britain would be at war with Germany.[132] There had been a delay as Chamberlain was trying to stiffen the French.[133] Inskip was to inform the dominions only about 9 a.m. that day. He

127 *Inskip Papers* 2, pp. 31–2, Diary, 1.9.1939 (copy).
128 *D O 114*, 98, Introduction, pp. 2–3.
129 *F O 371*, 23962, pp. 260–3, W12966/9831/68, Circular Telegram Z to 5 Dominions, 2.9.1939.
130 *D O 114*, 98, Introduction, pp. 2–3.
131 *Inskip Papers* 2, pp. 36–8, Diary, 2.9.1939 (copy).
132 *Cab 23*, 100, pp. 483–4, Cab 49 (39), Secret, 2.9.1939.
133 *Simon Papers* Diary 16, pp. 2–16, 2.9.1939.

thought it impossible to keep the dominions in the dark for so long, and notified them immediately after the cabinet had met.[134]

Australia issued a proclamation declaring a state of war on 3 September. New Zealand notified the existence of a state of war the same day.[135] It seemed certain that Canada would fight. That country declared war officially on 10 September. South Africa was awkward.

On 1 September Halifax raised the issue with te Water of South Africa severing diplomatic relations with Germany concurrently with Britain. Two issues were at stake: German diplomatic officials could pass on information to their governments about movement of ships which would be prejudicial to other commonwealth governments; the danger posed to South Africa by the protection of its trade with Britain and other friendly countries. Te Water thought that it might be preferable to defer consideration of this until after the South African parliament had met, but promised to communicate with his government. Te Water, however, felt that South Africa would, almost certainly, fight.[136]

On 2 September, after an interview with Smuts, the high commissioner suggested that Chamberlain might send a telegram to Hertzog emphasising the larger issues at stake.[137] A telegram was sent on 3 September. Chamberlain made a personal appeal to Hertzog for South Africa to support Britain in the same way as Australia, New Zealand and Canada had. Chamberlain suggested:

> Since I became prime minister efforts have, as you know been continually devoted to the preservation of peace but we have been left with no other course open to us than that which we have now taken. Events have shown that the cause for which we are fighting far transcends the Polish-German issues. It is nothing less than the re-establishment in the world of the rule of good faith and the renunciation of force.

The British government was prepared to intervene in South African political affairs. On 4 September Inskip saw Machtig of the dominions office and settled a telegram for the high commissioner to help Duncan refuse a dissolution if Hertzog asked for one. But the next day the news came through that Smuts was prime minister, and that Duncan had refused a dissolution. This move was not necessary.[138]

---

[134] *Cab 23*, 100, pp. 483–4, Cab 49 (39), Secret, 2.9.1939; *D O 114*, 98, Introduction, p. 3; *Inskip Papers* 2 pp. 39–40, Diary, 3.9.1939.

[135] *D O 114*, 98, Introduction, p. 3.

[136] Ibid., p. 38, No. 63, D28/46A, Harding to High Commissioner in South Africa, Telegram P No. 2. Secret and Personal, 1.9.1939.

[137] *F O 371*, 23964, pp. 105–7, High Commissioner in South Africa to Dominions Office, Telegram Most Immediate No. 2 Q Secret, 2.9.1939 (cypher).

[138] *Inskip Papers* 2, pp. 40–1, Diary, 8.9.1939 (copy).

Kennedy did suggest to Mallet on 3 September that if a dominion remained neutral arms could be purchased through that dominion from the United States. There seemed to be some vagueness among foreign office officials about the position of the dominions but O. E. Sargent minuted that he thought there might be something in the idea. Such an arrangement could not work through either of the 'disloyal' dominions, South Africa and Ireland. Canada would not accept neutrality for this purpose. Sargent thought Newfoundland a possibility, for although it was technically a dominion, it had a government under British control. Machtig of the dominions office considered Ireland best because of the relations between Ireland and the Irish Americans. The idea was not followed through as Hull pointed out that the neutrality act of 1937 forbade the export of arms to any neutral state for transmission to, or for the use of any belligerent state.[139]

Australia, New Zealand, South Africa and Canada fought alongside Britain. In March 1939 this might not have been the position. Throughout the negotiations with Russia the dominions were kept fully informed. Initially opposed to an agreement with Russia the dominions were brought around to recognising its advisability. The decisions on the policy towards Russia were cabinet decisions: Chamberlain had to give way under pressure from his colleagues. The cabinet and the foreign policy committee did consider the views of the dominions although they were not a crucial factor.

In assessing the influence of the dominions it is important to consider the role of the high commissioners in London. Their suggestions came close to a collective commonwealth foreign policy. At times their influence was more decisive than that of the official telegrams from the various dominion governments. Te Water, Massey and Bruce were particularly active and they all, in various degrees, continued to favour the appeasement of Europe to the end. In this they did reflect the attitude of their respective governments to some extent. Even Australia, though prepared to fight at the end of August, urged restraint on Poland. During this period some dominions even offered advice as to what British policy should be. This was the first time that this had happened.

Until May 1939 British contingency planning for possible war was based on the assumption that the dominions would fight. It was not until then that the committee of imperial defence tailored its plans to fit the

---

[139] *F O 371*, 23962, pp. 395–407, W13481/9831/68, Foreign Office Minutes, 3.9.1939 r. in r. 12.9.1939; Minute by O. E. Sargent, 4.9.1939; Minute by E. G. Machtig, 8.9.1939.

possible contingency of a dominion opting for neutrality. Ireland, however, was virtually not considered a dominion, and precautions were taken to prevent security leakage through that country.

There is evidence to suggest that the relay of information between the dominions office and the foreign office, and the dominions office and the various dominion governments, was not always as efficient as it might have been. Significant despatches were not passed on to the relevant source. But then this was true not only of the dominions: Vansittart's intelligence network warned of the Russian-German negotiations as early as May. The information from the United States on this did not reach the central department of the foreign office in time for it to throw light on the matter for the cabinet.

Inskip, as secretary of state for the dominions, seemed to sympathise with their position, and to place their case fairly to the British authorities. He acted as a spokesman for the dominions in the cabinet. During the last few days of peace this role that Inskip played was particularly evident. The British government was prepared to give careful consideration to the views of the dominion high commissioners in particular, but would not significantly alter policy because of them.

By early September it was evident to the cabinet that Roosevelt was prepared to favour Britain where he was not limited by congressional and public opinion. The cabinet, however, was not influenced by the United States to the extent of taking up the president's suggestion that there be no declaration of war so that he could possibly avoid implementing the neutrality acts.

Chamberlain's policy of deterrent alliances did not keep the peace. But the prime minister, when the time came, was ready to fight. He felt that Italy, at least, because of British policy, did not go to war alongside Germany over Poland.[140] The dreaded war on three fronts did not materialise immediately.

When war came Britain did have the support of four dominions and the ready sympathy of the United States. The months between Hitler's occupation of Prague and the march into Poland were crucial in bringing this about.

[140] Woodward claims that Italy did not fight as Mussolini was not ready for war and not sure that Hitler would win. See Llewellyn Woodward, *British Foreign Policy in the Second World War* 1 (London, 1970), pp. 20–1.

XI

THE DOMINIONS CONSOLIDATE

The Dominions Consolidate

HALIFAX, in a note written on the publication of the British documents recorded that the change of feeling in the dominions from the time of Munich to standing behind Britain on the outbreak of war, was 'the immediate consequence of Hitler's rape of Czechoslovakia in March 1939'.[1] For Halifax this was Chamberlain's great achievement.[2] The situation was more complex. Possibly the consolidation of opinion within the dominions was a result of the interaction of a developing awareness of the international situation and how it affected them, as well as the conviction that Chamberlain had tried all measures to preserve peace. In the case of South Africa it could be argued that Smuts saw his opportunity to seize the premiership. For Australia strategic vulnerability might have weighed. Sentimental ties of kinship and common heritage, as in New Zealand, played an incalculable, but probably convincing, role. The imperial factor still counted. The personal trust that individual leaders had gained in the British prime minister at the imperial conference was probably a decisive factor. This was certainly so with Mackenzie King. Halifax's assertion is a simplification.

In South Africa the position was uncertain until the day war was declared. It depended on the stand taken by Smuts. At no time did Smuts explicitly tell Hertzog that he felt that the cabinet agreement of September 1938 for neutrality was not binding.[3] In his speeches he might have satisfied the English speaking section by implying that South Africa would support Britain.[4] But in no instance was Smuts as definite as senator Clarkson, the minister of posts and telegraphs, who on 24 August said that: 'South Africa's interests are identical with those of the rest of the Empire, and South Africa will be in it up to the neck if anything happens.'[5] Smuts avoided the question in parliament. J. H. Hofmeyer who had resigned from the cabinet the previous September on the issue of the native representatives in parliament, raised the matter after Hitler's occupation of Prague.[6] Hofmeyer said that South Africa rightly supported

1 *Halifax Papers* A4 410 12 1, Foreign Policy an Unpublished Note, Undated.
2 Earl of Halifax, *Fullness of Days* (London, 1957), p. 198.
3 Oswald Pirow, *James Barry Munnik Hertzog* (Cape Town, 1958), p. 242.
4 W. K. Hancock, *Smuts, The Fields of Force, 1919–1950* (Cambridge, 1968), pp. 315–7.
5 *Daily Telegraph*, 25.8.1939.
6 E. A. Walker, *A History of Southern Africa* (London, 1957), p. 662. See *Lothian Papers* 391, pp. 386–7, B. K. Long to Lothian, 2.6.1939 for an Evaluation of Hofmeyer's position.

Chamberlain but that the policy of appeasement lay a 'shattered wreck'. Hofmeyer felt that the peace of the world could still be secured if the democratic nations bound themselves together to resist the 'onslaught of authoritarianism'. He was suggesting that the issue was now clear and that the time had come for the government to decide where it stood.[7] The Smuts wing and the Stallardites burst into cheers but their leader did not take the hint.[8]

Many had the impression that Smuts believed South Africa would be at war automatically if Britain fought.[9] By walking his tightrope Smuts succeeded in allowing his adversaries and his supporters to think what they wanted of him.

Smuts's personal correspondence offers few clues as to what stand he had decided to take if he had made a decision at all. He did not find fault with Chamberlain's guarantee to the eastern European countries, though he did hope that they could be turned into something in the nature of the league.[10] Smuts distrusted Russia, but felt that an agreement was desirable if it could preserve peace.

Smuts wrote to Lothian in a fairly optimistic mood on 25 May:

> I have never liked a Soviet agreement, but it may now be the only way out. If it comes about the result [may be? must be?] military stalemate and no war.

Smuts considered steps leading to a general settlement and disarmament.[11] Lothian replied that the position was better than six months previously. He felt that the Polish question would cause the next crisis of nerves but that war might be averted by a system of blockade. If this were so disarmament was not the next step: 'Peace depends . . . upon their being overwhelming superiority of power behind the law'.[12]

After Hitler's speech demanding Danzig and the Polish corridor Smuts decided that he was not in the mood for another Munich.[13] By 28 August he could not see how, in the long run, South Africa could keep out of the fight. He wrote:

> With us there is no enthusiasm for Poland, and less for Danzig and the corridor. Moreover, neutrality is even more firmly held as a faith than in the Middle West

---

7 Alan Paton, *Hofmeyer* (London, 1964), pp. 317–8.

8 Ibid., *loc. cit.*

9 *Manchester Guardian*, 5.5.1939.

10 *Smuts Papers* 60, No. 93, Smuts to E. Love, 30.5.1939. Quoted by Hancock, p. 311.

11 *Lothian Papers* 394, p. 603, Smuts to Lothian, 25.5.1939.

12 Ibid., pp. 606–10, Lothian to Smuts, 6.6.1939 (copy).

13 Hancock, pp. 311–3.

of U.S.A. And on the other side (which happens to be my own) there is the difficulty to understand how in the long run we could possibly keep out of the fight.[14]

But there was no clue as to what action Smuts would take.

South Africa's entry into the war was decided partly as well by the governor general, Patrick Duncan, who refused Hertzog a dissolution of parliament. Duncan did not like Chamberlain's policy of guarantees. Lothian, by then convinced that Vansittart had been proved correct in his estimate of the true nature of the national socialist regime,[15] tried to convince Duncan of the rightness of the new British policy. Duncan saw that the effect would be to give Hitler an excuse for further action and felt that Britain could not interfere in Europe with a mission of keeping the peace by force.[16] Lothian tried to explain to Duncan that national socialism was destructive of all values in which they believed, and sent him a copy of Dr. Hermann Rauschning's book on the fundamental nature of Hitlerism.[17] By the end of July Duncan still argued that British policy was on a 'thoroughly bad wicket' but ceded that criticisms by that time were 'academic'.[18]

Hertzog felt that the agreement of September 1938 did not mean that he should consult parliament if he decided not to go to war. This refinement was lost on his colleagues who believed that parliamentary consultation was implied whatever the decision.[19] The official united party organ, the *Suiderstem*, stated in May that neutrality was not possible in all cases and neither was participation: it was for parliament to decide.[20]

Parliament had to be summoned to extend the life of the senate which expired on 3 September. On a demand from Malan, Hertzog, on 2 September, promised to make a statement to the house on South Africa's position on 4 September. Pirow warned Hertzog that Smuts did not consider himself bound by the neutrality agreement, and that Louis Esselen had organised a majority in favour of war. Just before the cabinet met on 2 September Hertzog received a letter from Malan pledging the nationalist party's support for neutrality. Hertzog stated to the cabinet that he understood they were held by the decision for neutrality of the

14 *Smuts Papers* 60, No. 220, Smuts to M. C. Gillett, 28.8.1939. Quoted by Hancock, p. 314.

15 *Lothian Papers* 387, p. 840, Lothian to Vansittart, 11.5.1939 (copy).

16 Ibid., 389, pp. 185–8, Duncan to Lothian, 16.6.1939.

17 Ibid., pp. 189–91, Lothian to Duncan, 4.7.1939 (copy); Hermann Rauschning, Trans. E. W. Dickes, *Germany's Revolution of Destruction* (London, 1939).

18 *Lothian Papers* 389, p. 192, Duncan to Lothian, 21.7.1939.

19 Deneys Reitz, *No Outspan* (London, 1943), p. 237.

20 *Suiderstem*, 2.5.1939.

previous September. Smuts explained his opposition: he was convinced that Hitler threatened the peace and liberty of the world.[21] That evening Pirow saw Hertzog at Groote Schuur: Chamberlain had wired:

> You can adopt one of three alternatives: you can declare war on Germany, you can break off diplomatic relations with her or you can remain neutral. I beg of you not to follow the third course.

Pirow and Hertzog agreed that after the latter's speeches anything but neutrality was unthinkable.[22]

Smuts saw Clark, the British high commissioner, and told him that Hertzog had evolved a compromise neutrality plan: South Africa would stay out of war subject to the discharge of the obligations over Simonstown. Hertzog, arguing from a report sent to him by te Water of Inskip's appeal for South Africa to break off diplomatic relations and keep to the Simonstown agreement, felt that Britain might be satisfied with such action. Smuts felt that this was a misconception of what Inskip had said, and Clark concurred.[23] It was not a misconception, and Clark presumably knew this as he had been sent the telegram advising that action should be taken along these lines should South Africa verge towards neutrality.[24]

The cabinet met again on 3 September, after the British ultimatum had expired. Smuts thought that Chamberlain's alternative of breaking off diplomatic relations could be a way out. Hertzog would not accept this after what he had told the people on behalf of the government.[25] Hertzog claimed that it would savour of dependence if South Africa followed Britain's lead. He was prepared to give every condiseration to British shipping and men of war but the same had to apply to Germany. Pirow was prepared to send a squadron of aeroplanes to South West Africa and had plans for the prohibition of public meetings and press control. But after Hertzog spoke he stood by the prime minister. Havenga felt there would be a general election which would ensure that South Africa would become a republic. Hertzog refused to hold a party caucus.[26] The cabinet was split: seven for Smuts and six for Hertzog.[27] Pirow had seemingly

21 Paton, p. 321.
22 Pirow, p. 246. See also C. M. van der Heever, *Generaal J. B. M. Hertzog* (Johannesburg, 1944), pp. 697–700; Oswald Pirow, 'Generaal Hertzog as Staatsman' in P. J. Nienaber *et. al.*, *Gedenkboek Generaal J. B. M. Hertzog* (Johannesburg, 1965), pp. 280–321.
23 *D O 114*, 98, p. 44, No. 66, C6/49, High Commissioner in South Africa to Dominions Office, No. 267, Confidential, 13.9.1939 r. 9.10.1939.
24 See pp. 275–7.
25 Pirow, p. 246.
26 G. Heaton Nicholls, *South Africa in my Time* (London, 1961), p. 337.
27 Paton, p. 321.

told Hertzog that he could get a substantial majority for neutrality in the house. Stuttaford and Smuts spoke to some of the old South African party people who were wavering. That evening Smuts told Clark that he was prepared to move an amendment to Hertzog's statement in the house which would repudiate neutrality and declare war on Germany. The biggest unknown factor that worried Smuts was the attitude of the governor general. Hertzog could tender his resignation to the governor general, and form a new government, a move for which there was precedent, pledged to neutrality. The governor general could also grant Hertzog a dissolution of parliament. If the governor general were safe, Smuts had a majority in the house, and Hertzog could be defeated.[28]

Clark saw Duncan that night. The governor general was worried that Hertzog might press for a dissolution if he were defeated in the house. Duncan felt that he should, in the public interest, refuse such a request, though he doubted his constitutional right to do so. Clark cordially supported him in this attitude. Hertzog also saw Duncan that night and the prime minister said that he would probably have to ask for a dissolution. Duncan replied that if Smuts had a majority he would feel it his duty to refuse a dissolution. Hertzog then presented an embarrassing possibility that if he had a majority of only three or four he would ask for a dissolution and a general election as he would not have a working majority. Duncan did not see how he could refuse this, and Clark was unable to dispute Duncan's opinion. Clark saw Hertzog the next morning before the cabinet met to give him a message from Chamberlain,[29] and tried to persuade the prime minister that this was not merely one of England's wars. It was a 'forlorn hope'.[30]

On 4 September Hertzog moved in the house that South Africa remain neutral, except for Simonstown. Britain had declared war because it had obligations to Poland. South Africa had no such obligations. For Hertzog it was an issue of national independence. Furthermore he defended Hitler and blamed the treaty of Versailles. Implicitly referring to Smuts Hertzog said that those who differed from him might have let their views be known when there was still time.

Smuts replied by saying that nothing could be said for Hitler after the rape of Czechoslovakia. Hitler would next demand South West Africa:

[28] Nicholls, pp. 337–8. Quoting Diary, 3.9.1939.

[29] See p. 296.

[30] *D O 114*, 98, pp. 44–5, No. 66, C6/49, High Commissioner in South Africa to Dominions Office, No. 267, Confidential, 13.9.1939 r. 9.10.1939.

he was out for world domination. Smuts moved that South Africa sever relations with Germany.[31]

During the debate, Mr. Pocock, a member of parliament, came to see Clark on behalf of Smuts and said that Hertzog's supporters were spreading the rumour, that if Hertzog were defeated, Duncan would grant him a dissolution and a general election. It was thought that some of Smuts's would be supporters were hesitating. Clark wrote:

> General Smuts had very properly kept away from the Governor-General, but could I tell him anything? I was manifestly in a delicate position, but Mr. Pocock is a reliable man, and in the circumstances I felt justified in saying on information which had reached me I had good reason to think that the Governor-General would not grant a dissolution if General Smuts had a majority. Mr. Pocock probably read between the lines of the statement and went off satisfied.[32]

The vote was 80 to 67: Smuts won.[33]

Hertzog then asked Duncan for a dissolution. The governor general replied that Hertzog had lost the confidence of parliament. In this constitutional position he had no alternative but to deny the request and to send for Smuts.[34] The *Round Table* estimated that had an election been held Hertzog would have been returned to power.[35] Paton suggests that this might have led to civil war in South Africa.[36]

By a narrow majority of thirteen votes South Africa went to war a divided country. The governor general and the British high commissioner both played their parts in securing this. English speaking South Africa, for reasons of sentiment and ties of kin probably was always willing to fight for Britain. But it was in the minority. The vote was carried by those Afrikaners who still believed in the Smuts-Botha ideal of conciliation. Smuts's position is enigmatic. It is difficult to see what caused him to oppose neutrality in September 1939 when he had agreed to it a year previously. His personal correspondence suggests little enthusiasm for British foreign policy, but, by the end of August, a feeling that a stand had to be taken is discernible. Political speeches are, at best, ambiguous, and Smuts was a master of that art: he told English speaking South Africa what it wanted to hear without giving any firm pledge. In parliament he was silent. Perhaps Hertzog's complaint of Smuts's duplicity has foundation had

---

[31] Paton, pp. 322–3.
[32] *D O 114*, 98, p. 47, No. 66, C6/49, High Commissioner in South Africa to Dominions Office, No. 267, Confidential, 13.9.1939 r. 9.10.1939.
[33] Paton, pp. 322–3.
[34] Nicholls, p. 345.
[35] Anonymous, 'South Africa', *Round Table*, XXX (1939–40), pp. 200–14.
[36] Paton, p. 323.

Smuts changed his mind earlier than September 1939 on the neutrality issue. But the only firm evidence for such a change is discernible at the end of August. Smuts might have seen his chance to become prime minister. Smuts's lack of enthusiasm for Chamberlain's policy after Prague would suggest that he was not influenced by the British prime minister. The decision was Smuts's own, and on the available evidence it is difficult to assess his motivations. The only danger in the European situation for South Africa was possible German ambitions in South West Africa. Smuts made the most of this in his parliamentary speech.

South Africa declared war, but as R. H. Hadow minuted, it was 'torn asunder on social lines'. If Smuts could not heal the breach South Africa might react to a peace move by Hitler. That would be 'Hertzog's opportunity—or Malan's—for revenge'.[37] Twenty years later Pirow wrote that the cabinet meeting of 3 September made it a certainty 'that when the political pendulum swing back again, as it was bound to do, Malan's extremists would take over and the English speaking South Africans would become bywoners [aliens] in their own country'.[38]

Shortly after Hitler's occupation of Prague Lyons died and Menzies succeeded as premier in Australia. Menzies headed an uneasy coalition and faced personal hostility from the country party.[39] But there does not seem to have been much dissatisfaction with his continuance of the Lyons policy of support for the new British position.

Menzies made his first public pronouncement as prime minister on 26 April: in this he showed an awareness of the feeling that Australians should not fight outside their continent. He said:

> If Britain was at war, Australia was too, even though that war found Australians not on European battlefields but defending their own shores. He could not envisage the defence of an Australia which depended on British sea-power as its first element (thanks to which vital foreign trade and sea routes would be kept free), and yet which refused co-operation with Britain in time of danger. No Australian troops would be compelled to go on foreign battlefields: but let no one imagine that Australia could remain neutral in a war in which Britain was engaged.

Menzies, however, explained that in the Pacific Australia had its own responsibilities, and would have to be guided by its own decisions. The

[37] *F O 371*, 23964, pp. 103–7, W12857/9906/68, Garner to Hadow, G110/25, 30.8.1939 r. in r. 1.9.1939; p. 103, Minute by Hadow, 8.9.1939.
[38] Pirow, p. 246.
[39] Paul Hasluck, *The Government and the People* (Canberra, 1952), pp. 109–12; *Lothian Papers* 392, pp. 398–9, H. A. McClure Smith of the *Herald* to Lothian, 21.5.1939.

prime minister was considering the Japanese situation in which he perhaps felt Britain's interests were not primary.[40]

The position taken by Menzies was not seriously qualified by Sir Henry Gullett, the minister of external affairs, when he spoke to the house of representatives on 9 May. Gullett pointed out, with the concurrence of Menzies, that the speech of 26 April was not intended to mean that 'in any and every set of circumstances' Britain's foreign policy could automatically commit Australia to war: there was at that time 'no sort of disagreement' between Britain and Australia. Gullett did say that is was unlikely that Japan, Italy or Germany would fight.[41] He concluded, however, that Australia had been fully advised and consulted by Britain.

> If therefore, in pursuance of this policy, the Government of Britain is at any moment plunged into war, the Government will, on behalf of the Australian people, make common cause with the Mother Country in that war.

Curtin, the leader of the opposition, was in favour of genuine discussions with Italy and Germany.[42] He spoke also of the common interest of the British peoples in peace but stressed that the dominions should decide how, and to what extent they should participate in a war.[43]

The Menzies government preoccupied itself with accelerating rearmament, facilitating the supply of munitions, and the national registration bill. Australia spent £1 in every £4 on defence, whereas New Zealand spent only £1 in every £22, Canada £1 in £16 and South Africa £1 in £23.[44]

Although there was unease about the situation in Japan and British ability to defend Australia from attack, resulting in conciliatory moves towards Japan which tied in with British policy,[45] Australia generally welcomed a firm British stand on Europe. Halifax's statement that 'if international law and order are to be preserved, we must be prepared to fight in their defence' was approved by the Australian press.[46] An *Argus* editoral read:

> Every avenue of appeasement has been explored, every possibility of co-operation has been considered, every form of assistance has been proferred, with no response on the part of the axis Powers.[47]

[40] *Times*, 27.4.1939.
[41] *Sydney Morning Herald*, 10.5.1939; *Aust Parl Deb* 159, H or R, cols. 197–8, 9.5.1939.
[42] Ibid., col. 199.
[43] *Journal of the Parliaments of the Empire* 1939 20, p. 685; P. N. S. Mansergh, *Survey of British Commonwealth Affairs. Problems of External Policy 1931–1939* (Oxford, 1952), p. 175.
[44] Hasluck, p. 20; *Aust Parl Deb* 160, H or R, col. 1372, 7.6.1939.
[45] See p. 261.
[46] *Sydney Morning Herald*, 1.7.1939, Ed.; *Manchester Guardian*, 1.7.1939.
[47] *Argus*, 1.7.1939, Ed.

Chamberlain's tactics of exploring every avenue of peace probably helped to convince Australians. Certainly the press was sceptical of the campaign to include Churchill in the government in July. The *Age* pointed out that Churchill, in common with Eden and Duff Cooper belonged to that school of politicians whose political vision was restricted to Europe. Chamberlain was more aware of the dominions: the *Age* recalled the British prime minister's courage in implementing the policy of the appeasement of Europe, and recognised his determination to maintain Britain's own commitments.[48]

Even Menzies, so impressed by Germany during his visit in 1938,[49] had tempered his praise by August 1939. As late as 18 July 1939 Menzies spoke of the great things that Hitler and Mussolini had achieved for their countries, though he did not think the system suitable for Australia.[50] By 14 August Italy and Germany had become 'barbarous'. Menzies did insist that he favoured British policy of keeping the door of the international conference room open till the last moment.[51]

The Australian government was informed that Chamberlain had written to Hitler on 22 August that Britain intended to fulfil its obligations to Poland. The cabinet met on 24 August to draft the necessary emergency legislation for war.[52] Menzies publicly announced Australia's support for Britain, and the raising of a specially trained force of 14,000 within the militia to be called up before general mobilisation.[53] The threats of the labour opposition did not disturb Menzies as they had his predecessor. Curtin said that it would be a bold man who 'committed the lives of Australians as pawns in the fate of Poland. The safety of the Australian people impelled us to recognise our inability to send Australians overseas to take part in a European war'.[54] The *Daily News*, the labour organ whose influence and circulation were small, argued that war was 'wholly irrational'. The Australian government was becoming a dictatorship: it was for parliament to decide Australia's participation in any war. Menzies was only a servant of Downing Street.[55] The emergency committee of the Australian council of trade unions also felt that it should be given a

---

[48] *Age*, 19.7.1939, Ed.
[49] See p. 154.
[50] *Times*, 19.7.1939.
[51] *Sydney Morning Herald*, 14.8.1939.
[52] Hasluck, p. 149.
[53] *Manchester Guardian*, 24.8.1939.
[54] *Times*, 25.8.1939.
[55] *Daily News*, 30.8.1939, Ed.; *F O 371*, p. 23962, 216, W12703/9831/68, Dominions Office to Foreign Office, 26.8.1939 r. in r. 30.8.1939; Enclosing High Commissioner in Australia to Dominions Office, Telegram No. 16, 25.8.1939.

chance to express itself on the possibility of Australia becoming involved in hostilities overseas.[56]

Menzies was impervious to this criticism. A few minutes after Chamberlain announced that Britain was at war with Germany, Menzies broadcast: 'Britain is at war therefore Australia is at war'. The federal parliament was not summoned on this issue as the government felt that no separate declaration of war by Australia was required.[57]

Australia fought for king and country. Menzies, despite his insecure position, ignored labour criticism, and did not even concede that Australia had the constitutional right to make a separate declaration of war.

There had never been any question of New Zealand's loyalty and that it would fight with the mother country whether the cause be right or wrong. New Zealand had been awkward with its insistent belief in the ideals of the league of nations, and because of the pacifist convictions of its prime minister. During this period both these obstacles fell away.

Most crucial for this dominion was the conference of defence experts from Britain, Australia and New Zealand which met in Wellington in April 1939 to survey the commonwealth strategy in the Pacific. The meeting arose from a New Zealand suggestion at the imperial conference of 1937. The discussions caused an important personal conversation within the New Zealand cabinet, the prime minister, Savage being the key figure. Savage, optimistic and pacific, did not like to think of New Zealand men being sent to fight overseas. Consequently New Zealand's expanded defence preparations had emphasised the air force and the navy while neglecting the army. The Pacific defence conference convinced Savage of the need for an efficient army and during the following months he used his personal influence to achieve this. On 22 May Savage launched a recruiting campaign, and although opposition spokesmen urged universal military training, the government resisted peacetime conscription.[58]

At the defence conference New Zealand undertook to participate in a scheme for distributing and producing aircraft among British territories in the Pacific, to buy modern aircraft itself, to use British expertise to build up it army, and to have air personnel trained in Britain.[59] New Zealand was becoming absorbed into the British defence structure. With

[56] *Sydney Morning Herald*, 31.8.1939, Ed.
[57] Mansergh, p. 378.
[58] F. L. W. Wood, *The New Zealand People at War. Political and Extrenal Affairs* (Wellington, 1958), pp. 72–83; Mansergh, p. 200.
[59] Mansergh, p. 200.

the close co-ordination in defence New Zealand avoided any public clash with Britain on the Japanese situation.[60]

Chamberlain's efforts to educate New Zealand to the reality of the international situation and the weakness of the league,[61] worked. On 28 June, Viscount Galway, the governor general, in his speech from the throne said:

> But in the circumstances of to-day my Advisers have most reluctantly been forced to recognise the fact that a full and effective application of the Covenant is for the time being, impracticable.[62]

New Zealand took the decision to go to war as a unified country. On 23 August Mr. Hamilton, the leader of the opposition, assured the government of its unanimous backing 'in all and any action deemed necessary to meet the crisis'. Mr. Fraser, the acting prime minister, commented that war would find New Zealand 'united and solid'.[63] Fraser saw no difficulty about the estimates for defence since, when a country was threatened 'not only every human being but every penny in the Dominion and every ounce of property became part of the defence system of the country'.[64] New Zealand expressly approved the British decision to stand by the Polish guarantee on 28 August and just before midnight on 3 September the cabinet decided to go to war.[65]

New Zealand's unswerving loyalty to the imperial cause was never in question. In this dominion sentiment and ties of kinship were paramount. Defence considerations were only a factor. A united country was prepared to stand and fight by Britain's side. As a result of Chamberlain's careful education naive attachments to the ideals of the league were surmounted.

In Canada the key figure was Mackenzie King. At the imperial conference in 1937 he had been influenced by Chamberlain and thereafter felt that a special relationship existed between them.[66] Mackenzie King made overtures to Hitler in February 1939 about possible cultural exchanges between Canada and Germany. Hitler's reply that a number of Canadian students might visit Germany, only reached Mackenzie King on 21 July. Mackenzie King consulted the British about accepting it. At the time Hitler was using Danzig to provoke Poland and Senator

---

60 Ibid., *loc. cit.*
61 See pp. 44–5.
62 *N Z Parl Deb* 254, Leg Co, p. 4, 28.6.1939.
63 Ibid., 255, H of R, p. 492, 23.8.1939.
64 *Times*, 24.8.1939.
65 Wood, p. 97.
66 See p. 56.

Dandurand warned Mackenzie King that Canada should not be drawn into a conflict on that issue. The Canadian cabinet, however, decided not to tender advice to the British government unless asked to do so. Mackenzie King was horror-struck by the talk of bringing Churchill and Eden into the cabinet. Amidst these events, as Mackenzie King wrote to Chamberlain, Hitler's invitation seemed 'significant and sincere'. According to Eayrs it was also evidence of 'those "unseen forces", that invisible hand, which the Prime Minister of Canada increasingly believed to be in charge of the world's destiny, and of his own'. Mackenzie King planned to be a member of the visiting party but felt that it would have to wait till November, after the proposed general election.[67] Mackenzie King pursued the appeasement of Europe to the last. At the end of August he sent messages to Germany, Poland and Italy. He suggested an appeal by the king to Hitler.[68] But following the German-Russian agreement Mackenzie King warned the German consul general that the Canadian cabinet had decided unanimously to recommend to parliament that Canada should support Britain and France to the limit of its capacity.[69]

Mackenzie King is difficult to evaluate. His confidence in Chamberlain and the conviction that the British prime minister had done all that was possible to preserve peace, probably helped to convince Mackenzie King that he should lead his country into war. What cannot be assessed is the influence of spiritualism.

During this time Canada did participate in closer defence co-ordination with Britain. Colonel G. P. Loggie was sent to London as ordnance representative of the department of national defence. He could only attend meetings of the committee of imperial defence if authorised by Ottawa. Massey protested that this restriction made it impossible for Loggie to arrange for Canadian industry to co-operate fully in British defence plans. The high commissioner also urged that others were needed to deal with matters outside the restricted armaments area, such as raw materials and food. He informed Ottawa that the war office had stated that unless definite proposals were received within thirty days they would have to look elsewhere. Massey's request was acceded to, and at the beginning of 25 August Canadians arrived in London. The Duke of Devonshire and the senior supply officers of the three ministries conferred with the visitors about the supply of war materials from Canada.[70] Though there

[67] James Eayrs, *In Defence of Canada Appeasement and Rearmament* (Toronto, 1965), pp. 76–9; *Premier 1*, 334, Chamberlain to Mackenzie King, Telegram, Secret and Personal, 6.8.1939 (cypher).

[68] See p. 290.

[69] See p. 289.

[70] Vincent Massey, *What's Past is Prologue* (London, 1963), pp. 272–3, 278.

was initial reluctance on the part of the Canadian government to become involved, when pressed, it co-operated. Canada did not declare war until 10 September, as the declaration had to go through parliament, but in effect Canada was at war as soon as Britain as all war measures were in full operation. On 28 August the minister for national defence called out 10,000 men of the non permanent militia to man coastal defences. Aeroplanes were flown to Halifax for emergency duty.[71] As Gerald Campbell, the high commissioner in Canada wrote:

> co-operation with this office and with United Kingdom policy generally which . . . had in the past been at the best carefully pondered and at the worst flatly refused, now became the order of the day.

Campbell cited the instance of the crossing into Canada of aircraft ordered by Britain from the Lockheed factory in California.[72]

When Mackenzie King broadcast to Canada on 3 September he explained that 'no stone had been left unturned, no road unexplored in the patient search for peace'. He spoke in terms of the forces of good and evil:

> The forces of evil have been loosed in the world in a struggle between the pagan conception of a social order which ignores the individual and is based upon the doctrine of might and a civilisation based upon the Christian conception of the brotherhood of man with its regard for the sanctity of contractual relations and the sacredness of human personality.

He explained that he would seek authority from parliament for effective co-operation by Canada at the side of Britain, and had no doubt that this authority would be given. This co-operation was voluntary.[73] Mackenzie King repeated this theme of 'the conflict between the forces of good and evil' when he addressed parliament.[74] This debate settled controversy: the minister of justice, the leading representative of French Canada, declared that it was impossible to stay out of war; senator Meighen denounced those who thought Canada should and would take refuge under the wing of the United States. French Canada remained opposed to conscription, and the government promised not to introduce this

[71] Ibid., p. 278; *F O 371*, 23960, p. 183, High Commissioner in Canada to Dominions Office, Telegram No. 286, Important, 28.8.1939 r. 29.8.1939; *Documents on Canadian External Relations* 6, 1936–9, pp. 1238–43, No. 996, Memorandum Alternative Canadian Procedures if Great Britain Becomes at War, Secret, 24.8.1939.
[72] *D O 114*, 98, p. 39, No. 65, W G 3/1/2, High Commissioner in Canada to Dominions Office, No. 283, Very Confidential, 20.9.1939 r. 23.9.1939.
[73] *F O 371*, 23966, pp. 188–93, W13084/10478/68, Dominions Office to Foreign Office, 2.9.1939 r. in r. 4.9.1939; Enclosing Statement by Mackenzie King, 3.9.1939.
[74] Ibid., pp. 206–9, W13497/10478/68, Dominions Office to Foreign Office, G88/115, 9.9.1939 r. in r. 12.9.1939; Enclosing High Commissioner in Canada to Dominions Office, Telegram No. 329, Important, 8.9.1939.

measure, but apart from a few irreconcilables, there was little opposition from French Canadians who were resigned to participation in the war. Campbell wrote that they had 'a clear conviction that the forces which have brought on the present struggle are raising issues to which no democratic people . . . can remain indifferent'. The other minorities in Canada had no hesitation in deciding that Canada should participate in full strength.[75]

It seems strange that Canada did fight on this issue, particularly in the light of views frequently expressed about the dangers of becoming involved in British quarrels in Europe, and the possible internal repercussions within Canada. There was no strategic reason for Canada's fighting: Roosevelt had guaranteed Canada's security in his Kingston speech in September 1938.[76] The economic arguments are not convincing and were not raised. Perhaps, as had been evidenced during the Munich crisis, when it came to the choice, imperial solidarity still counted in Canada. The British element was strong and patriotic fervour was not lacking. The royal visit possibly played its part in consolidating public opinion. At the end of August a crowd of 20,000 in Toronto spontaneously sang *Land of Hope and Glory* at the end of the royal tour film.[77] By May Quebec was reportedly not unfavourably inclined towards fighting. But there were people like the Canadian minister in Washington, Herbert Marler, a Montrealer of Swiss extraction whose family had been in Quebec for generations. He was a nationalist and an isolationist, and advised the Canadian government that whatever Roosevelt might say the United States had no intention of becoming involved in European troubles.[78] In September 1938 it had been forecast that Canada would be divided if the cabinet recommended that it fight. A year later this danger was not so real. Perhaps Chamberlain's repeated efforts to find a peaceful solution helped to convince Canada of the justice of the British cause. Canada did not fight for a vague concept of collective security, but for the values of the commonwealth. As Campbell wrote:

> While it would be untrue to suggest that Canada guards her independence one whit less jealously to-day than she did a year ago and the ordeal which now faces the democracies of the world have served to show, if the lesson were needed as I think it was, in some quarters here, that equality of status is not incompatible

[75] *D O 114*, 98, pp. 39–43, No. 65, W G 3/1/2, High Commissioner in Canada to Dominions Office, No. 283, Very Confidential, 20.9.1939 r. 23.9.1939.

[76] See p. 140.

[77] *Daily Telegraph*, 29.8.1939.

[78] *Lothian Papers* 389, pp. 145–6, Grant Dexter Press Gallery H of C Canada to Lothian, 13.5.1939.

with co-operation in common aims, loyalty to a common allegiance, and the defence of common principles.[79]

It is true that when the crisis came, as Templewood observes, the commonwealth was united. This was possible largely as a result of convincing the dominions 'of our profound desire for peace and our unshakeable determination to resist an attack'.[80] But, perhaps, when it came to the choice what counted most were ties of sentiment and kin. The dominions were not immediately threatened by Hitler: they fought for Britain.

[79] *D O 114*, 98, p. 43, No. 65, W G3/1/2, High Commissioner in Canada to Dominions Office, No. 283, Very Confidential, 20.9.1939 r. 23.9.1939.
[80] Lord Templewood, *Nine Troubled Years* (London, 1954), p. 389.

XII

CONCLUSION

Conclusion

BEFORE the second world war Britain was still an imperial power. But it no longer had paramountcy over the dominions comparable to that in 1914. Britain too, in a limited way, was also a world power. The *Pax Britannica*, however, had passed. Perhaps not all in government in Britain realised that. With potential enemies in Europe and the far east, the British navy was not strong enough to face war on three fronts simultaneously with impunity. If at all possible, the co-operation of the United States had to be secured. Without this Britain would be particularly vulnerable on the sea. Every major foreign policy decision in Britain had to be considered in relation to its effect on opinion in the United States and the dominions. This did not mean that British policy was decided in other countries, but rather than an effort had to be made to educate the dominions as to the need for Britain's following a particular course of action, and at least to present policy on a high moral plane acceptable to a peculiarly self righteous and moralistic United States opinion.

Chamberlain directed British policy at this time. He gave it a sense of purpose and deciveness that it had lacked under Baldwin. But Chamberlain, as he wrote in January 1938, had to bridge the gulf between what was realistic and possible, and what he would have liked British policy to be:

> In the absence of any powerful ally, and until our armaments are completed, we must adjust our foreign policy to our circumstances.[1]

At all costs Chamberlain was determined that foreign policy should not be allowed to drift, as he felt it had done in the past. He was determined as prime minister to keep policy moving, and to take an active interest in it himself.[2] Though ageing and strong willed Chamberlain was not inflexible. An isolated, perhaps alienated figure, who had few, if any, close friends, but a devoted wife, he was happiest in solitude, fishing. Seemingly he was not on intimate terms with any of his cabinet colleagues even if he did feel a genuine warmth for them. Horace Wilson was his confident, but he was only Chamberlain's sounding board, someone on whom he could test his ideas. At times Chamberlain felt a sense of mission, that only he could prevent a European war:

---

[1] *Chamberlain Papers*, Chamberlain to Mrs. Morton Prince, 16.1.1939. Quoted by Keith Feiling, *The Life of Neville Chamberlain* (London, 1946), p. 324.

[2] *Templewood Papers* XIX (C) 11, Chamberlain to Hilda Chamberlain, 6.11.1938 (copy).

316

I know I can save the country and I do not believe that anyone else can. But I need a few more years for it.[3]

Chamberlain took initiatives on his own, put out feelers to find out how the dictators would react. In July 1937 he did not tell Eden of his note to Mussolini, just as in August 1939 he wrote to Hitler without the cabinet's knowledge. But British government at this time was still cabinet government. The flight to Berchtesgaden was not a cabinet decision as there was no time. But Chamberlain had sounded out various members of that body before he took the step. The crucial decisions during September 1938 were, in the end, cabinet decisions, and not those of the inner cabinet or one man. After his return from Godesberg Chamberlain explained that he would abide by the decision of his colleagues. The same was true of the Russian negotiations in 1939. Chamberlain might have formulated policy, but, on essential issues, the ultimate decision rested with the cabinet. Chamberlain, however, being a strong personality, had a considerable influence over the cabinet. But his methods were not dictatorial. He accepted criticism and opposition especially from Halifax, his chosen foreign secretary.

As prime minister Chamberlain probably expected too much from Roosevelt and the United States, and was disappointed when he did not get enough. At times this disappointment amounted to anger and even rejection. At the end of 1937 he wrote: 'It is always best and safest to count on nothing from the Americans but words'.[4] Again, in June 1938, Oliver Harvey records that Chamberlain was reported to have said, on the proposed appointment of an ambassador to the United States: 'the Americans are so rotten, and it does not therefore matter who we send them'.[5] This was possibly just gossip, and, in any case, it seems a remark rather out of character. Chamberlain probably only made such statements in moments of dejection.

Chamberlain had a real concern for the United States, and he made this known to the Americans before he became prime minister. It was this concern, and fears of disastrous consequences for Anglo-American relations, which caused him to turn down the proferred invitation to visit the United States in 1937, at a time when the possible outcome of the trade treaty negotiations might have proved awkward. In any case the

[3] *Chamberlain Papers*, Chamberlain, 12.3.1939.

[4] Quoted by Feiling, p. 325.

[5] Oliver Harvey, John Harvey, Ed., *The Diplomatic Diaries of Oliver Harvey 1937–1940* (London, 1970), p. 148, Diary, 1.6.1938.

invitation was seemingly more the work of Norman Davis than of Roosevelt. Chamberlain drafted the carefully worked refusal himself.[6] The prime minister explained his approach to the United States in a letter to Tweedsmuir on 19 November 1937:

> I have gone out of my way to encourage those sections of American opinion that seem to have welcomed the President's Chicago speech. I have done so because I wish to give the utmost possible support to any tendency towards a closer understanding and a more complete community of purpose between our two nations. Nevertheless I am very conscious of the difficulties that have still to be overcome by the President before it can be said that he has his people behind him. His Chicago speech can be regarded, I think, as evidence that he recognises the need for the education of public opinion; but I should doubt whether such education can yet be said to have proceeded very far and it would seem likely that its development must take time. . . . These considerations, however, should not deter us from pressing forward and I shall continue to do everything that lies in my powers to ensure improvement in our future relations.[7]

It was this realistic awareness of the limitations on Roosevelt of public and congressional opinion that partially caused Chamberlain to treat Roosevelt's proposed peace plan in January 1938 with caution, and, in the end, to break with Eden. Eden was obsessed with the need to involve the United States in European affairs, even through commitments in the far east if need be. Eden impetuous and single minded, was, perhaps, not as conscious of the realities of Britain's predicament as was Chamberlain.

Chamberlain always had United States opinion in mind. He secured Hitler's signature to the paper saying that the Munich agreement was a pledge that Britain and Germany would not fight in the hope that if Hitler broke his word the Americans would realise what kind of a man he was. British policy towards the refugees was dictated by a concern for United States opinion. Chamberlain even achieved the settlement with Ireland in 1938 with the Irish opinion in the United States in view. By 1939 all that Britain could do to help Roosevelt secure the repeal of the neutrality legislation was to keep quiet. British officials were careful to do just this. Chamberlain hoped that Roosevelt would succeed. The repeal of the neutrality laws would give added weight to the British policy of deterrence and efforts to contain Hitler. Chamberlain was disappointed when congress did not budge.

Roosevelt had a high regard for Chamberlain, and the knowledge of this obviously meant much to the prime minister. The president was

6 *Premier 1*, 261, Chamberlain to Roosevelt, 28.9.1937. Written in own Hand.
7 Ibid., 229, Chamberlain to Tweedsmuir, 19.11.1937.

anxious to help Britain, and through Colonel Arthur Murray Britain was able to let Roosevelt know what supplies it particularly needed. Consequently, when war came, Roosevelt told Britain that he would not declare engine blocks or aluminium sheets as aircraft parts.

Roosevelt, perhaps, was not an opportunist statesman in the A. J. P. Taylor sense.[8] By October 1937 he was aware of the dangers of the international situation and of the need to educate public opinion. The secret military staff conversations between Britain and the United States in January 1938 and May 1939 were indicative of the president's intentions. He was anxious to help Britain fight a war by blockade, as he suggested in September 1938 and again in August 1939. But Roosevelt was hampered by domestic crises, congress and public opinion. He said that he could go only as far as the public would allow him. He tried to go further. Roosevelt's plans were consistent from 1937–9.

Chamberlain was also particularly conscious of the need to educate the dominions to the realities of the European situation. Far away from the European theatre the dominions could not always understand Britain's concern with the dictators. But Britain was still, in a sense, an imperial power, and the dominions had to be carried along some how. The dominions were not bound by British policy decisions: they were informed rather than consulted. That—with the exception of Ireland which was hardly a dominion anyway—they fought, was little short of a miracle. Apart from New Zealand the dominions favoured the policy of the appeasement of Europe. They were not responsible for it: dominion opinion only confirmed Chamberlain on a course of action on which he had already decided. Over Czechoslovakia Chamberlain saw the reluctance of the dominions to fight, and the consequent break up of the commonwealth, as decisive. This was the view he put to the cabinet. As the European situation became more serious with Hitler's occupation of Prague, dominion influence was not so great. Their opinions were considered, and weighed against other factors. But care was taken to sift information on the European situation going to the dominions. In January 1937 Chamberlain was worried lest too gloomy a picture were painted for the dominions.[9] In March 1939 the worry was that the dominions would have too optimistic an impression. Information was selected accordingly.[10] The personal trust that some dominion leaders placed in Chamberlain

---

[8] See A. J. P. Taylor, *The Origins of the Second World War* (London, 1964).
[9] *Cab 2*, 6(2), Committee of Imperial Defence Minutes of 288th Meeting, Secret, 11.2.1937 (copy), No Dominion Representatives present.
[10] *F O 371*, 23053, pp. 293–5, C2298/691/18, Foreign Office Minute by Sargent, 22.2.1939.

after the imperial conference probably helped to secure dominion participation in the war. Another important factor was that Chamberlain did show the dominions that every means to preserve peace had been tried. This was essential as some dominions continued to favour the appeasement of Europe almost until the day war was declared.

British policy was limited by United States and dominion opinion. The imperial conference of 1937 convinced Chamberlain that his policy of preserving peace in Europe was the right one: South Africa, Canada, and Australia, far away from the European theatre, were unlikely to give even qualified support for any British involvement in a continental war. At that time little, if any, assistance could be expected from the United States. As MacDonald repeatedly warned the cabinet, the commonwealth and the United States were the only forces which could eventually check the dictators, and one day that combination might have to fight. It was largely Chamberlain's policy of appeasement which ensured that when war came in 1939 the commonwealth was united. Britain, too, had behind it a sympathetic United States, and Roosevelt's assurance that the industrial resources of his country would be at Britain's disposal. This was a considerable achievement.

BIBLIOGRAPHY

Bibliography

A. MANUSCRIPT SOURCES

BIRMINGHAM UNIVERSITY LIBRARY
Neville Chamberlain Papers
I have only been able to see extracts in the possession of Professor
A. Headlam-Morley, and the copies of letters from Neville Chamberlain
to his sister, Hilda, in the *Templewood Papers* XIX (C) 11.

CAMBRIDGE UNIVERSITY LIBRARY
Templewood Papers
XIX 12–4, Background Material and Letters and Notes on *Nine Troubled
Years*, 1948–57.
XIX (C) 11, *Nine Troubled Years*, Correspondence with Mrs. Chamber-
lain and Miss Hilda Chamberlain 1949–54 with Extracts from Neville
Chamberlain's Letters.

CHURCHILL COLLEGE, CAMBRIDGE
Inskip Papers
1–2, Copy of Extracts from Diaries, 1938–9.
Vansittart Papers
This collection, most of which was destroyed during the second world war,
contains little that has not been used by Ian Colvin in *Vansittart in Office*
(London, 1965).

INDIA OFFICE LIBRARY
Zetland Papers
MSS Eur D 609.
8–11, Letters from Zetland to Linlithgow, 1937–9.
25–6, Cabinet Papers.

HOUSE OF LORDS RECORD OFFICE
Samuel Papers

GARROWBY, YORKSHIRE
Halifax Papers
These are deposited in the York Public Library for inspection by arrange-
ment with the trustee.

Bibliography

LONDON UNIVERSITY, INSTITUTE OF HISTORICAL RESEARCH (now closed and in Lord Simon's custody).
Simon Papers
NATIONAL LIBRARY OF SCOTLAND, EDINBURGH
Elibank Papers
8808–9, Contain Correspondence between Colonel Arthur Murray and Roosevelt, 1937–9.

PUBLIC RECORD OFFICE, LONDON
Cab. 2, Minutes of the Committee of Imperial Defence
6 Pt 2, 7–9
Cab. 16, Papers for the Committee of Imperial Defence
183A.
Cab. 23, Minutes of the Cabinet
87–100
Cab. 24, Papers for the Cabinet
267–88
Cab. 27, Proceedings of Cabinet Committee on Foreign Policy
622–6, 646
Cab. 32, Imperial Conference
127–31, 136
Cab. 63, Hankey Papers
52–3
D O 3, Dominions Office, Indexes
101–4
D O 114, Dominions Office, Confidential Print
75, 77–8, 82–5, 87–8, 93–4, 96, 98.
F O 371, Foreign Office Files concerning Europe, the United States and the Far East.
20660–7, 20719–21, 20736–7, 20747, 20750–1, 20952–4, 20957, 20962–3, 21015–22, 21160, 21183, 21457, 21490–1, 21495–7, 21501, 21503–4, 21506–9, 21524–7, 21536, 21541, 21545, 21547–8, 21630, 21650, 21657, 21666, 21670, 21679, 21681–3, 21719, 21722, 21732, 21734, 21737–8, 21745, 21776–9, 21790–1, 22085, 22106, 22181, 22411–2, 22417, 22535, 22537, 22785–6, 22796–7, 22799–800, 228002–3, 22812–6, 22820–1, 22823, 22827, 22829, 22834, 22851, 22969, 22971–2, 22975, 22977, 22981, 23049, 23053, 23091, 23396–7, 23444, 23549, 23560–2, 23961–7.
F O 372, Foreign Office, Dominions Intelligence
3200–3, 3205, 3314–7, 3319.
F O 414, Further Correspondence respecting North America
275–6.

F O 800, Papers of Individual Foreign Office Officials
272, Sir Orme Sargent.
294, Cadogan.
296, Cranbourne.
298–9, Lord Inverchapel (Sir A. Clark Kerr).
309–10, 318, 324, Halifax.
395–7, General.
Premier 1, Papers for the Prime Minister
229, 238–9, 242, 259–62, 266A, 289, 291, 299–300, 309–10, 324, 334, 353, 366–7.

SCOTTISH RECORD OFFICE, EDINBURGH
Lothian Papers
203–4, 296, 322, 325–400, 404, 445.

B. PRINTED SOURCES

1. *Primary Sources*

OFFICIAL PAPERS
Cmd 5482, Imperial Conference, 1937. Summary of Proceedings, June 1937.
Documents on British Foreign Policy 1919–1939, 3rd Series, Butler, Rohan and J. P. T. Bury Eds. 10 Vols. London, 1949–61.
Documents on Canadian External Relations, Vol. 6, *1936–9*, Munro, John A.Ed. Ottawa, 1972.
Documents on German Foreign Policy, D.IV, *1918–1945*, London, 1951.
Foreign Relations of the United States, 1937–9, Washington, 1954–7.

PARLIAMENTARY DEBATES, 1937–9
Australian Parliamentary Debates
152–9
Canadian Parliamentary Debates House of Commons
Canadian Parliamentary Debates Senate
Journal of the Parliamentary Debates of the Empire
20
New Zealand Parliamentary Debates
248–56
South African Parliamentary Debates House of Assembly
29–35
South African Parliamentary Debates Senate
United Kingdom Parliamentary Debates House of Commons
5th Series, 317–51.
United Kingdom Parliamentary Debates House of Lords
5th Series, 104–14.
United States Congressional Record

SPEECHES, DIARIES AND PAPERS
Bullitt, William C. Bullitt, Orville E., Ed. *For the President. Personal and Secret Correspondence between Franklin D. Roosevelt and William C. Bullitt*. Boston, 1972.
Cadogan, Alexander. Dilks, David, Ed. *The Diaries of Sir Alexander Cadogan O.M. 1938–1945*. London, 1971.
Chamberlain, Neville. *The Struggle for Peace*, London, 1939.
Halifax, Earl of. Craster, H. H. E., Ed. *Speeches on Foreign Policy by Viscount Halifax*. Oxford, 1940.
Harvey, Oliver. Harvey, John, Ed. *The Diplomatic Diaries of Oliver Harvey 1937–1940*. London, 1970.

Hore-Belisha, Leslie. Minney, R. J., Ed. *The Private Papers of Hore-Belisha.* London, 1960.

Ironside, Lord. Macleod, Roderick and Dennis Kelly, Eds. *The Ironside Diaries 1937–1940.* London, 1962.

Lindbergh, Charles A. *The Wartime Journals of Charles A. Lindbergh.* New York, 1970.

Moffat, Jay Pierrepont. Hooker, Nancy Harrison, Ed. *The Moffat Papers Selections from the Diplomatic Journals of Jay Pierrepont Moffat 1919–1943*, Cambridge, Mass., 1956.

Pownall, Henry. Bond, Brian, Ed. *Chief of Staff. The Diaries of Lieutenant-General Sir Henry Pownall. Vol. I 1933–1940.* London, 1972.

Roosevelt, Franklin Delano. Roosevelt, Elliott, Ed. *F.D.R. His Personal Letters 1928–1845.* Vol. 2. New York, 1950.

NEWSPAPERS, 1937–9

Burger, (South Africa)

Cape Times (South Africa)

Chatham House Press Cuttings

Extracts from the following Newspapers:

Australia: Advertiser (Adelaide), *Age, Argus* (Melbourne), *Bulletin, Daily News* (incorporating *Labor Daily*), *Labor Daily, Sydney Morning Herald, West Australian.*

Britain: Daily Herald, Daily Telegraph, Evening Standard, Financial News, Manchester Guardian, Morning Post, News Chronicle, Observer, Sunday Times.

New Zealand: Press.

United States: New York Times, New York Herald Tribune.

Natal Witness (South Africa)

New York Times

North China Herald

Suiderstem (South Africa)

The Times

2. *Secondary Sources*

BOOKS

Adler, Selig. *The Isolationist Impulse.* London, 1957.

———. *The Uncertain Giant 1921–1941.* New York, 1965.

Aga Khan. *The Memoirs of Aga Khan. World Enough and Time.* London, 1954.

Amery, L. S. *The Unforgiving Years.* London, 1955.

Andrews, E. M. *Isolationism and Appeasement in Australia*. Canberra, 1970.

Aster, Sidney. *1939: The Making of the Second World War*. London, 1973.

Astor, Michael. *Tribal Feeling*. London, 1963.

Attlee, Clement Richard. *As it Happened*. London, 1964.

Beard, Charles A. *American Foreign Policy in the Making 1932–1940. A Study in Responsibilities*. New Haven, 1946.

Birkenhead, Earl of. *Halifax. The Life of Lord Halifax*. London, 1965.

Blum, John Morton. *From the Morgenthau Diaries. Years of Crisis, 1928–1939*. Boston, 1959.

Bohlen, Charles E. *Witness to History*. London, 1973.

Borg, Dorothy. *The United States and the Far Eastern Crisis of 1933–1938*. Cambridge, Mass., 1964.

Borg, Dorothy, Shumpei Okamoto and Dale K. A. Finlayson. *Pearl Harbor as History, Japanese-American Relations 1931–1941*. London, 1973.

Bowle, John. *Viscount Samuel*. London, 1957.

Bradley, P. *Can We Stay Out of War?* New York, 1936.

Brodwick, Alan Houghton. *Near to Greatness*. London, 1965.

Buhite, Russell D. *Nelson T. Johnson and American Policy toward China 1925–1941*. East Lansing, 1968.

Bullock, Alan. *Hitler. A Study in Tyranny*. London, 1962.

Burns, James MacGregor. *Roosevelt: The Lion and the Fox*. London, 1956.

Butler, J. R. M. *Lord Lothian (Philip Kerr) 1882–1940*. London, 1960.

Butler, Lord. *The Art of the Possible: The Memoirs of Lord Butler*. London, 1971.

Carter, Gwendolen. *The British Commonwealth and International Security*. Toronto, 1947.

Casey, R. G. *Friends and Neighbours*. Melbourne, 1954.

——. *Personal Experience 1939–1946*. London, 1962.

Churchill, Winston S. *The Gathering Storm*. London, 1948.

Citrine, Lord. *Men and Work*. London, 1964.

Clifford, Nicholas R. *Retreat from China. British Policy in the Far East 1937–1941*. London, 1967.

Cole, Wayne S. *Senator Gerald P. Nye and American Foreign Policy*. Minneapolis, 1962.

Collis, Maurice S. *Nancy Astor*. London, 1960.

Colvin, Ian. *The Chamberlain Cabinet*. London, 1971.

Conde, Alexander De. *Isolationism and Security*. Durham, N. Carolina, 1957.

Cook, Ramsey. *The Politics of John W. Dafoe and the Free Press.* Toronto, 1963.

Cooper, Duff. *Old Men Forget. The Autobiography of Duff Cooper,* London, 1953.

Coote, Colin. *A Companion of Honour. The Story of Walter Elliot.* London, 1965.

Connell, John. *Wavell Scholar and Soldier to June 1941.* London, 1964.

Craigie, Robert. *Behind the Japanese Mask.* London, 1945.

Crecraft, E. W. *Freedom of the Seas.* New York, 1935.

Dalton, Hugh. *The Fateful Years, Memoirs 1931–1945.* London, 1957.

Divine, Robert A. *The Illusion of Neutrality.* Chicago, 1962.

———. *Roosevelt and World War II.* Baltimore, 1969.

Drummond, Donald F. *The Passing of American Neutrality 1937–1941.* Ann Arbor, 1955.

Dulles, A. W. and H. F. Armstrong. *Can We Be Neutral?* New York, 1936.

Eayrs, James. *In Defence of Canada. Appeasement and Rearmament.* Toronto, 1965.

Eden, Anthony. *Facing the Dictators.* London, 1962.

———. *The Reckoning.* London, 1965.

Elliott, W. Y. and H. Duncan Hall, Eds. *The British Commonwealth at War.* New York, 1943.

Eubank, Keith. *Munich.* Oklahoma, 1963.

Feiling, Keith. *The Life of Neville Chamberlain.* London, 1946.

Gilbert, Martin. *Plough my Own Furrow, The Story of Lord Allan of Hurtwood.* London, 1965.

Gilbert, Martin and Richard Gott. *The Appeasers.* London, 1963.

Gladwyn, Lord. *The Memoirs of Lord Gladwyn.* London, 1972.

Graham, W. R. *Arthur Meighen.* Toronto, 1960.

Grew, Joseph C. *Ten Years in Japan.* London, 1944.

Grew, Joseph C. Hooker, Nancy Harvison, Ed. *Turbulent Era. A Diplomatic Record of Forty Years 1904–45.* Vol. 2. London, 1953.

Gunther, John. *Roosevelt in Retrospect.* London, 1950.

Halifax, Earl of. *Fullness of Days.* London, 1957.

Hancock, W. K. *Smuts. The Fields of Force, 1919–1950.* Cambridge, 1968.

Hankey, Lord. *Diplomacy by Conference.* London, 1946.

Hasluck, Paul. *The Government and the People 1939–1941.* Canberra, 1952.

Heinrichs, Waldo H., Jnr. *American Ambassador. Joseph C. Grew and the Development of the United States Diplomatic Tradition.* Boston, 1966.

Herzog, James H. *Closing the Open Door. American-Japanese Diplomatic Negotiations 1936–1941.* Annapolis, Maryland, 1973.

Bibliography

The History of the Times. *The 150th Anniversary and Beyond 1912–1948.* Vol. 4 Pt. 2. London, 1952.

Hodson, H. V., Ed. *The British Commonwealth and the Future. Proceedings of the Second Unofficial Conference on British Commonwealth Relations, Sydney, 3rd—17th September, 1938.* Oxford, 1939.

Howard, Michael. *The Continental Commitment.* London, 1974.

Hull, Cordell. *The Memoirs of Cordell Hull.* Vol. 1. London, 1948

Ismay, Lord. *The Memoirs of General the Lord Ismay.* London, 1960.

Jessup, P. C. *Neutrality, Today and Tomorrow.* New York, 1936.

Jonas, Manfred. *Isolationism and America 1935–1941.* New York, 1966.

Jones, Thomas. *A Diary with Letters.* London, 1954.

Kirby, Stanley Woodburn. *Singapore: The Chain of Disaster.* London, 1971.

——. *The War Against Japan.* Vol. 1 *The Loss of Singapore.* London, 1957.

Kirkpatrick, Ivone. *The Inner Circle.* London, 1959.

Koginos, Manny T. *The Panay Incident: Prelude to War.* Purdue, 1967.

Kottman, Richard W. *Reciprocity and the North Atlantic Triangle, 1932 1938.* Ithaca, New York, 1968.

Kreider, C. *The Anglo-American Trade Agreement.* Princeton, 1943.

Landecker, Manfred. *The President and Public Opinion. Leadership in Foreign Affairs.* Washington, 1968.

Langer, William L. and S. Everett Gleason. *The Challenge to Isolation, 1937–1940.* London, 1952.

Lee, Bradford A. *Britain and the Sino-Japanese War, 1937–1939. A Study in the Dilemmas of British Decline.* London, 1973.

Liddell Hart, Basil. *The Memoirs of Captain Liddell Hart.* Vol. 2. London, 1965.

Loewenheim, Francis L. *Peace of Appeasement. Hitler, Chamberlain and the Munich Crisis.* Boston, 1965.

Long, B. K. *In Smuts's Camp.* Oxford, 1945.

Louis, William Roger. *British Strategy in the Far East 1919–1939.* London, 1971.

Lyons, Enid. *So We Take Comfort.* London, 1965.

MacDonald, Malcolm. *People and Places.* London, 1969.

MacDonald, Tom. *Jan Hofmeyer. Heir to Smuts.* London, 1948.

McLachlan, Donald. *In the Chair: Barrington-Ward of The Times.* London, 1971.

Macleod, Ian. *Neville Chamberlain.* London, 1961.

Macmillan, Harold. *Winds of Change.* London, 1966.

Maddox, Robert James. *William E. Borah and American Foreign Policy.* Baton Rouge, 1969.

Mansergh, P. N. S. *The Commonwealth Experience.* London, 1969.

——. *Survey of British Commonwealth Affairs. Problems of External Policy 1931–1939.* Oxford, 1952.

Massey, Vincent. *What's Past is Prologue.* London, 1963.

Maugham, Viscount. *At the End of the Day.* London, 1953.

——. *The Truth About the Munich Crisis.* London, 1944.

Medlicott, W. N. *Contemporary England.* London, 1967.

Menzies, Robert. *Afternoon Light.* London, 1967.

Middlemas, Keith. *Diplomacy of Illusion: The British Government and Germany, 1937–39.* London, 1972.

Miller, J. D. B. *The Commonwealth and the World.* London, 1958.

Namier, Lewis B. *Diplomatic Prelude, 1938–1939.* London, 1948.

——. *Europe in Decay: A Study in Disintegration 1936–1940.* London, 1950.

Nash, Gerald D., Ed. *Franklin Delano Roosevelt.* Eaglewood Cliffs. N.J., 1967.

Nicholls, G. Heaton. *South Africa in My Time.* London, 1961.

Nienaber, P. J. *et. al. Gedenkboek Generaal J. B. M. Hertzog.* Johannesburg, 1965.

Northedge, F. S. *The Troubled Giant.* London, 1966.

Offner, Arnold A. *American Appeasement, United States Foreign Policy and Germany 1933–1938.* Cambridge, Mass., 1969.

Orvik, Nils. *The Decline of Neutrality 1914–1941.* 2nd Ed. London, 1971.

Osgood, Robert Endicott. *Ideals and Self-Interest in America's Foreign Relations.* Chicago, 1953.

Page, Earl. *Truant Surgeon.* Sydney, 1963.

Paton, Alan. *Hofmeyer.* London, 1964.

Pearson, Lester B. *Through Diplomacy to Politics. Memoirs 1897–1948.* London, 1973.

Perry, Hamilton Darby. *The Panay Incident: Prelude to Pearl Harbor.* New York, 1969.

Pickersgill, J. W. *The Mackenzie King Record 1939–1944.* Toronto, 1960.

Pirow, Oswald. *James Barry Munnik Hertzog.* Cape Town, 1958.

Pratt, Julius W. *Cordell Hull, 1933–44.* Vol. 1. New York, 1964.

Rauch, Basil. *Roosevelt. From Munich to Pearl Harbor.* New York, 1950.

Reitz, Denys. *No Outspan.* London, 1943.

Robbins, Keith. *Munich 1938.* London, 1968.

Robinson, Edgar Eugene. *The Roosevelt Leadership, 1933–1945.* New York, 1955.

Robinson, James A. *Congress and Foriegn Policy-Making. A Study in Legislative Influence and Initiative.* Illinois, 1962.

Robertson, Esmonde M., Ed. *The Origins of the Second World War.* London, 1971.

Rock, William R. *Appeasement on Trial. British Foreign Policy and its Critics, 1938–1939.* Hamden, Conn., 1966.

Rosenthal, E. *South African Diplomats Abroad.* Johannesburg, 1949.

Rosenman, Samuel I. *Working with Roosevelt.* New York, 1952.

Rothermere, Viscount. *Warnings and Predictions.* London, 1939.

Rowse, A. L. *All Souls and Appeasement.* London, 1961.

Samuel, Viscount. *Memoirs.* London, 1945.

Seton-Watson, R. W. *Britain and the Dictators.* Cambridge, 1938.

Shepardson, Whitney H. and William O. Scroggs. *The United States in World Affairs, 1936.* New York, 1937.

——, ——. *The United States in World Affairs, 1937–9.* New York, 1938–40.

Simon, Viscount *Retrospect.* London, 1952.

Skilling, H. Gordon. *Canadian Representation Abroad.* Toronto, 1945.

Smith, H. Lindsay. *Behind the Press in South Africa.* Cape Town, 1946.

Smith, J. Adam. *John Buchan.* London, 1965.

Soward, F. H., et. al. *Canada in World Affairs. The Pre-War Years.* London, 1941.

Strang, Lord. *Home and Abroad.* London, 1956.

Stromberg, Roland N *Collective Security and American Foreign Policy.* New York, 1963.

Tansill, Charles Callan. *Back Door to War. The Roosevelt Foreign Policy, 1933–1941.* Chicago, 1952.

Templewood, Lord. *Nine Troubled Years.* London, 1954.

Thompson, Neville. *The Anti-Appeasers: Conservative Opposition to Appeasement in the 1930's.* London, 1971.

Thorne, Christopher. *The Approach of War 1938–9.* London, 1967.

Taylor, A. J. P. *The Origins of the Second World War.* London, 1964.

Toynbee, Arnold J., Veronica M. Toynbee, and R. G. D. Laffan., Eds. *Survey of International Affairs.* 1937 2 Vols. 1938 3 Vols. 1939 vol.2. Oxford, 1938–58.

Toynbee, Arnold J. *Survey of International Affairs 1939. The World in March 1939.* Oxford, 1952.

Van den Heever, C. M. *Generaal J. B. M. Hertzog.* Johannesburg, 1944.

——. *General J. B. M. Hertzog.* Johannesburg, 1946.

Vansittart, Lord. *Bones of Contention.* London, Undated.

Wann, A. J. *The President as Chief Administrator. A Study of Franklin D. Roosevelt.* Washington, 1968.

Watt, Alan. *The Evolution of Australian Foreign Policy.* Cambridge, 1967.

Watt, D. C. *Personalities and Policies.* London, 1965.

Welles, Sumner. *Seven Major Decisions.* London, 1951.

——. *The Time for Decision.* London, 1944.

Whalen, Richard J. *The Founding Father: the Story of Joseph P. Kennedy.* London, 1965.

Wheeler-Bennett, John W. *Munich: Prologue to Tragedy.* London, 1948.

Wiltz, John E. *From Isolation to War, 1931–1941.* London, 1968.

Winterton, Earl of. *Orders of the Day.* London, 1953.

Wood, ·F. L. W. *The New Zealand People at War. Political and External Affairs. Official History of New Zealand in the Second World War, 1939–45.* Wellington, 1958.

Woodward, Llewellyn. *British Foreign Policy in the Second World War.* Vol. 1. London, 1970.

Woolton, Earl of. *The Memoirs of the Rt. Hon. the Earl of Woolton.* London, 1959.

Wrench, John Evelyn. *Geoffrey Dawson and Our Times.* London, 1955.

Young, Kenneth. *Sir Alec Douglas Home.* London, 1970.

ARTICLES

Altman, O. R. 'First Session of the Seventy-Fifth Congress, January 5, 1937 to August 21, 1937', *American Political Science Review*, XXXI (1937), pp. 1071–93.

Ashton-Gwatkin, F. T. A. 'The Personal Story of the Runciman Mission', *Listener*, XL (21.10.48), pp. 595–7.

Baturin, M. 'The United States and Munich', *International Affairs* Moscow V (1959), pp. 75–81.

Beloff, Max. 'Appeasement—For and Against', *Government and Opposition*, VII (1972), pp. 112–9.

Clifford, Nicholas R. 'Britain, America, and the Far East, 1937–1940: A Failure in Co-operation', *Journal of British Studies*, III (1963–4), pp. 137–54.

Cooper, Duff. 'A Cynical Act of Cold-blooded Butchery', *Listener*, XL (18.11.1948), pp. 757–8.

Current Notes on International Affairs. Vols. 4–5. Department of External Affairs. Canberra, 1938.

Dafoe, John W. 'The Imperial Conference of 1937', *University of Toronto Quarterly*, VII (1937–8), pp. 1–17.

Doherty, J. C. 'Die Dominions und die Britische Aussenpolitik von München bis zum Kriegsausbruch 1939', *Vierteljahrshefte für Zeitgeschichte*, XX (1972), pp. 209–34.

Fisher, Alan G. B. 'Economic Appeasement as a Means to Political Understanding and Peace', *Survey of International Affairs*, 1937, (1) pp. 56–109.

Garner, J. W. 'Recent Neutrality Legislation of the United States', *British Yearbook of International Law*, XVII (1936), pp. 45–9.

Haight, John McVickar Jnr. 'France, the United States, and the Munich Conference', *Journal of Modern History*, XXXII (Dec. 1960), pp. 340–58.

Headlam-Morley, Agnes. 'Was Neville Chamberlain's Foreign Policy Wrong?' *Listener*, XL (14.10.1948), pp. 551–3.

Henson, E. L. 'Britain, America and the Month of Munich', *International Relations*, 2 No. 5 (Apr. 1962), pp. 291–301.

Hodson, H. V. 'British Foreign Policy and the Dominions', *Foreign Affairs*, XVII (July 1939), pp. 753–63.

Lippmann, Walter. 'Rough-Hew Them how We will', *Foreign Affairs*, XV (July 1937), pp. 587–94.

Namier, Lewis B. 'Munich Survey: A Summing Up', *Listener*, XL (2.12.1948), pp. 835–6.

Phillips, Bradley. 'Current Neutrality Problems', *The American Political Science Review*, XXIX (Dec. 1935), pp. 1022–41.

Pratt, L. 'The Anglo-American Naval Conversations on the Far East of January 1938', *International Affairs*, XLVII (1971), pp. 745–63.

Round Table. Vols. XXVII–XXX (1937–9).

Shai, Aron. 'Was there a Far Eastern Munich?', *Journal of Contemporary History*, IX (July 1974), pp. 161–9.

Spencer, Robert. 'War Unpremeditated?', *The Canadian Historical Review*, XLIII (1962), pp. 136–44.

Tamchina, Rainer. 'Commonwealth und Appeasement: Die Politik der britischen Dominions', *Neue Politische Literatur*, (1972), pp. 471–89.

——. 'In Search of Common Causes: The Imperial Conference of 1937, *The Journal of Imperial and Commonwealth History*, I (1972), pp. 79–105.

Taylor, A. J. P. 'Brummagen Statesmanship', *Observer*, 10.1.1971.

Templewood, Lord. 'The Lesson of Munich' *Listener*, XL (9.12.48), p. 879.

Vansittart, Lord. 'A Morally Indefensible Agreement', *Listener*, XL (4.11.48), pp. 675–7.

Wallace, W. V. 'Roosevelt and British Appeasement, 1938', *Bulletin of the British Association of American Studies*, New Series V (Dec. 1962), pp. 4–30.

Watt, D. C. 'Appeasement. The Rise of a Revisionist School?', *Political Quarterly*, XXXVI (1965), pp. 191–213.

——. 'Der Einfluss der Dominions auf die Britische Auusenpolitik von München, 1938', *Vierteljahrshefte für Zeitgeschichte*, VIII (Jan. 1960), pp. 64–74.

——. 'Roosevelt and Neville Chamberlain: Two Appeasers', *International Journal*, XXVIII (1973), pp. 185–204.

Webster, Sir Charles. 'Munich Reconsidered, A Survey of British Policy', *International Affairs*, XXXVII (Apr. 1961), pp. 137–53.

Wilcox, Francis O. 'American Government and Politics. The Neutrality Fight in Congress, 1939', *The American Political Science Review*, XXXIII (1939), pp. 811–25.

INDEX

Abyssinia, 40, 168
  British policy in, 42
  Dominions on, 113–4
  Eden and British policy towards, 102,
    105, 110–1
  Italian-British relations and, 61–3, 97,
    101, 104–6
  Jordan and, 178–9
  New Zealand and, 134
  Smuts on, 220–1
Aden, 192
Adler, Selig, 9
Advertiser (Adelaide), 57
Aga Khan, 136–7
Age (Australia), 132, 308
Albania, 230–1
Aleutian Islands, 262
Amery, L.S., 7, 131, 166
  Influence on Smuts, 26
Anglo-German Friendship Association,
  26
Anglo-German Naval Agreement, 26,
  278
Anti Comintern Pact, 97
Arabia, 97
Argus (Melbourne), 132, 307
Arita Hachiro, 256–7
Ashton-Gwatkin, F.T.A., 7
  and Anglo-American co-operation, 139
  and Canada, 139
  and proposed trade agreement with
    United States, 16
Astor, Michael, 6
Attlee, Clement, 7
Australia, 86
  Abyssinia, 114, 184–5
  Anglo-American trade agreement, 17
  Anglo-Italian Agreement, 184–5
  Anglo-German naval agreement, 278
  Anglo-Russian negotiations, 272
  and British policy, 132, 202, 222, 227,
    237, 244–5, 247–9, 275, 287–8, 290,
    308, 320
  and British policy towards Czecho-
    slovakia, 132, 202
  and Churchill, 308
  Colonial compensation, 35
  Czechoslovakia, 119, 121, 124–5,
    132–4, 143–4, 146–7, 149, 154, 163,
    165–6, 168, 171, 174, 177, 221–2
  Declares war, 296, 300, 308–9
  Defence Policy, 211–2, 244–5, 275, 295
  Dominion consultation procedures,
    149–50, 21–2
  Dutch East Indies, 208
  France, 147, 279–80
  and Imperial conference (1937), 41–2,
    57–8
  and Imperial defence, 30–3, 49–51,
    57–8, 210

Japan and, 67, 132, 139, 240–1, 246,
    254, 259–60, 267
  Labour opposition in, 23, 57–8
  Mobilization (1938), 175
  Munich conference, 176, 179, 222
  Naval co-operation in far east, 91,
    240, 244
  Sanctions against Japan, 78, 83,
    259–61
Austria
  Anschluss, 109–110, 118, 126, 129, 136
  Australia and, 41
  British attitude to *Anschluss*, 45, 96
  Chamberlain's concern for, 111, 118
  Eden on British support for, 39
  in Eden's resignation decision, 112
  and Germany, 40, 55, 96
  Hertzog on, 42

Baldwin, Stanley, 14, 15, 33, 316
  Chairman of imperial conference
    (1937), 40
  Resigns as prime minister, 45
Balfour, J., 155, 293
Barrington-Ward, Robin, 6n, 153
Baruch, Barney, 19
Beard, Charles A., 10
Beck, Joseph, Polish foreign minister,
    228–9, 285, 291, 292
Beith, J. G. S., 88
Belgian Congo, 190
Belgium, 26, 54
  Chamberlain on British defence of, 120
  and Colonial compensation for
    Germany, 96, 108, 187
  Eden on British commitments to, 39
  and South Africa, 190
Benes, Edward, president of Czecho-
    slovakia, 123, 136, 144, 152, 159
  Australian views of, 147
  Bruce on, 124–5, 177–8
  and Henlein, 152
  Message from Roosevelt, 175
Bennett, R. B., leader of conservative
    party in Canada, 135–6
Berchtesgaden, 109, 152, 154, 155, 161,
    188, 317
Berlin, 95
  Irish representation in, 22
  South African representation in, 22
Bingham, Robert W., United States
    ambassador in London, 12, 16, 66,
    67, 79, 84
  on Eden/Chamberlain visit to United
    States, 17–8
  On far east and Anglo-American co-
    operation there, 68
Bloom bill in congress, 250
Blum, Léon, French statesman, 14
Bodenstein, H. J., secretary to Hertzog,
    25